# LEGAL AND ILLEGAL IMMIGRATION

ISSN 2327-9168

# LEGAL AND ILLEGAL IMMIGRATION

Mark Lane

**INFORMATION PLUS® REFERENCE SERIES**
Formerly Published by Information Plus, Wylie, Texas

Detroit • New York • San Francisco • New Haven, Conn • Waterville, Maine • London

**Legal and Illegal Immigration**

Mark Lane

Kepos Media, Inc.: Steven Long and Janice Jorgensen, Series Editors

Project Editors: Elizabeth Manar, Kathleen J. Edgar, Kimberley McGrath

Rights Acquisition and Management: Sheila Spencer

Composition: Evi Abou-El-Seoud, Mary Beth Trimper

Manufacturing: Rita Wimberly

For product information and technology assistance, contact us at
**Gale Customer Support, 1-800-877-4253.**
For permission to use material from this text or product,
submit all requests online at **www.cengage.com/permissions.**
Further permissions questions can be e-mailed to
**permissionrequest@cengage.com**

Cover photograph: © Jim Parkin/Shutterstock.com.

Gale
27500 Drake Rd.
Farmington Hills, MI 48331-3535

ISBN-13: 978-0-7876-5103-9 (set)          ISBN-10: 0-7876-5103-6 (set)
ISBN-13: 978-1-5699-5791-2                ISBN-10: 1-5699-5791-6

ISSN 2327-9168

This title is also available as an e-book.
ISBN-13: 978-1-5699-5838-4 (set)
ISBN-10: 1-5699-5838-6 (set)
Contact your Gale sales representative for ordering information.

Printed in the United States of America
1 2 3 4 5      17 16 15 14 13

# TABLE OF CONTENTS

# PREFACE

*Legal and Illegal Immigration* is part of the *Information Plus Reference Series*. The purpose of each volume of the series is to present the latest facts on a topic of pressing concern in modern American life. These topics include the most controversial and studied social issues of the 21st century: abortion, capital punishment, care of senior citizens, crime, the environment, genetics, health care, minorities, national security, social welfare, water, women, youth, and many more. Even though this series is written especially for high school and undergraduate students, it is an excellent resource for anyone in need of factual information on current affairs.

By presenting the facts, it is the intention of Gale, Cengage Learning to provide its readers with everything they need to reach an informed opinion on current issues. To that end, there is a particular emphasis in this series on the presentation of scientific studies, surveys, and statistics. These data are generally presented in the form of tables, charts, and other graphics placed within the text of each book. Every graphic is directly referred to and carefully explained in the text. The source of each graphic is presented within the graphic itself. The data used in these graphics are drawn from the most reputable and reliable sources, such as from the various branches of the U.S. government and from private organizations and associations. Every effort has been made to secure the most recent information available. Readers should bear in mind that many major studies take years to conduct and that additional years often pass before the data from these studies are made available to the public. Therefore, in many cases the most recent information available in 2013 is dated from 2010 or 2011. Older statistics are sometimes presented as well, if they are landmark studies or of particular interest and no more-recent information exists.

Although statistics are a major focus of the *Information Plus Reference Series*, they are by no means its only content. Each book also presents the widely held positions and important ideas that shape how the book's subject is discussed in the United States. These positions are explained in detail and, where possible, in the words of their proponents. Some of the other material to be found in these books includes historical background, descriptions of major events related to the subject, relevant laws and court cases, and examples of how these issues play out in American life. Some books also feature primary documents or have pro and con debate sections that provide the words and opinions of prominent Americans on both sides of a controversial topic. All material is presented in an evenhanded and unbiased manner; readers will never be encouraged to accept one view of an issue over another.

## HOW TO USE THIS BOOK

The United States is known as a melting pot, a place where people of different nationalities, cultures, ethnicities, and races have come together to form one nation. This process has been shaped by both legal and illegal immigration, and American attitudes toward immigrants have varied over time. Whether in the country legally or not, immigrants have faced discrimination based on prevailing social and political trends. For example, unprecedented immigration from Mexico, much of it illegal, began dramatically reshaping the United States in the latter decades of the 20th century. The resulting anxieties and cultural tensions not only shaped the lives of immigrants but also had major policy implications well into the 21st century. This book discusses these and other legal, social, and political aspects of immigration.

*Legal and Illegal Immigration* consists of nine chapters and five appendixes. Each chapter is devoted to a particular aspect of immigration in the United States. For a summary of the information that is covered in each chapter, please see the synopses that are provided in the Table of Contents. Chapters generally begin with an overview of the basic facts and background information on the chapter's topic, then proceed to examine subtopics of particular interest. For example, Chapter 6, The Costs and Benefits of Immigration, begins with a discussion of the ongoing debates surrounding the size of the economic contributions immigrants make relative to the costs their presence imposes on the country. The chapter then delves into the opposing calculations that drive these debates, offering perspective on federal, state, and local expenses in areas such as border security, entitlement benefits, and education. It then discusses an emerging consensus among economists suggesting that the benefits of immigration to the economy are greater than previously believed, and it addresses the projected economic impact of various immigration reform proposals. Readers can find their way through a chapter by looking for the section and subsection headings, which are clearly set off from the text. They can also refer to the book's extensive Index, if they already know what they are looking for.

**Statistical Information**

The tables and figures featured throughout *Legal and Illegal Immigration* will be of particular use to readers in learning about this topic. These tables and figures represent an extensive collection of the most recent and valuable statistics on the subject—for example, graphics cover the number of immigrant orphans adopted by U.S. citizens, the percentage of native-born and foreign-born workers employed in various industries, estimates of the unauthorized immigrant population, and the cost per apprehension of each unauthorized immigrant. Gale, Cengage Learning believes that making this information available to readers is the most important way to fulfill the goal of this book: to help readers understand the issues and controversies surrounding immigration and illegal immigrants in the United States and to reach their own conclusions.

Each table or figure has a unique identifier appearing above it for ease of identification and reference. Titles for the tables and figures explain their purpose. At the end of each table or figure, the original source of the data is provided.

To help readers understand these often complicated statistics, all tables and figures are explained in the text. References in the text direct readers to the relevant statistics. Furthermore, the contents of all tables and figures are fully indexed. Please see the opening section of the Index at the back of this volume for a description of how to find tables and figures within it.

**Appendixes**

Besides the main body text and images, *Legal and Illegal Immigration* has five appendixes. The first is a reproduction of a pamphlet published by the U.S. Depart-

ment of Justice titled *Federal Protections against National Origin Discrimination—U.S. Department of Justice: Potential Discrimination against Immigrants Based on National Origin*. The second appendix features maps of the world to assist readers in pinpointing the places of birth of the United States' immigrant population. The third is the Important Names and Addresses directory. Here, readers will find contact information for a number of government and private organizations that can provide further information on aspects of immigration and illegal immigrants. The fourth appendix is the Resources section, which can also assist readers in conducting their own research. In this section the author and editors of *Legal and Illegal Immigration* describe some of the sources that were most useful during the compilation of this book. The final appendix is the Index. It has been greatly expanded from previous editions and should make it even easier to find specific topics in this book.

**ADVISORY BOARD CONTRIBUTIONS**

The staff of Information Plus would like to extend its heartfelt appreciation to the Information Plus Advisory Board. This dedicated group of media professionals provides feedback on the series on an ongoing basis. Their comments allow the editorial staff who work on the project to make the series better and more user-friendly. The staff's top priority is to produce the highest-quality and most useful books possible, and the Information Plus Advisory Board's contributions to this process are invaluable.

The members of the Information Plus Advisory Board are:

- Kathleen R. Bonn, Librarian, Newbury Park High School, Newbury Park, California

- Madelyn Garner, Librarian, San Jacinto College, North Campus, Houston, Texas

- Anne Oxenrider, Media Specialist, Dundee High School, Dundee, Michigan

- Charles R. Rodgers, Director of Libraries, Pasco-Hernando Community College, Dade City, Florida

- James N. Zitzelsberger, Library Media Department Chairman, Oshkosh West High School, Oshkosh, Wisconsin

**COMMENTS AND SUGGESTIONS**

The editors of the *Information Plus Reference Series* welcome your feedback on *Legal and Illegal Immigration* Please direct all correspondence to:

Editors
*Information Plus Reference Series*
27500 Drake Rd.
Farmington Hills, MI 48331-3535

# CHAPTER 1
# IMMIGRATION IN U.S. HISTORY

The United States has always been a land of immigrants. The nation was founded by people from other countries seeking free choice of worship and new opportunities, and as it grew it was populated to a large degree by those escaping from cruel governments elsewhere or seeking relief from war, famine, or poverty. All came with dreams of a better life for themselves and their families. In spite of their diverse backgrounds, customs, and beliefs, the United States has accommodated its many immigrant peoples, though not without considerable friction along the way.

On the eastern shore of the peninsula that is now Florida, Spanish conquistadors established a settlement in 1565. The city of St. Augustine survived to become the oldest continuously occupied settlement of European origin in North America. It was the northern colonies, however, that expanded rapidly and became central to the development of the nation. In *Immigration: From the Founding of Virginia to the Closing of Ellis Island* (2002), Dennis Wepman chronicles the immigrants who shaped the United States. Not long after English settlers established the first permanent colony on the James River in Virginia in 1607, the French developed a settlement on the St. Lawrence River at what is now Quebec, Canada. Dutch explorers soon built a fur trading post, Fort Nassau, on the Hudson River at what is now Albany, New York. Swedes settled on the Delaware River near present-day Wilmington, Delaware. German Quakers and Mennonites joined William Penn's (1644–1718) experimental Pennsylvania colony. Jews from Brazil, Protestant Huguenots from France, and Puritans and Catholics from England all came to escape persecution of their religious beliefs and practices.

During the colonial period many immigrants came as indentured servants—meaning they were required to work for four to seven years to earn back the cost of their passage. To the great aggravation of the colonists, some were convicts who accepted being shipped across the ocean as an alternative to imprisonment or death. Wepman estimates that as many as 50,000 British felons were sent to the colonies as indentured servants. The first Africans arrived in Jamestown in 1619 as indentured servants, but other Africans were soon brought in chains and sold as slaves.

A continual flow of immigrants provided settlers to develop communities along the Atlantic coast, pioneers to push the United States westward, builders for the Erie Canal and the transcontinental railways, pickers for cotton in the South and vegetables in the Southwest, laborers for U.S. industrialization, and intellectuals in all fields. Together, these immigrants built, in the opinion of many people, the most diverse nation in the world.

According to Campbell Gibson and Kay Jung of the U.S. Census Bureau, in *Historical Census Statistics on Population Totals by Race, 1790 to 1990, and by Hispanic Origin, 1970 to 1990, for the United States, Regions, Divisions, and States* (September 2002, http://www.census.gov/population/www/documentation/twps0056/twps0056.pdf), the 1790 census in the United States showed a population of 3.2 million whites and 757,000 blacks, of whom about 60,000 were free and the rest slaves. (See Table 1.1.) The white U.S. population was predominantly of English heritage, but also included people of Dutch, French, German, Irish, Scottish, and Spanish descent. Native Americans were not counted.

## EARLY ATTITUDES TOWARD IMMIGRANTS

Even though immigration was the way of life in the country's first century, negative attitudes began to appear among the already settled English-heritage population. Officially, with the major exception of the Alien and Sedition Acts of 1798, the United States encouraged immigration. The Articles of Confederation, drafted in 1777, made anyone who was a citizen of one state a citizen of every other state. The U.S. Constitution (adopted in 1787) made only one direct reference to immigration. Article 1, Section 9, Clause

# TABLE 1.1

**Race and Hispanic origin of the U.S. population, 1790–1990**

| Census year | Total Population | Race | | | | | Hispanic origin (of any race) | White, not of Hispanic origin |
|---|---|---|---|---|---|---|---|---|
| | | White | Black | American Indian, Eskimo, and Aleut | Asian and Pacific Islander | Other race | | |
| **Number** | | | | | | | | |
| 1990 | 248,709,873 | 199,686,070.0 | 29,986,060 | 1,959,234 | 7,273,662 | 9,804,847 | 22,354,059 | 188,128,296 |
| Sample | 248,709,873 | 199,827,064.0 | 29,930,524 | 2,015,143 | 7,226,986 | 9,710,156 | 21,900,089 | 188,424,773 |
| 1980 | 226,545,805 | 188,371,622.0 | 26,495,025 | 1,420,400 | 3,500,439 | 6,758,319 | 14,608,673 | 180,256,366 |
| Sample | 226,545,805 | 189,035,012.0 | 26,482,349 | 1,534,336 | 3,726,440 | 5,767,668 | 14,603,683 | 180,602,838 |
| 1970 | 203,211,926 | 177,748,975.0 | 22,580,289 | 792,730 | 1,369,412 | 720,520 | (NA) | (NA) |
| 15% sample[a] | 203,210,158 | 178,119,221.0 | 22,539,362 | 760,572 | 1,356,967 | 434,036 | 9,589,216 | 169,023,068 |
| 5% sample | 203,193,774 | 178,081,520.0 | 22,565,377 | (NA) | (NA) | (NA) | 9,072,602 | 169,615,394 |
| 1960[b] | 179,323,175 | 158,831,732.0 | 18,871,831 | 523,591 | 877,934 | 218,087 | (NA) | (NA) |
| 1960[c] | 178,464,236 | 158,454,956.0 | 18,860,117 | 508,675 | 565,443 | 75,045 | (NA) | (NA) |
| 1950 | 150,697,361 | 134,942,028.0 | 15,042,286 | 343,410 | 259,397 | 110,240 | (NA) | (NA) |
| 1940[d] | 131,669,275 | 118,214,870.0 | 12,865,518 | 333,969 | 254,918 | (X) | 1,858,027 | 116,356,846 |
| 5% sample[d] | (NA) | 118,392,040.0 | (NA) | (NA) | (NA) | (X) | 1,861,400 | 116,530,640 |
| 1930 | 122,775,046 | 110,286,740.0 | 11,891,143 | 332,397 | 264,766 | (X) | (NA) | (NA) |
| 1920 | 105,710,620 | 94,820,915.0 | 10,463,131 | 244,437 | 182,137 | (X) | (NA) | (NA) |
| 1910 | 91,972,266 | 81,731,957.0 | 9,827,763 | 265,683 | 146,863 | (X) | (NA) | (NA) |
| 1900 | 75,994,575 | 66,809,196.0 | 8,833,994 | 237,196 | 114,189 | (X) | (NA) | (NA) |
| 1890[e] | 62,947,714 | 55,101,258.0 | 7,488,676 | 248,253 | 109,527 | (X) | (NA) | (NA) |
| 1890[f] | 62,622,250 | 54,983,890.0 | 7,470,040 | 58,806 | 109,514 | (X) | (NA) | (NA) |

| Census year | Total Population | White | Black | American Indian, Eskimo, and Aleut | Asian and Pacific Islander | Black | | |
|---|---|---|---|---|---|---|---|---|
| | | | | | | Total | Free | Slave |
| 1880 | 50,155,783 | 43,402,970.0 | 6,580,793 | 66,407 | 105,613 | | | |
| 1870 | 38,558,371 | 33,589,377.0 | 4,880,009 | 25,731 | 63,254 | | | |
| 1860 | 31,443,321 | 26,922,537.0 | 4,441,830 | 44,021 | 34,933 | 4,441,830 | 488,070 | 3,953,760 |
| 1850 | 23,191,876 | 19,553,068.0 | 3,638,808 | (NA) | (NA) | 3,638,808 | 434,495 | 3,204,313 |
| 1840 | 17,063,353 | 14,189,705.0 | 2,873,648 | (NA) | (NA) | 2,873,648 | 386,293 | 2,487,355 |
| 1830 | 12,860,702 | 10,532,060.0 | 2,328,642 | (NA) | (NA) | 2,328,642 | 319,599 | 2,009,043 |
| 1820 | 9,638,453 | 7,866,797.0 | 1,771,656 | (NA) | (NA) | 1,771,656 | 233,634 | 1,538,022 |
| 1810 | 7,239,881 | 5,862,073.0 | 1,377,808 | (NA) | (NA) | 1,377,808 | 186,446 | 1,191,362 |
| 1800 | 5,308,483 | 4,306,446.0 | 1,002,037 | (NA) | (NA) | 1,002,037 | 108,435 | 893,602 |
| 1790 | 3,929,214 | 3,172,006.0 | 757,208 | (NA) | (NA) | 757,208 | 59,527 | 697,681 |

| Census year | Total Population | White | Black | American Indian, Eskimo, and Aleut | Asian and Pacific Islander | Other race | Hispanic origin (of any race) | White, not of Hispanic origin |
|---|---|---|---|---|---|---|---|---|
| **Percent** | | | | | | | | |
| 1990 | 100.0 | 80.3 | 12.1 | 0.8 | 2.9 | 3.9 | 9.0 | 75.6 |
| Sample | 100.0 | 80.3 | 12.0 | 0.8 | 2.9 | 3.9 | 8.8 | 75.8 |
| 1980 | 100.0 | 83.1 | 11.7 | 0.6 | 1.5 | 3.0 | 6.4 | 79.6 |
| Sample | 100.0 | 83.4 | 11.7 | 0.7 | 1.6 | 2.5 | 6.4 | 79.7 |
| 1970 | 100.0 | 87.5 | 11.1 | 0.4 | 0.7 | 0.4 | (NA) | (NA) |
| 15% sample[a] | 100.0 | 87.7 | 11.1 | 0.4 | 0.7 | 0.2 | 4.7 | 83.2 |
| 5% sample | 100.0 | 87.6 | 11.1 | (NA) | (NA) | (NA) | 4.5 | 83.5 |
| 1960[b] | 100.0 | 88.6 | 10.5 | 0.3 | 0.5 | 0.1 | (NA) | (NA) |
| 1960[c] | 100.0 | 88.8 | 10.6 | 0.3 | 0.3 | — | (NA) | (NA) |
| 1950 | 100.0 | 89.5 | 10.0 | 0.2 | 0.2 | 0.1 | (NA) | (NA) |
| 1940[d] | 100.0 | 89.8 | 9.8 | 0.3 | 0.2 | (X) | 1.4 | 88.4 |
| 5% sample[d] | (NA) | 100.0 | (NA) | (NA) | (NA) | (X) | 1.4 | 88.5 |
| 1930 | 100.0 | 89.8 | 9.7 | 0.3 | 0.2 | (X) | (NA) | (NA) |
| 1920 | 100.0 | 89.7 | 9.9 | 0.2 | 0.2 | (X) | (NA) | (NA) |
| 1910 | 100.0 | 88.9 | 10.7 | 0.3 | 0.2 | (X) | (NA) | (NA) |
| 1900 | 100.0 | 87.9 | 11.6 | 0.3 | 0.2 | (X) | (NA) | (NA) |
| 1890[e] | 100.0 | 87.5 | 11.9 | 0.4 | 0.2 | (X) | (NA) | (NA) |
| 1890[f] | 100.0 | 87.8 | 11.9 | 0.1 | 0.2 | (X) | (NA) | (NA) |

| Census year | Total Population | White | Black | American Indian, Eskimo, and Aleut | Asian and Pacific Islander | Black | | |
|---|---|---|---|---|---|---|---|---|
| | | | | | | Total | Free | Slave |
| 1880 | 100.0 | 86.5 | 13.1 | 0.1 | 0.2 | | | |
| 1870 | 100.0 | 87.1 | 12.7 | 0.1 | 0.2 | | | |
| 1860 | 100.0 | 85.6 | 14.1 | 0.1 | 0.1 | 100.0 | 11.0 | 89.0 |
| 1850 | 100.0 | 84.3 | 15.7 | (NA) | (NA) | 100.0 | 11.9 | 88.1 |
| 1840 | 100.0 | 83.2 | 16.8 | (NA) | (NA) | 100.0 | 13.4 | 86.6 |
| 1830 | 100.0 | 81.9 | 18.1 | (NA) | (NA) | 100.0 | 13.7 | 86.3 |
| 1820 | 100.0 | 81.6 | 18.4 | (NA) | (NA) | 100.0 | 13.2 | 86.8 |
| 1810 | 100.0 | 81.0 | 19.0 | (NA) | (NA) | 100.0 | 13.5 | 86.5 |
| 1800 | 100.0 | 81.1 | 18.9 | (NA) | (NA) | 100.0 | 10.8 | 89.2 |
| 1790 | 100.0 | 80.7 | 19.3 | (NA) | (NA) | 100.0 | 7.9 | 92.1 |

1 provided that the "migration or importation of such persons as any of the states now existing shall think proper to admit, shall not be prohibited by the Congress prior to the year one thousand eight hundred and eight, but a tax or duty may be imposed on such importation, not exceeding ten dollars for each person." Article 1 also gave Congress power to establish "a uniform rule of naturalization" to grant U.S. citizenship.

## Alien and Sedition Acts

Early federal legislation established basic criteria for naturalization: five years' residence in the United States,

(X) = Not applicable.
(NA) = Not available.
[a]Hispanic origin based on Spanish language.
[b]Includes Alaska and Hawaii.
[c]Excludes Alaska and Hawaii.
[d]Hispanic origin based on the white population of Spanish mother tongue. Percentages shown based on sample data prorated to the 100-percent count of the white population and on the 100-percent count of the total population. These estimates are in italics.
[e]Includes Indian territory and Indian reservations.
[f]Excludes Indian territory and Indian reservations.

SOURCE: Campbell Gibson and Kay Jung, "Table A-1. Race and Hispanic Origin for the United States: 1790 to 1990," in *Historical Census Statistics on Population Totals by Race, 1790 to 1990, and by Hispanic Origin, 1970 to 1990, for the United States, Regions, Divisions, and States*, U.S. Census Bureau, Population Division, September 2002, http://www.census.gov/population/www/documentation/twps0076/twps0076.pdf (accessed March 20, 2013)

good moral character, and loyalty to the U.S. Constitution. These requirements were based on state naturalization laws. In 1798 the Federalist-controlled Congress proposed four laws, collectively called the Alien and Sedition Acts:

- The Naturalization Act lengthened the residence requirement for naturalization from five to 14 years.

- The Alien Act authorized the president to arrest and/ or expel allegedly dangerous aliens (noncitizens).

- The Alien Enemies Act allowed the imprisonment or deportation of aliens who were subjects of an enemy nation during wartime.

- The Sedition Act authorized fines and imprisonment for acts of treason, by immigrants or citizens, including "any false, scandalous and malicious writing."

The Sedition Act was used by the Federalist administration of President John Adams (1735–1826) to arrest and silence a number of newspaper editors who publicly opposed the new laws. The strong public outcry against the Alien and Sedition Acts was partly responsible for the election of Thomas Jefferson (1743–1826), the Democratic-Republican presidential candidate, in 1800. Jefferson pardoned the individuals who had been convicted under the Sedition Act. The Naturalization Act was repealed by Congress in 1802, and the other three laws were allowed to lapse.

## THE FIRST CENTURY OF IMMIGRATION

During the early 1800s U.S. territory more than doubled in size with the addition of 828,000 square miles (2.1 million square kilometers) of land with the Louisiana Purchase. Reports of rich farmland and virgin forests provided by explorers such as Meriwether Lewis (1774–1809) and William Clark (1770–1838) enticed Europeans from all walks of life—farmers, craftsmen, merchants, miners, laborers, and wealthy investors—to leave Europe for the land of opportunity. The U.S. Department of Homeland Security's (DHS) Office of Immigration Statistics reports in *Yearbook of Immigration Statistics: 2011* (September 2012, http://www.dhs .gov/sites/default/files/publications/immigrationstatistics/

yearbook/2011/ois_yb_2011.pdf) that in 1820, the first year immigration records were kept, only 8,385 immigrants were granted legal permanent residence in the United States. (See Table 1.2.) The number rose slowly at first and then more rapidly, with substantial year-to-year variations. In 1828, for example, 27,382 immigrants were granted legal permanent residence, and then between 1829 and 1831 the totals fluctuated between 22,000 and 23,500 annually, before jumping to 60,482 in 1832.

### Wave of Irish and German Immigration

Europe experienced a population explosion during the 1800s. As land in Europe became more and more scarce, tenant farmers were pushed off their farms and forced into poverty. Some of these farmers immigrated to the United States to start a new life. This situation was made worse in Ireland when a fungus that caused potato crops to rot struck in 1845. Many poor Irish farmers depended on potatoes for food. They suffered greatly from famine, and epidemics of cholera and typhoid spread among the malnourished from village to village. The potato famine forced people to choose between starving to death and leaving their country. In the 10-year period between 1830 and 1839, 170,672 Irish immigrants arrived in the United States. (See Table 1.3.) Driven by the potato famine, the number of Irish immigrants rose to 656,145 between 1840 and 1849, an increase of 284%. The flow of emigrants from Ireland to the United States peaked at a little over 1 million during the 1850s.

Increasing numbers of German immigrants, who were affected by a potato famine as well as by failed political revolutions, also came to the United States in large numbers. Between 1850 and 1859 the number of German immigrants (976,072) approached that of Irish immigrants. (See Table 1.3.) The influx of Germans peaked at 1.4 million immigrants between 1880 and 1889.

### Immigration, Politics, and the Civil War

This new wave of immigration led to intense anti-Irish, anti-German, and anti-Catholic sentiments among

**TABLE 1.2**

**Immigrants granted legal permanent resident status, fiscal years 1820–2011**

| Year | Number | Year | Number | Year | Number | Year | Number |
|------|--------|------|--------|------|--------|------|--------|
| 1820 | 8,385 | 1870 | 387,203 | 1920 | 430,001 | 1970 | 373,326 |
| 1821 | 9,127 | 1871 | 321,350 | 1921 | 805,228 | 1971 | 370,478 |
| 1822 | 6,911 | 1872 | 404,806 | 1922 | 309,556 | 1972 | 384,685 |
| 1823 | 6,354 | 1873 | 459,803 | 1923 | 522,919 | 1973 | 398,515 |
| 1824 | 7,912 | 1874 | 313,339 | 1924 | 706,896 | 1974 | 393,919 |
| 1825 | 10,199 | 1875 | 227,498 | 1925 | 294,314 | 1975 | 385,378 |
| 1826 | 10,837 | 1876 | 169,986 | 1926 | 304,488 | 1976* | 499,093 |
| 1827 | 18,875 | 1877 | 141,857 | 1927 | 335,175 | 1977 | 458,755 |
| 1828 | 27,382 | 1878 | 138,469 | 1928 | 307,255 | 1978 | 589,810 |
| 1829 | 22,520 | 1879 | 177,826 | 1929 | 279,678 | 1979 | 394,244 |
| 1830 | 23,322 | 1880 | 457,257 | 1930 | 241,700 | 1980 | 524,295 |
| 1831 | 22,633 | 1881 | 669,431 | 1931 | 97,139 | 1981 | 595,014 |
| 1832 | 60,482 | 1882 | 788,992 | 1932 | 35,576 | 1982 | 533,624 |
| 1833 | 58,640 | 1883 | 603,322 | 1933 | 23,068 | 1983 | 550,052 |
| 1834 | 65,365 | 1884 | 518,592 | 1934 | 29,470 | 1984 | 541,811 |
| 1835 | 45,374 | 1885 | 395,346 | 1935 | 34,956 | 1985 | 568,149 |
| 1836 | 76,242 | 1886 | 334,203 | 1936 | 36,329 | 1986 | 600,027 |
| 1837 | 79,340 | 1887 | 490,109 | 1937 | 50,244 | 1987 | 599,889 |
| 1838 | 38,914 | 1888 | 546,889 | 1938 | 67,895 | 1988 | 641,346 |
| 1839 | 68,069 | 1889 | 444,427 | 1939 | 82,998 | 1989 | 1,090,172 |
| 1840 | 84,066 | 1890 | 455,302 | 1940 | 70,756 | 1990 | 1,535,872 |
| 1841 | 80,289 | 1891 | 560,319 | 1941 | 51,776 | 1991 | 1,826,595 |
| 1842 | 104,565 | 1892 | 579,663 | 1942 | 28,781 | 1992 | 973,445 |
| 1843 | 52,496 | 1893 | 439,730 | 1943 | 23,725 | 1993 | 903,916 |
| 1844 | 78,615 | 1894 | 285,631 | 1944 | 28,551 | 1994 | 803,993 |
| 1845 | 114,371 | 1895 | 258,536 | 1945 | 38,119 | 1995 | 720,177 |
| 1846 | 154,416 | 1896 | 343,267 | 1946 | 108,721 | 1996 | 915,560 |
| 1847 | 234,968 | 1897 | 230,832 | 1947 | 147,292 | 1997 | 797,847 |
| 1848 | 226,527 | 1898 | 229,299 | 1948 | 170,570 | 1998 | 653,206 |
| 1849 | 297,024 | 1899 | 311,715 | 1949 | 188,317 | 1999 | 644,787 |
| 1850 | 369,980 | 1900 | 448,572 | 1950 | 249,187 | 2000 | 841,002 |
| 1851 | 379,466 | 1901 | 487,918 | 1951 | 205,717 | 2001 | 1,058,902 |
| 1852 | 371,603 | 1902 | 648,743 | 1952 | 265,520 | 2002 | 1,059,356 |
| 1853 | 368,645 | 1903 | 857,046 | 1953 | 170,434 | 2003 | 703,542 |
| 1854 | 427,833 | 1904 | 812,870 | 1954 | 208,177 | 2004 | 957,883 |
| 1855 | 200,877 | 1905 | 1,026,499 | 1955 | 237,790 | 2005 | 1,122,257 |
| 1856 | 200,436 | 1906 | 1,100,735 | 1956 | 321,625 | 2006 | 1,266,129 |
| 1857 | 251,306 | 1907 | 1,285,349 | 1957 | 326,867 | 2007 | 1,052,415 |
| 1858 | 123,126 | 1908 | 782,870 | 1958 | 253,265 | 2008 | 1,107,126 |
| 1859 | 121,282 | 1909 | 751,786 | 1959 | 260,686 | 2009 | 1,130,818 |
| 1860 | 153,640 | 1910 | 1,041,570 | 1960 | 265,398 | 2010 | 1,042,625 |
| 1861 | 91,918 | 1911 | 878,587 | 1961 | 271,344 | 2011 | 1,062,040 |
| 1862 | 91,985 | 1912 | 838,172 | 1962 | 283,763 | | |
| 1863 | 176,282 | 1913 | 1,197,892 | 1963 | 306,260 | | |
| 1864 | 193,418 | 1914 | 1,218,480 | 1964 | 292,248 | | |
| 1865 | 248,120 | 1915 | 326,700 | 1965 | 296,697 | | |
| 1866 | 318,568 | 1916 | 298,826 | 1966 | 323,040 | | |
| 1867 | 315,722 | 1917 | 295,403 | 1967 | 361,972 | | |
| 1868 | 138,840 | 1918 | 110,618 | 1968 | 454,448 | | |
| 1869 | 352,768 | 1919 | 141,132 | 1969 | 358,579 | | |

*Includes the 15 months from July 1, 1975 to September 30, 1976 because the end date of fiscal years was changed from June 30 to September 30.

SOURCE: "Table 1. Persons Obtaining Legal Permanent Resident Status: Fiscal Years 1820 to 2011," in *Yearbook of Immigration Statistics: 2011*, U.S. Department of Homeland Security, Office of Policy, Office of Immigration Statistics, September 2012, http://www.dhs.gov/sites/default/files/publications/immigration-statistics/yearbook/2011/ois_yb_2011.pdf (accessed March 5, 2013)

Americans, even among those whose families had been in the United States for only a few generations. It also triggered the creation of secret nativist societies (groups professing to protect the interests of the native-born against immigrants). Out of these groups grew a new political party, the Know Nothing movement (later known as the American Party), which claimed to support the rights of Protestant, American-born voters. The American Party managed to win 75 seats in Congress and six governorships in 1855 before it dissolved.

In contrast to the nativists, the Republican Party was welcoming to immigrants. The "Republican Party Platform of 1864" (2013, http://www.presidency.ucsb.edu/ws/index.php?pid=29621), which was written in part by Abraham Lincoln (1809–1865), stated, "Resolved, That foreign immigration, which in the past has added so much to the wealth, development of resources and increase of power to the nation, the asylum of the oppressed of all nations, should be fostered and encouraged by a liberal and just policy."

In 1862 Lincoln signed the Homestead Law, which offered 160 acres (65 hectares) of free land to any adult citizen or prospective citizen who agreed to occupy and improve the land for five years. Wepman notes that between

TABLE 1.3

## Immigration by region and selected country of last residence, fiscal years 1820–2011

| Region and country of last residence[a] | 1820 to 1829 | 1830 to 1839 | 1840 to 1849 | 1850 to 1859 | 1860 to 1869 | 1870 to 1879 | 1880 to 1889 | 1890 to 1899 | 1900 to 1909 | 1910 to 1919 | 1920 to 1929 |
|---|---|---|---|---|---|---|---|---|---|---|---|
| **Total** | **128,502** | **538,381** | **1,427,337** | **2,814,554** | **2,081,261** | **2,742,137** | **5,248,568** | **3,694,294** | **8,202,388** | **6,347,380** | **4,295,510** |
| Europe | 99,618 | 422,853 | 1,369,423 | 2,622,617 | 1,880,389 | 2,252,050 | 4,638,684 | 3,576,411 | 7,572,569 | 4,985,411 | 2,560,340 |
| Austria-Hungary[b, c] | — | — | — | — | 3,375 | 60,127 | 314,787 | 534,059 | 2,001,376 | 1,154,727 | 60,891 |
| Austria[b, c] | — | — | — | — | 2,700 | 54,529 | 204,805 | 268,218 | 532,416 | 589,174 | 31,392 |
| Hungary[b, c] | — | — | — | — | 483 | 5,598 | 109,982 | 203,350 | 685,567 | 565,553 | 29,499 |
| Belgium | 28 | 20 | 3,996 | 5,765 | 5,785 | 6,991 | 18,738 | 19,642 | 37,429 | 32,574 | 21,511 |
| Bulgaria[d] | — | — | — | — | — | — | — | 52 | 34,651 | 27,180 | 2,824 |
| Czechoslovakia[e] | — | — | — | — | — | — | — | — | — | — | 101,182 |
| Denmark | 173 | 927 | 671 | 3,227 | 13,553 | 29,278 | 85,342 | 56,671 | 61,227 | 45,830 | 34,406 |
| Finland[f] | — | — | — | — | 3 | 286 | 9,617 | 36,719 | — | — | 16,922 |
| France | 7,694 | 39,330 | 75,300 | 81,778 | 35,938 | 71,901 | 48,193 | 35,616 | 67,735 | 60,335 | 54,842 |
| Germany[c] | 5,753 | 124,726 | 385,434 | 976,072 | 723,734 | 751,769 | 1,445,181 | 579,072 | 328,722 | 174,227 | 386,634 |
| Greece | 17 | 49 | 17 | 32 | 51 | 209 | 1,807 | 12,732 | 145,402 | 198,108 | 60,774 |
| Ireland[g] | 51,617 | 170,672 | 656,145 | 1,029,486 | 427,419 | 422,264 | 674,061 | 405,710 | 344,940 | 166,445 | 201,644 |
| Italy | 430 | 2,225 | 1,476 | 8,643 | 9,853 | 46,296 | 267,660 | 603,761 | 1,930,475 | 1,229,916 | 528,133 |
| Netherlands | 1,105 | 1,377 | 7,624 | 11,122 | 8,387 | 14,267 | 52,715 | 29,349 | 42,463 | 46,065 | 29,397 |
| Norway-Sweden[h] | 91 | 1,149 | 12,389 | 22,202 | 82,937 | 178,823 | 586,441 | 334,058 | 426,981 | 192,445 | 170,329 |
| Norway[h] | — | — | — | — | — | 88,644 | 185,111 | 96,810 | 182,542 | 79,488 | 70,327 |
| Sweden[h] | — | — | — | — | — | 90,179 | 401,330 | 237,248 | 244,439 | 112,957 | 100,002 |
| Poland[c] | 19 | 366 | 105 | 1,087 | 1,886 | 11,016 | 42,910 | 107,793 | — | — | 224,420 |
| Portugal[f] | 252 | 896 | 359 | 4,218 | 4,741 | 13,990 | 15,189 | 25,874 | 65,154 | 82,489 | 44,829 |
| Romania | — | — | — | — | — | — | 5,842 | 6,808 | 57,322 | 13,566 | 67,810 |
| Russia[c, f, i] | 86 | 280 | 520 | 423 | 1,667 | 34,977 | 173,081 | 413,382 | 1,501,301 | 1,106,998 | 61,604 |
| Spain | 2,866 | 2,016 | 1,917 | 8,803 | 6,970 | 5,571 | 3,999 | 9,189 | 24,818 | 53,262 | 47,109 |
| Switzerland | 3,148 | 4,430 | 4,819 | 24,423 | 21,124 | 25,212 | 81,151 | 37,020 | 32,541 | 22,839 | 31,772 |
| United Kingdom[k] | 26,336 | 74,350 | 218,572 | 445,322 | 532,956 | 578,447 | 810,900 | 328,759 | 469,518 | 371,878 | 342,762 |
| Yugoslavia[l] | — | — | — | — | — | — | — | — | — | — | 49,215 |
| Other Europe | 3 | 40 | 79 | 14 | 10 | 626 | 1,070 | 145 | 514 | 6,527 | 21,330 |
| Asia | 34 | 55 | 121 | 36,080 | 54,408 | 134,071 | 71,152 | 61,304 | 300,441 | 269,736 | 126,740 |
| China | 3 | 8 | 32 | 35,933 | 54,028 | 133,139 | 65,797 | 15,268 | 19,884 | 20,916 | 30,648 |
| Hong Kong | — | — | — | — | — | — | — | — | — | — | — |
| India | 9 | 38 | 33 | 42 | 50 | 166 | 247 | 102 | 3,026 | 3,478 | 2,076 |
| Iran | — | — | 7 | — | 4 | 17 | 18 | 26 | — | — | 208 |
| Israel | — | — | — | — | — | — | — | — | — | — | — |
| Japan | — | — | — | — | 138 | 193 | 1,583 | 13,998 | 139,712 | 77,125 | 42,057 |
| Jordan | — | — | — | — | — | — | — | — | — | — | — |
| Korea[m] | — | — | — | — | — | — | — | — | — | — | — |
| Philippines | — | — | — | — | — | 4 | 1 | 19 | 605 | — | — |
| Syria[n] | — | — | — | — | 2 | 7 | 140 | — | — | — | — |
| Taiwan | — | — | — | — | — | — | — | — | — | — | 5,307 |
| Turkey | 19 | 8 | 45 | 94 | 129 | 382 | 2,478 | 27,510 | 127,999 | 160,717 | 40,374 |
| Vietnam | — | — | — | — | — | — | — | — | — | — | — |
| Other Asia | 3 | 1 | 4 | 11 | 57 | 163 | 888 | 4,381 | 9,215 | 7,500 | 6,070 |
| America | 9,656 | 31,911 | 50,527 | 84,201 | 130,427 | 345,889 | 529,845 | 38,756 | 277,882 | 1,070,539 | 1,591,278 |
| Canada and Newfoundland[o, p, q] | 2,297 | 11,875 | 34,285 | 64,171 | 117,975 | 323,974 | 492,508 | 2,668 | 123,067 | 708,715 | 949,286 |
| Mexico[p, q] | 3,835 | 7,187 | 3,069 | 3,446 | 1,957 | 5,133 | 2,405 | 734 | 31,188 | 185,334 | 498,945 |
| Caribbean | 3,061 | 11,792 | 11,803 | 12,447 | 8,809 | 14,592 | 27,600 | 31,885 | 100,960 | 120,860 | 83,482 |
| Cuba | — | — | — | — | 3,420 | 8,705 | 20,134 | 23,669 | — | — | 12,769 |
| Dominican Republic | — | — | — | — | — | — | — | — | — | — | — |
| Haiti | — | — | — | — | 78 | 149 | 124 | 101 | — | — | — |
| Jamaica[r] | — | — | — | — | 61 | 257 | 355 | 223 | — | — | — |
| Other Caribbean[r] | 3,061 | 11,792 | 11,803 | 12,447 | 5,250 | 5,481 | 6,987 | 7,892 | 100,960 | 120,860 | 70,713 |
| Central America | 57 | 94 | 297 | 512 | 70 | 202 | 359 | 674 | 7,341 | 15,692 | 16,511 |
| Belize | — | — | — | — | 9 | 26 | 80 | 25 | 583 | 40 | 285 |
| Costa Rica | — | — | — | — | 2 | 4 | 1 | 4 | — | — | — |
| El Salvador | — | — | — | — | — | 3 | — | 7 | — | — | — |
| Guatemala | — | — | — | — | 1 | 10 | 3 | 9 | — | — | — |
| Honduras | — | — | — | — | — | 11 | 4 | 4 | — | — | — |
| Nicaragua | — | — | — | — | — | 1 | 1 | 3 | — | — | — |
| Panama[s] | — | — | — | — | — | — | — | — | — | — | — |
| Other Central America | 57 | 94 | 297 | 512 | 58 | 147 | 270 | 622 | 6,758 | 15,652 | 16,226 |
| South America | 405 | 957 | 1,062 | 3,569 | 1,536 | 1,109 | 1,954 | 1,389 | 15,253 | 39,938 | 43,025 |
| Argentina | — | — | — | — | 7 | 58 | 64 | 36 | — | — | — |
| Bolivia | — | — | — | — | — | 5 | — | — | — | — | — |
| Brazil | — | — | — | — | 32 | 219 | 199 | 92 | — | — | 4,627 |
| Chile | — | — | — | — | 25 | 92 | 44 | 66 | — | — | — |
| Colombia | — | — | — | — | 2 | 196 | 1,210 | 607 | — | — | — |
| Ecuador | — | — | — | — | — | 7 | 14 | 33 | — | — | — |
| Guyana | — | — | — | — | 41 | 95 | 68 | 27 | — | — | — |
| Paraguay | — | — | — | — | — | 2 | — | — | — | — | — |

# TABLE 1.3

**Immigration by region and selected country of last residence, fiscal years 1820–2011** [CONTINUED]

| Region and country of last residence[a] | 1820 to 1829 | 1830 to 1839 | 1840 to 1849 | 1850 to 1859 | 1860 to 1869 | 1870 to 1879 | 1880 to 1889 | 1890 to 1899 | 1900 to 1909 | 1910 to 1919 | 1920 to 1929 |
|---|---|---|---|---|---|---|---|---|---|---|---|
| Peru | — | — | — | — | 35 | 127 | 25 | 79 | — | — | — |
| Suriname | — | — | — | — | — | 22 | 4 | 144 | — | — | — |
| Uruguay | — | — | — | — | — | — | — | — | — | — | — |
| Venezuela | — | — | — | — | 36 | 190 | 248 | — | — | — | — |
| Other South America | 405 | 957 | 1,062 | 3,569 | 1,358 | 96 | 78 | 305 | 15,253 | 39,938 | 38,398 |
| Other America | 1 | 6 | 11 | 56 | 80 | 879 | 5,019 | 1,406 | 73 | — | 29 |
| Africa | 19 | 66 | 67 | 104 | 458 | 441 | 768 | 432 | 6,326 | 8,867 | 6,362 |
| Egypt | — | — | — | 5 | 8 | 29 | 145 | 51 | — | — | 1,063 |
| Ethiopia | — | — | — | — | — | — | — | — | — | — | — |
| Liberia | 1 | 8 | 5 | 7 | 43 | 52 | 21 | 9 | — | — | — |
| Morocco | — | 4 | 1 | — | — | 15 | 12 | 9 | — | — | — |
| South Africa | — | — | — | — | 79 | 48 | 23 | 9 | — | — | — |
| Other Africa | 18 | 54 | 61 | 92 | 328 | 297 | 567 | 354 | 6,326 | 8,867 | 5,299 |
| Oceania | 2 | 1 | 3 | 110 | 107 | 9,094 | 7,341 | 3,279 | 11,677 | 12,339 | 9,860 |
| Australia | 2 | 1 | 2 | 104 | 96 | 8,933 | 7,250 | 3,098 | 11,191 | 11,280 | 8,404 |
| New Zealand[t] | — | — | — | 2 | 6 | 39 | 21 | 12 | — | — | 935 |
| Other Oceania | — | — | 1 | 4 | 5 | 122 | 70 | 169 | 486 | 1,059 | 521 |
| Not specified[u] | 19,173 | 83,495 | 7,196 | 71,442 | 15,472 | 592 | 778 | 14,112 | 33,493 | 488 | 930 |

| Region and country of last residence[a] | 1930 to 1939 | 1940 to 1949 | 1950 to 1959 | 1960 to 1969 | 1970 to 1979 | 1980 to 1989 | 1990 to 1999 | 2000 to 2009 | 2010 | 2011 |
|---|---|---|---|---|---|---|---|---|---|---|
| **Total** | **699,375** | **856,608** | **2,499,268** | **3,213,749** | **4,248,203** | **6,244,379** | **9,775,398** | **10,299,430** | **1,042,625** | **1,062,040** |
| Europe | 444,404 | 472,524 | 1,404,973 | 1,133,443 | 826,327 | 669,694 | 1,349,219 | 1,349,609 | 95,429 | 90,712 |
| Austria-Hungary[b,c] | 13,902 | 13,677 | 113,015 | 27,590 | 20,387 | 20,437 | 27,529 | 33,929 | 4,325 | 4,703 |
| Austria[b,c] | 6,678 | 8,496 | 81,354 | 17,571 | 14,239 | 15,374 | 18,234 | 21,151 | 3,319 | 3,654 |
| Hungary[b,c] | 7,224 | 5,181 | 31,661 | 10,019 | 6,148 | 5,063 | 9,295 | 12,778 | 1,006 | 1,049 |
| Belgium | 4,013 | 12,473 | 18,885 | 9,647 | 5,413 | 7,028 | 7,077 | 8,157 | 732 | 700 |
| Bulgaria[d] | 1,062 | 449 | 97 | 598 | 1,011 | 1,124 | 16,948 | 40,003 | 2,465 | 2,549 |
| Czechoslovakia[e] | 17,757 | 8,475 | 1,624 | 2,758 | 5,654 | 5,678 | 8,970 | 18,691 | 1,510 | 1,374 |
| Denmark | 3,470 | 4,549 | 10,918 | 9,797 | 4,405 | 4,847 | 6,189 | 6,049 | 545 | 473 |
| Finland[f] | 2,438 | 2,230 | 4,923 | 4,310 | 2,829 | 2,569 | 3,970 | 3,970 | 414 | 398 |
| France | 13,761 | 36,954 | 50,113 | 46,975 | 27,018 | 32,894 | 36,552 | 45,637 | 7,929 | 7,072 |
| Germany[c] | 117,736 | 119,403 | 576,905 | 209,616 | 77,142 | 85,752 | 92,207 | 122,373 | 966 | 1,196 |
| Greece | 10,599 | 8,605 | 45,153 | 74,173 | 102,370 | 37,729 | 25,403 | 16,841 | 1,610 | 1,533 |
| Ireland[g] | 28,195 | 15,701 | 47,189 | 37,788 | 11,461 | 22,210 | 65,384 | 15,642 | 2,956 | 2,670 |
| Italy | 85,053 | 50,509 | 189,061 | 200,111 | 150,031 | 55,562 | 75,992 | 28,329 | 1,520 | 1,258 |
| Netherlands | 7,791 | 13,877 | 46,703 | 37,918 | 10,373 | 11,234 | 13,345 | 17,351 | 1,662 | 1,530 |
| Norway-Sweden[h] | 13,452 | 17,326 | 44,231 | 36,150 | 10,298 | 13,941 | 17,825 | 19,382 | — | — |
| Norway[h] | 6,901 | 8,326 | 22,813 | 17,371 | 3,927 | 3,835 | 5,211 | 4,599 | 363 | 405 |
| Sweden[h] | 6,551 | 9,000 | 21,418 | 18,779 | 6,371 | 10,106 | 12,614 | 14,783 | 1,299 | 1,125 |
| Poland[c] | 26,460 | 7,774 | 6,498 | 55,773 | 33,699 | 63,483 | 172,249 | 117,921 | 7,391 | 6,634 |
| Portugal[f] | 3,518 | 6,765 | 13,928 | 70,568 | 104,754 | 42,685 | 25,497 | 11,479 | 759 | 878 |
| Romania | 5,264 | 1,254 | 914 | 2,339 | 10,774 | 24,753 | 48,136 | 52,154 | 3,735 | 3,679 |
| Russia[c,f,i] | 2,473 | 605 | 453 | 2,329 | 28,132 | 33,311 | 433,427 | 167,152 | 7,502 | 8,548 |
| Spain | 3,669 | 2,774 | 6,880 | 40,793 | 41,718 | 22,783 | 18,443 | 17,695 | 2,040 | 2,319 |
| Switzerland | 5,990 | 9,904 | 17,577 | 19,193 | 8,536 | 8,316 | 11,768 | 12,173 | 868 | 861 |
| United Kingdom[k] | 61,813 | 131,794 | 195,709 | 220,213 | 133,218 | 153,644 | 156,182 | 171,979 | 14,781 | 13,443 |
| Yugoslavia[l] | 6,920 | 2,039 | 6,966 | 17,990 | 31,862 | 16,267 | 57,039 | 131,831 | 4,772 | 4,611 |
| Other Europe | 9,068 | 5,387 | 7,231 | 6,814 | 5,242 | 3,447 | 29,087 | 290,871 | 22,608 | 20,316 |
| Asia | 19,292 | 34,532 | 135,844 | 358,563 | 1,406,526 | 2,391,356 | 2,859,899 | 3,470,835 | 410,209 | 438,580 |
| China | 5,874 | 16,072 | 8,836 | 14,060 | 17,627 | 170,897 | 342,058 | 591,711 | 67,634 | 83,603 |
| Hong Kong | — | — | 13,781 | 67,047 | 117,350 | 112,132 | 116,894 | 57,583 | 3,263 | 3,149 |
| India | 554 | 1,692 | 1,922 | 18,638 | 148,018 | 231,649 | 352,528 | 590,464 | 66,185 | 66,331 |
| Iran | 198 | 1,144 | 3,195 | 9,059 | 33,763 | 98,141 | 76,899 | 76,755 | 9,078 | 9,015 |
| Israel | — | 98 | 21,376 | 30,911 | 36,306 | 43,669 | 41,340 | 54,081 | 5,172 | 4,389 |
| Japan | 2,683 | 1,557 | 41,968 | 40,956 | 52,812 | 44,150 | 66,582 | 84,552 | 7,100 | 6,751 |
| Jordan | — | 3 | 4,919 | 9,230 | 25,541 | 28,928 | 42,755 | 53,550 | 9,327 | 8,211 |
| Korea[m] | — | 83 | 4,845 | 27,048 | 241,192 | 322,708 | 179,770 | 209,758 | 22,022 | 22,748 |
| Philippines | 457 | 4,099 | 17,245 | 70,660 | 337,726 | 502,056 | 534,338 | 545,463 | 56,399 | 55,251 |
| Syria[n] | 2,188 | 1,179 | 1,091 | 2,432 | 8,086 | 14,534 | 22,906 | 30,807 | 7,424 | 7,983 |
| Taiwan | — | — | 721 | 15,657 | 83,155 | 119,051 | 132,647 | 92,657 | 6,785 | 6,206 |
| Turkey | 1,314 | 754 | 2,980 | 9,464 | 12,209 | 19,208 | 38,687 | 48,394 | 7,435 | 9,040 |
| Vietnam | — | — | 290 | 2,949 | 121,716 | 200,632 | 275,379 | 289,616 | 30,065 | 33,486 |
| Other Asia | 6,024 | 7,851 | 12,675 | 40,452 | 171,025 | 483,601 | 637,116 | 745,444 | 112,320 | 122,417 |
| America | 230,319 | 328,435 | 921,644 | 1,674,185 | 1,903,636 | 2,694,504 | 5,137,142 | 4,441,529 | 426,981 | 423,277 |
| Canada and Newfoundland[o,p,q] | 162,703 | 160,911 | 353,169 | 433,128 | 179,267 | 156,313 | 194,788 | 236,349 | 19,491 | 19,506 |
| Mexico[p,q] | 32,709 | 56,158 | 273,847 | 441,824 | 621,218 | 1,009,586 | 2,757,418 | 1,704,166 | 138,717 | 142,823 |
| Caribbean | 18,052 | 46,285 | 115,869 | 427,843 | 708,643 | 789,343 | 1,004,114 | 1,053,357 | 139,389 | 133,012 |
| Cuba | 10,641 | 25,976 | 73,221 | 202,030 | 256,497 | 132,552 | 159,037 | 271,742 | 33,372 | 36,261 |

**TABLE 1.3**

**Immigration by region and selected country of last residence, fiscal years 1820–2011** [CONTINUED]

| Region and country of last residence[a] | 1930 to 1939 | 1940 to 1949 | 1950 to 1959 | 1960 to 1969 | 1970 to 1979 | 1980 to 1989 | 1990 to 1999 | 2000 to 2009 | 2010 | 2011 |
|---|---|---|---|---|---|---|---|---|---|---|
| Dominican Republic | 1,165 | 4,802 | 10,219 | 83,552 | 139,249 | 221,552 | 359,818 | 291,492 | 53,890 | 46,036 |
| Haiti | 207 | 823 | 3,787 | 28,992 | 55,166 | 121,406 | 177,446 | 203,827 | 22,336 | 21,802 |
| Jamaica[r] | — | — | 7,397 | 62,218 | 130,226 | 193,874 | 177,143 | 172,523 | 19,439 | 19,298 |
| Other Caribbean[r] | 6,039 | 14,684 | 21,245 | 51,051 | 127,505 | 119,959 | 130,670 | 113,773 | 10,352 | 9,615 |
| Central America | 6,840 | 20,135 | 40,201 | 98,569 | 120,376 | 339,376 | 610,189 | 591,130 | 43,597 | 43,249 |
| Belize | 193 | 433 | 1,133 | 4,185 | 6,747 | 14,964 | 12,600 | 9,682 | 997 | 933 |
| Costa Rica | 580 | 1,965 | 4,044 | 17,975 | 12,405 | 25,017 | 17,054 | 21,571 | 2,306 | 2,230 |
| El Salvador | 712 | 4,885 | 5,094 | 14,405 | 29,428 | 137,418 | 273,017 | 251,237 | 18,547 | 18,477 |
| Guatemala | 632 | 1,303 | 4,197 | 14,357 | 23,837 | 58,847 | 126,043 | 156,992 | 10,263 | 10,795 |
| Honduras | 809 | 1,874 | 5,320 | 15,087 | 15,653 | 39,071 | 72,880 | 63,513 | 6,381 | 6,053 |
| Nicaragua | 564 | 4,393 | 7,812 | 10,383 | 10,911 | 31,102 | 80,446 | 70,015 | 3,476 | 3,314 |
| Panama[s] | 1,774 | 5,282 | 12,601 | 22,177 | 21,395 | 32,957 | 28,149 | 18,120 | 1,627 | 1,447 |
| Other Central America | 1,576 | — | — | — | — | — | — | — | | |
| South America | 9,990 | 19,662 | 78,418 | 250,754 | 273,529 | 399,803 | 570,596 | 856,508 | 85,783 | 84,687 |
| Argentina | 1,397 | 3,108 | 16,346 | 49,384 | 30,303 | 23,442 | 30,065 | 47,955 | 4,312 | 4,335 |
| Bolivia | 77 | 893 | 2,759 | 6,205 | 5,635 | 9,798 | 18,111 | 21,921 | 2,211 | 2,113 |
| Brazil | 1,468 | 3,653 | 11,547 | 29,238 | 18,600 | 22,944 | 50,744 | 115,404 | 12,057 | 11,643 |
| Chile | 568 | 1,320 | 4,669 | 12,384 | 15,032 | 19,749 | 18,200 | 19,792 | 1,940 | 1,854 |
| Colombia | 1,278 | 3,454 | 15,567 | 68,371 | 71,265 | 105,494 | 137,985 | 236,570 | 21,861 | 22,130 |
| Ecuador | 320 | 2,207 | 8,574 | 34,107 | 47,464 | 48,015 | 81,358 | 107,977 | 11,463 | 11,068 |
| Guyana | 193 | 596 | 1,131 | 4,546 | 38,278 | 85,886 | 74,407 | 70,373 | 6,441 | 6,288 |
| Paraguay | 36 | 85 | 576 | 1,249 | 1,486 | 3,518 | 6,082 | 4,623 | 449 | 501 |
| Peru | 460 | 1,273 | 5,980 | 19,783 | 25,311 | 49,958 | 110,117 | 137,614 | 14,063 | 13,836 |
| Suriname | 33 | 130 | 299 | 612 | 714 | 1,357 | 2,285 | 2,363 | 202 | 167 |
| Uruguay | 153 | 754 | 1,026 | 4,089 | 8,416 | 7,235 | 6,062 | 9,827 | 1,286 | 1,521 |
| Venezuela | 1,360 | 2,182 | 9,927 | 20,758 | 11,007 | 22,405 | 35,180 | 82,087 | 9,497 | 9,229 |
| Other South America | 2,647 | 7 | 17 | 28 | 18 | 2 | — | 2 | 1 | 2 |
| Other America | 25 | 25,284 | 60,140 | 22,076 | 603 | 83 | 37 | 19 | 4 | — |
| Africa | 2,120 | 6,720 | 13,016 | 23,780 | 71,405 | 141,987 | 346,410 | 759,734 | 98,246 | 97,429 |
| Egypt | 781 | 1,613 | 1,996 | 5,581 | 23,543 | 26,744 | 44,604 | 81,564 | 9,822 | 9,096 |
| Ethiopia | 10 | 28 | 302 | 804 | 2,588 | 12,927 | 40,097 | 87,207 | 13,853 | 13,985 |
| Liberia | 35 | 37 | 289 | 841 | 2,391 | 6,420 | 13,587 | 23,316 | 2,924 | 3,117 |
| Morocco | 110 | 1,463 | 3,293 | 2,880 | 1,967 | 3,471 | 15,768 | 40,844 | 4,847 | 4,249 |
| South Africa | 312 | 1,022 | 2,278 | 4,360 | 10,002 | 15,505 | 21,964 | 32,221 | 2,705 | 2,754 |
| Other Africa | 872 | 2,557 | 4,858 | 9,314 | 30,914 | 76,920 | 210,390 | 494,582 | 64,095 | 64,228 |
| Oceania | 3,240 | 14,262 | 11,319 | 23,659 | 39,983 | 41,432 | 56,800 | 65,793 | 5,946 | 5,825 |
| Australia | 2,260 | 11,201 | 8,275 | 14,986 | 18,708 | 16,901 | 24,288 | 32,728 | 3,077 | 3,062 |
| New Zealand[t] | 790 | 2,351 | 1,799 | 3,775 | 5,018 | 6,129 | 8,600 | 12,495 | 1,046 | 1,006 |
| Other Oceania | 190 | 710 | 1,245 | 4,898 | 16,257 | 18,402 | 23,912 | 20,570 | 1,823 | 1,757 |
| Not specified[u] | — | 135 | 12,472 | 119 | 326 | 305,406 | 25,928 | 211,930 | 5,814 | 6,217 |

—Represents zero or not available.

[a]Data for years prior to 1906 refer to country of origin; data from 1906 to 2011 refer to country of last residence.

Because of changes in country boundaries, data for a particular country may not necessarily refer to the same geographic area over time.

[b]Data for Austria and Hungary not reported separately for all years during 1860 to 1869, 1890 to 1899, and 1900 to 1909.

[c]From 1899 to 1919, data for Poland included in Austria, Germany, Hungary, and Russia.

[d]From 1899 to 1919, data for Bulgaria included Serbia and Montenegro.

[e]Currently includes Czech Republic, Czechoslovakia (former), and Slovakia.

[f]From 1899 to 1919, data for Finland included in Russia.

[g]Prior to 1925, data for Northern Ireland included in Ireland.

[h]Data for Norway and Sweden not reported separately until 1861.

[i]From 1892 to 1952, data for Cape Verde included in Portugal.

[j]From 1820 to 1920, data refer to the Russian Empire. Between 1920 and 1990 data refer to the Soviet Union. From 1991 to 1999, data refer to Russia, Armenia, Azerbaijan, Belarus, Georgia, Kazakhstan, Kyrgyzstan, Moldova, Tajikistan, Turkmenistan, Ukraine, and Uzbekistan. Beginning in 2000, data refer to Russia only.

[k]Since 1925, data for United Kingdom refer to England, Scotland, Wales and Northern Ireland.

[l]Currently includes Bosnia-Herzegovina, Croatia, Kosovo, Macedonia, Montenegro, Serbia, Serbia and Montenegro, and Slovenia.

[m]Korea includes both North and South Korea.

[n]From 1886 to 1923, data for Syria included in Turkey.

[o]Includes British North America and Canadian provinces.

[p]Land arrivals not completely enumerated until 1908.

[q]No data available for Canada or Mexico from 1886 to 1893.

[r]From 1892 to 1952, Jamaica was included in British West Indies.

[s]From 1932 to 1972, data for the Panama Canal Zone included in Panama.

[t]From 1892 to 1924, data for New Zealand included in Australia.

[u]Includes 32,897 persons returning in 1906 to their homes in the United States.

Note: Official recording of immigration to the United States begin in 1820 after the passage of the Act of March 2, 1819. From 1820 to 1867, figures represent alien passenger arrivals at seaports; from 1868 to 1891 and 1895 to 1897, immigrant alien arrivals; from 1892 to 1894 and 1898 to 2011, immigrant aliens admitted for permanent residence; from 1892 to 1903, aliens entering by cabin class were not counted as immigrants. Land arrivals were not completely enumerated until 1908. For this table, Fiscal Year 1843 covers 9 months ending September 30, 1843; Fiscal Years 1832 and 1850 cover 15 months ending December 31 of the respective years; and Fiscal Year 1868 covers 6 months ending June 30, 1868; and Fiscal Year 1976 covers 15 months ending September 30, 1976.

SOURCE: "Table 2. Persons Obtaining Legal Permanent Resident Status by Region and Selected Country of Last Residence: Fiscal Years 1820–2011," in *Yearbook of Immigration Statistics: 2011*, U.S. Department of Homeland Security, Office of Policy, Office of Immigration Statistics, September 2012, http://www.dhs.gov/sites/default/files/publications/immigration-statistics/yearbook/2011/ois_yb_2011.pdf (accessed March 5, 2013)

1862 and 1904 over 147 million acres (59.5 million hectares) of western land were claimed by adventurous citizens and eager new immigrants. In addition, efforts to complete a transcontinental railroad during the 1860s provided work for predominantly Irish and Chinese laborers.

The Civil War (1861–1865) initially restricted the flow of immigrants to the United States, but then growth of the immigrant population returned to prewar levels. As Table 1.2 shows, the number of immigrants granted legal permanent resident status dropped from 153,640 in 1860 to just under 92,000 in both 1861 and 1862, before rising to 176,282 in 1863, 193,418 in 1864, and 248,120 in 1865.

## Post–Civil War Growth in Immigration

During the Industrial Revolution, which began in the United States in the early 1800s, factory machines and large-scale manufacturing replaced hand tools and small craft shops. These changes accelerated after the Civil War, fueling the need for workers in the nation's flourishing factories. The number of arriving immigrants averaged around 335,000 annually between 1866 and 1874. (See Table 1.2.) After a short falloff in immigration between 1875 and 1879, the numbers continued their climb in the 1880s. Throughout this period the bulk of the immigrant population came from Germany, Ireland, and the United Kingdom, and the numbers of Canadians immigrating to the United States began to rival these other groups. (See Table 1.3.) Opposition to immigration continued among some factions of established citizens. Secret societies of white supremacists, such as the Ku Klux Klan, formed throughout the South to oppose not only African-American suffrage but also the influence of the Roman Catholic Church and rapid naturalization of foreign immigrants.

## East European Influx during the 1880s

The decade from 1880 to 1889 marked a new era in immigration to the United States. The volume of immigrants nearly doubled, from 2.7 million in the 1870s to 5.2 million in the 1880s. (See Table 1.3.) German arrivals peaked, and the numbers arriving from Norway, Sweden, and the United Kingdom also reached their highest levels. At the same time, a new wave of immigrants began to arrive from Russia (including a significant number of Jews fleeing massacres called pogroms), Poland, Austria-Hungary, and Italy. The mass exodus from eastern Europe foretold of events that would result during World War I (1914–1918). These newcomers came from countries with limited public education and, in some cases, less sense of social equality than previous immigrants' countries of origin. They were often unskilled and illiterate. They tended to form tight ethnic communities within large cities, where they maintained their own language and customs, which further limited their ability to assimilate into U.S. culture.

## A Developing Federal Role in Immigration

The increasing numbers of immigrants prompted a belief that there should be some type of administrative order to the ever-growing influx. In 1864 Congress created the Commission of Immigration under the U.S. Department of State. A one-person office was set up in New York City to oversee immigration.

The 1870s witnessed a national debate over the importation of contract labor and limiting immigration for such purposes. In 1875, after considerable debate, Congress passed the Page Law. As the first major piece of restrictive immigration legislation, it prohibited alien convicts and prostitutes from entering the country.

With the creation of the Commission of Immigration, the federal government began to play a central role in immigration, which had previously been handled by the individual states. Beginning in 1849 court decisions had strengthened the federal government's role and limited the states' role in regulating immigration. In 1875 the U.S. Supreme Court ultimately ruled in *Henderson v. Mayor of the City of New York* (92 U.S. 259) and *Chy Lung v. Freeman* (92 U.S. 275) that the immigration laws of New York, Louisiana, and California were unconstitutional. This ended the rights of states to regulate immigration and exclude undesirable aliens. Thereafter, the federal government had complete responsibility for immigration.

In 1882 Congress passed the first general immigration law. The Immigration Act of 1882 established a centralized immigration administration under the U.S. secretary of the treasury. The law also allowed the exclusion of "undesirables," such as paupers, criminals, and the insane. A head tax was added at $0.50 per arriving immigrant to defray the expenses of immigration regulation and caring for the immigrants after their arrival in the United States.

## Influx of Immigrants from Asia

Before the discovery of gold in California in 1848, few Asians (only 121 between 1840 and 1849) came to the United States. (See Table 1.3.) Between 1849 and 1852 large numbers of Asian immigrants began arriving in the United States. These early arrivals came mostly from southern China, spurred on by economic depression, famine, war, and flooding. Thousands of Chinese immigrants were recruited to build railroads and work in mines, construction, and manufacturing. Many became domestic servants. Former mining-camp cooks who had saved some of their income opened restaurants. Others invested small amounts in equipment to operate laundries, performing a service few other people wanted to tackle. Between 1850 and 1879, 223,100 immigrants from China arrived in the United States, whereas only a few thousand arrived from other Asian countries.

Some people became alarmed by this increase in Chinese immigration. Their fears were fueled by a combination of racism and concerns among American-born workers that employers were bringing over foreign workers to replace them and keep unskilled wages low. The public began to call for restrictions on Chinese immigration.

### Chinese Exclusion Act

In 1882 Congress passed the Chinese Exclusion Act, which prohibited further immigration of Chinese laborers to the United States for 10 years. Exceptions included teachers, diplomats, students, merchants, and tourists. This act marked the first time the United States barred immigration of a national group. The law also prohibited Chinese immigrants in the United States from becoming naturalized U.S. citizens. As a result, the law dramatically reduced Chinese immigration. Between 1890 and 1899 only 15,268 Chinese immigrants arrived, compared with the 133,139 Chinese immigrants who had arrived in the decade before the act was passed. (See Table 1.3.)

Four other laws that prohibited the immigration of Chinese laborers followed the Chinese Exclusion Act. The Geary Act of 1892 extended the Chinese Exclusion Act for 10 more years. In cases brought before the U.S. Supreme Court, the court upheld the constitutionality of these two laws. The Immigration Act of 1904 made the Chinese exclusion laws permanent. Under the Immigration Act of 1917 the United States suspended the immigration of laborers from almost all Asian countries.

During World War II (1939–1945) the United States and China became allies against the Japanese in Asia. As a gesture of goodwill, President Franklin D. Roosevelt (1882–1945) signed in December 1943 the Act to Repeal the Chinese Exclusion Acts, to Establish Quotas, and for Other Purposes. The new law lifted the ban on the naturalization of Chinese nationals but established a quota (a prescribed number) of 105 Chinese immigrants to be admitted per year.

### Beginning of Japanese Immigration

Until the passage of the Chinese Exclusion Act, Japanese immigration was hardly noticeable, with the total flow at 331 between 1860 and 1879. (See Table 1.3.) Because Japanese immigrants were not covered by the Chinese Exclusion Act, Japanese laborers were brought in to replace Chinese workers. Consequently, Japanese immigration increased from 1,583 during the 1880s to 139,712 during the first decade of the 20th century.

The same anti-Asian attitudes that led to the Chinese Exclusion Act of 1882 culminated in President Theodore

Roosevelt's (1858–1919) Gentlemen's Agreement of 1907, an informal arrangement between the United States and Japan that cut the flow of Japanese immigration to a trickle. This anti-Asian attitude resurfaced a generation later in the National Origins Act of 1924. The immigration quota for any nationality group had been based on the number of people of that nationality that were residents in the United States during the 1910 census. The new law reduced quotas from 3% to 2% and shifted the base for quota calculations from 1910 to 1890. Because few Asians lived in the United States in 1890, the 1924 reduction in Asian immigration was particularly dramatic. Asian immigration was not permitted to increase until after World War II.

### Greater Federal Control

In "U.S. Immigration and Naturalization Service—Populating a Nation: A History of Immigration and Naturalization" (2013, http://www.cbp.gov/xp/cgov/about/history/legacy/ins_history.xml), the U.S. Customs and Border Protection, the largest law enforcement agency within the DHS, provides a short history of immigration policy in the United States. It states that in 1891 the federal government assumed total control over immigration issues. The Immigration Act of 1891 authorized the establishment of the U.S. Office of Immigration under the U.S. Department of the Treasury. This first comprehensive immigration law added to the list of inadmissible people those suffering from certain contagious diseases, polygamists (married people who have more than one spouse at the same time), and aliens convicted of minor crimes. The law also prohibited using advertisements to encourage immigration.

On January 1, 1892, a new federal immigration station began operating on Ellis Island in New York City. During its years of operation, from 1892 to 1954, more than 12 million immigrants were processed through Ellis Island. This figure represents nearly half of the more than 23 million total immigrants who arrived during that period.

In 1895 the Office of Immigration became the Bureau of Immigration under the commissioner-general of immigration. In 1903 the Bureau of Immigration was transferred to the U.S. Department of Commerce and Labor. The Basic Naturalization Act of 1906 consolidated the immigration and naturalization functions of the federal government under the Bureau of Immigration and Naturalization. When the Department of Commerce and Labor was separated into two cabinet departments in 1913, two bureaus were formed: the Bureau of Immigration and the Bureau of Naturalization. In 1933 the two bureaus were reunited as the U.S. Immigration and Naturalization Service (INS).

## A MILLION IMMIGRANTS PER YEAR BY 1905

By the 1890s the origins of those arriving in the United States had changed. Fewer immigrants came from northern Europe, whereas immigrants from southern, central, and eastern Europe increased every year. Of the 7.6 million European immigrants who arrived between 1900 and 1909, 5.4 million (71%) came from Austria-Hungary, Italy, and Russia. (See Table 1.3.) The exodus of Jews from eastern Europe was particularly significant. The American Immigration Law Foundation notes in "AILF Overview of U.S. Jewish Immigration History" (December 6, 2004, http://www.ailf.org/exhibits/jewish2004/jewish_history.shtml) that many of these Jewish immigrants were merchants, shopkeepers, craftsmen, and professionals, contrary to the stereotype of poor, uneducated immigrants arriving from eastern Europe.

As Table 1.2 shows, the nation's already high immigration rate at the turn of the 20th century nearly doubled between 1902 and 1907. Immigration reached a million per year in 1905, 1906, 1907, 1910, 1913, and 1914, but declined to less than 327,000 per year from 1915 through 1919 because of World War I. Many Americans worried about the growing influx of immigrants, whose customs seemed unfamiliar and strange to most of the native population. Anti-Catholic sentiments, distrust of political radicalism (usually expressed as antisocialism), and racist movements gained prevalence and spurred a resurgence of nativism.

The Immigration Act of 1907 barred the immigration of "feeble-minded" people, people with physical or mental defects that might prevent them from earning a living, and people with tuberculosis. Besides increasing the head tax on each arriving immigrant to $5, the 1907 law also officially classified the arriving aliens as either immigrants (people planning to take up residence in the United States) or nonimmigrants (people visiting for a short period to attend school, conduct business, or travel as tourists). All arrivals were required to declare their intentions for permanent or temporary stays in the United States. The law further authorized the president to refuse admission to people he considered harmful to the labor conditions in the nation.

Reflecting national concerns about conflicts between old and new immigrant groups, the Bureau of Immigration and Naturalization proposed in annual reports that the immigrants should be more widely dispersed throughout the rest of the country, instead of being concentrated mostly in the northeastern urban areas of the United States. Not only would such a distribution of aliens help relieve the nation's urban problems but also the bureau thought it might promote greater racial and cultural assimilation.

## Immigration Act of 1917

The mounting negative feelings toward immigrants resulted in the Immigration Act of 1917, which was passed despite President Woodrow Wilson's (1856–1924) veto. Besides codifying previous immigration legislation, the 1917 act required that immigrants over the age of 16 years be able to pass a literacy test, which proved to be a controversial clause. The new act also cited the following groups to the inadmissible classes of immigrants:

> All idiots, imbeciles, feeble-minded persons, epileptics, insane persons … persons with chronic alcoholism; paupers; professional beggars; vagrants; persons afflicted with tuberculosis in any form or a loathsome or dangerous contagious disease; persons not comprehended within any of the foregoing excluded classes who are found to be and are certified by the examining surgeon as being mentally or physically defective, such physical defect being of a nature which may affect the ability of such alien to earn a living; persons who have been convicted … of a felony or other crime or misdemeanor involving moral turpitude; polygamists, or persons who practice polygamy or believe in and advocate the practice of polygamy; anarchists, or persons who advocate the overthrow by force or violence of the Government of the United States, or of all forms of law … or who advocate the assassination of public officials, or who advocate and teach the unlawful destruction of property…; prostitutes, or persons coming to the United States for the purpose of prostitution or immoral purposes.

The act also specifically disqualified those coming from the designated Asiatic "barred zone," which encompassed most of Asia and the Pacific Islands. This provision was a continuation of the Chinese Exclusion Act of 1882 and the Gentlemen's Agreement of 1907, in which the Japanese government had agreed to stop the flow of workers to the United States. In 1918 a presidential proclamation announced that passports were required for all entries into the United States.

## Denied Entry

Despite increasingly restrictive immigration legislation, only a small percentage of those attempting to immigrate to the United States were turned away. As Table 1.4 shows, 650,252 people were denied entry for a variety of reasons between 1892 and 1990. The largest excluded group consisted of 219,399 people who were considered "likely to become public charge," followed closely by the 204,943 who "attempted entry without inspection or without proper documents" beginning in the 1920s. The 30-year period from 1901 to 1930 was the peak era for exclusion of immigrants deemed likely to become public charges and those considered to be mentally or physically defective or immoral. The 1917 ban on illiterate immigrants excluded 13,679 people over the next 50 years.

# TABLE 1.4

## Immigrants denied entry by reason for denial, fiscal years 1892–1990

| Year | Total | Subversive or anarchist | Criminal or narcotics violations | Immoral | Mental or physical defect | Likely to become public charge | Stowaway | Attempted entry without inspection or without proper documents | Contract laborer | Unable to read (over 16 years of age) | Other |
|---|---|---|---|---|---|---|---|---|---|---|---|
| 1892–1990 | 650,252 | 1,369 | 17,465 | 8,209 | 82,590 | 219,399 | 16,240 | 204,943 | 41,941 | 13,679 | 44,417 |
| 1892–1900 | 22,515 | — | 65 | 89 | 1,309 | 15,070 | — | — | 5,792 | — | 190 |
| 1901–1910 | 108,211 | 10 | 1,681 | 1,277 | 24,425 | 63,311 | — | — | 12,991 | — | 4,516 |
| 1911–1920 | 178,109 | 27 | 4,353 | 4,824 | 42,129 | 90,045 | 1,904 | — | 15,417 | 5,083 | 14,327 |
| 1921–1930 | 189,307 | 9 | 2,082 | 1,281 | 11,044 | 37,175 | 8,447 | 94,084 | 6,274 | 8,202 | 20,709 |
| 1931–1940 | 68,217 | 5 | 1,261 | 253 | 1,530 | 12,519 | 2,126 | 47,858 | 1,235 | 258 | 1,172 |
| 1941–1950 | 30,263 | 60 | 1,134 | 80 | 1,021 | 1,072 | 3,182 | 22,441 | 219 | 108 | 946 |
| 1951–1960 | 20,585 | 1,098 | 2,017 | 361 | 956 | 149 | 376 | 14,657 | 13 | 26 | 932 |
| 1961–1970 | 4,831 | 128 | 383 | 24 | 145 | 27 | 175 | 3,706 | — | 2 | 241 |
| 1971–1980 | 8,455 | 32 | 814 | 20 | 31 | 31 | 30 | 7,237 | — | — | 260 |
| 1981–1990 | 19,759 | NA | 3,675 | NA | NA | NA | NA | 14,960 | — | — | 1,124 |
| 1981 | 659 | NA | 152 | NA | NA | NA | NA | 486 | — | — | 21 |
| 1982 | 698 | NA | 183 | NA | NA | NA | NA | 478 | — | — | 37 |
| 1983 | 979 | NA | 205 | NA | NA | NA | NA | 728 | — | — | 46 |
| 1984 | 1,089 | NA | 160 | NA | NA | NA | NA | 870 | — | — | 59 |
| 1985 | 1,747 | NA | 297 | NA | NA | NA | NA | 1,351 | — | — | 99 |
| 1986 | 2,278 | NA | 270 | NA | NA | NA | NA | 1,904 | — | — | 104 |
| 1987 | 1,994 | NA | 426 | NA | NA | NA | NA | 1,423 | — | — | 145 |
| 1988 | 2,693 | NA | 482 | NA | NA | NA | NA | 2,043 | — | — | 168 |
| 1989 | 3,893 | NA | 712 | NA | NA | NA | NA | 2,973 | — | — | 208 |
| 1990 | 3,729 | NA | 788 | NA | NA | NA | NA | 2,704 | — | — | 237 |

—Represents zero.

NA = Not available.

Note: From 1941–53, statistics represent all exclusions at sea and air ports and exclusions of aliens seeking entry for 30 days or longer at land ports. After 1953, includes aliens excluded after formal hearings.

SOURCE: Adapted from "Table 44. Aliens Excluded by Administrative Reason for Exclusion: Fiscal Years 1892–1990," in Yearbook of Immigration Statistics: 2004, U.S. Department of Homeland Security, Office of Policy, Office of Immigration Statistics, January 2006, http://www.dhs.gov/yearbook-immigration-statistics-2004 (accessed March 20, 2013)

World War I temporarily slowed the influx of immigrants. As Table 1.2 shows, 1,218,480 immigrants arrived in 1914; a year later the number dropped to 326,700. By 1918, the final year of the war, 110,618 immigrants ventured to the United States. However, the heavy flow of immigration started again after the war as people fled the war-ravaged European continent. In 1921, 805,228 immigrants arrived in the United States.

## First Quota Law

Concern over whether the United States could continue to absorb such huge numbers of immigrants led Congress to introduce a major change in U.S. immigration policy. Other factors influencing Congress included racial fears about the new immigrants and apprehension over some of the immigrants' politically radical ideas.

The Quota Law of 1921 was the first quantitative immigration law. Congress limited the number of aliens of any nationality who could enter the United States to 3% of the number of foreign-born people of that nationality who lived in the United States in 1910 (based on the U.S. census). By 1910, however, many south and east Europeans had already entered the country, a fact legislators had overlooked. Consequently, to restructure the makeup of the immigrant population Congress approved the National Origins Act of 1924. This act set the first permanent limitation on immigration, called the national origins quota system. The law immediately limited the number of people of each nationality to 2% of the population of that nationality who lived in the United States in 1890.

The 1924 law provided that after July 1, 1927, an overall cap would allow a total of 150,000 immigrants per year. Quotas for each national origin group were to be developed based on the 1920 census. Exempted from the quota limitation were spouses or dependents of U.S. citizens, returning alien residents, or natives of Western Hemisphere countries not subject to quotas (natives of Mexico, Canada, or other independent countries of Central or South America). The 1924 law further required that all arriving nonimmigrants present visas (government authorizations permitting entry into a country for a specific purpose and for a finite amount of time) obtained from a U.S. consulate abroad. U.S. immigration policies adhered to the 1917 and 1924 acts until 1952.

## Impact of Quotas

The new laws also barred all Asian immigration, which soon led to a shortage of farm and sugar plantation workers. Filipinos filled the gap because the Philippines was a U.S. territory at the time, and they did not come under the immigration quota laws. In addition, large numbers of Caribbean immigrants arrived, peaking during the 1910 to 1919 period, when 120,860 Caribbean immigrants entered the United States. (See Table 1.3.)

Before World War I, Caribbean workers had moved among the islands and to parts of South and Central America. Following the war many went north in search of work. Similarly, after World War II, when agricultural changes in the Caribbean forced many people off farms and into cities, many traveled on to the United States or the United Kingdom.

With the new quota laws, the problem of illegal immigrants arose for the first time. Previously, only a few who had failed the immigration standards tried to sneak in, usually across the U.S.-Mexican or U.S.-Canadian land borders. With the new laws, the number of illegal immigrants began to increase. Subsequently, Congress created the U.S. Border Patrol in 1924 (under the Labor Appropriation Act) to oversee the nation's borders and prevent illegal immigrants from coming into the United States.

## IMMIGRATION DURING WORLD WAR II

Immigration dropped well below 100,000 arrivals per year during the Great Depression (1929–1939) because the United States offered no escape from the unemployment that was rampant throughout most of the world. However, in the latter half of the 1930s Nazi persecution caused a new round of immigrants to flee Europe. In 1940 the INS was transferred from the U.S. Department of Labor to the U.S. Department of Justice. This move reflected the growing fear of war, making the surveillance of aliens a question of national security rather than one of how many to admit. The job of the INS shifted from the exclusion of aliens to combating alien criminal and subversive elements. This required closer cooperation with the U.S. attorney general's office and the Federal Bureau of Investigation.

## Alien Registration

World War II began with the German invasion of Poland in September 1939. Growing concern about an increase in refugees that might result from the war in Europe led Congress to pass the Alien Registration Act of 1940 (also known as the Smith Act). Among its provisions, this act required all aliens in the United States to register. Those over 14 years old also had to be fingerprinted. All registration and fingerprinting took place at local post offices between August 27 and December 26, 1940. Each alien was identified by an alien registration number, known as an A-number. For the first time, the government had a means of identifying individual immigrants. The law has been challenged by the courts, but the A-number system was still in use in 2013. Following registration, each alien received by mail an Alien Registration Receipt Card, which he or she was required to keep to prove registration. Each alien was also required to report any change of address within five days. Managing such a vast number of registrants and documents in a short time created a monumental challenge for the federal government. The ranks of employees in the Alien Registration Division of the INS increased dramatically in late 1940 and early 1941.

The United States officially entered World War II on December 8, 1941, the day after the Japanese attack on the U.S. naval station in Pearl Harbor, Hawaii. President Roosevelt immediately proclaimed all "nationals and subjects" of nations with which the country was at war to be enemy aliens. According to the INS, on January 14, 1942, the president issued a proclamation requiring further registration of aliens from enemy nations (primarily Germany, Italy, and Japan). All such aliens aged 14 years and older were directed to apply for a Certificate of Identification during the month of February 1942.

Alien registrations were used by a variety of government agencies and private industry to locate possible enemy subversives, such as aliens working for defense contractors, aliens with radio operator licenses, and aliens trained to pilot aircraft. The INS notes that one out of every 23 workers in U.S. industry at that time was a noncitizen.

### Japanese Internment

Following the recommendation of military advisers, President Roosevelt issued Executive Order 9066 on February 19, 1942, which authorized the forcible internment of people of Japanese ancestry. Lieutenant General John L. DeWitt (1880–1962) was placed in charge of removal of the Japanese to internment camps, which were located in remote areas in western states, including Arizona, California, Colorado, Idaho, Utah, and Wyoming. Two camps were also established in Arkansas. In *Final Report: Japanese Evacuation from the West Coast 1942* (1943), DeWitt stated that during a period of less than 90 days 110,442 people of Japanese ancestry were evacuated from the West Coast. More than two-thirds were U.S. citizens. Relocation began in April 1942. The last camp was vacated in March 1946.

Even though the United States was also at war with Germany and Italy, only people of Japanese descent were forced into internment camps. Noncitizens and citizens alike were forced to sell their homes and possessions and to leave their jobs. They lived in tiny, single-room accommodations, sometimes for many years. This treatment, based on fear of Japanese disloyalty, was later widely disparaged as unfair, demeaning, and ineffective as a national-security measure.

Executive Order 9066 was not formally terminated after the war ended. Over the years many Japanese-Americans expressed concern that it could be implemented again. In 1976 President Gerald R. Ford (1913–2006) issued a proclamation that officially terminated the provisions of Executive Order 9066 retroactive to December 31, 1946. In 1988 President Ronald Reagan (1911–2004) signed a bill into law that provided $20,000 in restitution (monetary compensation) to each of the surviving internees.

## POSTWAR IMMIGRATION LAW

A growing fear of communist infiltration, called the Red Scare, arose during the post–World War II period. One result was the passage of the Internal Security Act of 1950, which made membership in communist or totalitarian organizations cause for exclusion (denial of an alien's entry into the United States), deportation, or denial of naturalization. The law also required resident aliens to report their addresses annually and made reading, writing, and speaking English prerequisites for naturalization.

The Immigration and Nationality Act of 1952 added preferences for relatives and skilled aliens, gave immigrants and aliens certain legal protections, made all races eligible for immigration and naturalization, and absorbed most of the Internal Security Act of 1950. The act changed the national origin quotas to only one-sixth of 1% of the number of people in the United States in 1920 whose ancestry or national origin was attributable to a specific area of the world. It also allowed aliens to be excluded on ideological grounds, homosexuality, health restrictions, criminal records, narcotics addiction, and involvement in terrorism.

Once again, countries within the Western Hemisphere were not included in the quota system. President Harry S. Truman (1884–1972) vetoed the legislation, but Congress overrode his veto. Even though there were major amendments, the Immigration and Nationality Act remained the basic statute governing who could gain entry into the United States until the passage of new laws following the September 11, 2001, terrorist attacks against the United States.

During the 1950s a half-dozen special laws allowed the entrance of additional refugees. Many of the laws resulted from World War II, but some stemmed from new developments, including laws that relaxed the quotas for refugees fleeing the failed 1956 Hungarian revolution and those seeking asylum following the 1959 Cuban revolution.

## A TWO-HEMISPHERE SYSTEM

In 1963 President John F. Kennedy (1917–1963) submitted a plan to change the quota system. Two years later Congress passed the Immigration and Nationality Act Amendments of 1965. Since 1924 sources of immigration had changed. During the 1950s immigration from Asia to the United States nearly quadrupled from 34,532 (between 1940 and 1949) to 135,844 (between 1950 and 1959). (See Table 1.3.) During the same period immigrants to the United States from North, Central, and South America increased dramatically.

The 1965 legislation canceled the national origins quota system and made visas available on a first-come, first-served basis. A seven-category preference system was implemented for families of U.S. citizens and permanent resident aliens for the purpose of family reunification. In addition, the law set visa allocations for people with special occupational skills, abilities, or training needed in the United States. It also established an annual ceiling of 170,000 Eastern Hemisphere immigrants with a 20,000 per-country limit, and an annual limit of 120,000 for the Western Hemisphere without a per-country limit or preference system.

The Immigration and Nationality Act Amendments of 1976 extended the 20,000 per-country limit to Western Hemisphere countries. Some legislators were concerned that the 20,000-person limit for Mexico was inadequate, but their objections were overruled. The Immigration and Nationality Act Amendments of 1978 combined the separate ceilings for the Eastern and Western Hemispheres into a single worldwide ceiling of 290,000.

## PROGRAMS FOR REFUGEES

Official U.S. refugee programs began in response to the devastation of World War II, which created millions of refugees and displaced people (DPs). (A displaced person is a person living in a foreign country as a result of having been driven from his or her home country because of war or political unrest.) This was the first time the United States formulated policy to admit people fleeing persecution. The Presidential Directive of December 22, 1945, gave priority in issuing visas to about 40,000 DPs. The directive was followed by the Displaced Persons Act of 1948, which authorized the admission of 202,000 people from Eastern Europe, and the Refugee Relief Act of 1953, which approved entry of another 209,000 defectors from communist countries over a three-year period. The Displaced Persons Act counted the refugees in the existing immigration quotas, whereas the Refugee Relief Act admitted them outside the quota system.

### Parole Authority: A Temporary Admission Policy

In 1956 the U.S. attorney general used the parole authority (temporary admission) under section 212(d) (15) of the Immigration and Nationality Act of 1952 for the first time on a large scale. This section authorized the attorney general to temporarily admit any alien to the United States. Even though parole was not admission for permanent residence, it could lead to permanent resident or immigrant status. Aliens already in the United States on a temporary basis could apply for asylum (to stay in the United States) on the grounds they were likely to suffer persecution if returned to their native land. The

attorney general was authorized to withhold deportation on the same grounds.

In *Americans at the Gate: The United States and Refugees during the Cold War* (2008), Carl J. Bon Tempo estimates that this parole authority was used to admit approximately 32,000 of the 38,000 Hungarians who fled the failed 1956 Hungarian revolution. The other 6,000 entered under the Refugee Relief Act of 1953 and were automatically admitted as permanent residents. Similarly, in *Defining America through Immigration Policy* (2004), Bill Ong Hing notes that the parole provision was used to accommodate 15,000 refugees leaving China following the communist revolution there in 1949, and was used again in 1962 to admit several thousand Chinese refugees from Hong Kong to the United States.

### Refugees as Conditional Entrants

In 1965, under the Immigration and Nationality Act Amendments, Congress added section 203(a) (7) to the Immigration and Nationality Act of 1952, creating a group of conditional entrant refugees from communist or Middle Eastern countries, with status similar to the refugee parolees. Sections 203(a) (7) and 212(d) (15) were used to admit thousands of refugees, including Czechoslovakians escaping their failed revolution in 1968, Ugandans fleeing their dictatorship during the 1970s, and Lebanese avoiding the civil war in their country during the 1980s.

The United States did not have a general policy governing the admission of refugees until the Refugee Act of 1980. This act eliminated refugees as a category in the preference system and set a worldwide ceiling on immigration of 270,000, not counting refugees. It also removed the requirement that refugees had to originate from a communist or Middle Eastern nation.

## ILLEGAL IMMIGRATION BECOMES A MAJOR ISSUE

During wartime, the Department of Labor authorized the admission of temporary workers, mainly from Mexico. For example, during World War I nearly 77,000 Mexican workers were admitted to the United States, but only about half of them returned to Mexico. The other half remained in the United States illegally. Then, amid soaring unemployment during the Great Depression, hundreds of thousands of Mexicans were deported or otherwise forced to leave the United States

As the national economy strengthened during World War II, there was a shortage of labor, and President Roosevelt initiated what later came to be known as the Bracero ("manual laborer") Program, which allowed temporary agricultural laborers from Mexico to come to the United States to work. The program expired at the end of the war but was continued via a number of legislative and executive acts before finally being discontinued in 1964. The National Museum of American History indicates in "Opportunity or Exploitation: The Bracero Program" (2013, http://americanhistory.si.edu/onthemove/themes/story_51_5.html) that over 4.5 million Mexicans came to the United States during the 22 years that the Bracero Program was in effect, and the program reinforced existing migration patterns, so that even after it was discontinued, many Mexican workers had come to rely on seasonal agricultural employment in the United States. In the absence of the legal framework for seeking seasonal work in the United States, many Mexicans continued to cross the border illegally. The population of unauthorized immigrants began to grow.

During the 1970s the Vietnam War (1954–1975) divided the nation, oil prices skyrocketed, and gasoline shortages caused long waiting lines at gas stations. Price controls were implemented and removed to control rampant inflation. In this period of political, social, and economic uncertainty many people saw immigrants as straining the already limited welfare and educational systems. States with growing immigrant populations, such as California, Florida, Illinois, New York, and Texas, pushed Congress for immigration reform.

A surge of refugees from Vietnam and Cambodia as well as Cubans escaping the Fidel Castro (1926–) regime during the mid-1970s added to Americans' concerns. The major source of immigrants had changed from Europe to Latin America and Asia. Many people were uncomfortable with the faces and cultures of these new arrivals.

President Ford established the cabinet-level Domestic Council Committee on Illegal Aliens. Its December 1976 report recommended sanctions against employers who knowingly hired undocumented workers, increased border enforcement, and called for legalization for certain unauthorized immigrants who had arrived in the United States before July 1, 1968. In 1979 Congress established the Select Commission on Immigration and Refugee Policy. The commission spent the next two years evaluating the problem. Its 1981 *Final Report* fostered ideas that would become part of major new immigration reform legislation in 1986.

Well into the 21st century, however, Congress and the nation were still struggling to come to a consensus on issues such as border security, which took on new importance in the years after the September 11, 2001, terror attacks. Likewise, there were ongoing debates about whether and how to integrate not only those immigrants who had entered the United States legally but also the millions of unauthorized immigrants already in the United States. Legislation aimed at addressing the integration of unauthorized immigrants, such as the Development, Relief, and Education for Alien Minors Act, had many prominent supporters in Congress and in the nation at large, but as of May 2013 comprehensive immigration reform remained elusive. This later period of immigration history is examined in Chapter 2.

# IMMIGRATION LAWS AND POLICIES SINCE 1980

In "Immigration: Shaping and Reshaping America" (*Population Bulletin*, vol. 61, no. 4, December 2006), Philip Martin and Elizabeth Midgley point out that before the 1980s U.S. immigration laws might have changed once in a generation, but the quickening pace of global change after 1980 brought major new immigration legislation in 1986, 1990, and 1996. The September 11, 2001 (9/11), terrorist attacks against the United States led to antiterrorism laws that had considerable impact on immigration policies and procedures and that effected changes to immigration legislation. This chapter covers the most significant immigration laws and policies from the 1980s through 2013.

## GREEN CARDS

A legal permanent resident (LPR) card, which is issued by the U.S. Citizenship and Immigration Services (USCIS) and commonly known as a "green card," gives individuals the right to permanently live in the United States. An LPR carries this document as proof of legal status in the country.

What is known as a green card has come in a variety of different colors at different times in history. The first receipt card, Form AR-3, resulted from the Alien Registration Act of 1940, a national defense measure that was enacted during World War II (1939–1945). The act required all non-U.S. citizens (aliens) to register at post offices. From there the registration forms were forwarded to the U.S. Immigration and Naturalization Service (INS). The receipt card was mailed to each alien as proof of his or her compliance with the law. These receipts were printed on white paper.

When the war ended, alien registration became part of the regular immigration procedure. Aliens registered at ports of entry and the INS issued different types of Alien Registration Receipt Cards based on each alien's admission status. For example, temporary foreign laborers received an I-100a card, visitors received an I-94c card, and permanent residents received an I-151 card. The cards were different colors to make it easy to identify the immigration status of each alien. The permanent resident card, which was necessary to obtain employment, was green.

The Internal Security Act of 1950 made the I-151 card even more valuable. Effective April 17, 1951, any alien holding an AR-3 card (the type that was issued to all aliens during World War II) had to apply to have it replaced with the green I-151 card. Anyone who could not prove his or her legal admission to the United States did not qualify for a green card and could be subject to prosecution for violation of immigration laws.

By 1951 the green card represented security for an immigrant because it indicated the right to permanently live and work in the United States. The Alien Registration Receipt Card, Form I-151, became commonly known to immigrants, immigration attorneys, enforcement officers, and employers by its color. The term *green card* designated not only the document but also the official status so desired by many legal nonimmigrants (students, tourists, and temporary workers) and by unauthorized immigrants.

The green card was so desirable that counterfeiting became a problem. In response to this counterfeiting, the INS issued 19 different designs of the card between 1940 and 1977. The 1964 version was pale blue, and in 1965 the card became dark blue. In January 1977 the INS introduced the machine-readable Alien Registration Receipt Card, Form I-551, which has since been issued in a variety of colors, including pink and a pink and blue combination. Form I-151 and its successor, Form I-551, have such vital meaning to immigrants that despite changes in form number, design, and color, it will probably always be known as a green card.

## IMMIGRATION REFORM AND CONTROL ACT OF 1986

In November 1986, after a six-year effort to send an acceptable immigration bill through both houses of

Congress, President Ronald Reagan (1911–2004) signed the Immigration Reform and Control Act (IRCA) into law. To control illegal immigration, the IRCA adopted three major strategies:

- Legalization of a portion of the undocumented population, thereby reducing the number of immigrants illegally resident in the United States

- Sanctions against employers who knowingly hire illegal immigrants

- Additional border enforcement to impede further unlawful entries

Two groups of immigrants became eligible to apply for legalization under the IRCA. The largest group consisted of immigrants who could prove that they had continuously resided in the United States without authorization since January 1, 1982. This group had entered the United States in one of two ways: they arrived as unauthorized immigrants before January 1, 1982, or they arrived on temporary visas (government authorizations permitting entry into a country) that expired before January 1, 1982.

To adjust to the legal status of permanent resident, immigrants were required to prove eligibility for admission and have at least a minimal understanding and knowledge of the English language, U.S. history, and the U.S. government. They could apply for citizenship five years from the date permanent resident status was granted.

The second group of immigrants that became eligible to apply for legalization under the IRCA were referred to as special agricultural workers (SAWs). This category was created because many fruit and vegetable farmers feared they would lose their workers, many of whom were undocumented, if the IRCA provisions regarding length of continuous residence were applied to seasonal laborers. Most of these workers were migrants who returned home to live in Mexico when there was no work available in the fields. The SAW program permitted unauthorized immigrants who had performed labor in perishable agricultural commodities for a minimum of 90 days between May 1985 and May 1986 to apply for legalization.

### How Many Were Legalized?

In *IRCA Legalization Effects: Lawful Permanent Residence and Naturalization through 2001* (October 25, 2002, http://www.dhs.gov/xlibrary/assets/statistics/publications/irca0114int.pdf), Nancy Rytina of the INS estimates that 3 million to 5 million undocumented immigrants were living in the United States in 1986. More than 3 million of these applied for temporary residence status under the IRCA, and nearly 2.7 million (88%) were eventually approved for permanent residence. By 2001 one-third (33%,

or 889,033) of these residents had become naturalized citizens. Rytina notes that a majority (75%) of applicants under the IRCA provisions were born in Mexico.

The IRCA barred newly legalized immigrants from receiving most federally funded public assistance for five years. Exceptions included access to emergency care and access to Medicaid for children, pregnant women, the elderly, and the handicapped. The State Legalization Impact Assistance Grant program reimbursed state and local governments the costs for providing public assistance, education, and public health services to the legalized immigrants.

### Employer Sanctions

The employer sanctions provision of the IRCA was intended to correct a double standard that prohibited unauthorized immigrants from working in the United States but permitted employers to hire them. The IRCA prohibited employers from hiring, recruiting, or referring for a fee those known to be unauthorized to work in the United States. Employers who violated the law were subject to a series of civil fines or criminal penalties when a pattern or practice of violations was found.

DOCUMENTING ELIGIBILITY FOR EMPLOYMENT. The burden of proof was on employers to demonstrate that their employees had valid proof of identity and were authorized to work. The IRCA required employers to complete the Employment Eligibility Verification form, known as Form I-9, for each employee hired. In completing the form the employer certified that the employee had presented valid proof of identity and eligibility for employment and that these documents appeared genuine. The IRCA also required employers to retain the completed I-9 forms and produce them in response to an official government request.

Form I-9 was revised a number of times after its 1986 introduction. As of 2013, it consisted of three parts. (See Figure 2.1.) Section One, to be completed by the employee, required the disclosure of basic personal information and an attestation of legal authorization to work in the United States. Section Two, to be completed by the employer, provided information about the official documents used to establish the employee's legal authorization to work. Section Three was to be completed by employers who were rehiring an employee within three years of the date the original I-9 form had been completed or when official documents provided on an employee's I-9 form had expired. Form I-9 was available in English and Spanish, but only employers in Puerto Rico could have employees complete the Spanish version for their records. Employers in the 50 states and other U.S. territories were allowed to use the Spanish version as a translation guide for Spanish-speaking employees, but the English version was required for company

**FIGURE 2.1**

## Form I-9, Employment Eligibility Verification

# Employment Eligibility Verification
### Department of Homeland Security
U.S. Citizenship and Immigration Services

USCIS
Form I-9

OMB No. 1615-0047
Expires 03/31/2016

▶**START HERE. Read instructions carefully before completing this form. The instructions must be available during completion of this form.**
**ANTI-DISCRIMINATION NOTICE:** It is illegal to discriminate against work-authorized individuals. Employers **CANNOT** specify which document(s) they will accept from an employee. The refusal to hire an individual because the documentation presented has a future expiration date may also constitute illegal discrimination.

**Section 1. Employee Information and Attestation** (*Employees must complete and sign Section 1 of Form I-9 no later than the first day of employment, but not before accepting a job offer.*)

| Last Name (*Family Name*) | First Name (*Given Name*) | Middle Initial | Other Names Used (*if any*) |
|---|---|---|---|
| | | | |

| Address (*Street Number and Name*) | Apt. Number | City or Town | State ▼ | Zip Code |
|---|---|---|---|---|
| | | | | |

| Date of Birth (*mm/dd/yyyy*) | U.S. Social Security Number | E-mail Address | Telephone Number |
|---|---|---|---|
| | ☐☐☐-☐☐-☐☐☐☐ | | |

**I am aware that federal law provides for imprisonment and/or fines for false statements or use of false documents in connection with the completion of this form.**

**I attest, under penalty of perjury, that I am (check one of the following):**

☐ A citizen of the United States

☐ A noncitizen national of the United States (*See instructions*)

☐ A lawful permanent resident (Alien Registration Number/USCIS Number): _____

☐ An alien authorized to work until (expiration date, if applicable, mm/dd/yyyy) _____ . Some aliens may write "N/A" in this field.
(*See instructions*)

*For aliens authorized to work, provide your Alien Registration Number/USCIS Number* **OR** *Form I-94 Admission Number:*

1. Alien Registration Number/USCIS Number: _____

**OR**

2. Form I-94 Admission Number: _____

If you obtained your admission number from CBP in connection with your arrival in the United States, include the following:

Foreign Passport Number: _____

Country of Issuance: _____ ▼

Some aliens may write "N/A" on the Foreign Passport Number and Country of Issuance fields. (*See instructions*)

> **3-D Barcode**
> **Do Not Write in This Space**

| Signature of Employee: | Date (*mm/dd/yyyy*): |
|---|---|
| | |

**Preparer and/or Translator Certification** (*To be completed and signed if Section 1 is prepared by a person other than the employee.*)

**I attest, under penalty of perjury, that I have assisted in the completion of this form and that to the best of my knowledge the information is true and correct.**

| Signature of Preparer or Translator: | Date (*mm/dd/yyyy*): |
|---|---|
| | |

| Last Name (*Family Name*) | First Name (*Given Name*) |
|---|---|
| | |

| Address (*Street Number and Name*) | City or Town | State ▼ | Zip Code |
|---|---|---|---|
| | | | |

**STOP** *Employer Completes Next Page* **STOP**

Form I-9 03/08/13 N

Page 7 of 9

**FIGURE 2.1**

## Form I-9, Employment Eligibility Verification [CONTINUED]

### Section 2. Employer or Authorized Representative Review and Verification
*(Employers or their authorized representative must complete and sign Section 2 within 3 business days of the employee's first day of employment. You must physically examine one document from List A OR examine a combination of one document from List B and one document from List C as listed on the "Lists of Acceptable Documents" on the next page of this form. For each document you review, record the following information: document title, issuing authority, document number, and expiration date, if any.)*

**Employee Last Name, First Name and Middle Initial from Section 1:**

| List A | OR | List B | AND | List C |
|---|---|---|---|---|
| Identity and Employment Authorization | | Identity | | Employment Authorization |

| List A | List B | List C |
|---|---|---|
| Document Title: | Document Title: | Document Title: |
| Issuing Authority: | Issuing Authority: | Issuing Authority: |
| Document Number: | Document Number: | Document Number: |
| Expiration Date (*if any*) (*mm/dd/yyyy*): | Expiration Date (*if any*) (*mm/dd/yyyy*): | Expiration Date (*if any*) (*mm/dd/yyyy*): |
| Document Title: | | |
| Issuing Authority: | | |
| Document Number: | | |
| Expiration Date (*if any*) (*mm/dd/yyyy*): | | |
| Document Title: | | 3-D Barcode Do Not Write in This Space |
| Issuing Authority: | | |
| Document Number: | | |
| Expiration Date (*if any*) (*mm/dd/yyyy*): | | |

### Certification

I attest, under penalty of perjury, that (1) I have examined the document(s) presented by the above-named employee, (2) the above-listed document(s) appear to be genuine and to relate to the employee named, and (3) to the best of my knowledge the employee is authorized to work in the United States.

**The employee's first day of employment (*mm/dd/yyyy*):** _____ (***See instructions for exemptions.***)

| Signature of Employer or Authorized Representative | Date (*mm/dd/yyyy*) | Title of Employer or Authorized Representative |
|---|---|---|
| Last Name (*Family Name*) | First Name (*Given Name*) | Employer's Business or Organization Name |

| Employer's Business or Organization Address (*Street Number and Name*) | City or Town | State ▼ | Zip Code |
|---|---|---|---|

### Section 3. Reverification and Rehires *(To be completed and signed by employer or authorized representative.)*

| A. New Name (*if applicable*)    Last Name (*Family Name*)    First Name (*Given Name*)    Middle Initial | B. Date of Rehire (*if applicable*) (*mm/dd/yyyy*): |
|---|---|

C. If employee's previous grant of employment authorization has expired, provide the information for the document from List A or List C the employee presented that establishes current employment authorization in the space provided below.

| Document Title: | Document Number: | Expiration Date (*if any*) (*mm/dd/yyyy*): |
|---|---|---|

I attest, under penalty of perjury, that to the best of my knowledge, this employee is authorized to work in the United States, and if the employee presented document(s), the document(s) I have examined appear to be genuine and to relate to the individual.

| Signature of Employer or Authorized Representative: | Date (*mm/dd/yyyy*): | Print Name of Employer or Authorized Representative: |
|---|---|---|

Form I-9 03/08/13 N

Page 8 of 9

## FIGURE 2.1

**Form I-9, Employment Eligibility Verification** [CONTINUED]

### LISTS OF ACCEPTABLE DOCUMENTS
#### All documents must be UNEXPIRED

Employees may present one selection from List A or a combination of one selection from List B and one selection from List C.

| LIST A | | LIST B | | LIST C |
|---|---|---|---|---|
| **Documents that Establish Both Identity and Employment Authorization** | **OR** | **Documents that Establish Identity** | **AND** | **Documents that Establish Employment Authorization** |

| LIST A | LIST B | LIST C |
|---|---|---|
| 1. U.S. Passport or U.S. Passport Card | 1. Driver's license or ID card issued by a State or outlying possession of the United States provided it contains a photograph or information such as name, date of birth, gender, height, eye color, and address | 1. A Social Security Account Number card, unless the card includes one of the following restrictions: <br>(1) NOT VALID FOR EMPLOYMENT <br>(2) VALID FOR WORK ONLY WITH INS AUTHORIZATION <br>(3) VALID FOR WORK ONLY WITH DHS AUTHORIZATION |
| 2. Permanent Resident Card or Alien Registration Receipt Card (Form I-551) | | |
| 3. Foreign passport that contains a temporary I-551 stamp or temporary I-551 printed notation on a machine-readable immigrant visa | 2. ID card issued by federal, state or local government agencies or entities, provided it contains a photograph or information such as name, date of birth, gender, height, eye color, and address | 2. Certification of Birth Abroad issued by the Department of State (Form FS-545) |
| 4. Employment Authorization Document that contains a photograph (Form I-766) | | 3. Certification of Report of Birth issued by the Department of State (Form DS-1350) |
| 5. For a nonimmigrant alien authorized to work for a specific employer because of his or her status: | 3. School ID card with a photograph | 4. Original or certified copy of birth certificate issued by a State, county, municipal authority, or territory of the United States bearing an official seal |
| a. Foreign passport; and | 4. Voter's registration card | |
| b. Form I-94 or Form I-94A that has the following: | 5. U.S. Military card or draft record | |
| (1) The same name as the passport; and | 6. Military dependent's ID card | 5. Native American tribal document |
| (2) An endorsement of the alien's nonimmigrant status as long as that period of endorsement has not yet expired and the proposed employment is not in conflict with any restrictions or limitations identified on the form. | 7. U.S. Coast Guard Merchant Mariner Card | 6. U.S. Citizen ID Card (Form I-197) |
| | 8. Native American tribal document | 7. Identification Card for Use of Resident Citizen in the United States (Form I-179) |
| | 9. Driver's license issued by a Canadian government authority | 8. Employment authorization document issued by the Department of Homeland Security |
| 6. Passport from the Federated States of Micronesia (FSM) or the Republic of the Marshall Islands (RMI) with Form I-94 or Form I-94A indicating nonimmigrant admission under the Compact of Free Association Between the United States and the FSM or RMI | **For persons under age 18 who are unable to present a document listed above:** | |
| | 10. School record or report card | |
| | 11. Clinic, doctor, or hospital record | |
| | 12. Day-care or nursery school record | |

**Illustrations of many of these documents appear in Part 8 of the Handbook for Employers (M-274).**

**Refer to Section 2 of the instructions, titled "Employer or Authorized Representative Review and Verification," for more information about acceptable receipts.**

Form I-9 03/08/13 N                                                                 Page 9 of 9

SOURCE: "Form I-9, Employment Eligibility Verification," U.S. Department of Homeland Security, U.S. Citizenship and Immigration Services, March 8, 2013, http://www.uscis.gov/files/form/I-9.pdf (accessed March 21, 2013)

records. Employees were entitled, however, to use a translator/preparer to assist them in completing the form.

## IMMIGRATION MARRIAGE FRAUD AMENDMENTS OF 1986

Before 1986 the INS granted permanent residence fairly quickly to the foreign spouses of U.S. citizens or LPRs. However, a number of marriages between Americans and foreigners occurred purely to attain U.S. permanent residence

status for the foreigner. Some U.S. citizens or LPRs agreed to marry immigrants for money, and then the marriages were dissolved once the immigrant obtained LPR status. Other cases involved unauthorized immigrants entering into marriages by deceiving citizens or LPRs with declarations of love.

The Immigration Marriage Fraud Amendments of 1986 specified that individuals basing their immigrant status on a marriage of less than two years were considered conditional immigrants. To remove the conditional immigrant status, the individual had to apply for permanent residence within 90 days after the second-year anniversary of receiving conditional status. The conditional immigrant and his or her spouse were required to show that the marriage was and continued to be a valid one; otherwise, conditional immigrant status was terminated and the individual could be deported.

The U.S. Immigration and Customs Enforcement (ICE) is responsible for enforcement of the anti-marriage fraud policy. It does not keep detailed statistics regarding the number of fraudulent marriage cases it investigates or prosecutes. However, Wendy Koch notes in "Va. Case Highlights Fraudulent Marriages" (USAToday.com, November 8, 2006) that between fiscal years (FYs) 2004 and 2006 ICE investigated 700 cases of marriage fraud. A typical case involved marriage fraud "rings," in which individuals charged a fee to arrange marriages between citizens and foreign nationals for the purpose of gaining citizenship.

### Battered Brides

Spousal abuse sometimes results during the two-year period of conditional immigrant status. Particularly in cases of mail-order brides and brides from countries where women have few, if any, rights, husbands sometimes take advantage of the power they have as the wife's sponsor. The new wife is dependent on her husband to obtain permanent U.S. residence. The U.S. Department of Justice finds cases of alien wives who are virtual prisoners, afraid they will be deported if they defy their husband or report abuse. In addition, some of the women come from cultures in which divorced women are outcasts with no place in society.

The Violence against Women Act of 1994 (which is part of the Violent Crime Control and Law Enforcement Act of 1994) and the Victims of Trafficking and Violence Prevention Act of 2000 were enacted to address the plight of such abused women and their children. The 1994 law allows the women and/or children to self-petition for immigrant status without the abuser's participation or consent. Abused males can also file a self-petition under this law. The 2000 law created a new nonimmigrant U visa for victims of serious crimes. Recipients of the U visa, including victims of crimes against women, can adjust to LPR status based on humanitarian grounds as determined by the U.S. attorney general.

### IMMIGRATION ACT OF 1990

Shortly after the IRCA was passed, Senators Edward M. Kennedy (1932–2009; D-MA) and Alan K. Simpson (1931–; R-WY) began work to change the Immigration and Nationality Act Amendments of 1965, which provided the framework for legal immigration into the United States. The senators asserted that its family-oriented system allowed one legal immigrant to bring too many relatives into the country. They proposed to cut the number of dependents admitted and replace them with individuals who had the skills or money to immediately benefit the U.S. economy. The result of their efforts was the Immigration Act (IMMACT) of 1990.

Enacted in November 1990, IMMACT represented a major overhaul of immigration law. The focus of the new law was to raise the annual number of immigrants allowed from 500,000 to 700,000 and give greater priority to employment-based immigration. A diversity program encouraged applications from countries with low immigration history by allotting 50,000 visas per year in this category.

### Diversity Visa Program

The IMMACT diversity program was introduced as a transitional measure from 1992 to 1994. Ruth Ellen Wasem and Karma Ester of the Congressional Research Service explain in "Immigration: Diversity Visa Lottery" (April 22, 2004, http://www.ilw.com/immigdaily/news/2005,0809-crs.pdf) that under the permanent program, which began in 1995, no country was permitted more than 7% of the total number of diversity visas, and Northern Ireland was treated as a separate state rather than included within the United Kingdom. To be eligible, aliens were required to have at least a high school education or equivalent, or have at least two years of work experience in an occupation that required a minimum of two years' training or two years' experience within the past five years. An alien selected under the lottery program could apply for permanent residence and, if granted, was authorized to work in the United States. The alien's spouse and unmarried children under the age of 21 years were also allowed to enter the United States.

Beginning in FY 1999, 5,000 of the annual diversity-program visas were reserved for participants in the 1997 Nicaraguan Adjustment and Central American Relief Act. This law provided various immigration benefits and relief from deportation to certain Nicaraguans, Cubans, Salvadorans, Guatemalans, nationals of former Soviet-bloc countries, and their dependents. Beginning in 2000, the overall number of visas available under the diversity program was reduced to 50,000.

### Changing Grounds for Exclusion

IMMACT changed the political and ideological grounds for exclusion and deportation. The law repealed the ban against the admission of communists and representatives of other totalitarian regimes that had been in place since 1950. In addition, immigration applicants who had been excluded previously because of associations with communism were provided exceptions if the applicants had been involuntary members of the communist party, had terminated membership, or merely had close relationships with people affiliated with communism.

## Temporary Protected Status

IMMACT authorized the U.S. attorney general to grant temporary protected status (TPS) to undocumented aliens present in the United States when a natural disaster, ongoing armed conflict, or other extraordinary occurrence in their country posed a danger to their personal safety.

TPS lasts for six to 18 months unless conditions in the alien national's country warrant an extension of stay. TPS does not lead to permanent resident status, although such aliens can obtain work authorization. Once the TPS designation ends, the foreign nationals resume the same immigrant status they had before TPS (unless that status has expired) or any new status they obtained while in TPS. According to the USCIS, in "Temporary Protected Status" (April 3, 2013, http://www.uscis.gov/), in 2013 applicants from the following countries were eligible for TPS: El Salvador, Haiti, Honduras, Nicaragua, Somalia, Sudan, South Sudan, and Syria.

## ILLEGAL IMMIGRATION REFORM AND IMMIGRANT RESPONSIBILITY ACT OF 1996

The Illegal Immigration Reform and Immigrant Responsibility Act (IIRIRA) went into effect in September 1996. Among many other provisions, the IIRIRA attempted to combat illegal immigration by making the following changes to immigration law:

- Doubling the number of Border Patrol agents to 5,000 by 2001 and increasing equipment and technology at air and land ports of entry

- Authorizing improvements of southwestern border barriers

- Toughening penalties for immigrant smuggling (up to 10 years in prison, 15 years for third and subsequent offenses) and document fraud (up to 15 years in prison)

- Increasing the number of INS investigators for worksite enforcement, tracking aliens who overstay visas, and investigating alien smuggling

- Instituting a new "expedited removal" proceeding (denial of an alien's entry into the United States without a hearing) to speed deportation of aliens with no documents or with fraudulent documents

- Authorizing three voluntary pilot programs to enable employers to verify the immigrant status of job applicants and to reduce the number and types of documents needed for identification and employment eligibility

- Instituting a bar on admissibility for aliens seeking to reenter the United States after having been unlawfully present in the country—a bar of three years for aliens unlawfully present from six months to a year and a bar of 10 years for those unlawfully present for more than a year

## Verifying Employee Eligibility for Work

To assist employers in complying with the IIRIRA as well as with workplace provisions of the IRCA, the Social Security Administration began in 1997 the Basic Pilot Program, a computerized system that allowed employers to check the validity of Social Security numbers (SSNs) presented by new hires. The system was tested with employers who volunteered in California, Florida, Illinois, and Texas before being expanded on December 1, 2004, to employers who volunteered in all states. The program returned a tentative nonconfirmation (known as a TNC) if the name, date of birth, or gender of the new hire did not match Social Security records; if the SSN had never been issued; or if records indicated the person issued that SSN was deceased. The new hire had a set time limit for resolving the problem with the Social Security Administration before the employer could terminate the individual's employment.

In "Illegal Immigrants at Center of New Identity Theft Crackdown" (NYTimes.com, December 14, 2006), Rachel L. Swarns reports that in December 2006 the U.S. Department of Homeland Security (DHS) raided six Swift & Company meat processing plants. It detained 1,282 illegal immigrants and charged 65 people with identity theft. Swift & Company had participated in the Basic Pilot Program for several years, but the raids showed that the system did not recognize identity theft. The Basic Pilot Program confirmed the validity of the SSN but did not check to see how many times and in what locations the number had been used for employment. Thus, several people could be using the same number on fraudulent identification (ID).

The Basic Pilot Program was renamed E-Verify in 2007 and expanded to include a feature that would allow employers to scan a new hire's photo identification to be compared against images stored in DHS immigration databases. Even though the program remained voluntary according to federal law, 16 states mandated the use of E-Verify in some form as of 2012. Jon Feere of the Center for Immigration Studies notes in "An Overview of E-Verify Policies at the State Level" (July 2012, http://cis.org/e-verify-at-the-state-level) that six of these states had laws in place mandating the use of E-Verify by most or all businesses: Alabama, Arizona, Georgia, Mississippi, North Carolina, and South Carolina. Five additional states required public employers and public contractors to use the system: Indiana, Missouri, Nebraska, Oklahoma, and Virginia. Three states (Louisiana, Minnesota, and Pennsylvania) required public contractors alone to use the system;

FIGURE 2.2

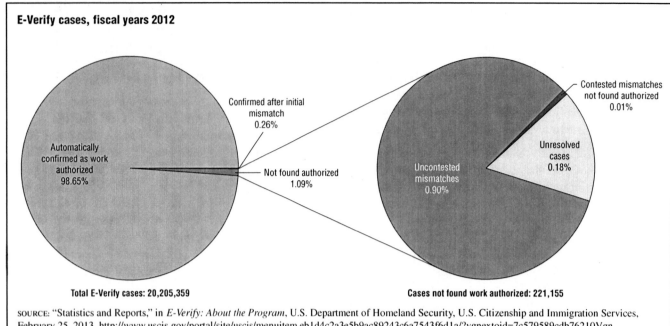

**E-Verify cases, fiscal years 2012**

Confirmed after initial mismatch
0.26%

Automatically confirmed as work authorized
98.65%

Not found authorized
1.09%

Contested mismatches not found authorized
0.01%

Unresolved cases
0.18%

Uncontested mismatches
0.90%

**Total E-Verify cases: 20,205,359**

**Cases not found work authorized: 221,155**

SOURCE: "Statistics and Reports," in *E-Verify: About the Program*, U.S. Department of Homeland Security, U.S. Citizenship and Immigration Services, February 25, 2013, http://www.uscis.gov/portal/site/uscis/menuitem.eb1d4c2a3e5b9ac89243c6a7543f6d1a/?vgnextoid=7c579589cdb76210Vgn VCM100000b92ca60aRCRD&vgnextchannel=7c579589cdb76210VgnVCM100000b92ca60aRCRD (accessed March 22, 2013)

one state (Idaho) required only public employers to use the system; and one state (Florida) required only agencies under the governor's direction to use the system.

According to the USCIS, in FY 2012 E-Verify was used to determine work eligibility in 20.2 million cases nationally. (See Figure 2.2.) Of these employees, 98.7% were found to be authorized to work within 24 hours. The remaining 1.4% of cases were split between those whose eligibility was initially contested and who were able to prove that they were in fact authorized (0.3%) and those who were conclusively determined to be unauthorized (1.1%).

## PATRIOT ACT OF 2001

Following 9/11 it became apparent that some, if not all, of the perpetrators had entered the United States legally, and many had overstayed their visas with no notice taken by the INS or any other enforcement agency. As a result, several laws were enacted to address immigration concerns related to terrorism. The first such law was the Uniting and Strengthening America by Providing Appropriate Tools Required to Intercept and Obstruct Terrorism Act (known as the Patriot Act), which was signed into law in October 2001. With reference to immigration, the act:

• Mandated that the number of personnel at the northern border be tripled, appropriated funds for technology improvements, and gave the INS access to the Federal Bureau of Investigation's (FBI) criminal databases. The INS was to begin the task of locating hundreds of thousands of foreigners who had been

ordered deported and entering their names into the FBI database.

• Amended the Immigration and Nationality Act of 1952 to clarify that an alien who solicited funds or membership or provided material support to a certified terrorist organization could be detained or removed from the country.

• Directed the U.S. attorney general to implement an entry-exit system, with particular focus on biometric information gathered during the visa application process, and develop tamper-resistant documents. The new system would require certain nonimmigrants to register with the INS and submit fingerprints and photographs on arrival in the United States; report to the INS in person within 30 days of arrival and annually thereafter; and notify an INS agent of their departure. Those who failed to comply could face criminal prosecution.

• Appropriated $36.8 million to implement a foreign-student monitoring system with mandatory participation by all institutions of higher education that enrolled foreign students or exchange visitors. The act expanded the list of participating institutions to include air flight schools, language training schools, and vocational schools.

• Established provisions to ensure that the immigration status of 9/11 victims and their families was not adversely affected as a result of the attacks. The family members of some victims were facing deportation.

The Patriot Act was amended several times over the following decade, and its central features were reauthorized by Congress and President George W. Bush (1946–) in 2006. In 2011 President Barack Obama (1961–) signed a bill reauthorizing, through 2015, three key provisions that were set to expire.

## HOMELAND SECURITY ACT OF 2002

In November 2002 President George W. Bush signed into law the Homeland Security Act, which implemented the largest restructuring of the government in several decades. This act created the cabinet-level U.S. Department of Homeland Security, which consolidated the functions of more than 20 federal agencies into one department that employs over 170,000 people. One of the affected agencies was the INS.

### INS Reorganization

Title IV, Section 402 of the Homeland Security Act transferred the responsibilities of the INS from the Justice Department to the DHS. The INS was renamed the U.S. Citizenship and Immigration Services on March 1, 2003; the new service no longer had responsibility for law enforcement, but became solely responsible for processing visas and petitions for naturalization, asylum, and refugee status. Immigration enforcement became the responsibility of ICE.

### Border Security

Section 402 of the Homeland Security Act outlined the responsibilities of the undersecretary for border and transportation security. These included:

- Preventing the entry of terrorists and the instruments of terrorism into the United States

- Securing the borders, territorial waters, ports, terminals, waterways, and air, land, and sea transportation systems of the United States

- Administering the immigration and naturalization laws of the United States, including the establishment of rules governing the granting of visas and other forms of permission to enter the United States to individuals who are not citizens or LPRs

- Administering the customs laws of the United States

- Ensuring the speedy, orderly, and efficient flow of lawful traffic and commerce in carrying out these responsibilities

## OTHER POST-9/11 CHANGES

Since 9/11 hundreds of policy changes have been inaugurated by the Justice Department, the U.S. Department of State, the DHS, and the INS/USCIS. Among the most prominent are changes affecting the issuing of nonimmigrant visas to residents of certain countries and to students, as well as changes authorizing local law enforcement agents to participate in the enforcement of immigration law.

In November 2001 the State Department mandated background checks on all male visa applicants between the ages of 16 and 45 from 26 mostly Muslim countries. The Enhanced Border Security and Visa Entry Reform Act of 2002 prohibited issuing nonimmigrant visas to nationals of seven countries (Cuba, Iran, Iraq, Libya, North Korea, Sudan, and Syria) unless it was determined after a thorough background check that the individuals were not security threats. The list of prohibited countries could change as directed by the U.S. attorney general.

After 9/11 the United States also increased visa restrictions for foreign students. The IIRIRA had mandated the creation of a database that stored information about international students, but the system had not yet been launched when 9/11 occurred. In May 2002 the INS launched the Student and Exchange Visitor Information System (SEVIS), an Internet-based system to track foreign nationals who enter the country on student visas. SEVIS, which was overseen by ICE after the creation of the DHS, came online in 2003. A drastic improvement of previous decentralized systems for tracking student visa recipients, the system compiled information across agencies and allowed federal immigration authorities to monitor not only individuals but also the schools and exchange programs that brought students to the United States. According to the Student Exchange Visitor Program (SEVP; the division of ICE that oversees SEVIS), in *Student and Exchange Visitor Information System: General Summary Quarterly Review* (January 2, 2013, http://www.ice.gov/doclib/sevis/pdf/by-the-numbers.pdf), as of January 2013 there were records for 10.3 million current and former student visa holders in the system. The SEVP further notes that with the increase in the amount and comprehensiveness of the data in the system, it has seen a steady increase in the number of government agencies, notably among them the ICE Counterterrorism and Criminal Exploitation Unit, that regularly request SEVIS information.

Yet another post-9/11 change in immigration policy came when the Justice Department ruled that effective August 2002 local police could detain individuals for immigration violations, a right formerly reserved for federal agents. The measure, like that pertaining to the foreign-student database, was a part of the IIRIRA that had never been finalized. Florida became the test state, initiating a Memorandum of Understanding with the Justice Department, which authorized specially trained local police officers to assist federal agents in locating and detaining wanted aliens.

## INTELLIGENCE REFORM AND TERRORISM PREVENTION ACT AND REAL ID ACT

In late 2002 the National Commission on Terrorist Attacks on the United States (also known as the 9/11 Commission) was created by Congress and the president to prepare a complete account of the circumstances surrounding the 9/11 terrorist attacks and the nation's response. The commission was also mandated to provide recommendations that were designed to guard against future attacks. One of the commission's recommendations was to create a national identification program. In December 2004 President Bush signed the Intelligence Reform and Terrorism Prevention Act. This act set national standards for driver's licenses, Social Security cards, and birth certificates.

In May 2005 President Bush signed the REAL ID Act, which mandated federal standards for state-issued driver's licenses. The new act transferred responsibility for driver's license security from the U.S. Department of Transportation to the DHS.

The new law required states to develop security upgrades and security clearances for Department of Motor Vehicles personnel; verify all documents with the original issuing agency and verify U.S. citizenship or lawful immigration status before issuing a driver's license or nondriver's ID card; redesign driver's licenses and ID cards so that they contain certain types of security features; and establish new data management, storage, and sharing protocols. States were prohibited from accepting any foreign documents other than an official passport for identity purposes. States were required to be certified by May 11, 2008, in compliance with the DHS and the Transportation Department.

Civil libertarians objected to the REAL ID Act on the basis of its invasion of privacy and lack of safeguards for personal and private information. The American Civil Liberties Union explains in "What's Wrong with REAL ID" (2013, http://www.realnightmare.org/) that it objects to REAL ID because the law will "increase the threat of identity theft, enable the routine tracking of individuals, and propel us toward a surveillance society." Another concern is that the act will cost billions to implement. *The REAL ID Act: National Impact Analysis* (September 2006, http://www.ncsl.org/print/statefed/real_id_impact_report_final_sept19.pdf), the result of a survey jointly sponsored by the National Governors Association, the National Conference of State Legislatures (NCSL), and the National Association of Motor Vehicle Administrators, projected that full implementation of the act would cost more than $11 billion between 2005 and 2010. Besides new applicants, all current holders of state driver's licenses or ID cards would be required to make a personal visit to a Department of Motor Vehicles office to present original documents verifying identity and be reenrolled in the state's computer system. The cost of additional staff and

work hours necessary to reenroll that number of people was an estimated $8.5 billion. Upgrading state and national systems to facilitate verification of each document presented by a driver's license applicant or reenrollee was estimated to cost a further $1.4 billion, and the cost of license redesign to comply with required security features was projected at $1.1 billion. Other items, such as security clearances and fraudulent document training for employees processing license applications, added an additional $40 million to the price tag for compliance.

Reports on the impact of the REAL ID Act generated a stir in state legislatures, and several introduced legislation that prohibited its implementation, either by directing state agencies not to implement it or by denying the funding necessary for its implementation. The NCSL notes in "State Legislative Activity in Opposition to the Real ID" (http://www.ncsl.org/documents/standcomm/sctran/REALIDComplianceReport.pdf) that as of June 2012, 27 states had enacted anti–REAL ID legislation or resolutions.

The 2008 deadline for compliance with the REAL ID Act was extended several times. In the press release "DHS Determines 13 States Meet REAL ID Standards" (http://www.dhs.gov/news/2012/12/20/dhs-determines-13-states-meet-real-id-standards), the DHS notes that as of December 2012, 13 states had met the standards outlined by the REAL ID Act. A previous extension of the act's deadline for compliance had established January 15, 2013, as the final deadline past which noncompliant state IDs would no longer be valid for boarding commercial aircraft and other federally regulated purposes. The DHS reports, however, that states not in compliance by the deadline would be granted temporary deferments and that the fall of 2013 was the established target for the release of a new implementation schedule, with actual implementation to begin "at a suitable date thereafter."

## DEFERRED ACTION FOR CHILDHOOD ARRIVALS PROGRAM

Although the general trend in post-9/11 immigration legislation had been to restrict the flow of immigrants and/or to enhance border security provisions, there were also frequent calls for legislation that relaxed the legal sanctions imposed on certain unauthorized immigrants. The most prominent legislative attempt to provide relief to the unauthorized population was the Development, Relief, and Education for Alien Minors (DREAM) Act, introduced in 2001 by Senators Dick Durbin (1944–; D-IL) and Orrin Hatch (1934–; R-UT). The bill would allow certain young people brought to the United States as children who had graduated from high school and demonstrated good character to remain in the United States for college or to enlist in the military, after which point they would qualify for citizenship. Several versions of the bill appeared in both houses of Congress in the decade that followed, but none mustered sufficient support for passage.

On June 15, 2012, however, Janet Napolitano (1957–), the secretary of homeland security, announced that the United States would cease deporting those young people who met certain criteria outlined in DREAM Act legislation. The Obama administration's new policy was called the Deferred Action for Childhood Arrivals program. It went into effect on August 15 of that year. The USCIS explains in "Consideration of Deferred Action for Childhood Arrivals Process" (January 18, 2013, http://www.uscis.gov/) that the program offered the possibility of relief from deportation to individuals between the ages of 15 and 30 years who met the following criteria:

- Was under the age of 16 years at the time of arrival in the United States

- Had continuously resided in the United States for a minimum of five years preceding June 15, 2012, and was physically present in the United States on that date

- Was currently a student, a high school graduate, a recipient of a general education development certificate, or an honorably discharged veteran of the military or the U.S. Coast Guard

- Had never been convicted of a felony or of multiple or significant misdemeanors and posed no threat to national security or public safety

The USCIS states that individuals who met these criteria were eligible to apply for deferred action, which consisted of relief from the threat of deportation for two years. Those granted deferred-action status could apply for renewal at the end of that period. They would be eligible for work authorization. Eligibility to apply for deferred action, however, did not guarantee receipt of that status; applicants were to be judged on a case-by-case basis. The Deferred Action for Childhood Arrivals program fell short of DREAM Act proposals in that it did not offer beneficiaries a path to legal permanent residence or citizenship. Additionally, immediate family members and dependents of those granted deferred-action status were ineligible for deferred action. Those who came to the United States after June 15, 2012, were not eligible for deferred action.

Jeffrey S. Passel and Mark Hugo Lopez of the Pew Hispanic Center assess the possible outcome of the Deferred Action for Childhood Arrivals program in *Up to 1.7 Million Unauthorized Immigrant Youth May Benefit from New Deportation Rules* (August 14, 2012, http://www.pewhispanic.org/files/2012/12/unauthroized_immigrant_youth_update.pdf). Of the 4.4 million unauthorized immigrants aged 30 years and younger at the time the program went into effect, an estimated 1.7 million were likely eligible for deferred action. (See Figure 2.3.) Approximately 950,000 of these

FIGURE 2.3

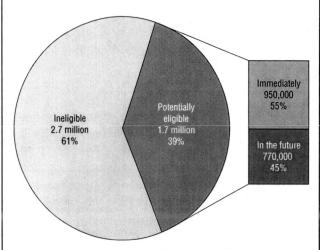

**Unauthorized immigrants ages 30 and under eligible for Deferred Action for Childhood Arrivals program, 2012**

Ineligible 2.7 million 61%

Potentially eligible 1.7 million 39%

Immediately 950,000 55%

In the future 770,000 45%

Note: There are 4.4 million unauthorized immigrants in the U.S. ages 30 and under. The Pew Hispanic Center estimates 1.7 million could potentially be eligible for relief from deportation.

SOURCE: Jeffrey S. Passel and Mark Hugo Lopez, "Figure 1. Unauthorized Immigrants Ages 30 and under Eligible for Deportation Relief," in *Up to 1.7 Million Unauthorized Immigrant Youth May Benefit from New Deportation Rules*, Pew Research Center, Pew Hispanic Center, August 14, 2012, http://www.pewhispanic.org/files/2012/12/unauthroized_immigrant_youth_update.pdf (accessed March 14, 2013)

were believed to be eligible immediately, and the remaining 770,000 were expected to become eligible in the future, as a result of reaching the age of 15 years or meeting the eligibility requirements by enrolling in school. Of the 2.7 million unauthorized immigrants aged 30 years and younger who were ineligible for deferred action, 2.4 million were ineligible because they came to the United States after the age of 15 years or had not been in the United States for five years as of June 15, 2012. (See Table 2.1.) Another 280,000 of those ineligible were under 15 years of age but had not been in the United States for five years. In addition, Passel and Lopez estimate that there were 6.8 million illegal immigrants who did not qualify for the program because they were aged 31 years and older.

## IMMIGRATION LEGISLATION IN THE STATES

Beginning in the 1990s populist concern about the rising numbers of unauthorized immigrants, especially in border states, led to the proposal of a range of restrictive laws at the state level. In 1994 California, with more than double the foreign-born population of any other state, made an unsuccessful attempt to restrict illegal immigration. A decade later Arizona began implementing a series of laws that imposed unprecedentedly severe restrictions on immigrants. Other states that had not historically been home to large immigrant

**TABLE 2.1**

**Deferred Action for Childhood Arrivals eligibility, by individual characteristics, 2012**

[In thousands]

| | |
|---|---|
| **Unauthorized immigrants ages 30 and under** | **4,410** |
| **Potentially eligible** | **1,730** |
| Potentially eligible now | |
|     Ages 18–30 in high school or with high school diploma | 700 |
|     Ages 15–17, enrolled in high school | 250 |
| Not eligible now, but potentially eligible in future | |
|     Ages 5–14 | 450 |
|     Ages 16–30, no high school diploma or GED and not enrolled in school | 320 |
| **Ineligible** | **2,680** |
| Under age 15, but have been in U.S. less than 5 years | 280 |
| Ages 15 and older and arrived in U.S. after age 15* | 2,400 |

Note: All estimates rounded independently to nearest 10,000. Estimates shown do not take into account military or Coast Guard service and do not take into account felony or misdemeanor status. Both are criteria used by the U.S. Department of Homeland Security to determine eligibility.
*Includes some unauthorized immigrants who arrived before age 16 but have not been in the U.S. for five years.
GED = General equivalency diploma

SOURCE: Jeffrey S. Passel and Mark Hugo Lopez, "Table 1. Deferred Action for Childhood Arrivals Eligibility among Unauthorized Immigrants Ages 30 and Under," in *Up to 1.7 Million Unauthorized Immigrant Youth May Benefit from New Deportation Rules*, Pew Research Center, Pew Hispanic Center, August 14, 2012, http://www.pewhispanic.org/files/2012/12/unauthroized_immigrant_youth_update.pdf (accessed March 14, 2013).

populations began to see influxes of immigrants during the first decade of the 21st century, and many of these states passed restrictive immigration laws that were modeled on Arizona's. Like California's attempt to restrict immigration before them, these laws raised civil rights issues as well as issues related to the balance of power between the federal government and the states. The constitutionality of Arizona's laws were eventually decided by the U.S. Supreme Court.

## California's Efforts to Suppress Illegal Immigration

Increasing concern about the effects of illegal immigration in California culminated in November 1994, when voters approved Proposition 187. The ballot initiative prohibited unauthorized immigrants and their children from receiving any welfare services, education, or emergency health care. It further required local law enforcement authorities, educators, medical professionals, and social service workers to report suspected unauthorized immigrants to federal and state authorities. It also considered the manufacture, distribution, and sale of fraudulent documents to be a state felony punishable by up to five years in prison.

The day after California voters approved Proposition 187, civil rights groups filed suit in federal district court to block implementation of the ballot initiative. One week later a temporary restraining order was issued. In November 1995 the U.S. district judge Mariana R. Pfaelzer (1926–) ruled unconstitutional Proposition 187's provision that denied elementary and secondary education for undocumented children. Pfaelzer cited the U.S. Supreme Court decision in *Plyler v. Doe* (457 U.S. 202 [1982]), which held that the equal protection clause of the 14th Amendment prohibits states from denying education to illegal immigrants. Civil rights and education groups had argued that states had no legal rights to regulate immigration, which was a federal responsibility.

In March 1998 Pfaelzer permanently barred Proposition 187's restrictions on benefits for unauthorized immigrants and declared much of the legislation unconstitutional. Pfaelzer did allow, however, the criminal provision to consider as a felony the manufacture, distribution, and use of false documents.

## Arizona Succeeds Where California Failed

In November 2004 Arizona voters approved Proposition 200, which required proof of citizenship when registering to vote and applying for public benefits. It also required state, county, and municipal employees to report suspected undocumented immigrants to the authorities. The Mexican American Legal Defense and Educational Fund filed suit to block implementation of Proposition 200. In December 2004 the U.S. district judge David C. Bury (1942–) lifted a temporary order barring implementation of Proposition 200, which allowed it to become law in Arizona.

Proposition 200 proved to be just the beginning of Arizona's restrictive immigration laws. In 2007 Arizona passed one of the toughest immigration laws in the country, the Legal Arizona Workers Act (LAWA), which became effective on January 1, 2008. LAWA provided for the suspension and revocation of the business licenses of Arizona employers who knowingly employ illegal immigrants. It also required employers to verify the work status of newly hired workers through E-Verify.

In 2010 Arizona passed the most restrictive immigration law on record to that date, Arizona Senate Bill 1070 (SB 1070). Signed into law by Governor Jan Brewer (1944–) on April 23, 2010, and subsequently modified, SB 1070 required police officers to determine immigration status during "lawful contact," such as routine traffic stops. The law also required legal immigrants to carry registration documents at all times, making failure to do so a state crime; authorized police to arrest illegal immigrants if they had probable cause to believe that the person had committed an offense that would lead to deportation; and made it illegal for unauthorized workers to solicit or perform work.

SB 1070 faced legal challenges almost immediately. Particular outrage was directed at the so-called show me your papers provision, which required law enforcement agencies to ask suspected immigrants for proof of their authorization to be in the United States. Critics argued that the provision legalized racial profiling by essentially requiring police to question the immigration status of anyone who looked Hispanic. In addition to a number of other lawsuits attempting to block implementation of the law, the Justice Department filed suit against the state of Arizona in July 2010, asserting that only the federal government had the authority to regulate immigration. Lower courts ruled in favor of the Justice Department, but Arizona appealed and was ultimately granted a hearing before the U.S. Supreme Court. In June 2012 the court issued a 5–3 ruling in *Arizona v. United States* (567 U.S. ___) that struck down much of the law on the grounds that it conflicted with federal law. However, the court upheld the legality of the "show me your papers" provision. The majority opinion, written by Justice Anthony M. Kennedy (1936–), suggested that this provision could later be struck down if a documented pattern of racial profiling resulted from its implementation.

## Other State Immigration Legislation

Arizona's success at passing restrictive immigration laws beginning in 2004 led other states to follow suit. According to the NCSL, the number of immigration-related bills and resolutions introduced in state legislatures and laws enacted both jumped sharply in 2007 and peaked in 2011, before falling somewhat in 2012. (See Table 2.2.) In 2011, 1,607 bills related to immigration were proposed in state legislatures and 318 laws or resolutions were passed; in 2012, those numbers stood at 983 and 168, respectively. The NCSL notes that immigration laws related to state budgets, law enforcement, employment, and identification and driver's licenses were among the most frequently passed forms of immigration legislation between 2010 and 2012. (See Table 2.3.)

While Arizona's SB 1070 was tied up in the courts, the state of Alabama made national headlines by passing an immigration law that was widely considered to be the most restrictive on record. Modeled on SB 1070, Alabama's House Bill 56 (HB 56) was signed into law by Governor Robert Bentley (1943–) in June 2011. HB 56

contained a "show me your papers" provision similar to Arizona's, and it prohibited unauthorized immigrants from receiving any public services, from attending public colleges and universities, and from applying for jobs. Employers were required to use the E-Verify system to confirm the immigration status of all employees, and the refusal to hire a legal resident while employing an unauthorized immigrant was declared a discriminatory practice. The law prohibited the transportation or harboring of illegal immigrants and the renting of property to illegal immigrants. Meanwhile, primary and secondary public school officials were required to ascertain the immigration status of students and report the number of suspected illegal immigrants to state education officials. Many backers of the law were overt about the intent of HB 56: to make everyday life so difficult for unauthorized immigrants that they would leave the state voluntarily or "self-deport." Josh Lederman reports in "Co-author of Arizona Immigration Law Says 'Self-Deportation' Working" (TheHill.com, February 11, 2012) that Kris Kobach (1966–), the secretary of state of Kansas, claimed in February 2012 that HB 56 and SB 1070 had encouraged many illegal immigrants to leave Alabama and Arizona rather than risk arrest and deportation. Kobach helped write both laws.

Much like SB 1070, HB 56 was met with a broad array of legal challenges. A number of HB 56's provisions were temporarily blocked pending the outcome of the court cases, and in August 2012 the U.S. Court of Appeals for the 11th Circuit invalidated as unconstitutional many of the measures meant to make everyday life difficult for illegal immigrants, including the measures requiring school officials to report students that they suspected of being undocumented. Alabama's appeal of this ruling to the U.S. Supreme Court was denied. As in Arizona, however, the controversial "show me your papers" provision was upheld.

**TABLE 2.2**

**State legislation related to immigrants, 2005–12**

| Year | Introduced | Passed legislatures | Vetoed/ (pending) | Enacted | Resolutions | Total laws & resolutions |
|---|---|---|---|---|---|---|
| 2005 | 300 | 45 | 6 | 39 | 0 | 39 |
| 2006 | 570 | 90 | 6 | 84 | 12 | 96 |
| 2007 | 1,562 | 252 | 12 | 240 | 50 | 290 |
| 2008 | 1,305 | 209 | 3 | 206 | 64 | 270 |
| 2009 | 1,500[a] | 373 | 20 | 222 | 131 | 353 |
| 2010 | 1,400[a] | 356 | 10 | 208 | 138 | 346 |
| 2011 | 1,607 | 318 | 15 | 197 | 109 | 306 |
| 2012 | 983 | 168 | 11(1)[b] | 156 | 111 | 267 |

[a]2009–2010 estimates
[b]One bill was sent to the governor Dec. 27, 2012 and enacted in 2013.

SOURCE: "Table 1. State Legislation Related to Immigrants, 2005–2012," in *2012 Immigration-Related Laws and Resolutions in the States (Jan. 1–Dec. 31, 2012)*, National Conference of State Legislatures, January 2013, http://www.ncsl.org/issues-research/immig/2012-immigration-related-laws-jan-december-2012.aspx (accessed March 5, 2013)

**TABLE 2.3**

**Immigration laws and resolutions passed by state legislatures, by type, 2010–12**

| Main sub-topics | 2010 Number of laws enacted | 2010 Number of states | 2011 Number of laws enacted (vetoed) | 2011 Number of states | 2012 Number of laws enacted (vetoed) (pending) | 2012 Number of states |
|---|---|---|---|---|---|---|
| Budgets | 49 | 29 | 19 (2) | 15 | 38 | 21 |
| Education | 17 | 11 | 20 (1) | 11 | 13 (2) | 11 |
| Employment | 27 | 20 | 27 (3) | 18 | 14 (4) | 13 |
| Health | 17 | 13 | 23 (2) | 15 | 12 | 8 |
| Human trafficking | 8 | 8 | 5 | 5 | 9 | 7 |
| ID/driver's licenses and other licenses | 26 | 21 | 27 | 18 | 14 | 12 |
| Law enforcement | 37 | 19 | 39 (5) | 20 | 26 (1) | 16 |
| Miscellaneous | 20 | 15 | 12 (1) | 9 | 10 (1) | 9 |
| Omnibus/multi-issue measures | 2 | 1 | 6 | 5 | 1 | 1 |
| Public benefits | 9 | 8 | 15 (1) | 11 | 16 (1) | 9 |
| Voting | 6 | 3 | 4 | 4 | 3 (2) (1) | 4 |
| **Total enacted laws** | **218** | **43** | **197 (15)** | **42 (& PR)** | **156 (12)** | **44 (& PR)** |
| Resolutions | 138 | 27 | 109 | 26 | 111 | 31 |
| **Total laws and resolutions passed/adopted by state legislatures** | **356** | **47** | **321** | **42 (& PR)** | **279** | **44 (& PR)** |
| Vetoed by governors | 10 | 2 | 15 | 8 | 12* | 6 |
| **Total enacted laws and adopted resolutions** | **346** | | **306** | | **267** | |

*One pending bill in 2012 on voting was enacted in January 2013.
PR = Puerto Rico.

SOURCE: "Table 2. Laws and Resolutions on Immigration Passed by Legislatures from 2010–2012," in *2012 Immigration-Related Laws and Resolutions in the States (Jan. 1–Dec. 31, 2012)*, National Conference of State Legislatures, January 2013, http://www.ncsl.org/issues-research/immig/2012-immigration-related-laws-jan-december-2012.aspx (accessed March 5, 2013)

# CHAPTER 3
# CURRENT IMMIGRATION STATISTICS

Although the United States has always been a nation of immigrants, the size, characteristics, and geographical distribution of the foreign-born population have changed dramatically with time. The U.S. Census Bureau notes in "How Do We Know? America's Foreign Born in the Last 50 Years" (2013, http://www.census.gov/how/infographics/foreign_born.html) that in 1960 there were an estimated 9.7 million foreign-born residents in the United States. Immigrants at that time represented one out of every 20 U.S. residents, most were from Europe, and they were concentrated in the Northeast and the Midwest. In 2010, by contrast, there were approximately 40 million foreign-born U.S. residents. Immigrants at that time represented one out of every eight U.S. residents, most were from Latin America and Asia, and they were increasingly concentrated in the West and the South.

These changes occurred rapidly and represent a profound shift in the character of the country. However, the relative sizes of the foreign-born and native-born populations in 2010 were not historically unique. Although the percentage of the total population that was foreign born increased steadily between 1970 and 2010, from 4.7% to 12.9%, this last percentage remained below its historic high. (See Figure 3.1.) In decennial census counts from 1860 to 1920, the immigrant population was never less than 13.2% of the total U.S. population, and in 1890 the figure stood at an all-time high of 14.8%. The Census Bureau projects that immigrants will constitute 13.3% of the total population by 2050 and 10.9% by 2100. (See Table 3.1.)

To understand the scope of the immigration issue in the United States, it is important to know the number of immigrants in the country, where they came from, why they came, and why some did not get to stay. Because immigrant statistics have been the basis for legislation and project funding, information about immigrants' ages, skills, ability to work, and location of settlement in the

United States is collected in a variety of forms by a number of different federal agencies.

## COUNTING IMMIGRANTS

Elizabeth M. Grieco et al. of the Census Bureau provide an overview of the immigrant population of the United States in *The Foreign-Born Population in the United States: 2010* (May 2012, http://www.census.gov/prod/2012pubs/acs-19.pdf). Of the estimated 40 million foreign-born individuals who were living in the United States in 2010, 17.5 million were naturalized citizens and 22.5 million were noncitizens. (See Table 3.2.) The noncitizen category included both those authorized to live in the United States on a temporary or permanent basis and those who had come to the country illegally, either by overstaying their visas (government permits allowing individuals to enter a country and remain for specific purposes and finite periods) or by entering the country without authorization. In "Unauthorized Immigrants: 11.1 Million in 2011" (December 6, 2012, http://www.pewhispanic.org/2012/12/06/unauthorized-immigrants-11-1-million-in-2011/), Jeffrey Passel and D'Vera Cohn of the Pew Hispanic Center (a project of the Pew Research Center whose immigration counts are widely cited) state there were approximately 11.2 million unauthorized immigrants in the United States in 2010 and 11.1 million in 2011.

In 2010 more than half (53.1%, or 21.2 million) of the 40 million foreign-born U.S. residents were originally from Latin America and the Caribbean, and 11.7 million of these immigrants (29.3% of the total) were from Mexico. (See Table 3.3.) Approximately 11.3 million (28.2%) foreign-born residents were from Asia, and 4.8 million (12.1%) were from Europe. Another 1.6 million (4%) were from Africa. Immigrants from Northern America (a Census Bureau classification that includes Canada, Bermuda, Greenland, and the French North Atlantic island territory St. Pierre and Miquelon) made up 807,000 (2%) of the

FIGURE 3.1

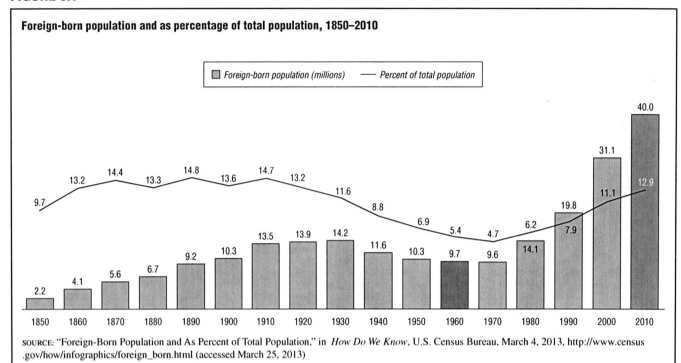

**Foreign-born population and as percentage of total population, 1850–2010**

SOURCE: "Foreign-Born Population and As Percent of Total Population," in *How Do We Know*, U.S. Census Bureau, March 4, 2013, http://www.census.gov/how/infographics/foreign_born.html (accessed March 25, 2013)

## TABLE 3.1

**Population projections for native and foreign-born, selected years 2010–2100**

| | July 1 2010 | July 1 2025 | July 1 2050 | July 1 2075 | July 1 2100 |
|---|---|---|---|---|---|
| **Total** | | | | | |
| Population | 299,861 | 337,814 | 403,686 | 480,504 | 570,954 |
| Percent of total | 100.0 | 100.0 | 100.0 | 100.0 | 100.0 |
| Native population | 266,359 | 296,999 | 349,890 | 420,957 | 508,694 |
| Percent of total | 88.8 | 87.9 | 86.7 | 87.6 | 89.1 |
| Foreign-born population | 33,502 | 40,814 | 53,796 | 59,546 | 62,259 |
| Percent of total | 11.2 | 12.1 | 13.3 | 12.4 | 10.9 |

SOURCE: Adapted from "Projections of the Resident Population by Race, Hispanic Origin, and Nativity: Middle Series, 1999–2100 (NP-T5-C; NP-T5-F; NP-T5-G; NP-T5-H)," in *Population Projections*, U.S. Census Bureau, January 13, 2000, http://www.census.gov/population/www/projections/natsum-T5.html (accessed January 1, 2013)

## TABLE 3.2

**Native and foreign-born populations, 2010**

[Numbers in thousands]

| Nativity and citizenship | Population[a] | Margin of error[b] (±) | Percent | Margin of error[b] (±) |
|---|---|---|---|---|
| **Total** | **309,350** | (X) | **100.0** | (X) |
| Native | 269,394 | 115 | 87.1 | — |
| Foreign born | 39,956 | 115 | 12.9 | — |
| Naturalized citizen | 17,476 | 82 | 5.6 | — |
| Noncitizen | 22,480 | 120 | 7.3 | — |

(X) Not applicable.
—Represents or rounds to zero.
[a]Population as of July 1, 2010.
[b]Data are based on a sample and are subject to sampling variability. A margin of error is a measure of an estimate's variability. The larger the margin of error in relation to the size of the estimates, the less reliable the estimate. When added to and subtracted from the estimate, the margin of error forms the 90 percent confidence interval.

SOURCE: Elizabeth M. Grieco et al., "Table 1. Population by Nativity Status and Citizenship: 2010," in *The Foreign-Born Population in the United States: 2010*, U.S. Department of Commerce, Economics and Statistics Administration, U.S. Census Bureau, May 2012, http://www.census.gov/prod/2012pubs/acs-19.pdf (accessed March 6, 2013)

foreign-born population, and immigrants from Oceania accounted for 217,000 (0.5%).

In 2010 California was home to more than a quarter (25.4%) of the national foreign-born population, while another 30% of foreign-born residents were split between New York (10.8%), Texas (10.4%), and Florida (9.2%). (See Figure 3.2.) Other states with large immigrant populations were New Jersey (where 4.6% of the total immigrant population lived), Illinois (4.4%), Massachusetts (2.5%), Georgia (2.4%), Virginia (2.3%), and Washington (2.2%). The remaining 26% of the foreign-born population was dispersed among the other 40 states and the District of Columbia.

The presence of immigrants has a marked influence on the character of the individual states to which they were primarily drawn. Grieco et al. indicate that immigrants represented 27% of all California residents, 22% of all New York residents, and 21% of all New Jersey residents in 2010. The percentage of the foreign-born population exceeded the national average of 12.9% in 14 states and the District of Columbia. (See Figure 3.3.) According to the Center for American Progress, in "The Facts

TABLE 3.3

**Foreign-born population by region of birth, 2010**

[Numbers in thousands]

| Region of birth | Population | Margin of error[a] (±) | Percent | Margin of error[a] (±) |
|---|---|---|---|---|
| Total[b] | 39,956 | 115 | 100.0 | (X) |
| Africa | 1,607 | 33 | 4.0 | 0.1 |
| Asia | 11,284 | 47 | 28.2 | 0.1 |
| Europe | 4,817 | 44 | 12.1 | 0.1 |
| Latin America and the Caribbean | 21,224 | 90 | 53.1 | 0.1 |
| Mexico | 11,711 | 83 | 29.3 | 0.2 |
| Other Central America | 3,053 | 46 | 7.6 | 0.1 |
| South America | 2,730 | 42 | 6.8 | 0.1 |
| Caribbean | 3,731 | 42 | 9.3 | 0.1 |
| Northern America | 807 | 16 | 2.0 | — |
| Oceania | 217 | 10 | 0.5 | — |

(X) Not applicable.

—Represents or rounds to zero.

[a]Data are based on a sample and are subject to sampling variability. A margin of error is a measure of an estimate's variability. The larger the margin of error in relation to the size of the estimates, the less reliable the estimate. When added to and subtracted from the estimate, the margin of error forms the 90 percent confidence interval.

[b]Excludes 181 persons who reported they were born at sea.

Note: Percentages do not sum to 100.0 due to rounding.

SOURCE: Elizabeth M. Grieco et al., "Table 2. Foreign-Born Population by Region of Birth: 2010," in *The Foreign-Born Population in the United States: 2010*, U.S. Department of Commerce, Economics and Statistics Administration, U.S. Census Bureau, May 2012, http://www.census.gov/prod/2012pubs/acs-19.pdf (accessed March 6, 2013)

FIGURE 3.2

**Foreign-born population by state, 2010**

[Percent distribution. Data based on sample.]

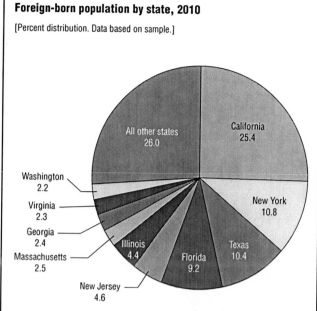

Note: Percentages do not sum to 100.0 due to rounding.

SOURCE: Elizabeth M. Grieco et al., "Figure 2. Foreign-Born Population by State: 2010," in *The Foreign-Born Population in the United States: 2010*, U.S. Department of Commerce, Economics and Statistics Administration, U.S. Census Bureau, May 2012, http://www.census.gov/prod/2012pubs/acs-19.pdf (accessed March 6, 2013)

on Immigration Today" (July 6, 2012, http://www.americanprogress.org/issues/immigration/report/2012/07/06/11888/the-facts-on-immigration-today/), 15 states—Alabama, Arkansas, Colorado, Delaware, Georgia, Idaho, Kentucky, Minnesota, Nebraska, Nevada, New Mexico, North Carolina, South Carolina, Tennessee, and Utah—saw their immigrant populations increase by 200% or more between 1990 and 2009.

**Marriage and Families**

Grieco et al. indicate that immigrants were more likely than native-born residents to be married. Figure 3.4 shows that in 2010, 58.5% of foreign-born people were married, compared with 47% of native-born people. Smaller percentages of immigrants than natives were widowed (5.1% versus 6.2%), divorced (7.5% versus 11.5%), or never married (25.8% versus 33.2%). There was significant variation in marital status among different immigrant populations, however. Immigrants born in Asia were more likely than immigrants as a whole to be married (66% versus 58.5%), whereas immigrants born in Latin America were less likely than immigrants as a whole to be married (53.9% versus 58.5%). The percentage of immigrants from Mexico who were married (57.7%) was approximately equivalent to the figure for immigrants as a whole.

Immigrant women were also significantly more likely to have children than were native-born women. As Figure 3.5 shows, 70.3 of every 1,000 foreign-born

women aged 15 to 50 years had given birth in the 12 months preceding the Census Bureau's 2010 survey, compared with 51.5 of every 1,000 native-born women. As with marital status, there were significant variations in the fertility rate among different foreign-born populations. The fertility rate was highest among women from Africa (97.3 of every 1,000), Oceania (77.8), and Latin America (75). Women from Mexico had a higher fertility rate (85.2) than the average for women from Latin America. Female immigrants from Asia (62.5), Northern America (57.3), and Europe (55) had lower fertility rates than immigrant women as a whole. These latter three groups were also the least likely of all immigrant groups to have given birth out of wedlock, and immigrant women as a whole were significantly less likely than native-born women to have given birth out of wedlock.

The Census Bureau tracks most people's living arrangements in terms of households. A single household consists of everyone who lives together in a home or apartment. (People living in group quarters, such as a dormitory, are not counted as being members of a household.) The Census Bureau further distinguishes between types of households, such as family households (consisting of related individuals) and nonfamily households (e.g., people living alone and roommates). Foreign-born people were more likely to live in family households in 2010 than were native-born people, and immigrant family households were more likely to be

**FIGURE 3.3**

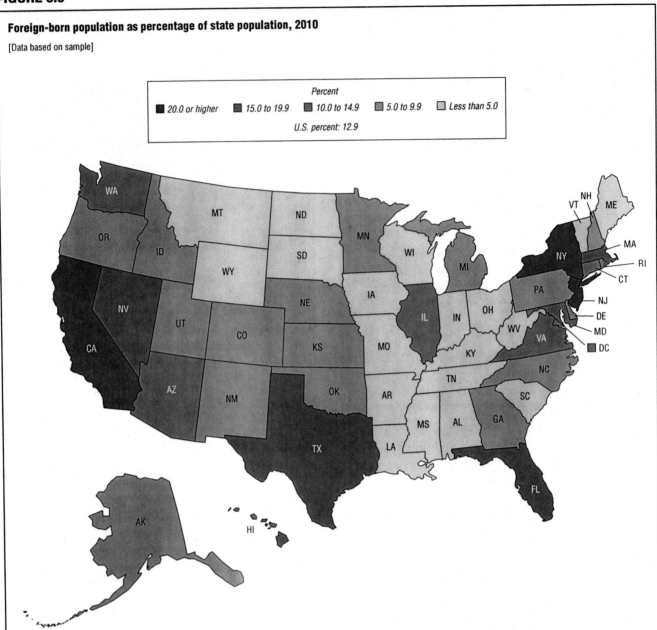

**Foreign-born population as percentage of state population, 2010**

[Data based on sample]

Percent

■ *20.0 or higher*  ■ *15.0 to 19.9*  ■ *10.0 to 14.9*  ■ *5.0 to 9.9*  □ *Less than 5.0*

*U.S. percent: 12.9*

SOURCE: Elizabeth M. Grieco et al., "Figure 1. Foreign-Born Population As Percent of State Population: 2010," in *The Foreign-Born Population in the United States: 2010*, U.S. Department of Commerce, Economics and Statistics Administration, U.S. Census Bureau, May 2012, http://www.census.gov/prod/2012pubs/acs-19.pdf (accessed March 6, 2013)

headed by a married couple. Approximately 77% of foreign-born people lived in a family household, compared with 65% of native-born people; and 55.2% of immigrant family households were headed by a married couple, compared with 47.6% of native households. (See Figure 3.6.) Among foreign-born households, those with origins in Asia (63.1%) and Oceania (62.4%) were the most likely to be headed by a married couple. An estimated 52.4% of families originating from Latin American were headed by a married couple. Families originating from Mexico were the most likely (58.4%) among Latin American families to be headed by a married couple.

In light of these marital and family characteristics, it is perhaps unsurprising that on average immigrants lived in larger households than native-born residents. In 2010, 28% of the native-born population lived in one-person households and 35% lived in two-person households. (See Figure 3.7.) By comparison, only 18% of the foreign-born population lived in one-person households and only 24% lived in two-person households. A higher percentage of foreign-born individuals lived in three-person households (19% versus 15% for the native-born), four-person households (19% versus 13%), five-person households (11% versus 6%), six-person households (5% versus 2%), and households with seven or more members (4% versus 1%).

FIGURE 3.4

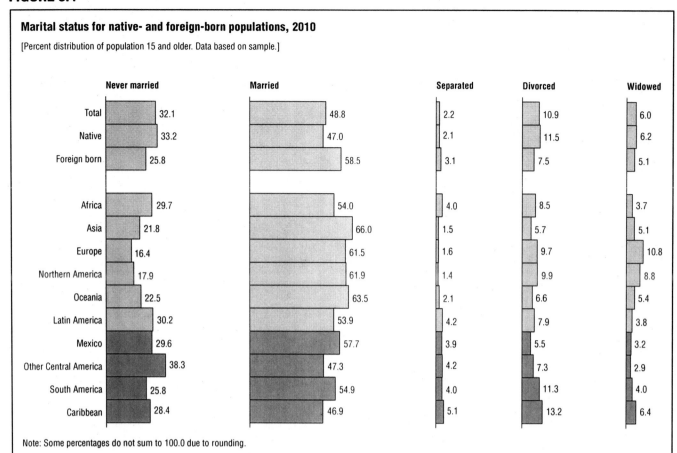

**Marital status for native- and foreign-born populations, 2010**

[Percent distribution of population 15 and older. Data based on sample.]

Note: Some percentages do not sum to 100.0 due to rounding.

SOURCE: Elizabeth M. Grieco et al., "Figure 5. Marital Status: 2010," in *The Foreign-Born Population in the United States: 2010*, U.S. Department of Commerce, Economics and Statistics Administration, U.S. Census Bureau, May 2012, http://www.census.gov/prod/2012pubs/acs-19.pdf (accessed March 6, 2013)

## Employment, Education, Income, and Poverty

In the press release "Foreign-Born Workers: Labor Force Characteristics—2011" (May 24, 2012, http://www.bls.gov/news.release/pdf/forbrn.pdf), the Bureau of Labor Statistics (BLS) states that in 2011 foreign-born workers made up 15.9% of the U.S. labor force, up slightly from the previous year's figure of 15.8%. Hispanics accounted for nearly half (49%) of the foreign-born labor force while non-Hispanic Asians were the second-largest group in the foreign-born labor force at 22.3%. As Table 3.4 shows, immigrants were more likely to be part of the labor force than native-born Americans, although the participation rates varied by gender. Approximately 67% of all foreign-born individuals aged 16 years and older were either working or actively seeking work in 2011, compared with 63.6% of native-born Americans. Foreign-born men participated in the labor force at rates well outpacing those of native-born men (79.5% versus 68.8%), but native-born women were more likely to be in the labor force than foreign-born women (58.7% versus 54.6%). The unemployment rate for foreign-born workers (9.1%) was slightly higher than the unemployment rate for native-born workers (8.9%),

although the unemployment rates for both groups had fallen measurably since 2010 in keeping with the improved employment situation as the effects of the Great Recession (which officially began in late 2007 and lasted until mid-2009) faded.

Compared with native-born workers, in 2011 foreign-born workers tended to be concentrated in service occupations; production, transportation, and material moving occupations; and natural resources, construction, and maintenance occupations. For example, 24.6% of foreign-born workers were employed in service occupations—such as health care support, building and grounds cleaning and maintenance, food preparation and serving, and personal care—whereas only 16.4% of native-born workers were employed in this field. (See Table 3.5.) Similarly, 15.8% of foreign-born workers were employed in production, transportation, and material moving occupations, compared with 11% of native-born workers. By contrast, native-born workers tended to be more highly concentrated in management, professional, and related occupations (39.3% of native-born workers compared with 28.6% of foreign-born workers) and sales and office occupations

**FIGURE 3.5**

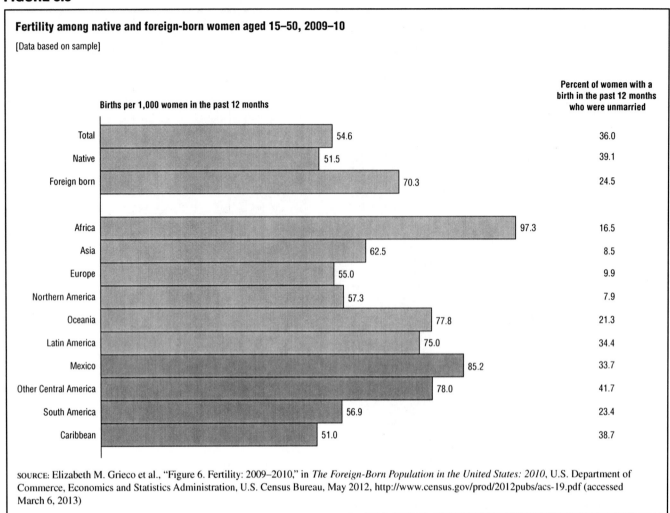

**Fertility among native and foreign-born women aged 15–50, 2009–10**

[Data based on sample]

Births per 1,000 women in the past 12 months

Percent of women with a birth in the past 12 months who were unmarried

| | Births per 1,000 | Percent unmarried |
|---|---|---|
| Total | 54.6 | 36.0 |
| Native | 51.5 | 39.1 |
| Foreign born | 70.3 | 24.5 |
| Africa | 97.3 | 16.5 |
| Asia | 62.5 | 8.5 |
| Europe | 55.0 | 9.9 |
| Northern America | 57.3 | 7.9 |
| Oceania | 77.8 | 21.3 |
| Latin America | 75.0 | 34.4 |
| Mexico | 85.2 | 33.7 |
| Other Central America | 78.0 | 41.7 |
| South America | 56.9 | 23.4 |
| Caribbean | 51.0 | 38.7 |

SOURCE: Elizabeth M. Grieco et al., "Figure 6. Fertility: 2009–2010," in *The Foreign-Born Population in the United States: 2010*, U.S. Department of Commerce, Economics and Statistics Administration, U.S. Census Bureau, May 2012, http://www.census.gov/prod/2012pubs/acs-19.pdf (accessed March 6, 2013)

(24.8% of native-born workers compared with 17.5% of foreign-born workers).

The best predictor of economic success is educational attainment, and in 2010 immigrants were far more likely to lack a high school diploma than native-born residents of the United States. According to Audrey Singer of the Brookings Institution, in "Immigrant Workers in the U.S. Labor Force" (March 15, 2012, http://www.brookings.edu/research/papers/2012/03/15-immigrant-workers-singer), 28.9% of the foreign-born population aged 25 to 64 years did not have a high school diploma or the equivalent in 2010, compared with 7.4% of the native-born population of the same age. Immigrants aged 25 to 64 years were, however, almost as likely as natives of the same age to have a bachelor's degree (18.6% versus 21.4%) or a master's or professional degree (9.1% versus 9.5%). Moreover, 1.9% of immigrants aged 25 to 64 years had doctoral degrees, compared with 1.2% of natives.

In 2011 the median weekly income for foreign-born workers aged 25 years and older was $628, 75.6% of the median weekly income for native-born workers of the same age. (See Table 3.6.) Even though immigrants with a bachelor's degree or higher made almost the same median weekly wage as their native-born counterparts ($1,148 versus $1,151), there were significant disparities between immigrant and native-born earnings at every other stage of educational attainment, and the high proportion of immigrants without a high school education brought down the overall foreign-born median weekly wage substantially. Similar disparities appear when the yearly incomes of foreign-born families are compared with those of native-born families. As Figure 3.8 shows, the median yearly income (half of all people earned more and half earned less) of foreign-born families ($50,341) was substantially less than that of native-born families ($63,231) in 2010. The median income for foreign-born noncitizen families, many of which were headed by unauthorized immigrants working for low wages, lagged far behind that of native-born Americans, as did the median income of immigrant families that had come to the United States in the preceding 10 years. Among families headed by immigrants who had become naturalized citizens, however, the median income was $61,333, almost equal to that of native-born families.

Despite the fact that foreign-born workers were more likely than native-born workers to participate in the labor

FIGURE 3.6

### Household type for native and foreign-born populations, 2010

[Percent distribution. Households are classified by nativity and region of birth of the householder. Data are based on sample.]

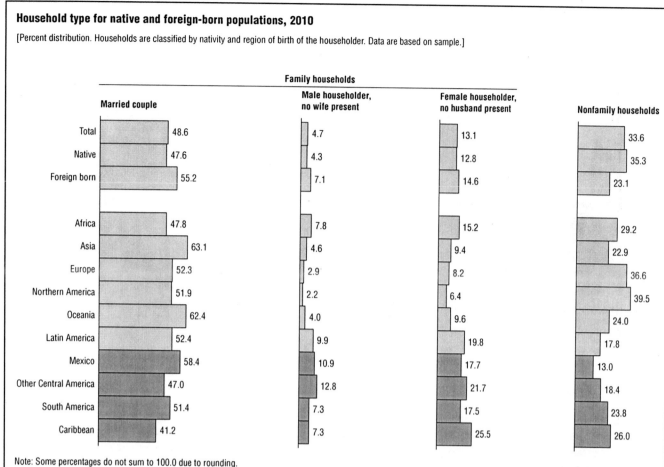

Note: Some percentages do not sum to 100.0 due to rounding.

SOURCE: Elizabeth M. Grieco et al., "Figure 10. Household Type: 2010," in *The Foreign-Born Population in the United States: 2010*, U.S. Department of Commerce, Economics and Statistics Administration, U.S. Census Bureau, May 2012, http://www.census.gov/prod/2012pubs/acs-19.pdf (accessed March 6, 2013)

force, foreign-born people were more likely to be poor than were native-born people in 2010. (See Figure 3.9.) In that year, 19% of foreign-born residents had incomes below the poverty level, compared with 13.6% of native-born residents. As with the family income trends among different groups of immigrants, the foreign-born individuals most likely to be living in poverty were noncitizens and those who had arrived in the preceding 10 years. These two groups experienced poverty at rates of 25.1% and 25.6%, respectively. Meanwhile, naturalized immigrants were less likely to be poor than native-born citizens; only 10.8% of the naturalized population were living below the poverty level in 2010.

## IMMIGRANT STATUS AND ADMISSIONS

Although the term *immigrant* is used commonly to refer to any foreign-born person living in the United States, federal law defines an immigrant as a person who is legally admitted for permanent residence in the United States. Many other foreign-born people live in the United States, some legally under the terms of non-immigrant temporary visas and some illegally, without

government authorization. Among those considered immigrants under the federal definition of the term, some arrive in the country with immigrant visas issued abroad by U.S. Department of State consular offices, and others who are already residents in the United States become immigrants when they adjust their status from temporary to permanent residence. The latter category includes individuals who enter the country as foreign students, temporary workers, refugees and asylees (those seeking asylum), and some unauthorized immigrants.

There are various ways to qualify for immigration to the United States and receive a green card, but as the U.S. Citizenship and Immigration Services (USCIS) notes in "Green Card Eligibility" (2013, http://www.uscis.gov/), immigrant admissions fall into four major categories:

• Family-based

• Employment-based

• Refugee- or asylum-based

• Other ways (a category consisting of specific qualifying groups discussed in this section)

FIGURE 3.7

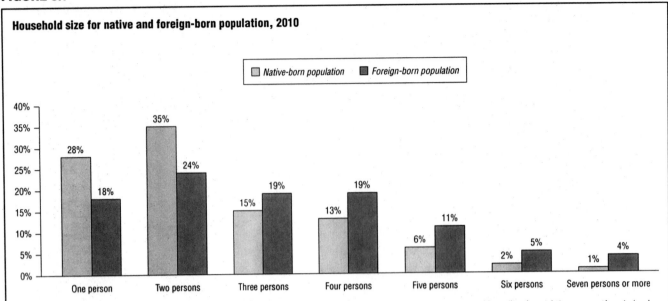

**Household size for native and foreign-born population, 2010**

Note: As of March. The foreign-born population includes anyone who is not a U.S. citizen at birth. This includes legal permanent residents (immigrants), temporary migrants (such as students), humanitarian migrants (such as refugees), and persons llegally present in the United States. Based on Current Population Survey, Annual Social and Economic Supplement which includes the civilian noninstitutional population plus armed forces living off post or with their families on post.

SOURCE: Adapted from "Table 40. Native and Foreign-Born Populations by Selected Characteristics: 2010," in *Statistical Abstract of the United States: 2012*, 131st ed., U.S. Census Bureau, 2011, http://www.census.gov/compendia/statab/2012/tables/12s0040.pdf (accessed March 5, 2013)

There are different visa limits for the different categories as well as hierarchies of preference within each category. Immediate relatives of U.S. citizens (a category that includes parents, spouses, and unmarried children under the age of 21 years) are granted the highest priority of all classes of immigrants. Visas are always made available for them, and they do not have to wait. Other family members of citizens may apply for family-based visas, but these are subject to availability and the legal priority status of various family relationships. Under the Immigration and Nationality Act (INA) of 1952, a minimum of 226,000 family-based visas are issued each year.

Job- and employment-based immigrants may apply for visas while abroad based on an offer from an employer, but they are subject to preference rankings and must wait accordingly for available visas. There are 140,000 green cards allocated for employment-based immigrants each year, but the number actually issued is larger in some years, as unused family-based visas can be allotted to this category. Workers with "extraordinary abilities, outstanding professors and researchers, and certain multinational executives and managers" are among the individuals who fall into the highest-priority category among job- and employment-based green-card applicants. In descending order of preference, the other employment-based priority categories include workers with advanced degrees, skilled professionals, those affiliated with religious orders, and investors or entrepreneurs.

Foreign-born individuals who are admitted as refugees may apply for green cards one year after entering

the United States as a refugee. Likewise, foreign-born residents granted asylum status while already in the United States may apply for a green card one year after being granted asylum status. The spouses and children of refugees and asylees are also eligible for legal permanent resident (LPR) status at the same time. Refugees must apply for a green card at that time to remain within the law. Asylees are not required to apply for a green card on that same time frame, but because changed circumstances in their countries of origin can result in the termination of their asylum status, they are encouraged to do so upon becoming eligible. Refugees and asylees (and their spouses and children) applying for green cards must have been physically present in the United States for an entire year following their arrival or granting of status, and their refugee or asylum status must still be current. There are no limits on the number of green cards issued in this category.

Although these three categories represent the bulk of the green cards issued in most years, there are also numerous other ways to obtain LPR status. There are 50,000 diversity visas granted annually to applicants from countries with low historic rates of immigration to the United States. Also, a number of small, specific groups of immigrants were eligible for green cards in 2013. Among these specific groups were children of U.S. citizens born in Korea, Vietnam, Laos, Kampuchea (Cambodia), or Thailand during the years encompassing U.S. military action in Korea and Vietnam; individuals who had served as witnesses or informants for U.S. law

# TABLE 3.4

## Employment status of the foreign-born and native-born populations by selected characteristics, 2010–11

[Numbers in thousands]

| Characteristic | 2010 Civilian noninstitutional population | 2010 Civilian labor force Total | 2010 Participation rate | 2010 Employed | 2010 Unemployed Number | 2010 Unemployment rate | 2011 Civilian noninstitutional population | 2011 Civilian labor force Total | 2011 Participation rate | 2011 Employed | 2011 Unemployed Number | 2011 Unemployment rate |
|---|---|---|---|---|---|---|---|---|---|---|---|---|
| **Total** | | | | | | | | | | | | |
| **Total, 16 years and over** | **237,830** | **153,889** | **64.7** | **139,064** | **14,825** | **9.6** | **239,618** | **153,617** | **64.1** | **139,869** | **13,747** | **8.9** |
| Men | 115,174 | 81,985 | 71.2 | 73,359 | 8,626 | 10.5 | 116,317 | 81,975 | 70.5 | 74,290 | 7,684 | 9.4 |
| Women | 122,656 | 71,904 | 58.6 | 65,705 | 6,199 | 8.6 | 123,300 | 71,642 | 58.1 | 65,579 | 6,063 | 8.5 |
| **Foreign born** | | | | | | | | | | | | |
| **Total, 16 years and over** | **35,869** | **24,356** | **67.9** | **21,969** | **2,387** | **9.8** | **36,420** | **24,391** | **67.0** | **22,183** | **2,208** | **9.1** |
| Men | 17,936 | 14,375 | 80.1 | 12,946 | 1,429 | 9.9 | 18,090 | 14,379 | 79.5 | 13,120 | 1,260 | 8.8 |
| Women | 17,934 | 9,981 | 55.7 | 9,023 | 958 | 9.6 | 18,331 | 10,012 | 54.6 | 9,063 | 949 | 9.5 |
| **Age** | | | | | | | | | | | | |
| 16 to 24 years | 3,533 | 1,975 | 55.9 | 1,661 | 314 | 15.9 | 3,631 | 1,971 | 54.3 | 1,695 | 276 | 14.0 |
| 25 to 34 years | 7,714 | 5,936 | 77.0 | 5,387 | 550 | 9.3 | 7,562 | 5,758 | 76.1 | 5,255 | 503 | 8.7 |
| 35 to 44 years | 8,470 | 6,884 | 81.3 | 6,265 | 619 | 9.0 | 8,492 | 6,843 | 80.6 | 6,301 | 542 | 7.9 |
| 45 to 54 years | 6,949 | 5,719 | 82.3 | 5,172 | 547 | 9.6 | 7,089 | 5,799 | 81.8 | 5,274 | 525 | 9.1 |
| 55 to 64 years | 4,528 | 3,011 | 66.5 | 2,727 | 284 | 9.4 | 4,737 | 3,161 | 66.7 | 2,870 | 290 | 9.2 |
| 65 years and over | 4,674 | 831 | 17.8 | 757 | 74 | 8.9 | 4,909 | 860 | 17.5 | 788 | 72 | 8.3 |
| **Race and Hispanic or Latino ethnicity[a]** | | | | | | | | | | | | |
| White non-Hispanic or Latino | 7,363 | 4,470 | 60.7 | 4,138 | 332 | 7.4 | 7,617 | 4,583 | 60.2 | 4,237 | 346 | 7.6 |
| Black non-Hispanic or Latino | 2,898 | 2,162 | 74.6 | 1,893 | 269 | 12.4 | 3,002 | 2,137 | 71.2 | 1,870 | 267 | 12.5 |
| Asian non-Hispanic or Latino | 8,073 | 5,315 | 65.8 | 4,928 | 386 | 7.3 | 8,306 | 5,449 | 65.6 | 5,086 | 363 | 6.7 |
| Hispanic or Latino ethnicity | 17,162 | 12,152 | 70.8 | 10,776 | 1,376 | 11.3 | 17,132 | 11,963 | 69.8 | 10,751 | 1,212 | 10.1 |
| **Educational attainment** | | | | | | | | | | | | |
| **Total, 25 years and over** | **32,336** | **22,381** | **69.2** | **20,308** | **2,073** | **9.3** | **32,790** | **22,420** | **68.4** | **20,488** | **1,932** | **8.6** |
| Less than a high school diploma | 9,620 | 5,930 | 61.6 | 5,219 | 712 | 12.0 | 9,532 | 5,721 | 60.0 | 5,086 | 634 | 11.1 |
| High school graduates, no college[b] | 8,284 | 5,663 | 68.4 | 5,087 | 576 | 10.2 | 8,488 | 5,674 | 66.8 | 5,145 | 529 | 9.3 |
| Some college or associate degree | 5,200 | 3,818 | 73.4 | 3,463 | 355 | 9.3 | 5,389 | 3,927 | 72.9 | 3,584 | 343 | 8.7 |
| Bachelor's degree and higher[c] | 9,232 | 6,970 | 75.5 | 6,539 | 431 | 6.2 | 9,381 | 7,098 | 75.7 | 6,673 | 425 | 6.0 |
| **Native born** | | | | | | | | | | | | |
| **Total, 16 years and over** | **201,960** | **129,533** | **64.1** | **117,095** | **12,438** | **9.6** | **203,197** | **129,226** | **63.6** | **117,686** | **11,539** | **8.9** |
| Men | 97,238 | 67,610 | 69.5 | 60,414 | 7,196 | 10.6 | 98,228 | 67,595 | 68.8 | 61,170 | 6,425 | 9.5 |
| Women | 104,722 | 61,923 | 59.1 | 56,682 | 5,242 | 8.5 | 104,970 | 61,630 | 58.7 | 56,516 | 5,115 | 8.3 |
| **Age** | | | | | | | | | | | | |
| 16 to 24 years | 34,415 | 18,960 | 55.1 | 15,417 | 3,543 | 18.7 | 34,567 | 19,026 | 55.0 | 15,668 | 3,358 | 17.7 |
| 25 to 34 years | 33,189 | 27,678 | 83.4 | 24,842 | 2,836 | 10.2 | 33,801 | 27,967 | 82.7 | 25,282 | 2,685 | 9.6 |
| 35 to 44 years | 31,620 | 26,482 | 83.8 | 24,398 | 2,084 | 7.9 | 31,006 | 25,817 | 83.3 | 23,970 | 1,847 | 7.2 |
| 45 to 54 years | 37,348 | 30,242 | 81.0 | 28,019 | 2,223 | 7.4 | 36,753 | 29,560 | 80.4 | 27,593 | 1,967 | 6.7 |
| 55 to 64 years | 31,357 | 20,286 | 64.7 | 18,909 | 1,377 | 6.8 | 32,250 | 20,604 | 63.9 | 19,315 | 1,289 | 6.3 |
| 65 years and over | 34,032 | 5,886 | 17.3 | 5,511 | 375 | 6.4 | 34,819 | 6,252 | 18.0 | 5,858 | 393 | 6.3 |
| **Race and Hispanic or Latino ethnicity[a]** | | | | | | | | | | | | |
| White non-Hispanic or Latino | 153,448 | 99,478 | 64.8 | 91,483 | 7,994 | 8.0 | 153,541 | 98,751 | 64.3 | 91,609 | 7,142 | 7.2 |
| Black non-Hispanic or Latino | 24,691 | 14,996 | 60.7 | 12,529 | 2,467 | 16.5 | 24,911 | 14,973 | 60.1 | 12,526 | 2,447 | 16.3 |
| Asian non-Hispanic or Latino | 2,900 | 1,782 | 61.5 | 1,641 | 141 | 7.9 | 2,917 | 1,793 | 61.5 | 1,647 | 147 | 8.2 |
| Hispanic or Latino ethnicity | 16,551 | 10,596 | 64.0 | 9,130 | 1,467 | 13.8 | 17,306 | 10,934 | 63.2 | 9,518 | 1,417 | 13.0 |

# TABLE 3.4

## Employment status of the foreign-born and native-born populations by selected characteristics, 2010–11 [CONTINUED]

[Numbers in thousands]

| | 2010 | | | | | | 2011 | | | | | |
| | | Civilian labor force | | | | | | Civilian labor force | | | | |
| | | | | | Unemployed | | | | | | Unemployed | |
| Characteristic | Civilian noninstitutional population | Total | Participation rate | Employed | Number | Unemployment rate | Civilian noninstitutional population | Total | Participation rate | Employed | Number | Unemployment rate |
|---|---|---|---|---|---|---|---|---|---|---|---|---|
| **Educational attainment** | | | | | | | | | | | | |
| **Total, 25 years and over** | **167,546** | **110,573** | **66.0** | **101,679** | **8,895** | **8.0** | **168,630** | **110,200** | **65.4** | **102,019** | **8,181** | **7.4** |
| Less than a high school diploma | 16,046 | 5,949 | 37.1 | 4,896 | 1,053 | 17.7 | 15,590 | 5,878 | 37.7 | 4,881 | 998 | 17.0 |
| High school graduates, no college[b] | 53,753 | 32,573 | 60.6 | 29,206 | 3,367 | 10.3 | 53,444 | 31,670 | 59.3 | 28,679 | 2,992 | 9.4 |
| Some college or associate degree | 47,022 | 33,022 | 70.2 | 30,284 | 2,738 | 8.3 | 47,700 | 32,904 | 69.0 | 30,310 | 2,594 | 7.9 |
| Bachelor's degree and higher[c] | 50,724 | 39,029 | 76.9 | 37,293 | 1,736 | 4.4 | 51,896 | 39,747 | 76.6 | 38,149 | 1,598 | 4.0 |

[a]Data for race/ethnicity groups do not sum to totals because data are not presented for all races.
[b]Includes persons with a high school diploma or equivalent.
[c]Includes persons with bachelor's, master's, professional, and doctoral degrees.
Note: Updated population controls are introduced annually with the release of January data.

SOURCE: "Table 1. Employment Status of the Foreign-Born and Native-Born Populations by Selected Characteristics, 2010–2011 Annual Averages," in *Foreign-Born Workers: Labor Force Characteristics—2011*, U.S. Department of Labor, Bureau of Labor Statistics, May 24, 2012, http://www.bls.gov/news.release/pdf/forbn.pdf (accessed March 5, 2013)

**TABLE 3.5**

**Employed foreign-born and native-born persons, by occupation and sex, 2011**

[Percent distribution]

| | Foreign born | | | Native born | | |
|---|---|---|---|---|---|---|
| Occupation | Total | Men | Women | Total | Men | Women |
| Total employed (in thousands) | 22,183 | 13,120 | 9,063 | 117,686 | 61,170 | 56,516 |
| **Occupation as a percent of total employed** | | | | | | |
| Total employed | 100.0 | 100.0 | 100.0 | 100.0 | 100.0 | 100.0 |
| Management, professional, and related occupations | 28.6 | 26.5 | 31.6 | 39.3 | 36.1 | 42.7 |
| Management, business, and financial operations occupations | 11.0 | 11.2 | 10.7 | 16.3 | 17.7 | 14.8 |
| Management occupations | 7.6 | 8.5 | 6.3 | 11.5 | 13.6 | 9.3 |
| Business and financial operations occupations | 3.4 | 2.6 | 4.5 | 4.7 | 4.1 | 5.5 |
| Professional and related occupations | 17.6 | 15.4 | 20.9 | 23.0 | 18.4 | 27.9 |
| Computer and mathematical occupations | 3.5 | 4.5 | 2.0 | 2.4 | 3.4 | 1.3 |
| Architecture and engineering occupations | 2.0 | 2.8 | 0.7 | 2.0 | 3.3 | 0.6 |
| Life, physical, and social science occupations | 1.0 | 0.9 | 1.2 | 0.9 | 0.9 | 0.9 |
| Community and social service occupations | 0.9 | 0.7 | 1.2 | 1.8 | 1.2 | 2.5 |
| Legal occupations | 0.4 | 0.2 | 0.7 | 1.4 | 1.4 | 1.4 |
| Education, training, and library occupations | 3.7 | 2.1 | 5.9 | 6.6 | 3.3 | 10.3 |
| Arts, design, entertainment, sports, and media occupations | 1.4 | 1.4 | 1.3 | 2.1 | 2.1 | 2.1 |
| Healthcare practitioner and technical occupations | 4.8 | 2.6 | 7.9 | 5.7 | 2.7 | 8.9 |
| Service occupations | 24.6 | 19.3 | 32.2 | 16.4 | 13.7 | 19.4 |
| Healthcare support occupations | 2.6 | 0.7 | 5.4 | 2.4 | 0.5 | 4.3 |
| Protective service occupations | 0.9 | 1.3 | 0.4 | 2.5 | 3.9 | 1.1 |
| Food preparation and serving related occupations | 7.9 | 7.8 | 7.9 | 5.1 | 4.1 | 6.2 |
| Building and grounds cleaning and maintenance occupations | 8.8 | 8.0 | 10.0 | 3.0 | 3.8 | 2.2 |
| Personal care and service occupations | 4.3 | 1.5 | 8.4 | 3.4 | 1.4 | 5.6 |
| Sales and office occupations | 17.5 | 12.6 | 24.5 | 24.8 | 17.6 | 32.6 |
| Sales and related occupations | 8.7 | 7.4 | 10.7 | 11.4 | 11.1 | 11.7 |
| Office and administrative support occupations | 8.7 | 5.2 | 13.8 | 13.4 | 6.6 | 20.8 |
| Natural resources, construction, and maintenance occupations | 13.5 | 21.8 | 1.5 | 8.5 | 15.7 | 0.7 |
| Farming, fishing, and forestry occupations | 1.9 | 2.4 | 1.0 | 0.5 | 0.8 | 0.2 |
| Construction and extraction occupations | 8.5 | 14.1 | 0.3 | 4.5 | 8.3 | 0.2 |
| Installation, maintenance, and repair occupations | 3.2 | 5.2 | 0.2 | 3.6 | 6.6 | 0.3 |
| Production, transportation, and material moving occupations | 15.8 | 19.8 | 10.1 | 11.0 | 16.9 | 4.7 |
| Production occupations | 8.7 | 9.3 | 7.7 | 5.3 | 7.5 | 2.9 |
| Transportation and material moving occupations | 7.2 | 10.5 | 2.4 | 5.7 | 9.3 | 1.8 |

Note: Updated population controls are introduced annually with the release of January data. Effective with January 2011 data, occupations reflect the introduction of the 2010 Census occupational classification system into the Current Population Survey, or household survey. This classification system is derived from the 2010 Standard Occupational Classification (SOC). No historical data have been revised. Data for 2011 are not strictly comparable with earlier years.

SOURCE: "Table 4. Employed Foreign-Born and Native-Born Persons 16 Years and over by Occupation and Sex, 2011 Annual Averages," in *Foreign-Born Workers: Labor Force Characteristics—2011*, U.S. Department of Labor, Bureau of Labor Statistics, May 24, 2012, http://www.bls.gov/news.release/pdf/forbrn.pdf (accessed March 5, 2013)

enforcement agencies; Afghan and Iraqi translators who had served the U.S. government; battered spouses, children, and parents of citizens or green-card holders; victims of criminal activity and human trafficking; and many others.

## The Characteristics of Legal Permanent Residents

The U.S. Department of Homeland Security's (DHS) Office of Immigration Statistics (OIS) states in *2011 Yearbook of Immigration Statistics* (September 2012, http://www.dhs.gov/sites/default/files/publications/immigration-statistics/yearbook/2011/ois_yb_2011.pdf) that slightly fewer than 1.1 million people obtained LPR status in fiscal year (FY) 2011. (See Table 3.7.) This number was up less than 20,000 from the year before and down significantly from a prerecession peak of 1.3 million in 2006. Figure 3.10 shows the trends in flows of LPRs over the course of the 20th and early 21st centuries. LPR admissions spiked to their all-time highest levels around 1990 as a

result of the 2.7 million people admitted under the Immigration Reform and Control Act of 1986.

The United States offers two general methods for foreign-born people to obtain immigrant status. In the first method an alien living abroad can apply for an immigrant visa and then become a legal resident when approved for admission at a U.S. port of entry. The second method of gaining immigrant status is by adjustment of status. This procedure allows certain foreign-born individuals already in the United States to apply for immigrant status, including certain undocumented residents, temporary workers, foreign students, and refugees. Of the total number of LPR applications granted in 2011, 580,092 (54.6%) were status adjustments and 481,948 were new arrivals. (See Table 3.7.)

As Table 3.7 shows, each year a majority of green cards go to the family members of U.S. citizens and LPRs. Without fail, the largest group annually granted

**TABLE 3.6**

**Educational attainment and median weekly earnings by foreign-born and native-born workers aged 25 and older, 2011**

[Numbers in thousands]

| | 2011 | | | | |
|---|---|---|---|---|---|
| | Foreign born | | Native born | | |
| Characteristic | Number | Median weekly earnings | Number | Median weekly earnings | Earnings of foreign born as percent of native born[a] |
| **Educational attainment** | | | | | |
| Total, 25 years and over | **15,361** | **628** | **76,373** | **831** | **75.6** |
| Less than a high school diploma | 3,822 | 417 | 3,197 | 497 | 83.9 |
| High school graduates, no college[b] | 3,828 | 530 | 21,328 | 661 | 80.2 |
| Some college or associate degree | 2,580 | 665 | 22,625 | 746 | 89.2 |
| Bachelor's degree and higher[c] | 5,131 | 1,148 | 29,222 | 1,151 | 99.8 |

[a]These figures are computed using unrounded medians and may differ slightly from percents computed using the rounded medians displayed in this table.
[b]Includes persons with a high school diploma or equivalent.
[c]Includes persons with bachelor's, master's, professional, and doctoral degrees.
Note: Updated population controls are introduced annually with the release of January data.

SOURCE: Adapted from "Table 5. Median Usual Weekly Earnings of Full-Time Wage and Salary Workers for the Foreign Born and Native Born by Selected Characteristics, 2010–11 Annual Averages," in *Foreign-Born Workers: Labor Force Characteristics—2011*, U.S. Department of Labor, Bureau of Labor Statistics, March 19, 2010, http://www.bls.gov/news.release/pdf/forbrn.pdf (accessed March 5, 2013)

**FIGURE 3.8**

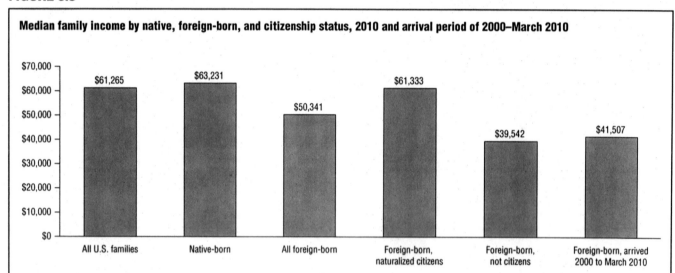

**Median family income by native, foreign-born, and citizenship status, 2010 and arrival period of 2000–March 2010**

Note: As of March. The foreign-born population includes anyone who is not a U.S. citizen at birth. This includes legal permanent residents (immigrants), temporary migrants (such as students), humanitarian migrants (such as refugees), and persons illegally present in the United States. Based on Current Population Survey, Annual Social and Economic Supplement which includes the civilian noninstitutional population plus armed forces living off post or with their families on post.

SOURCE: Adapted from "Table 40. Native and Foreign-Born Populations by Selected Characteristics: 2010," in *Statistical Abstract of the United States: 2012*, 131st ed., U.S. Census Bureau, 2011, http://www.census.gov/compendia/statab/2012/tables/12s0040.pdf (accessed March 5, 2013)

LPR status consists of the immediate family members of U.S. citizens. Of the approximately 1.1 million individuals issued green cards in FY 2011, 453,158 (42.7%) were part of this category. An additional 234,931 people were granted family-based LPR status as members of a citizen's or LPR's extended family. In all, 688,089 (64.8%) green cards were issued based on family relationships.

After these family-based categories, the most commonly issued classes of green cards are employment based: 139,339 applicants were granted LPR status in FY 2011 based on employment. (See Table 3.7.) Of these, 124,384 were status adjustments and 14,955 were new arrivals.

Meanwhile, green cards issued to refugees and asylees are all adjustments of status, because individuals in this category only become eligible for LPR status after one continuous year of residence in the United States. In FY 2011, 113,045 refugees and 55,415 asylees were granted LPR status. Another 50,103 immigrants were granted diversity visas. Diversity visas overwhelmingly go to new arrivals: the FY 2011 total in this category consisted of 48,486 new arrivals and 1,617 adjustments of status.

As Table 3.8 shows, Asia and North America together supplied approximately 70% or more of LPRs in FYs 2009, 2010, and 2011. In FY 2011, 42.5% of

FIGURE 3.9

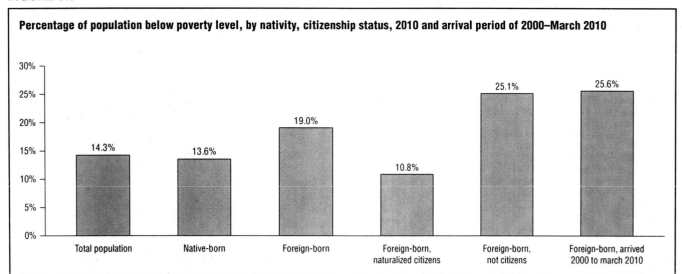

**Percentage of population below poverty level, by nativity, citizenship status, 2010 and arrival period of 2000–March 2010**

Note: As of March. Excludes unrelated individuals under age 15, and persons whose poverty status is unknown. The foreign-born population includes anyone who is not a U.S. citizen at birth. This includes legal permanent residents (immigrants), temporary migrants (such as students), humanitarian migrants (such as refugees), and persons illegally present in the United States. Based on Current Population Survey, Annual Social and Economic Supplement which includes the civilian noninstitutional population plus armed forces living off post or with their families on post.

SOURCE: Adapted from "Table 40. Native and Foreign-Born Populations by Selected Characteristics: 2009," in *Statistical Abstract of the United States: 2012*, 131st ed., U.S. Census Bureau, 2011, http://www.census.gov/compendia/statab/2012/tables/12s0040.pdf (accessed March 5, 2013)

LPRs were Asian and 31.4% were North American. In FY 2011 another 9.5% of new LPRs came from Africa, 8.1% were from South America, and 7.9% were from Europe, while only 0.5% originated from Oceania. The leading country of origin for new LPR admissions in FY 2011 was Mexico, with 13.5% of the total. Other leading countries of origin among those receiving LPR status were China (the country of origin for 8.2% of new LPRs), India (6.5%), the Philippines (5.4%), and the Dominican Republic (4.3%).

Most of the individuals granted LPR status in FY 2011 resided in high-population states that were already home to large immigrant communities. (See Table 3.9.) Roughly one-fifth (19.8%) of LPRs admitted that year lived in California, 14% in New York, 10.3% in Florida, 8.9% in Texas, and 5.2% in New Jersey. The New York City region was the leading metropolitan area of residence for new green-card holders in FY 2011, with 17.3% of new LPRs, followed by the Los Angeles metro area (8.1%), the Miami area (6.8%), the Washington, D.C., area (3.7%), and the Chicago area (3.3%). (See Table 3.10.)

According to Randall Monger and James Yankay, in "U.S. Legal Permanent Residents: 2011" (April 2012, http://www.dhs.gov/xlibrary/assets/statistics/publications/lpr_fr_2011.pdf), LPRs are typically younger than the native population and are more likely to be female. In FY 2011, 3.6% of new LPRs were under five years of age, 11.6% were aged five to 14 years, 18.7% were aged 15 to 24 years, and 23.8% were aged 25 to 34 years. (See Table 3.11.) The median age for new LPRs was 31, whereas the median age for the native-born population was 35. Of LPRs admitted in FY 2011, 54.7% were female and 45.3% were

male. (See Table 3.12.) A majority (56.4%) were married. (See Table 3.13.)

**New Arrivals by Adoption**

One subgroup of LPRs of particular interest to many observers are children who arrive in the United States via international adoption. These children have received LPR status under the family-based allotment of visas since October 2000, when Congress passed the Child Citizenship Act. This act granted automatic U.S. citizenship to foreign-born biological and adopted children of U.S. citizens, and international adoption became a growing trend in the years that followed.

The adoption of foreign-born children reached a peak in FY 2004 with a total of 22,991 children admitted as citizens. (See Figure 3.11.) By FY 2011 the number of foreign-born children admitted to the United States through adoption had dropped to 9,319, a decline of almost 60%. This decline was in no small part the result of laws passed in China in 2007 that established tougher criteria for foreigners looking to adopt there. The State Department indicates in "Statistics" (2013, http://adoption.state.gov/about_us/statistics.php) that adoptions from China fell from 7,903 in FY 2005 to 2,587 in FY 2011. Guatemala is another country that was once the source of many adoptions. In FY 2008 the State Department reports that it was the leading country of origin for international adoptions, with 4,112 total. However, the State Department explains in "Guatemala" (March 2013, http://adoption.state.gov/country_information/country_specific_info.php?country-select=guatemala) that the

TABLE 3.7

**Persons obtaining legal permanent resident status by type and major class of admission, fiscal years 2002–11**

| Type and class of admission | 2002 | 2003 | 2004 | 2005 | 2006 | 2007 | 2008 | 2009 | 2010 | 2011 |
|---|---|---|---|---|---|---|---|---|---|---|
| **Total** | | | | | | | | | | |
| Total | 1,059,356 | 703,542 | 957,883 | 1,122,257 | 1,266,129 | 1,052,415 | 1,107,126 | 1,130,818 | 1,042,625 | 1,062,040 |
| Family-sponsored preferences | 186,880 | 158,796 | 214,355 | 212,970 | 222,229 | 194,900 | 227,761 | 211,859 | 214,589 | 234,931 |
| First: Unmarried sons/daughters of U.S. citizens and their children | 23,517 | 21,471 | 26,380 | 24,729 | 25,432 | 22,858 | 26,173 | 23,965 | 26,998 | 27,299 |
| Second: Spouses, children, and unmarried sons/daughters of alien residents | 84,785 | 53,195 | 93,609 | 100,139 | 112,051 | 86,151 | 103,456 | 98,567 | 92,088 | 108,618 |
| Third: Married sons/daughters of U.S. citizens and their spouses and children | 21,041 | 27,287 | 28,695 | 22,953 | 21,491 | 20,611 | 29,273 | 25,930 | 32,817 | 27,704 |
| Fourth: Brothers/sisters of U.S. citizens (at least 21 years of age) and their spouses and children | 57,537 | 56,843 | 65,671 | 65,149 | 63,255 | 65,280 | 68,859 | 63,397 | 62,686 | 71,310 |
| Immediate relatives of U.S. citizens | 483,676 | 331,286 | 417,815 | 436,115 | 580,348 | 494,920 | 488,483 | 535,554 | 476,414 | 453,158 |
| Spouses | 293,219 | 183,796 | 252,193 | 259,144 | 339,843 | 274,358 | 265,671 | 317,129 | 271,909 | 258,320 |
| Children* | 96,941 | 77,948 | 88,088 | 94,858 | 120,064 | 103,828 | 101,342 | 98,270 | 88,297 | 80,311 |
| Parents | 93,516 | 69,542 | 77,534 | 82,113 | 120,441 | 116,734 | 121,470 | 120,155 | 116,208 | 114,527 |
| Employment-based preferences | 173,777 | 81,714 | 155,317 | 246,865 | 159,075 | 161,733 | 164,741 | 140,903 | 148,343 | 139,339 |
| First: Priority workers | 34,168 | 14,453 | 31,291 | 64,731 | 36,960 | 26,697 | 36,678 | 40,924 | 41,055 | 25,251 |
| Second: Professionals with advanced degrees or aliens of exceptional ability | 44,316 | 15,406 | 32,534 | 42,597 | 21,911 | 44,162 | 70,046 | 45,552 | 53,946 | 66,831 |
| Third: Skilled workers, professionals, and unskilled workers | 88,002 | 46,415 | 85,969 | 129,070 | 89,922 | 85,030 | 48,903 | 40,398 | 39,762 | 37,216 |
| Fourth: Certain special immigrants | 7,149 | 5,376 | 5,394 | 10,121 | 9,533 | 5,038 | 7,754 | 10,341 | 11,100 | 6,701 |
| Fifth: Employment creation (investors) | 142 | 64 | 129 | 346 | 749 | 806 | 1,360 | 3,688 | 2,480 | 3,340 |
| Diversity | 42,820 | 46,335 | 50,084 | 46,234 | 44,471 | 42,127 | 41,761 | 47,879 | 49,763 | 50,103 |
| Refugees | 115,601 | 34,362 | 61,013 | 112,676 | 99,609 | 54,942 | 90,030 | 118,836 | 92,741 | 113,045 |
| Asylees | 10,197 | 10,402 | 10,217 | 30,286 | 116,845 | 81,183 | 76,362 | 58,532 | 43,550 | 55,415 |
| Parolees | 6,018 | 4,196 | 7,121 | 7,715 | 4,569 | 1,999 | 1,172 | 2,385 | 1,592 | 1,147 |
| Children born abroad to alien residents | 783 | 743 | 707 | 571 | 623 | 597 | 637 | 587 | 716 | 633 |
| Nicaraguan Adjustment and Central American Relief Act (NACARA) | 9,307 | 2,498 | 2,292 | 1,155 | 661 | 340 | 296 | 296 | 248 | 158 |
| Cancellation of removal | 23,642 | 28,990 | 32,702 | 20,785 | 29,516 | 14,927 | 11,128 | 8,156 | 8,180 | 7,430 |
| Haitian Refugee Immigration Fairness Act (HRIFA) | 5,345 | 1,406 | 2,451 | 2,820 | 3,375 | 2,448 | 1,580 | 552 | 386 | 154 |
| Other | 1,310 | 2,814 | 3,809 | 4,065 | 4,808 | 2,299 | 3,175 | 5,279 | 6,103 | 6,527 |
| **Adjustments of status** | | | | | | | | | | |
| Total | 675,067 | 345,209 | 583,921 | 738,302 | 819,248 | 621,047 | 640,568 | 667,776 | 566,576 | 580,092 |
| Family-sponsored preferences | 63,363 | 29,032 | 64,427 | 70,459 | 79,709 | 52,059 | 56,899 | 39,787 | 26,279 | 28,346 |
| First: Unmarried sons/daughters of U.S. citizens and their children | 8,648 | 5,241 | 7,782 | 6,389 | 8,275 | 7,358 | 5,650 | 5,112 | 3,922 | 3,343 |
| Second: Spouses, children, and unmarried sons/daughters of alien residents | 44,888 | 17,966 | 45,669 | 55,362 | 62,507 | 37,046 | 41,881 | 24,597 | 11,716 | 11,985 |
| Third: Married sons/daughters of U.S. citizens and their spouses and children | 3,583 | 2,370 | 4,672 | 4,164 | 3,954 | 3,126 | 3,811 | 3,306 | 4,465 | 3,085 |
| Fourth: Brothers/sisters of U.S. citizens (at least 21 years of age) and their spouses and children | 6,244 | 3,455 | 6,304 | 4,544 | 4,973 | 4,529 | 5,557 | 6,772 | 6,176 | 9,933 |
| Immediate relatives of U.S. citizens | 305,304 | 177,192 | 269,964 | 266,851 | 357,127 | 277,188 | 251,090 | 309,073 | 252,842 | 243,174 |
| Spouses | 238,367 | 137,659 | 209,358 | 208,758 | 275,676 | 211,843 | 191,197 | 242,123 | 189,460 | 178,868 |
| Children* | 35,251 | 20,944 | 30,706 | 30,738 | 43,826 | 31,351 | 25,465 | 28,586 | 22,750 | 20,288 |
| Parents | 31,686 | 18,589 | 29,900 | 27,355 | 37,625 | 33,994 | 34,428 | 38,364 | 40,632 | 44,018 |
| Employment-based preferences | 133,755 | 52,139 | 128,232 | 219,987 | 121,586 | 133,082 | 149,527 | 127,121 | 136,010 | 124,384 |
| First: Priority workers | 24,587 | 8,089 | 27,060 | 60,240 | 32,060 | 23,802 | 35,082 | 39,420 | 39,070 | 23,605 |
| Second: Professionals with advanced degrees or aliens of exceptional ability | 38,993 | 12,969 | 31,134 | 41,109 | 20,939 | 42,991 | 68,832 | 44,336 | 52,388 | 65,140 |
| Third: Skilled workers, professionals, and unskilled workers | 64,554 | 26,962 | 65,875 | 109,713 | 60,390 | 62,642 | 38,981 | 33,525 | 34,433 | 29,757 |
| Fourth: Certain special immigrants | 5,530 | 4,094 | 4,094 | 8,737 | 7,917 | 3,332 | 6,301 | 8,855 | 9,384 | 5,306 |
| Fifth: Employment creation (investors) | 91 | 25 | 69 | 188 | 280 | 315 | 331 | 985 | 735 | 576 |
| Diversity | 1,986 | 2,591 | 2,031 | 1,850 | 1,853 | 1,360 | 1,440 | 1,277 | 1,571 | 1,617 |
| Refugees | 115,601 | 34,362 | 61,013 | 112,676 | 99,609 | 54,942 | 90,030 | 118,836 | 92,741 | 113,045 |
| Asylees | 10,197 | 10,402 | 10,217 | 30,286 | 116,845 | 81,183 | 76,362 | 58,532 | 43,550 | 55,415 |
| Parolees | 6,018 | 4,196 | 7,121 | 7,715 | 4,569 | 1,999 | 1,172 | 2,385 | 1,592 | 1,147 |
| Children born abroad to alien residents | — | — | — | — | — | — | — | — | — | — |
| Nicaraguan Adjustment and Central American Relief Act (NACARA) | 9,307 | 2,498 | 2,292 | 1,155 | 661 | 340 | 296 | 296 | 248 | 158 |
| Cancellation of removal | 23,642 | 28,990 | 32,702 | 20,785 | 29,516 | 14,927 | 11,128 | 8,156 | 8,180 | 7,430 |
| Haitian Refugee Immigration Fairness Act (HRIFA) | 5,345 | 1,406 | 2,451 | 2,820 | 3,375 | 2,448 | 1,580 | 552 | 386 | 154 |
| Other | 549 | 2,401 | 3,471 | 3,718 | 4,398 | 1,519 | 1,044 | 1,761 | 3,177 | 5,222 |

United States stopped approving adoptions from Guatemala at the end of 2007 because of problems with that country's adoption system. The only adoptions from Guatemala that have gone forward since then were those already in process before December 31, 2007.

**TABLE 3.7**

**Persons obtaining legal permanent resident status by type and major class of admission, fiscal years 2002–11 [CONTINUED]**

| Type and class of admission | 2002 | 2003 | 2004 | 2005 | 2006 | 2007 | 2008 | 2009 | 2010 | 2011 |
|---|---|---|---|---|---|---|---|---|---|---|
| **New arrivals** | | | | | | | | | | |
| Total | 384,289 | 358,333 | 373,962 | 383,955 | 446,881 | 431,368 | 466,558 | 463,042 | 476,049 | 481,948 |
| Family-sponsored preferences | 123,517 | 129,764 | 149,928 | 142,511 | 142,520 | 142,841 | 170,862 | 172,072 | 188,310 | 206,585 |
| First: Unmarried sons/daughters of U.S. citizens and their children | 14,869 | 16,230 | 18,598 | 18,340 | 17,157 | 15,500 | 20,523 | 18,853 | 23,076 | 23,956 |
| Second: Spouses, children, and unmarried sons/daughters of alien residents | 39,897 | 35,229 | 47,940 | 44,777 | 49,544 | 49,105 | 61,575 | 73,970 | 80,372 | 96,633 |
| Third: Married sons/daughters of U.S. citizens and their spouses and children | 17,458 | 24,917 | 24,023 | 18,789 | 17,537 | 17,485 | 25,462 | 22,624 | 28,352 | 24,619 |
| Fourth: Brothers/sisters of U.S. citizens (at least 21 years of age) and their spouses and children | 51,293 | 53,388 | 59,367 | 60,605 | 58,282 | 60,751 | 63,302 | 56,625 | 56,510 | 61,377 |
| Immediate relatives of U.S. citizens | 178,372 | 154,094 | 147,851 | 169,264 | 223,221 | 217,732 | 237,393 | 226,481 | 223,572 | 209,984 |
| Spouses | 54,852 | 46,137 | 42,835 | 50,386 | 64,167 | 62,515 | 74,474 | 75,006 | 82,449 | 79,452 |
| Children* | 61,690 | 57,004 | 57,382 | 64,120 | 76,238 | 72,477 | 75,877 | 69,684 | 65,547 | 60,023 |
| Parents | 61,830 | 50,953 | 47,634 | 54,758 | 82,816 | 82,740 | 87,042 | 81,791 | 75,576 | 70,509 |
| Employment-based preferences | 40,022 | 29,575 | 27,085 | 26,878 | 37,489 | 28,651 | 15,214 | 13,782 | 12,333 | 14,955 |
| First: Priority workers | 9,581 | 6,364 | 4,231 | 4,491 | 4,900 | 2,895 | 1,596 | 1,504 | 1,985 | 1,646 |
| Second: Professionals with advanced degrees or aliens of exceptional ability | 5,323 | 2,437 | 1,400 | 1,488 | 972 | 1,171 | 1,214 | 1,216 | 1,558 | 1,691 |
| Third: Skilled workers, professionals, and unskilled workers | 23,448 | 19,453 | 20,094 | 19,357 | 29,532 | 22,388 | 9,922 | 6,873 | 5,329 | 7,459 |
| Fourth: Certain special immigrants | 1,619 | 1,282 | 1,300 | 1,384 | 1,616 | 1,706 | 1,453 | 1,486 | 1,716 | 1,395 |
| Fifth: Employment creation (investors) | 51 | 39 | 60 | 158 | 469 | 491 | 1,029 | 2,703 | 1,745 | 2,764 |
| Diversity | 40,834 | 43,744 | 48,053 | 44,384 | 42,618 | 40,767 | 40,321 | 46,602 | 48,192 | 48,486 |
| Refugees | — | — | — | — | — | — | — | — | — | — |
| Asylees | — | — | — | — | — | — | — | — | — | — |
| Parolees | — | — | — | — | — | — | — | — | — | — |
| Children born abroad to alien residents | 783 | 743 | 707 | 571 | 623 | 597 | 637 | 587 | 716 | 633 |
| Nicaraguan Adjustment and Central American Relief Act (NACARA) | — | — | — | — | — | — | — | — | — | — |
| Cancellation of removal | — | — | — | — | — | — | — | — | — | — |
| Haitian Refugee Immigration Fairness Act (HRIFA) | — | — | — | — | — | — | — | — | — | — |
| Other | 761 | 413 | 338 | 347 | 410 | 780 | 2,131 | 3,518 | 2,926 | 1,305 |

—Represents zero.
*Includes orphans.

SOURCE: "Table 6. Persons Obtaining Legal Permanent Resident Status by Type and Major Class of Admission: Fiscal Years 2002 to 2011," in *Yearbook of Immigration Statistics: 2011*, U.S. Department of Homeland Security, Office of Policy, Office of Immigration Statistics, September 2012, http://www.dhs.gov/sites/default/files/publications/immigration-statistics/yearbook/2011/ois_yb_2011.pdf (accessed March 5, 2013)

**FIGURE 3.10**

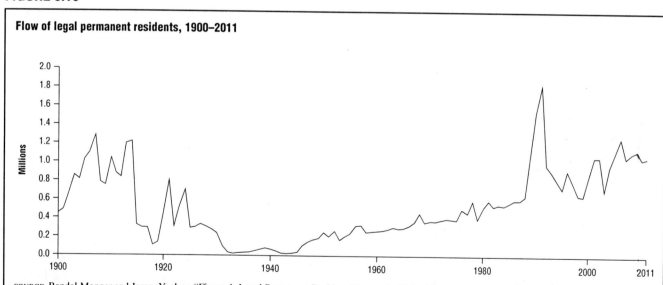

**Flow of legal permanent residents, 1900–2011**

SOURCE: Randal Monger and James Yankay, "Figure 1. Legal Permanent Resident Flow to the United States: 1900 to 2011," in *U.S. Legal Permanent Residents: 2011*, U.S. Department of Homeland Security, Office of Immigration Statistics, April 2012, http://www.dhs.gov/xlibrary/assets/statistics/publications/lpr_fr_2011.pdf (accessed March 6, 2013)

**TABLE 3.8**

**Legal permanent resident flow by region and country of birth, fiscal years 2009–11**

[Countries ranked by 2011 LPR flow]

| Region and country of birth | 2011 Number | 2011 Percent | 2010 Number | 2010 Percent | 2009 Number | 2009 Percent |
|---|---|---|---|---|---|---|
| **Region** | | | | | | |
| Total | 1,062,040 | 100.0 | 1,042,625 | 100.0 | 1,130,818 | 100.0 |
| Africa | 100,374 | 9.5 | 101,355 | 9.7 | 127,046 | 11.2 |
| Asia | 451,593 | 42.5 | 422,063 | 40.5 | 413,312 | 36.5 |
| Europe | 83,850 | 7.9 | 88,801 | 8.5 | 105,476 | 9.3 |
| North America | 333,902 | 31.4 | 336,553 | 32.3 | 375,180 | 33.2 |
| Caribbean | 133,680 | 12.6 | 139,951 | 13.4 | 146,071 | 12.9 |
| Central America | 43,707 | 4.1 | 43,951 | 4.2 | 47,868 | 4.2 |
| Other North America | 156,515 | 14.7 | 152,651 | 14.6 | 181,241 | 16.0 |
| Oceania | 4,980 | 0.5 | 5,345 | 0.5 | 5,578 | 0.5 |
| South America | 86,096 | 8.1 | 87,178 | 8.4 | 102,860 | 9.1 |
| Unknown | 1,245 | 0.1 | 1,330 | 0.1 | 1,366 | 0.1 |
| **Country** | | | | | | |
| Total | 1,062,040 | 100.0 | 1,042,625 | 100.0 | 1,130,818 | 100.0 |
| Mexico | 143,446 | 13.5 | 139,120 | 13.3 | 164,920 | 14.6 |
| China, People's Republic | 87,016 | 8.2 | 70,863 | 6.8 | 64,238 | 5.7 |
| India | 69,013 | 6.5 | 69,162 | 6.6 | 57,304 | 5.1 |
| Philippines | 57,011 | 5.4 | 58,173 | 5.6 | 60,029 | 5.3 |
| Dominican Republic | 46,109 | 4.3 | 53,870 | 5.2 | 49,414 | 4.4 |
| Cuba | 36,452 | 3.4 | 33,573 | 3.2 | 38,954 | 3.4 |
| Vietnam | 34,157 | 3.2 | 30,632 | 2.9 | 29,234 | 2.6 |
| Korea, South | 22,824 | 2.1 | 22,227 | 2.1 | 25,859 | 2.3 |
| Colombia | 22,635 | 2.1 | 22,406 | 2.1 | 27,849 | 2.5 |
| Haiti | 22,111 | 2.1 | 22,582 | 2.2 | 24,280 | 2.1 |
| Iraq | 21,133 | 2.0 | 19,855 | 1.9 | 12,110 | 1.1 |
| Jamaica | 19,662 | 1.9 | 19,825 | 1.9 | 21,783 | 1.9 |
| El Salvador | 18,667 | 1.8 | 18,806 | 1.8 | 19,909 | 1.8 |
| Bangladesh | 16,707 | 1.6 | 14,819 | 1.4 | 16,651 | 1.5 |
| Burma | 16,518 | 1.6 | 12,925 | 1.2 | 13,621 | 1.2 |
| Pakistan | 15,546 | 1.5 | 18,258 | 1.8 | 21,555 | 1.9 |
| Iran | 14,822 | 1.4 | 14,182 | 1.4 | 18,553 | 1.6 |
| Peru | 14,064 | 1.3 | 14,247 | 1.4 | 16,957 | 1.5 |
| Ethiopia | 13,793 | 1.3 | 14,266 | 1.4 | 15,462 | 1.4 |
| Canada | 12,800 | 1.2 | 13,328 | 1.3 | 16,140 | 1.4 |
| All other countries | 357,554 | 33.7 | 359,506 | 34.5 | 415,996 | 36.8 |

LPR = Lawful Permanent Resident.

SOURCE: Randal Monger and James Yankay, "Table 3. Legal Permanent Resident Flow by Region and Country of Birth, Fiscal Years 2009 to 2011," in *U.S. Legal Permanent Residents: 2011*, U.S. Department of Homeland Security, Office of Immigration Statistics, April 2012, http://www.dhs.gov/xlibrary/assets/statistics/publications/lpr_fr_2011.pdf (accessed March 6, 2013)

As Figure 3.12 shows, in FY 2011 the largest share of foreign-born children adopted by U.S. citizens came from Asia (45.5%), followed by Africa (27.1%) and Europe (19.4%). In "Statistics," the State Department shows that in FY 2011 the leading countries of origin for international adoptees were China, Ethiopia, Russia, South Korea, and Ukraine.

## NATURALIZATION

Naturalization refers to the conferring of U.S. citizenship on a person after birth. A naturalization court grants citizenship if the naturalization occurs within the United States, whereas a representative of the USCIS confers citizenship when naturalization occurs outside the United States. Beginning in 1992 the Immigration Act (IMMACT) of 1990 also permitted people to naturalize through administrative hearings with the U.S. Immigration and Naturalization Service (now the USCIS). When individuals become U.S. citizens, they pledge allegiance to the United States and renounce allegiance to their former country.

To naturalize, most immigrants must meet certain general requirements. They must be at least 18 years old, have been legally admitted to the United States for permanent residence, and have lived in the country continuously for at least five years. They must also be able to speak, read, and write English; know how the U.S. government works; have a basic knowledge of U.S. history; and be of good moral character.

The naturalization test covers reading and writing in English as well as basic U.S. history and government. The USCIS provides study materials for both the English test and the civics test at "Study for the Test" (2013, http://www.uscis.gov/). Study materials available for the English portion of the test include reading and writing flashcards and the official list of vocabulary words. The

**TABLE 3.9**

**Legal permanent resident flow by state of residence, fiscal years 2009–11**

[Ranked by 2011 LPR flow]

| State of residence | 2011 Number | 2011 Percent | 2010 Number | 2010 Percent | 2009 Number | 2009 Percent |
|---|---|---|---|---|---|---|
| Total | 1,062,040 | 100.0 | 1,042,625 | 100.0 | 1,130,818 | 100.0 |
| California | 210,591 | 19.8 | 208,446 | 20.0 | 227,876 | 20.2 |
| New York | 148,426 | 14.0 | 147,999 | 14.2 | 150,722 | 13.3 |
| Florida | 109,229 | 10.3 | 107,276 | 10.3 | 127,006 | 11.2 |
| Texas | 94,481 | 8.9 | 87,750 | 8.4 | 95,384 | 8.4 |
| New Jersey | 55,547 | 5.2 | 56,920 | 5.5 | 58,879 | 5.2 |
| Illinois | 38,325 | 3.6 | 37,909 | 3.6 | 41,889 | 3.7 |
| Massachusetts | 32,236 | 3.0 | 31,069 | 3.0 | 32,607 | 2.9 |
| Virginia | 27,767 | 2.6 | 28,607 | 2.7 | 29,825 | 2.6 |
| Georgia | 27,015 | 2.5 | 24,833 | 2.4 | 28,396 | 2.5 |
| Maryland | 25,778 | 2.4 | 26,450 | 2.5 | 26,722 | 2.4 |
| Other* | 292,645 | 27.6 | 285,366 | 27.4 | 311,512 | 27.5 |

*Includes unknown, U.S. territories and armed forces posts.
LPR = Lawful Permanent Resident.

SOURCE: Randal Monger and James Yankay, "Table 4. Legal Permanent Resident Flow by State of Residence: Fiscal Years 2009 to 2011," in *U.S. Legal Permanent Residents: 2011*, U.S. Department of Homeland Security, Office of Immigration Statistics, April 2012, http://www.dhs.gov/xlibrary/assets/statistics/publications/lpr_fr_2011.pdf (accessed March 6, 2013)

**TABLE 3.10**

**Legal permanent resident flow by metropolitan area of residence, fiscal years 2009–11**

[Ranked by 2011 LPR flow]

| Metropolitan area of residence | 2011 Number | 2011 Percent | 2010 Number | 2010 Percent | 2009 Number | 2009 Percent |
|---|---|---|---|---|---|---|
| Total | 1,062,040 | 100.0 | 1,042,625 | 100.0 | 1,130,818 | 100.0 |
| New York-Northern New Jersey-Long Island, NY-NJ-PA | 183,681 | 17.3 | 186,084 | 17.8 | 189,849 | 16.8 |
| Los Angeles-Long Beach-Santa Ana, CA | 86,161 | 8.1 | 87,443 | 8.4 | 97,538 | 8.6 |
| Miami-Fort Lauderdale-Pompano Beach, FL | 71,775 | 6.8 | 69,420 | 6.7 | 83,936 | 7.4 |
| Washington-Arlington-Alexandria, DC-VA-MD-WV | 39,365 | 3.7 | 41,322 | 4.0 | 42,567 | 3.8 |
| Chicago-Joliet-Naperville, IL-IN-WI | 35,039 | 3.3 | 35,109 | 3.4 | 38,840 | 3.4 |
| San Francisco-Oakland-Fremont, CA | 32,433 | 3.1 | 31,761 | 3.0 | 32,302 | 2.9 |
| Houston-Sugar Land-Baytown, TX | 31,136 | 2.9 | 30,844 | 3.0 | 32,021 | 2.8 |
| Dallas-Fort Worth-Arlington, TX | 28,090 | 2.6 | 26,003 | 2.5 | 29,020 | 2.6 |
| Boston-Cambridge-Quincy, MA-NH | 25,909 | 2.4 | 24,969 | 2.4 | 26,346 | 2.3 |
| Atlanta-Sandy Springs-Marietta, GA | 22,035 | 2.1 | 20,445 | 2.0 | 23,343 | 2.1 |
| Other, including unknown | 506,416 | 47.7 | 489,225 | 46.9 | 535,056 | 47.3 |

Note: Metropolitan areas defined based on Core-based Statistical Areas (CBSAs).
LPR = Lawful Permanent Resident.

SOURCE: Randal Monger and James Yankay, "Table 5. Legal Permanent Resident Flow by Metropolitan Area of Residence: Fiscal Years 2009 to2011," in *U.S. Legal Permanent Residents: 2011*, U.S. Department of Homeland Security, Office of Immigration Statistics, April 2012, http://www.dhs.gov/xlibrary/assets/statistics/publications/lpr_fr_2011.pdf (accessed March 6, 2013)

civics study materials also consist of flash cards and exercises, as well as the booklet *Learn about the United States: Quick Civics Lessons for the Naturalization Test* (January 2013, http://www.uscis.gov/), which contains short lessons based on each of the 100 civics questions.

### Special Provisions

A small share of people are naturalized under special provisions of the naturalization laws that exempt them from one or more of the general requirements. For example, spouses of U.S. citizens can become naturalized in three years instead of the normal five. Children who

immigrated with their parents generally receive their U.S. citizenship through the naturalization of their parents. Aliens with LPR status who served honorably in the U.S. military are also entitled to certain exemptions from the naturalization requirements.

### Naturalization of Active-Duty Military

Under the terms of the INA, certain foreign-born members and veterans of the U.S. military are eligible for naturalization. The USCIS explains in "Citizenship for Military Members" (2010, http://www.uscis.gov/) that LPRs who have served honorably in any branch of

**TABLE 3.11**

## Legal permanent resident flow by age, fiscal years 2009–11

| Age | 2011 | | 2010 | | 2009 | |
|---|---|---|---|---|---|---|
| | Number | Percent | Number | Percent | Number | Percent |
| Total | 1,062,040 | 100.0 | 1,042,625 | 100.0 | 1,130,818 | 100.0 |
| Under 5 years | 38,378 | 3.6 | 37,592 | 3.6 | 38,177 | 3.4 |
| 5 to 14 years | 123,123 | 11.6 | 118,987 | 11.4 | 130,701 | 11.6 |
| 15 to 24 years | 199,114 | 18.7 | 191,328 | 18.4 | 209,682 | 18.5 |
| 25 to 34 years | 252,917 | 23.8 | 253,188 | 24.3 | 277,867 | 24.6 |
| 35 to 44 years | 197,377 | 18.6 | 195,209 | 18.7 | 210,901 | 18.7 |
| 45 to 54 years | 120,797 | 11.4 | 118,070 | 11.3 | 124,621 | 11.0 |
| 55 to 64 years | 77,198 | 7.3 | 75,817 | 7.3 | 80,208 | 7.1 |
| 65 years and over | 53,126 | 5.0 | 52,425 | 5.0 | 58,659 | 5.2 |
| Unknown age | 10 | — | 9 | — | 2 | — |
| Median age (years) | 31 | X | 31 | X | 31 | X |

X = Not applicable.
—Figure rounds to 0.0.

SOURCE: Randal Monger and James Yankay, "Table 6. Legal Permanent Resident Flow by Age, Fiscal Years 2009 to 2011," in *U.S. Legal Permanent Residents: 2011*, U.S. Department of Homeland Security, Office of Immigration Statistics, April 2012, http://www.dhs.gov/xlibrary/assets/statistics/publications/lpr_fr_2011.pdf (accessed March 6, 2013)

**TABLE 3.12**

## Legal permanent resident flow by gender, fiscal years 2009–11

| Gender | 2011 | | 2010 | | 2009 | |
|---|---|---|---|---|---|---|
| | Number | Percent | Number | Percent | Number | Percent |
| Total | 1,062,040 | 100.0 | 1,042,625 | 100.0 | 1,130,818 | 100.0 |
| Male | 480,679 | 45.3 | 471,849 | 45.3 | 513,015 | 45.4 |
| Female | 581,351 | 54.7 | 570,771 | 54.7 | 617,799 | 54.6 |
| Unknown | 10 | — | 5 | — | 4 | — |

—Figure rounds to 0.0.

SOURCE: Randal Monger and James Yankay, "Table 7. Legal Permanent Resident Flow by Gender, Fiscal Years 2009 to 2011," in *U.S. Legal Permanent Residents: 2011*, U.S. Department of Homeland Security, Office of Immigration Statistics, April 2012, http://www.dhs.gov/xlibrary/assets/statistics/publications/lpr_fr_2011.pdf (accessed March 6, 2013)

**TABLE 3.13**

## Legal permanent resident flow by marital status, fiscal years 2009–11

| Marital status | 2011 | | 2010 | | 2009 | |
|---|---|---|---|---|---|---|
| | Number | Percent | Number | Percent | Number | Percent |
| Total | 1,062,040 | 100.0 | 1,042,625 | 100.0 | 1,130,818 | 100.0 |
| Single | 405,164 | 38.1 | 390,470 | 37.5 | 417,232 | 36.9 |
| Married | 599,122 | 56.4 | 596,959 | 57.3 | 654,674 | 57.9 |
| Other* | 53,017 | 5.0 | 51,174 | 4.9 | 54,454 | 4.8 |
| Unknown | 4,737 | 0.4 | 4,022 | 0.4 | 4,458 | 0.4 |

*Other includes persons who are widowed, divorced, or separated.

SOURCE: Randal Monger and James Yankay, "Table 6. Legal Permanent Resident Flow by Marital Status, Fiscal Years 2009 to 2011," in *U.S. Legal Permanent Residents: 2011*, U.S. Department of Homeland Security, Office of Immigration Statistics, April 2012, http://www.dhs.gov/xlibrary/assets/statistics/publications/lpr_fr_2011.pdf (accessed March 6, 2013)

the armed forces for one year or more and who meet certain basic criteria are often eligible for "peacetime naturalization," and LPRs who have served any length of time (even one day) during hostilities and meet certain basic criteria are eligible for naturalization. The basic criteria for both forms of military naturalization include an ability to read, write, and speak English; a knowledge of civics; good moral character; and an attachment to the principles of the U.S. Constitution. Certain spouses and children of members of the armed forces are also eligible

## FIGURE 3.11

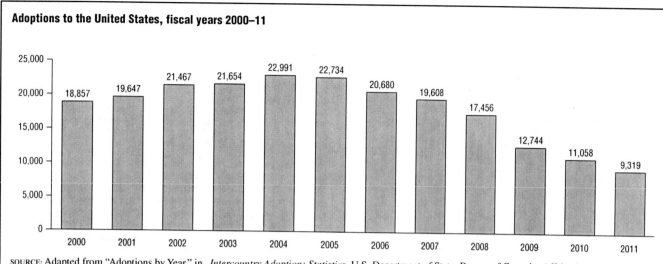

**Adoptions to the United States, fiscal years 2000–11**

SOURCE: Adapted from "Adoptions by Year," in *Intercountry Adoption: Statistics*, U.S. Department of State, Bureau of Consular Affairs, http://adoption .state.gov/about_us/statistics.php (accessed March 6, 2013)

## FIGURE 3.12

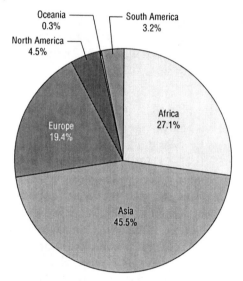

**Immigrant orphans adopted by U.S. citizens by region of birth, fiscal year 2011**

Note: Excludes 2 adoptees of unknown origin.

SOURCE: Adapted from "Table 12. Immigrant Orphans Adopted by U.S. Citizens by Gender, Age, and Region and Country of Birth, Fiscal Year 2011," in *Yearbook of Immigration Statistics: 2011*, U.S. Department of Homeland Security, Office of Policy, Office of Immigration Statistics, September 2012, http://www.dhs.gov/sites/default/files/ publications/immigration-statistics/yearbook/2011/ois_yb_2011.pdf (accessed March 6, 2013)

for expedited or overseas naturalization, and certain deceased members of the armed forces are eligible for posthumous naturalization.

Eligible candidates for peacetime naturalization must have been continuously in residence in the United States for five years and physically present for at least 30 months of the five years immediately preceding the date of their application. Naturalization during periods of hostility carries no such residency requirement: applicants who were either admitted as an LPR after entering the military or who were physically present in the United States prior to entering the military are eligible to apply. The periods of hostilities during which military service of any length qualified applicants for naturalization include World War II (1939–1945), the Korean War (1950–1953), the Vietnam War (1954–1975), the Persian Gulf War (1990–1991), and the entire period following September 11, 2001. This last designated period of hostilities had not been terminated as of May 2013; it would end only when the president issued an executive order to that effect.

In "Immigrants in the US Armed Forces" (May 2008, http://www.migrationinformation.org/USFocus/display.cfm ?ID=683), Jeanne Batalova of the Migration Policy Institute states that as of February 2008 there were 65,000 immigrants serving on active duty in the U.S. armed forces. Batalova also notes that between September 2001 and February 2008, 37,250 foreign-born service members had been naturalized. Another 111 were granted posthumous citizenship under the terms of the INA. About 5% of all active-duty personnel in 2008 were foreign born.

### Naturalization among Different Immigrant Groups

The OIS reports in *2011 Yearbook of Immigration Statistics* that in FY 2011 a total of 694,193 people became naturalized U.S. citizens. Figure 3.13 provides a percentage breakdown of their region of birth. More than one-third (249,940, or 36%) of that year's naturalized citizens were from Asia, and nearly as many (217,750, or 31.4%) were from North America. Lower proportions of people naturalized were from Europe (11.8%), Africa (10%), South America (10.1%), and Oceania (0.5%).

FIGURE 3.13

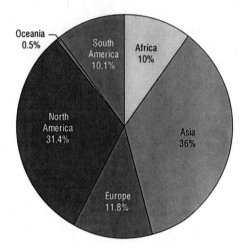

**Persons naturalized, by selected region of birth, 2011**

Oceania 0.5%
South America 10.1%
Africa 10%
North America 31.4%
Asia 36%
Europe 11.8%

Note: Does not include 337 individuals of unknown origin.

SOURCE: Adapted from "Table 21. Persons Naturalized by Region and Country of Birth: Fiscal Years 2002 to 2011," in *Yearbook of Immigration Statistics: 2011*, U.S. Department of Homeland Security, Office of Policy, Office of Immigration Statistics, September 2012, http://www.dhs.gov/sites/default/files/publications/immigration-statistics/yearbook/2011/ois_yb_2011.pdf (accessed March 6, 2013)

TABLE 3.14

**Persons naturalized, by country of birth, fiscal years 2007–11**

| Country of birth | 2007 | 2008 | 2009 | 2010 | 2011 |
| --- | --- | --- | --- | --- | --- |
| China | 33,134 | 40,017 | 37,130 | 33,969 | 32,864 |
| Colombia | 12,089 | 22,926 | 16,593 | 18,417 | 22,693 |
| Cuba | 15,394 | 39,871 | 24,891 | 14,050 | 21,071 |
| Dominican Republic | 20,645 | 35,251 | 20,778 | 15,451 | 20,508 |
| India | 46,871 | 65,971 | 52,889 | 61,142 | 45,985 |
| Mexico | 122,258 | 231,815 | 111,630 | 67,062 | 94,783 |
| Philippines | 38,830 | 58,792 | 38,934 | 35,465 | 42,520 |
| Vietnam | 27,921 | 39,584 | 31,168 | 19,313 | 20,922 |

SOURCE: Adapted from "Table 21. Persons Naturalized by Region and Country of Birth: Fiscal Years 2002 to 2011," in *Yearbook of Immigration Statistics: 2011*, U.S. Department of Homeland Security, Office of Policy, Office of Immigration Statistics, September 2012, http://www.dhs.gov/sites/default/files/publications/immigration-statistics/yearbook/2011/ois_yb_2011.pdf (accessed March 6, 2013)

Mexico was the country of origin for the largest number of naturalized citizens (94,783), followed by India (45,985), the Philippines (42,520), China (32,864), Colombia (22,693), Cuba (21,071), Vietnam (20,922), and the Dominican Republic (20,508). (See Table 3.14.) According to the OIS, these were among the most common countries of origin for naturalized citizens for FYs 2007 to 2011, with Mexico consistently leading all nations. El Salvador, South Korea, Jamaica, and Haiti also posted high totals in one or more of those fiscal years.

Naturalization rates vary significantly by country of origin, and the case of Mexican immigrants deserves special attention, given their prevalence among the total immigrant population, the population of LPRs, and the naturalized population. Ana Gonzalez-Barrera et al. of the Pew Hispanic Center report in *The Path Not Taken: Two-Thirds of Legal Mexican Immigrants Are Not U.S. Citizens* (February 4, 2013, http://www.pewhispanic.org/files/2013/02/Naturalizations_Jan_2013_FINAL.pdf) that Mexican immigrants accounted for 3.9 million of the total 12 million LPRs in 2011, but they became naturalized citizens at much lower rates than other immigrants. Although an increasing percentage of eligible Mexican immigrants chose to become naturalized citizens between 2000 and 2011, only 36% of those eligible in 2011 were naturalized, compared with 68% of the eligible non-Mexican immigrant population.

Gonzalez-Barrera et al. note that the number of Latin American and Caribbean immigrants who were eligible for naturalization but had not applied in 2011 (5.8 million) surpassed the number of immigrants from those regions who had naturalized to that date (5.6 million). It was not a lack of desire that drove the low rates of naturalization among the Hispanic immigrants Pew surveyed: 93% told researchers that they would naturalize if they could. The most commonly cited reasons for not applying for naturalization were personal and administrative barriers, chief among them an insufficient mastery of English and the cost of the application process.

## NONIMMIGRANTS

There is no cap on the total number of nonimmigrants allowed to enter the United States, although there are annual limits for some specific types of nonimmigrants. The United States, like most other countries, encourages tourism and tries to attract as many visitors as possible. Even though it is easy to get in, strict rules do apply to the conditions of the visit. For example, students can stay only long enough to complete their studies, and businesspeople can stay no longer than six months (although a six-month extension is available). Most nonimmigrants are not allowed to hold jobs while in the United States, although exceptions are made for students and the families of diplomats. An undetermined number of visitors, amounting to many tens of thousands by some estimates, overstay their nonimmigrant visas and continue to live in the United States illegally.

Visas are classified by the type of nonimmigrant visitor. For example, foreign diplomats have A visas, university students have F visas, and many temporary workers have H visas. Table 3.15 lists nonimmigrant admissions, nonimmigrant visa classifications, and the numbers of nonimmigrant visas that were issued by the State Department between FYs 2007 and 2011. In FY 2011, 158.5 million nonimmigrants were admitted to the

**TABLE 3.15**

## Nonimmigrant admissions by class of admission, fiscal years 2007–11

| Class of admission | 2007 | 2008 | 2009 | 2010 | 2011 |
|---|---|---|---|---|---|
| **Total all admissions** | **171,300,000** | **175,400,000** | **162,600,000** | **159,700,000** | **158,500,000** |
| Total I-94 admissions | 37,149,651 | 39,381,928 | 36,231,554 | 46,471,516 | 53,082,286 |
| Temporary workers and families | 1,932,075 | 1,949,695 | 1,703,697 | 2,816,525 | 3,385,775 |
| Temporary workers and trainees | 1,118,138 | 1,101,938 | 936,272 | 1,682,132 | 2,092,028 |
| Temporary workers in specialty occupations (H1B) | 461,730 | 409,619 | 339,243 | 454,763 | 494,565 |
| Chile and Singapore Free Trade Agreement aliens (H1B1) | 170 | 153 | 213 | 163 | 30 |
| Registered nurses participating in the Nursing Relief for Disadvantaged Areas (H1C) | 49 | 170 | 231 | 295 | 124 |
| Seasonal agricultural workers (H2A) | 87,316 | 173,103 | 149,763 | 139,406 | 188,411 |
| Seasonal nonagricultural workers (H2B) | 75,727 | 104,618 | 56,381 | 69,395 | 79,794 |
| Returning H2B workers (H2R) | 79,168 | 5,003 | 162 | 104 | 68 |
| Trainees (H3) | 5,540 | 6,156 | 4,168 | 3,078 | 3,279 |
| Spouses and children of H1, H2, or H3 (H4) | 144,136 | 122,423 | 105,429 | 141,575 | 155,936 |
| Workers with extraordinary ability or achievement (O1) | 36,184 | 41,238 | 45,600 | 49,995 | 51,775 |
| Workers accompanying and assisting in performance of O1 workers (O2) | 10,349 | 12,497 | 12,966 | 13,989 | 15,949 |
| Spouses and children of O1 and O2 (O3) | 5,377 | 6,386 | 6,533 | 6,764 | 6,985 |
| Internationally recognized athletes or entertainers (P1) | 53,050 | 57,030 | 54,432 | 72,917 | 84,545 |
| Artists or entertainers in reciprocal exchange programs (P2) | 4,835 | 4,358 | 4,028 | 11,213 | 13,359 |
| Artists or entertainers in culturally unique programs (P3) | 11,900 | 12,767 | 11,441 | 9,669 | 9,301 |
| Spouses and children of P1, P2, or P3 (P4) | 2,223 | 2,229 | 2,359 | 2,836 | 2,944 |
| Workers in international cultural exchange programs (Q1) | 2,412 | 3,231 | 2,555 | 2,430 | 2,331 |
| Workers in religious occupations (R1) | 25,162 | 25,106 | 17,362 | 21,043 | 19,683 |
| Spouses and children of R1 (R2) | 6,881 | 6,421 | 4,481 | 7,966 | 5,682 |
| North American Free Trade Agreement (NAFTA) professional workers (TN) | 85,142 | 88,382 | 99,018 | 634,121 | 899,455 |
| Spouses and children of TN (TD) | 20,787 | 21,048 | 19,907 | 40,410 | 57,812 |
| Intracompany transferees | 531,073 | 558,485 | 493,992 | 702,460 | 788,187 |
| Intracompany transferees (L1) | 363,536 | 382,776 | 333,386 | 502,732 | 562,776 |
| Spouses and children of L1 (L2) | 167,537 | 175,709 | 160,606 | 199,728 | 225,411 |
| Treaty traders and investors | 238,936 | 243,386 | 229,301 | 383,700 | 454,101 |
| Treaty traders and their spouses and children (E1) | 51,722 | 50,377 | 49,111 | 87,989 | 110,169 |
| Treaty investors and their spouses and children (E2) | 177,920 | 180,270 | 166,983 | 281,873 | 329,230 |
| Australian Free Trade Agreement principals, spouses and children (E3) | 9,294 | 12,739 | 13,207 | 13,838 | 14,702 |
| Representatives of foreign information media | 43,928 | 45,886 | 44,132 | 48,233 | 51,459 |
| Representatives of foreign information media and spouses and children (I1) | 43,928 | 45,886 | 44,132 | 48,233 | 51,459 |
| Students | 841,673 | 917,373 | 951,964 | 1,595,078 | 1,788,962 |
| Academic students (F1) | 787,756 | 859,169 | 895,392 | 1,514,783 | 1,702,730 |
| Spouses and children of F1 (F2) | 40,178 | 42,039 | 40,956 | 61,036 | 66,449 |
| Vocational students (M1) | 13,073 | 15,496 | 14,632 | 17,641 | 18,824 |
| Spouses and children of M1 (M2) | 666 | 669 | 984 | 1,618 | 959 |
| Exchange visitors | 489,286 | 506,138 | 459,408 | 543,335 | 526,931 |
| Exchange visitors (J1) | 443,482 | 459,126 | 413,150 | 484,740 | 469,993 |
| Spouses and children of J1 (J2) | 45,804 | 47,012 | 46,258 | 58,595 | 56,938 |
| Diplomats and other representatives | 303.290 | 314,920 | 323,183 | 380,241 | 377,830 |
| Ambassadors, public ministers, career diplomatic or consular officers and their families (A1) | 30,291 | 30,882 | 31,038 | 38,948 | 37,692 |
| Other foreign government officials or employees and their families (A2) | 131,583 | 136,699 | 142,315 | 173,293 | 175,651 |
| Attendants, servants, or personal employees of A1 and A2 and their families (A3) | 1,602 | 1,686 | 1,766 | 1,870 | 1,843 |
| Principals of recognized foreign governments (G1) | 15,099 | 15,348 | 14,876 | 16,452 | 15,649 |
| Other representatives of recognized foreign governments (G2) | 15,160 | 18,367 | 17,529 | 17,711 | 20,395 |
| Representatives of nonrecognized or nonmember foreign governments (G3) | 816 | 844 | 912 | 904 | 967 |
| International organization officers or employees (G4) | 88,374 | 89,711 | 92,878 | 105,040 | 100,858 |
| Attendants, servants, or personal employees of representatives (G5) | 1,477 | 1,399 | 1,389 | 1,385 | 1,509 |
| North Atlantic Treaty Organization (NATO) officials, spouses, and children (N1 to N7) | 18,888 | 19,984 | 20,480 | 24,638 | 23,266 |
| Temporary visitors for pleasure | 27,486,177 | 29,442,168 | 27,800,027 | 35,131,310 | 40,578,964 |
| Temporary visitors for pleasure (B2) | 13,087,974 | 13,371,671 | 12,680,504 | 19,144,042 | 23,806,138 |
| Visa Waiver Program—temporary visitors for pleasure (WT) | 13,469,851 | 15,099,059 | 14,272,553 | 14,821,569 | 15,706,067 |
| Guam Visa Waiver Program—temporary visitors for pleasure to Guam (GT) | 928,352 | 971,438 | 846,970 | 120,544 | X |
| Guam—Commonwealth of Northern Mariana Islands (CNMI) Visa Waiver Program—temporary visitors for pleasure to Guam or Northern Mariana Islands (GMT) | X | X | X | 1,045,155 | 1,066,759 |
| Temporary visitors for business | 5,418,884 | 5,603,668 | 4,390,888 | 5,205,980 | 5,694,809 |
| Temporary visitors for business (B1) | 2,928,875 | 3,052,581 | 2,408,092 | 2,944,397 | 3,055,932 |
| Visa Waiver Program—temporary visitors for business (WB) | 2,486,015 | 2,546,322 | 1,977,361 | 2,256,611 | 2,635,472 |
| Guam Visa Waiver Program—temporary visitors for business to Guam (GB) | 3,994 | 4,765 | 5,435 | 904 | X |
| Guam—Commonwealth of Northern Mariana Islands (CNMI) Visa Waiver Program—temporary visitors for business to Guam or Northern Mariana Islands (GMB) | X | X | X | 4,068 | 3,405 |

country, which was down slightly from the previous year's total of 159.7 million and down more substantially from 175.4 million in FY 2008. Two groups of visitors account for the bulk of nonimmigrant admissions each year: Canadians who visit the United States for business or pleasure, and Mexicans who have a Nonresident Alien

| Class of admission | 2007 | 2008 | 2009 | 2010 | 2011 |
|---|---|---|---|---|---|
| Transit aliens | 396,383 | 387,237 | 346,695 | 327,584 | 322,499 |
| Aliens in continuous and immediate transit through the United States (C1) | 376,451 | 365,958 | 326,704 | 304,023 | 296,636 |
| Aliens in transit to the United Nations (C2) | 2,914 | 2,646 | 2,613 | 2,987 | 4,397 |
| Foreign government officials, their spouses, children, and attendants in transit (C3) | 17,018 | 18,633 | 17,378 | 20,574 | 21,466 |
| Transit without visa (C4) | X | X | X | X | X |
| Commuter students | 310 | 1,102 | 6,488 | 53,711 | 108,894 |
| Canadian or Mexican national academic commuter students (F3) | 307 | 1,102 | 6,488 | 53,711 | 108,892 |
| Canadian or Mexican national vocational commuter students (M3) | 3 | — | — | — | D |
| Alien Fiancé(e)s of U.S. citizens and children | 38,507 | 34,863 | 32,009 | 34,893 | 27,700 |
| Fiancé(e)s of U.S. citizens (K1) | 32,991 | 29,916 | 27,754 | 30,445 | 24,112 |
| Children of K1 (K2) | 5,516 | 4,947 | 4,255 | 4,448 | 3,588 |
| Legal Immigration Family Equity (LIFE) Act | 37,594 | 24,172 | 20,960 | 38,810 | 30,099 |
| Spouses of U.S. citizens, visa pending (K3) | 15,065 | 12,849 | 12,937 | 25,615 | 17,874 |
| Children of U.S. citizens, visa pending (K4) | 3,430 | 2,845 | 2,578 | 4,557 | 3,103 |
| Spouses of permanent residents, visa pending (V1) | 6,960 | 3,609 | 2,482 | 3,620 | 3,659 |
| Children of permanent residents, visa pending (V2) | 5,435 | 2,270 | 1,424 | 2,206 | 2,546 |
| Dependents of V1 or V2, visa pending (V3) | 6,704 | 2,599 | 1,539 | 2,812 | 2,917 |
| Other | 100 | 103 | 74 | 92 | 93 |
| Unknown | 205,372 | 200,489 | 196,161 | 343,957 | 239,730 |

NA = Not available.
X = Not applicable.
D = Data withheld to limit disclosure.
—Represents zero.
Notes: Admissions represent counts of events, i.e., arrivals, not unique individuals; multiple entries of an individual on the same day are counted as one admission. The majority of short-term admissions from Canada and Mexico are excluded.

SOURCE: Adapted from "Table 25. Nonimmigrant Admissions by Class of Admission: Fiscal Years 2002 to 2011," in *Yearbook of Immigration Statistics: 2011*, U.S. Department of Homeland Security, Office of Policy, Office of Immigration Statistics, September 2012, http://www.dhs.gov/sites/default/files/publications/immigration-statistics/yearbook/2011/ois_yb_2011.pdf (accessed March 6, 2013)

Border Crossing Card (which allows for unlimited travel back and forth between the two countries). In FY 2011 these two groups accounted for 105.4 million (66.5%) of total nonimmigrant admissions. (Note that the DHS counts each admission, rather than each individual.) These two groups are not required to fill out the DHS's I-94 arrival/departure form, on which nonimmigrants must declare the purpose and length of their visits, their nationality, and other important information. Accordingly, the DHS does not collect detailed data about these visitors.

The remaining 53.1 million nonimmigrant admissions in FY 2011 represented the entries of foreign nationals required to fill out the I-94 form. (See Table 3.15.) These temporary admissions included vacationers (by far the largest group), business visitors, those authorized to work in the United States on a temporary basis, diplomats and their staffs and families, and students, among others. The number of admissions of temporary visitors for pleasure was 40.6 million, up substantially over the preceding four years, when total visitors for pleasure admissions numbered between 27.5 million and 35.1 million annually. The number of admissions of temporary visitors for business was 5.7 million, up from 5.2 million in FY 2010 and 4.4 million in FY 2009, but roughly consistent with the admissions of business visitors in FYs 2007 and 2008. There were 3.4 million temporary worker–related admissions in FY 2011, the highest number in five years. Foreign students accounted for a growing number of I-94 admissions as well.

There were 1.8 million student entries in FY 2011, up from 1.6 million the year before and more than double the FY 2007 number of 841,673.

**Temporary Foreign Workers**

A temporary worker is an foreign national coming to the United States to work for a limited period. Most legal temporary workers arrive with H-class visas, which include H-1B/H-1B1 and H-2/H-2A visas. The State Department's Bureau of Consular Affairs notes in *Report of the Visa Office 2012* (2012, http://www.travel.state.gov/visa/statistics/statistics_5861.html) that over half (52%) of individuals admitted to the United States on H-class visas in FY 2012 came from Asia. (See Figure 3.14.) North America (Canada, Mexico, Central America, and the Caribbean) contributed another 34.9% of these workers. Within these regions, certain countries predominated. For example, of the 175,003 Asian workers issued H-class visas that year, 135,608 (77.5%) came from India. Chinese nationals represented the second-largest group of temporary workers from Asia, at 14,778 (8.4%). Of the 116,592 North American workers issued H-class visas in FY 2012, 104,202 (89.4%) came from Mexico. Jamaica, with 5,280 H-class visa holders, contributed the second-highest percentage (4.5%) of temporary workers from North America.

**H-1 VISA PROGRAM.** The H-1 visa program is largely synonymous with the H-1B classification, which allows a temporary worker in a specialty occupation to remain in

FIGURE 3.14

**H class visas issued, by region, fiscal year 2012**

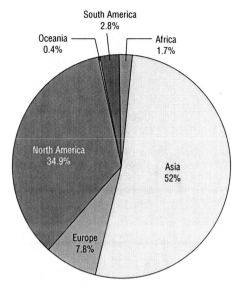

South America
2.8%

Oceania
0.4%

Africa
1.7%

North America
34.9%

Asia
52%

Europe
7.8%

Note: Does not add up to 100% due to rounding. Excludes 18 individuals or unknown nationality.

SOURCE: Adapted from "Table XVII. Nonimmigrant Visas Issued, Fiscal Year 2012," in *Report of the Visa Office 2012*, U.S. Department of State, Bureau of Consular Affairs, 2012, http://www.travel.state.gov/pdf/FY12AnnualReport-TableXVII.pdf (accessed March 6, 2013)

the United States for an extended period, generally not to exceed six years. There are other H-1 programs—H-1B1, a program specifically for workers from Chile and Singapore, and H-1C, a program for registered nurses—but these constitute a tiny fraction of the overall H-1 program petitions approved yearly by the USCIS.

The USCIS defines the scope of the H-1B program in its yearly report to Congress, *Characteristics of H-1B Specialty Occupation Workers: Fiscal Year 2011 Annual Report to Congress October 1, 2010–September 30, 2011* (March 12, 2012, http://www.uscis.gov/USCIS/Resources/Reports%20and%20Studies/H-1B/h1b-fy-11-characteristics.pdf):

> The H-1B nonimmigrant classification is a vehicle through which a qualified alien may seek admission to the United States on a temporary basis to work in his or her field of expertise. An H-1B petition can be filed for an alien to perform services in a specialty occupation, services relating to a Department of Defense (DoD) cooperative research and development project or coproduction project, or services of distinguished merit and ability in the field of fashion modeling. Prior to employing an H-1B temporary worker, the U.S. employer must first file a Labor Condition Application (LCA) with the Department of Labor (DOL) and then file an H-1B petition with USCIS. The LCA specifies the job, salary, length, and geographic location of employment. The employer must agree to pay the alien the greater of the actual or prevailing wage for the position.

The USCIS states that a foreign worker is allowed to remain in H-1 status for up to six continuous years, but each H-1B petition covers a maximum of three years. Employers must file new H-1B petitions to extend the H-1B holder's term of employment to the maximum six years. H-1B petitions may also be filed on behalf of a worker who already has H-1B status with a different employer, and petitions may be filed to revise previous petitions. Therefore, the total number of approved petitions in any given year is likely to exceed the number of foreign individuals who are actually working in the United States under the terms of the program. At the end of the six-year limit for H-1B status, a worker must either apply for a different immigration status, if eligible, or the individual must leave the United States. Following a year outside of the United States, these workers may be eligible to return to the country under H-1B status for another six-year period.

According to the USCIS, IMMACT set an annual cap on H-1B visas at 65,000 beginning in FY 1992. The USCIS explains, however, that "generally, a petition to extend an H-1B nonimmigrant's period of stay, change the conditions of [his or her] employment, or request new H-1B employment for an H-1B worker already in the United States will not count against the H-1B fiscal year cap." The American Competitiveness and Workforce Improvement Act of 1998 and the American Competitiveness in the Twenty-First Century Act of 2000 introduced important changes to the H-1B program, among them raising the H-1B cap and the introduction of exemptions to the cap. As a result of these initiatives the H-1B cap reached 195,000 in FY 2003, before reverting to the original total of 65,000 in FY 2004. It remained at this level in FY 2011. A number of exemptions remained on the books, however, including an exemption for an annual total of 20,000 foreign nationals who have earned master's or higher degrees in the United States.

As Table 3.16 shows, 269,653 H-1B petitions were approved in FY 2011. Most (61%, or 163,208) were for continuing employment. The other 39% (106,445) of approved petitions were for initial employment. The initial employment petitions were split roughly equally between workers living outside the United States, and those living inside the United States under the terms of student or other visas. The number of H-1B petitions approved in FY 2011 marked a significant increase over FYs 2009 and 2010, likely due to increased hiring among U.S. businesses as the effects of the Great Recession began to fade. Although the total number of H-1B petitions approved between FYs 2008 and 2011 fluctuated, the relative proportions allotted to initial and continuing employment held steady.

H-1B petitions were not distributed equally among different nationalities. As Table 3.17 shows, H-1B beneficiaries from India accounted for 156,317 (58%) of the total number of approved petitions in FY 2011, and for more than half of both initial and continuing employment petitions that year.

**TABLE 3.16**

**H-1B petitions approved by type, fiscal years 2008–11**

| Type of petition | Petitions approved | | | | | | | |
|---|---|---|---|---|---|---|---|---|
| | Fiscal year 2008 | Percent | Fiscal year 2009 | Percent | Fiscal year 2010 | Percent | Fiscal year 2011 | Percent |
| Total | 276,252 | 100 | 214,271 | 100 | 192,990 | 100 | 269,653 | 100 |
| Initial employment | 109,335 | 40 | 86,300 | 40 | 76,627 | 40 | 106,445 | 39 |
| Aliens outside U.S. | 55,893 | 20 | 33,283 | 16 | 34,848 | 18 | 48,665 | 18 |
| Aliens in U.S. | 53,442 | 19 | 53,017 | 25 | 41,779 | 22 | 57,780 | 21 |
| Continuing employment | 166,917 | 60 | 127,971 | 60 | 116,363 | 60 | 163,208 | 61 |

Note: Sum of the percent may not add to 100 due to rounding.

SOURCE: "Table 3. H-1B Petitions Approved by Type: Fiscal Years 2008 to 2011," in *Characteristics of H-1B Specialty Occupation Workers: Fiscal Year 2011 Annual Report to Congress, October 1, 2010–September 30, 2011*, U.S. Department of Homeland Security, U.S. Citizenship and Immigration Services, March 12, 2012, http://www.uscis.gov/USCIS/Resources/Reports%20and%20Studies/H-1B/h1b-fy-11-characteristics.pdf (accessed March 12, 2013)

---

**TABLE 3.17**

**H-1B petitions approved by country of birth and type, fiscal years 2010–11**

| Country of birth | All beneficiaries | | Initial employment | | Continuing employment | |
|---|---|---|---|---|---|---|
| | Fiscal year 2010 Number | Fiscal year 2011 Number | Fiscal year 2010 Number | Fiscal year 2011 Number | Fiscal year 2010 Number | Fiscal year 2011 Number |
| Total | 192,990 | 269,653 | 76,627 | 106,445 | 116,363 | 163,208 |
| India | 102,911 | 156,317 | 34,617 | 55,972 | 68,294 | 100,345 |
| China, People's Republic | 17,101 | 23,787 | 7,480 | 10,165 | 9,621 | 13,622 |
| Canada | 7,260 | 9,362 | 2,979 | 3,584 | 4,281 | 5,778 |
| Philippines | 6,172 | 7,582 | 2,104 | 2,020 | 4,068 | 5,562 |
| South Korea | 5,623 | 6,689 | 3,150 | 3,407 | 2,473 | 3,282 |
| United Kingdom | 3,848 | 4,629 | 2,125 | 2,573 | 1,723 | 2,056 |
| Mexico | 2,632 | 3,473 | 1,124 | 1,367 | 1,508 | 2,106 |
| Japan | 2,781 | 3,274 | 1,189 | 1,276 | 1,592 | 1,998 |
| Taiwan | 2,360 | 2,937 | 1,267 | 1,455 | 1,093 | 1,482 |
| France | 2,160 | 2,653 | 1,264 | 1,517 | 896 | 1,136 |
| Pakistan | 2,227 | 2,552 | 806 | 891 | 1,421 | 1,661 |
| Germany | 1,864 | 2,193 | 1,059 | 1,210 | 805 | 983 |
| Turkey | 1,934 | 2,161 | 948 | 967 | 986 | 1,194 |
| Brazil | 1,624 | 2,010 | 884 | 1,105 | 740 | 905 |
| Colombia | 1,527 | 1,786 | 652 | 705 | 875 | 1,081 |
| Venezuela | 1,507 | 1,734 | 752 | 846 | 755 | 888 |
| Nepal | 1,072 | 1,566 | 500 | 719 | 572 | 847 |
| Russia | 1,162 | 1,514 | 647 | 873 | 515 | 641 |
| Italy | 1,107 | 1,351 | 657 | 816 | 450 | 535 |
| Spain | 839 | 1,198 | 475 | 684 | 364 | 514 |
| Other countries | 25,279 | 30,885 | 11,948 | 14,293 | 13,331 | 16,592 |

Note: Countries of birth are ranked based on 2011 data.

SOURCE: "Table 4A. H-1B Petitions Approved by Country of Birth of Beneficiary and Type of Petition (Number): Fiscal Years 2010 and 2011," in *Characteristics of H-1B Specialty Occupation Workers: Fiscal Year 2011 Annual Report to Congress, October 1, 2010–September 30, 2011*, U.S. Department of Homeland Security, U.S. Citizenship and Immigration Services, March 12, 2012, http://www.uscis.gov/USCIS/Resources/Reports%20and%20Studies/H-1B/h1b-fy-11-characteristics.pdf (accessed March 12, 2013)

---

Workers from China accounted for the second-highest number of approved H-1B petitions, 23,787, or 8.8% of the total. The concentration of Indian and Chinese workers living in the United States under H-1B status was related to the distribution of jobs that qualified for the program. In FY 2011 nearly half of all H-1B jobs were in the computer industry. (See Table 3.18.) India's computer industry has grown explosively since the mid-1990s, and the country has developed a renowned infrastructure of educational and training programs that make it a leading international source for technology

talent. Likewise, another major source of H-1B petitions, the engineering industry, represents an area in which China's educational system and economy are among the world's strongest.

H-2 VISA PROGRAM. The H-2 Temporary Agricultural Worker Program was authorized by the INA to provide a flexible response to seasonal agricultural labor demands. Since 1964 it has been the only legal program in the United States for temporary foreign agricultural workers. In 1986 the H-2 program was amended to create separate

TABLE 3.18

**H-1B petitions approved by occupation and type, fiscal years 2010–11**

| Occupational category | All beneficiaries | | Initial employment | | Continuing employment | |
|---|---|---|---|---|---|---|
| | Fiscal year 2010 Number | Fiscal year 2011 Number | Fiscal year 2010 Number | Fiscal year 2011 Number | Fiscal year 2010 Number | Fiscal year 2011 Number |
| Total | 192,990 | 269,653 | 76,627 | 106,445 | 116,363 | 163,208 |
| Occupation known | 191,165 | 265,365 | 75,825 | 105,395 | 115,340 | 159,970 |
| Computer-related occupations | 90,802 | 134,873 | 31,661 | 51,570 | 59,141 | 83,303 |
| Occupations in Architecture, Engineering and Surveying | 19,781 | 29,695 | 7,869 | 11,950 | 11,912 | 17,745 |
| Occupations in Education | 19,713 | 24,321 | 8,626 | 9,081 | 11,087 | 15,240 |
| Occupations in Administrative Specializations | 16,516 | 21,240 | 7,637 | 9,553 | 8,879 | 11,687 |
| Occupations in Medicine and Health | 14,997 | 18,704 | 6,224 | 6,037 | 8,773 | 12,667 |
| Managers and Officials N.E.C.* | 6,744 | 7,341 | 2,999 | 3,187 | 3,745 | 4,154 |
| Occupations in Life Sciences | 5,102 | 6,375 | 2,466 | 2,992 | 2,636 | 3,383 |
| Occupations in Mathematics and Physical Sciences | 4,480 | 5,968 | 1,945 | 2,450 | 2,535 | 3,518 |
| Miscellaneous Professional, Technical, and Managerial | 4,013 | 4,944 | 1,819 | 2,315 | 2,194 | 2,629 |
| Occupations in Social Sciences | 4,011 | 4,928 | 1,911 | 2,346 | 2,100 | 2,582 |
| Occupations in Art | 2,116 | 3,013 | 1,084 | 1,577 | 1,032 | 1,436 |
| Occupations in Law and Jurisprudence | 1,136 | 1,325 | 562 | 692 | 574 | 633 |
| Occupations in Writing | 745 | 943 | 385 | 486 | 360 | 457 |
| Fashion Models | 250 | 761 | 194 | 676 | 56 | 85 |
| Occupations in Entertainment and Recreation | 452 | 556 | 249 | 270 | 203 | 286 |
| Occupations in Museum, Library & Archival Sciences | 147 | 202 | 71 | 93 | 76 | 109 |
| Occupations in Religion and Theology | 160 | 176 | 123 | 120 | 37 | 56 |
| Occupation unknown | 1,825 | 4,288 | 802 | 1,050 | 1,023 | 3,238 |

Notes: Occupations ranked based on 2011 data.
*N.E.C. indicates *not elsewhere classified.*

SOURCE: "Table 8A. H-1B Petitions Approved by Major Occupation Group of Beneficiary and Type of Petition (Number): Fiscal Years 2010 and 2011," in *Characteristics of H-1B Specialty Occupation Workers: Fiscal Year 2011 Annual Report to Congress, October 1, 2010–September 30, 2011,* U.S. Department of Homeland Security, U.S. Citizenship and Immigration Services, March 12, 2012, http://www.uscis.gov/USCIS/Resources/Reports%20and%20Studies/H-1B/h1b-fy-11-characteristics.pdf (accessed March 12, 2013)

categories of workers: H-2A visas were for temporary workers who performed agricultural services, H-2B visas were for workers who performed other services, and H-2R visas were for former H-2B workers authorized to return to the United States. The H-2R program was discontinued in 2007, but the H-2A and H-2B programs as conceived in 1986 remained in effect in 2013.

The H-2A program is based on employer needs and has no set numerical limits, while the H-2B program is capped at 66,000 new visas per year. According to the U.S. Government Accountability Office, in *H-2A Visa Program: Modernization and Improved Guidance Could Reduce Employer Application Burden* (September 2012, http://www.gao.gov/assets/650/648175.pdf), approximately 55,000 H-2A visas were issued in FY 2011, almost all of them to workers from Mexico. H-2B visa numbers typically exceed the statutory cap, as numerous exemptions exist. For example, workers who are already in the United States on an H-2B visa and who are authorized to extend their visa are not counted against the cap, nor are workers in certain categories of jobs periodically identified as exempt. Both H-2A and H-2B certifications are typically granted for 10-month periods, but both are subject to renewal for a period of up to three years.

Agricultural employers who anticipate a shortage of domestic workers file an application for H-2A certification with the U.S. Department of Labor. These employers must certify that there are not enough U.S. workers able,

qualified, and willing to do the work. The employer must also certify that the jobs are not vacant due to a labor dispute. Employers in other industries are eligible to petition for H-2B workers if their need for labor under the program is considered temporary. An employer's need for employees is considered temporary if it is a one-time occurrence, a seasonal need, a peak-load need (a need related to an anticipated spike in business), or an intermittent need.

Employers utilizing the H-2A and H-2B programs are required to pay wages at a rate that will not adversely affect the prevailing wages for U.S. citizens and permanent residents. These wage floors are typically set as equal to the highest of the following: the average wage paid to local workers in the industry, the federal minimum wage, the state minimum wage, or the local minimum wage. Both programs are also subject to restrictions regarding the countries of origin of participating workers. Each year the DHS publishes a list of countries whose citizens or nationals are authorized to participate in the two programs. As of May 2013, the list included 59 countries. Changes in the list of approved countries does not affect workers currently employed under the program unless they apply for an extension of their visas.

Figure 3.15 shows the top-10 crops worked by H-2A visa holders in FY 2011. Tobacco farmers successfully requested 5,890 H-2A visa recipients, followed by growers of hay (4,780), oranges (4,080), and apples

FIGURE 3.15

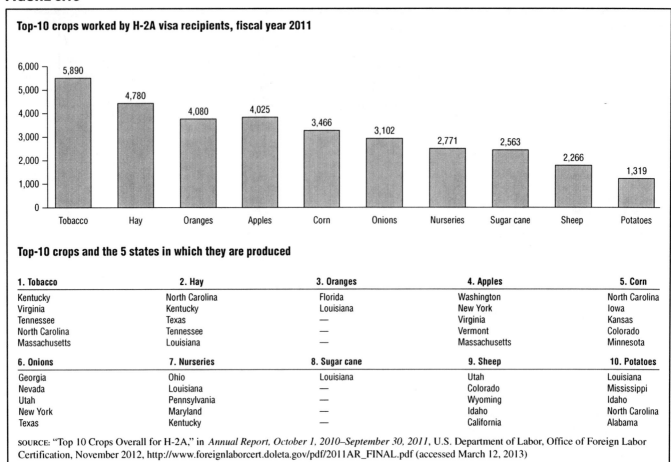

**Top-10 crops worked by H-2A visa recipients, fiscal year 2011**

**Top-10 crops and the 5 states in which they are produced**

| 1. Tobacco | 2. Hay | 3. Oranges | 4. Apples | 5. Corn |
|---|---|---|---|---|
| Kentucky | North Carolina | Florida | Washington | North Carolina |
| Virginia | Kentucky | Louisiana | New York | Iowa |
| Tennessee | Texas | — | Virginia | Kansas |
| North Carolina | Tennessee | — | Vermont | Colorado |
| Massachusetts | Louisiana | — | Massachusetts | Minnesota |

| 6. Onions | 7. Nurseries | 8. Sugar cane | 9. Sheep | 10. Potatoes |
|---|---|---|---|---|
| Georgia | Ohio | Louisiana | Utah | Louisiana |
| Nevada | Louisiana | — | Colorado | Mississippi |
| Utah | Pennsylvania | — | Wyoming | Idaho |
| New York | Maryland | — | Idaho | North Carolina |
| Texas | Kentucky | — | California | Alabama |

SOURCE: "Top 10 Crops Overall for H-2A," in *Annual Report, October 1, 2010–September 30, 2011*, U.S. Department of Labor, Office of Foreign Labor Certification, November 2012, http://www.foreignlaborcert.doleta.gov/pdf/2011AR_FINAL.pdf (accessed March 12, 2013)

(4,025). Tobacco, hay, and orange farming were concentrated in the southern states; and sugarcane, a crop for which 2,563 H-2A recipients were certified to work, was exclusive to Louisiana. Otherwise H-2A workers were employed in scattered locations across the United States.

Figure 3.16 shows the occupations for which H-2B visas were most commonly certified, as well as the average hourly wage for each position. The Labor Department's Office of Foreign Labor Certification cleared 17,661 individuals to work as groundskeepers in FY 2011, by far the most common occupation for H-2B visa holders. Nearly equal numbers of forest workers (7,963) and landscape laborers (7,840) were certified, and over 5,000 certifications each went to housekeepers and amusement park workers. Among all the top-10 H-2B jobs, the highest average hourly wage was $9.90 (for forest workers), and the lowest was $7.74 (meat trimmers).

**Foreign Students at Institutions of Higher Education**

According to the Institute of International Education (IIE), in *Open Doors Data* (2012, http://www.iie.org/Research-and-Publications/Open-Doors/Data), during the 1948–49 school year there were an estimated 25,464 international students in U.S. colleges and universities, amounting to 1.1% of the total population of 2.4 million higher-education students. (See Table 3.19.) After hovering between 1.3% and 1.6% of

the total student population for most of the next three decades, in the late 1970s the foreign-student population surpassed 2% of the total student population. This percentage continued to rise through the 2001–02 school year. It then dropped off somewhat over the next several years before rebounding. During the 2011–12 academic year there were 764,495 students enrolled in U.S. colleges and universities, accounting for 3.7% of all college and university students.

As Table 3.20 shows, well over half (489,970) of all international students enrolled at U.S. colleges and universities during the 2011–12 academic year were from Asia, and China was by far the leading country of origin among international students. An estimated 194,029 Chinese students were enrolled in American institutions of higher learning, up 11.4% from the preceding school year. India was the second-leading country of origin for international students with 100,270 enrolled during the 2011–12 school year, down slightly from the preceding year. Other leading countries of origin included South Korea (72,295 students), Saudi Arabia (34,139), Canada (26,821), Taiwan (23,250), Japan (19,966), Vietnam (15,572), and Mexico (13,893).

Table 3.21 shows the concentration of international students in different fields of study according to their

FIGURE 3.16

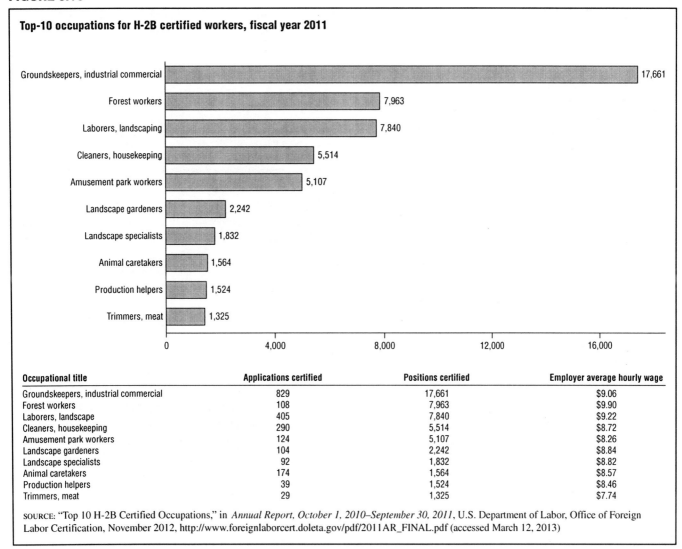

**Top-10 occupations for H-2B certified workers, fiscal year 2011**

| Occupational title | Applications certified | Positions certified | Employer average hourly wage |
|---|---|---|---|
| Groundskeepers, industrial commercial | 829 | 17,661 | $9.06 |
| Forest workers | 108 | 7,963 | $9.90 |
| Laborers, landscape | 405 | 7,840 | $9.22 |
| Cleaners, housekeeping | 290 | 5,514 | $8.72 |
| Amusement park workers | 124 | 5,107 | $8.26 |
| Landscape gardeners | 104 | 2,242 | $8.84 |
| Landscape specialists | 92 | 1,832 | $8.82 |
| Animal caretakers | 174 | 1,564 | $8.57 |
| Production helpers | 39 | 1,524 | $8.46 |
| Trimmers, meat | 29 | 1,325 | $7.74 |

SOURCE: "Top 10 H-2B Certified Occupations," in *Annual Report, October 1, 2010–September 30, 2011*, U.S. Department of Labor, Office of Foreign Labor Certification, November 2012, http://www.foreignlaborcert.doleta.gov/pdf/2011AR_FINAL.pdf (accessed March 12, 2013)

country of origin. The tendency of international students to come to the United States to study business and management was pronounced. This was the most common field of study among students from Brazil, China, France, Germany, Hong Kong, Indonesia, Japan, Mexico, Nepal, Russia, South Korea, Taiwan, Thailand, the United Kingdom, Venezuela, and Vietnam. Engineering was also a common field of study among international students. This was the most common field of study among students from India, Iran, Malaysia, Nigeria, Pakistan, Saudi Arabia, and Turkey, and it was the second-most-common field among students in a number of other countries including China.

## VISA FEES

In "Fees and Reciprocity Tables" (2013, http://travel.state.gov/visa/fees/fees_1341.html), the Bureau of Consular Affairs explains that there are two types of fees associated with U.S. visas: service fees and issuance fees. Service fees are charged upon application for a visa or for certain special services. They vary depending on the class of visa and, with

a few exceptions, are paid by all applicants. For example, as of May 2013, nonimmigrant visas not requiring petitions (with the exception of E visas) cost $160. Petition-based nonimmigrant visas, including H visas for temporary workers, cost $190. Filing an immigrant visa petition for a relative cost $420, while employment-based immigrant visa applications cost $405.

Issuance fees apply only to nonimmigrant visas and are based on reciprocity. Under this concept, the State Department tracks what other countries charge U.S. citizens for various types of visas. For any country where the amount exceeds the U.S. service fee for that type of visa, the United States assesses an issuance fee on visa applicants from that country to make up the cost difference. In other words, issuance fees ensure that any foreigner applying for a nonimmigrant visa to visit the United States pays at least as much for that visa as a U.S. citizen would pay for a visa to visit that foreigner's country of origin. Unlike service fees, issuance fees are only assessed after a visa application has been approved.

TABLE 3.19

**International student enrollment in colleges and universities, school years 1948–49 to 2011–12**

[1948–2012]

| Year | International students | Annual % change | Total enrollment[a] | % Int'l |
|------|------|------|------|------|
| 1948/49 | 25,464 | — | 2,403,400 | 1.1 |
| 1949/50 | 26,433 | 3.8 | 2,445,000 | 1.1 |
| 1950/51 | 29,813 | 12.8 | 2,281,000 | 1.3 |
| 1951/52 | 30,462 | 2.2 | 2,102,000 | 1.4 |
| 1952/53 | 33,675 | 10.5 | 2,134,000 | 1.6 |
| 1953/54 | 33,833 | 0.5 | 2,231,000 | 1.5 |
| 1954/55 | 34,232 | 1.2 | 2,447,000 | 1.4 |
| 1955/56 | 36,494 | 6.6 | 2,653,000 | 1.4 |
| 1956/57 | 40,666 | 11.4 | 2,918,000 | 1.4 |
| 1957/58 | 43,391 | 6.7 | 3,324,000 | 1.3 |
| 1958/59 | 47,245 | 8.9 | no data | — |
| 1959/60 | 48,486 | 2.6 | 3,640,000 | 1.3 |
| 1960/61 | 53,107 | 9.5 | no data | — |
| 1961/62 | 58,086 | 9.4 | 4,146,000 | 1.4 |
| 1962/63 | 64,705 | 11.4 | no data | — |
| 1963/64 | 74,814 | 15.6 | 4,780,000 | 1.6 |
| 1964/65 | 82,045 | 9.7 | 5,280,000 | 1.6 |
| 1965/66 | 82,709 | 0.8 | 5,921,000 | 1.4 |
| 1966/67 | 100,262 | 21.2 | 6,390,000 | 1.6 |
| 1967/68 | 110,315 | 10.0 | 6,912,000 | 1.6 |
| 1968/69 | 121,362 | 10.0 | 7,513,000 | 1.6 |
| 1969/70 | 134,959 | 11.2 | 8,005,000 | 1.7 |
| 1970/71 | 144,708 | 7.2 | 8,581,000 | 1.7 |
| 1971/72 | 140,126 | −3.2 | 8,949,000 | 1.6 |
| 1972/73 | 146,097 | 4.3 | 9,215,000 | 1.6 |
| 1973/74 | 151,066 | 3.4 | 9,602,000 | 1.6 |
| 1974/75[b] | 154,580 | 2.3 | 10,224,000 | 1.5 |
| 1975/76 | 179,344 | 16.0 | 11,185,000 | 1.6 |
| 1976/77 | 203,068 | 13.2 | 11,012,000 | 1.8 |
| 1977/78 | 235,509 | 16.0 | 11,286,000 | 2.1 |
| 1978/79 | 263,938 | 12.1 | 11,260,000 | 2.3 |
| 1979/80 | 286,343 | 8.5 | 11,570,000 | 2.5 |
| 1980/81 | 311,882 | 8.9 | 12,097,000 | 2.6 |
| 1981/82 | 326,299 | 4.6 | 12,372,000 | 2.6 |
| 1982/83 | 336,985 | 3.3 | 12,426,000 | 2.7 |
| 1983/84 | 338,894 | 0.6 | 12,465,000 | 2.7 |
| 1984/85 | 342,113 | 0.9 | 12,242,000 | 2.8 |
| 1985/86 | 343,777 | 0.5 | 12,247,000 | 2.8 |
| 1986/87 | 349,609 | 1.7 | 12,504,000 | 2.8 |
| 1987/88 | 356,187 | 1.9 | 12,767,000 | 2.8 |
| 1988/89 | 366,354 | 2.9 | 13,055,000 | 2.8 |
| 1989/90 | 386,851 | 5.6 | 13,539,000 | 2.9 |
| 1990/91 | 407,529 | 5.3 | 13,819,000 | 2.9 |
| 1991/92 | 419,585 | 3.0 | 14,359,000 | 2.9 |
| 1992/93 | 438,618 | 4.5 | 14,487,000 | 3.0 |
| 1993/94 | 449,749 | 2.5 | 14,305,000 | 3.1 |
| 1994/95 | 452,635 | 0.6 | 14,279,000 | 3.2 |
| 1995/96 | 453,787 | 0.3 | 14,262,000 | 3.2 |
| 1996/97 | 457,984 | 0.9 | 14,368,000 | 3.2 |
| 1997/98 | 481,280 | 5.1 | 14,502,000 | 3.3 |
| 1998/99 | 490,933 | 2.0 | 14,507,000 | 3.4 |
| 1999/00 | 514,723 | 4.8 | 14,791,000 | 3.5 |
| 2000/01 | 547,867 | 6.4 | 15,312,000 | 3.6 |
| 2001/02 | 582,996 | 6.4 | 15,928,000 | 3.7 |
| 2002/03 | 586,323 | 0.6 | 16,612,000 | 3.5 |
| 2003/04 | 572,509 | −2.4 | 16,911,000 | 3.4 |
| 2004/05 | 565,039 | −1.3 | 17,272,000 | 3.3 |
| 2005/06 | 564,766 | −0.05 | 17,487,000 | 3.2 |
| 2006/07 | 582,984 | 3.2 | 17,759,000 | 3.3 |
| 2007/08 | 623,805 | 7.0 | 18,248,000 | 3.4 |
| 2008/09 | 671,616 | 7.7 | 19,103,000 | 3.5 |
| 2009/10 | 690,923 | 2.9 | 20,428,000 | 3.4 |
| 2010/11 | 723,277 | 4.7 | 20,550,000 | 3.5 |
| 2011/12 | 764,495 | 5.7 | 20,625,000 | 3.7 |

## FOREIGN NATIONALS NOT ADMITTED TO THE UNITED STATES

State Department officials in foreign countries screen applicants and deny visas for a variety of reasons. An

TABLE 3.19

**International student enrollment in colleges and universities, school years 1948–49 to 2011–12** [CONTINUED]

[1948–2012]

[a]Data from the National Center for Education Statistics.
[b]The data collection process was changed in 1974/75. Refugees were counted from 1975/76 to 1990/91.

SOURCE: "International Student Enrollment Trends, 1948/49–2011/12," in *Open Doors Report on International Educational Exchange*, Institute of International Education, 2012, http://www.iie.org/opendoors (accessed March 11, 2013)

applicant refused a visa can then attempt to "overcome" the issue(s) that caused the denial. In *Report of the Visa Office 2012*, the Bureau of Consular Affairs breaks down the number of foreign nationals refused entry to the United States in FY 2012 according to the reasons for denial. By far the most common reason for denying visas to immigrants was an application's failure to comply with the INA or related regulations. Among the 311,835 applications for immigrant visas that were refused in FY 2012, 303,166 were initially refused on this basis. (See Table 3.22.) However, 197,489 applicants overcame denials issued for this reason, approximately two-thirds the number of applicants that were refused. It should be noted that applications can be denied for more than one reason and that applicants can be denied more than once in a fiscal year, so the total number of denials catalogued in Table 3.22 exceeds the number of individual applicants. Additionally, an applicant can be refused one year and overcome the refusal the following year, so the number of visas refused and the number of refusals overcome in a given year do not refer to identical pools of individuals. The second-most-common reason for denying an immigrant application involved an individual's unlawful presence in the United States: 27,524 applications were denied because the applicant had been illegally present for 365 or more days in the preceding 10 years. Again, many applicants (21,673, or 78.7% of the number refused for this reason in FY 2012) managed to overcome this problem. Other reasons immigrant visas were denied in FY 2012 include an individual's infection by a communicable disease, lack of required vaccinations, history of drug abuse, prior criminal convictions, misrepresentation, and unlawful presence in the United States after previous immigration violations.

The most common reason for initial denial of a nonimmigrant visa in FY 2012 was an application's failure to demonstrate that the individual was entitled to nonimmigrant status. Over 1.3 million nonimmigrant visas were denied in FY 2012 for this reason, while only 16,563 applicants managed to overcome this issue. (See Table 3.22.) A large number of nonimmigrant applications (806,773) were denied for failure to comply with the INA or subsequent regulations, but most of the applicants (724,217) managed to overcome this problem. Other reasons that sizable numbers of nonimmigrant applications were denied in

TABLE 3.20

**Number of international students by place of origin, school years 2010–11 and 2011–12**

| Place of origin | 2010/11 | 2011/12 | % change |
|---|---|---|---|
| **Africa** | **36,890** | **35,502** | **−3.8** |
| **East Africa** | **8,863** | **7,827** | **−11.7** |
| Burundi | 123 | 103 | −16.3 |
| Djibouti | 11 | 8 | −27.3 |
| Eritrea | 120 | 110 | −8.3 |
| Ethiopia | 1,392 | 1,334 | −4.2 |
| Kenya | 4,666 | 3,898 | −16.5 |
| Rwanda | 457 | 465 | 1.8 |
| Seychelles | 6 | 10 | 66.7 |
| Somalia | 26 | 34 | 30.8 |
| Sudan | 236 | 180 | −23.7 |
| Tanzania | 1,006 | 906 | −9.9 |
| Uganda | 820 | 779 | −5.0 |
| **Central Africa** | **2,831** | **2,778** | **−1.9** |
| Cameroon | 1,659 | 1,530 | −7.8 |
| Central African Republic | 29 | 28 | −3.4 |
| Chad | 99 | 84 | −15.2 |
| Congo, Rep. of the | 240 | 249 | 3.8 |
| Congo, Dem. Rep. of the | 252 | 320 | 27.0 |
| Equatorial Guinea | 119 | 164 | 37.8 |
| Gabon | 431 | 402 | −6.7 |
| São Tomé & Príncipe | 2 | 1 | −50.0 |
| **North Africa** | **5,420** | **5,456** | **0.7** |
| Algeria | 158 | 177 | 12.0 |
| Egypt | 2,181 | 2,201 | 0.9 |
| Libya | 1,494 | 1,328 | −11.1 |
| Morocco | 1,201 | 1,305 | 8.7 |
| Tunisia | 386 | 445 | 15.3 |
| **Southern Africa** | **5,330** | **5,196** | **−2.5** |
| Angola | 699 | 779 | 11.4 |
| Botswana | 229 | 175 | −23.6 |
| Comoros | 23 | 9 | −60.9 |
| Lesotho | 51 | 46 | −9.8 |
| Madagascar | 146 | 133 | −8.9 |
| Malawi | 269 | 258 | −4.1 |
| Mauritius | 247 | 205 | −17.0 |
| Mozambique | 76 | 67 | −11.8 |
| Namibia | 73 | 63 | −13.7 |
| Reunion | 7 | 1 | −85.7 |
| South Africa | 1,669 | 1,610 | −3.5 |
| Swaziland | 146 | 154 | 5.5 |
| Zambia | 560 | 535 | −4.5 |
| Zimbabwe | 1,135 | 1,161 | 2.3 |
| **West Africa** | **14,446** | **14,245** | **−1.4** |
| Benin | 289 | 313 | 8.3 |
| Burkina Faso | 626 | 631 | 0.8 |
| Cape Verde | 55 | 87 | 58.2 |
| Côte d'Ivoire/Ivory Coast | 904 | 955 | 5.6 |
| Gambia | 385 | 383 | −0.5 |
| Ghana | 2,900 | 2,769 | −4.5 |
| Guinea | 139 | 104 | −25.2 |
| Guinea-Bissau | 12 | 12 | 0.0 |
| Liberia | 172 | 159 | −7.6 |
| Mali | 481 | 402 | −16.4 |
| Mauritania | 60 | 61 | 1.7 |
| Niger | 247 | 279 | 13.0 |
| Nigeria | 7,148 | 7,028 | −1.7 |
| Saint Helena | 4 | 1 | −75.0 |
| Senegal | 600 | 681 | 13.5 |
| Sierra Leone | 183 | 130 | −29.0 |
| Togo | 241 | 250 | 3.7 |

FY 2012 include the applicant having been unlawfully present in the United States 365 or more days within the preceding 10 years, misrepresentation, crimes involving moral turpitude, controlled substance trafficking and other violations, smuggling, the applicant having been unlawfully

| Place of origin | 2010/11 | 2011/12 | % change |
|---|---|---|---|
| **Asia** | **461,790** | **489,970** | **6.1** |
| **East Asia** | **286,925** | **319,515** | **11.4** |
| China | 157,558 | 194,029 | 23.1 |
| Hong Kong | 8,136 | 8,032 | −1.3 |
| Japan | 21,290 | 19,966 | −6.2 |
| Macau | 497 | 505 | 1.6 |
| Mongolia | 1,259 | 1,423 | 13.0 |
| North Korea | 16 | 15 | −6.3 |
| South Korea | 73,351 | 72,295 | −1.4 |
| Taiwan | 24,818 | 23,250 | −6.3 |
| **South and Central Asia** | **128,845** | **124,392** | **−3.5** |
| Afghanistan | 429 | 371 | −13.5 |
| Bangladesh | 2,873 | 3,314 | 15.3 |
| Bhutan | 115 | 100 | −13.0 |
| India | 103,895 | 100,270 | −3.5 |
| Kazakhstan | 1,890 | 1,938 | 2.5 |
| Kyrgyzstan | 279 | 254 | −9.0 |
| Maldives | 34 | 29 | −14.7 |
| Nepal | 10,301 | 9,621 | −6.6 |
| Pakistan | 5,045 | 4,600 | −8.8 |
| Sri Lanka | 2,965 | 2,902 | −2.1 |
| Tajikistan | 249 | 298 | 19.7 |
| Turkmenistan | 210 | 209 | −0.5 |
| Uzbekistan | 560 | 486 | −13.2 |
| **Southeast Asia** | **46,020** | **46,063** | **0.1** |
| Brunei | 66 | 69 | 4.5 |
| Cambodia | 340 | 333 | −2.1 |
| East Timor | 48 | 40 | −16.7 |
| Indonesia | 6,942 | 7,131 | 2.7 |
| Laos | 49 | 43 | −12.2 |
| Malaysia | 6,735 | 6,743 | 0.1 |
| Myanmar | 796 | 807 | 1.4 |
| Philippines | 3,604 | 3,194 | −11.4 |
| Singapore | 4,316 | 4,505 | 4.4 |
| Thailand | 8,236 | 7,626 | −7.4 |
| Vietnam | 14,888 | 15,572 | 4.6 |
| **Europe** | **84,296** | **85,423** | **1.3** |
| Albania | 697 | 659 | −5.5 |
| Andorra | 14 | 24 | 71.4 |
| Armenia | 350 | 363 | 3.7 |
| Austria | 1,019 | 989 | −2.9 |
| Azerbaijan | 440 | 460 | 4.5 |
| Belarus | 347 | 358 | 3.2 |
| Belgium | 904 | 880 | −2.7 |
| Bosnia and Herzegovina | 356 | 341 | −4.2 |
| Bulgaria | 1,957 | 1,694 | −13.4 |
| Croatia | 583 | 552 | −5.3 |
| Cyprus | 470 | 438 | −6.8 |
| Czech Republic | 765 | 701 | −8.4 |
| Denmark | 1,149 | 1,233 | 7.3 |
| Estonia | 228 | 241 | 5.7 |
| Finland | 639 | 640 | 0.2 |
| France | 8,098 | 8,232 | 1.7 |
| Georgia | 460 | 481 | 4.6 |
| Germany | 9,458 | 9,347 | −1.2 |
| Gibraltar | 2 | 4 | 100.0 |
| Greece | 1,874 | 1,922 | 2.6 |
| Hungary | 670 | 655 | −2.2 |
| Iceland | 369 | 391 | 6.0 |
| Ireland | 1,167 | 1,106 | −5.2 |
| Italy | 4,308 | 4,284 | −0.6 |
| Kosovo | 121 | 114 | −5.8 |
| Latvia | 324 | 308 | −4.9 |
| Liechtenstein | 5 | 14 | 180.0 |
| Lithuania | 338 | 288 | −14.8 |
| Luxembourg | 59 | 68 | 15.3 |
| Macedonia | 257 | 222 | −13.6 |
| Malta | 19 | 41 | 115.8 |

| Place of origin | 2010/11 | 2011/12 | % change |
|---|---|---|---|
| Moldova | 411 | 416 | 1.2 |
| Monaco | 22 | 43 | 95.5 |
| Montenegro | 85 | 112 | 31.8 |
| Netherlands | 1,833 | 1,975 | 7.7 |
| Norway | 1,822 | 2,016 | 10.6 |
| Poland | 1,852 | 1,838 | −0.8 |
| Portugal | 981 | 970 | −1.1 |
| Romania | 1,883 | 1,607 | −14.7 |
| Russia | 4,692 | 4,805 | 2.4 |
| San Marino | 2 | 3 | 50.0 |
| Serbia | 1,067 | 1,068 | 0.1 |
| Slovakia | 419 | 424 | 1.2 |
| Slovenia | 178 | 171 | −3.9 |
| Spain | 4,330 | 4,924 | 13.7 |
| Sweden | 3,236 | 3,926 | 21.3 |
| Switzerland | 1,287 | 1,362 | 5.8 |
| Turkey | 12,184 | 11,973 | −1.7 |
| Ukraine | 1,583 | 1,535 | −3.0 |
| United Kingdom | 8,947 | 9,186 | 2.7 |
| Vatican City/Holy See | 4 | 1 | −75.0 |
| Europe, unspecified | 31 | 18 | −41.9 |
| **Latin America** | **64,169** | **64,021** | **−0.2** |
| **Caribbean** | 11,644 | 10,987 | −5.6 |
| Anguilla | 43 | 29 | −32.6 |
| Antigua and Barbuda | 193 | 183 | −5.2 |
| Aruba | 94 | 67 | −28.7 |
| Bahamas | 1,720 | 1,737 | 1.0 |
| Barbados | 332 | 267 | −19.6 |
| British Virgin Islands | 94 | 116 | 23.4 |
| Cayman Islands | 165 | 181 | 9.7 |
| Cuba | 62 | 57 | −8.1 |
| Dominica | 256 | 261 | 2.0 |
| Dominican Republic | 1,393 | 1,610 | 15.6 |
| Grenada | 189 | 261 | 38.1 |
| Guadeloupe | 14 | 15 | 7.1 |
| Haiti | 888 | 889 | 0.1 |
| Jamaica | 3,172 | 2,694 | −15.1 |
| Martinique | 8 | 3 | −62.5 |
| Montserrat | 8 | 2 | −75.0 |
| Netherlands Antilles | 201 | 155 | −22.9 |
| St. Kitts and Nevis | 217 | 269 | 24.0 |
| St. Lucia | 526 | 352 | −33.1 |
| St. Vincent and the Grenadines | 105 | 95 | −9.5 |
| Trinidad and Tobago | 1,882 | 1,689 | −10.3 |
| Turks and Caicos | 82 | 55 | −32.9 |
| **Mexico and Central America** | 20,361 | 20,432 | 0.3 |
| Belize | 388 | 370 | −4.6 |
| Costa Rica | 1,105 | 1,078 | −2.4 |
| El Salvador | 1,157 | 1,151 | −0.5 |
| Guatemala | 1,042 | 1,048 | 0.6 |
| Honduras | 1,349 | 1,407 | 4.3 |
| Mexico | 13,713 | 13,893 | 1.3 |
| Nicaragua | 434 | 363 | −16.4 |
| Panama | 1,173 | 1,122 | −4.3 |
| **South America** | 32,164 | 32,602 | 1.4 |
| Argentina | 2,105 | 1,888 | −10.3 |
| Bolivia | 977 | 1,025 | 4.9 |
| Brazil | 8,777 | 9,029 | 2.9 |
| Chile | 2,164 | 2,203 | 1.8 |
| Colombia | 6,456 | 6,295 | −2.5 |
| Ecuador | 2,150 | 2,160 | 0.5 |
| French Guiana | 28 | 1 | −96.4 |
| Guyana | 272 | 224 | −17.6 |
| Paraguay | 322 | 342 | 6.2 |
| Peru | 2,939 | 2,702 | −8.1 |
| Suriname | 94 | 92 | −2.1 |
| Uruguay | 389 | 360 | −7.5 |
| Venezuela | 5,491 | 6,281 | 14.4 |

**TABLE 3.20**

Number of international students by place of origin, school years 2010–11 and 2011–12 [CONTINUED]

| Place of origin | 2010/11 | 2011/12 | % change |
|---|---|---|---|
| **Middle East** | **42,543** | **56,664** | **33.2** |
| Bahrain | 409 | 438 | 7.1 |
| Iran | 5,626 | 6,982 | 24.1 |
| Iraq | 616 | 809 | 31.3 |
| Israel | 2,701 | 2,490 | −7.8 |
| Jordan | 2,002 | 2,062 | 3.0 |
| Kuwait | 2,998 | 3,722 | 24.1 |
| Lebanon | 1,462 | 1,350 | −7.7 |
| Oman | 313 | 538 | 71.9 |
| Palestinian Territories | 331 | 331 | 0.0 |
| Qatar | 716 | 979 | 36.7 |
| Saudi Arabia | 22,704 | 34,139 | 50.4 |
| Syria | 526 | 458 | −12.9 |
| United Arab Emirates | 1,871 | 2,097 | 12.1 |
| Yemen | 268 | 269 | 0.4 |
| **North America** | **27,941** | **27,210** | **−2.6** |
| Bermuda | 395 | 389 | −1.5 |
| Canada | 27,546 | 26,821 | −2.6 |
| **Oceania** | **5,610** | **5,697** | **1.6** |
| Australia | 3,777 | 3,848 | 1.9 |
| Cook Islands | 4 | 6 | 50.0 |
| Fiji | 138 | 122 | −11.6 |
| French Polynesia | 30 | 42 | 40.0 |
| Kiribati | 31 | 48 | 54.8 |
| Marshall Islands | 52 | 39 | −25.0 |
| Micronesia | 131 | 98 | −25.2 |
| Nauru | 11 | 7 | −36.4 |
| New Caledonia | 13 | 8 | −38.5 |
| New Zealand | 1,164 | 1,204 | 3.4 |
| Niue | 8 | 8 | 0.0 |
| Palau | 31 | 21 | −32.3 |
| Papua New Guinea | 50 | 60 | 20.0 |
| Samoa | 49 | 51 | 4.1 |
| Solomon Islands | 7 | 13 | 85.7 |
| Tonga | 103 | 104 | 1.0 |
| Tuvalu | 2 | 3 | 50.0 |
| Vanuatu | 8 | 8 | 0.0 |
| Wallis and Futuna | 1 | 7 | 600.0 |
| **Stateless** | 10 | 8 | −20.0 |
| **World total** | **723,249** | **764,495** | **5.7** |

SOURCE: "International Student Totals by Place of Origin, 2010/11–2011/12," in *Open Doors Report on International Educational Exchange*, Institute of International Education, 2012, http://www.iie.org/opendoors (accessed March 12, 2013)

present in the United States following a prior immigration violation, and falsely claiming citizenship.

## Returns and Removals

Having a U.S. visa does not guarantee entry. A visa allows a traveler arriving at a U.S. port of entry to request permission to enter. U.S. Customs and Border Protection inspectors determine the admissibility of aliens who arrive at any of the approximately 300 U.S. ports of entry. Those who arrive without required documents, present improper or fraudulent documents, or are on criminal wanted lists are deemed inadmissible. The Illegal Immigration Reform and Immigrant Responsibility Act (IIRIRA) of 1996 provides two options for dealing with the inadmissible individual: removal proceedings and returns (voluntary departure).

**TABLE 3.21**

## Fields of study of international students by place of origin, school year 2011–2012

[2011/12]

| Place of origin | Business/ management | Education | Engineering | Fine/ applied arts | Health professions | Humanities | Intensive English | Math/ computer science | Physical/ life sciences | Social sciences | Other | Undeclared | Total students |
|---|---|---|---|---|---|---|---|---|---|---|---|---|---|
| | | | | | | Percent of total | | | | | | | |
| Brazil | 26.3 | 2.6 | 7.9 | 8.0 | 4.1 | 5.5 | 2.8 | 3.2 | 6.1 | 10.8 | 19.6 | 3.1 | 9,029 |
| Canada | 15.4 | 5.4 | 7.7 | 7.2 | 15.8 | 4.9 | 0.0 | 2.7 | 8.5 | 13.8 | 15.8 | 2.8 | 26,821 |
| China | 28.7 | 1.7 | 19.6 | 3.8 | 1.5 | 1.3 | 2.8 | 11.2 | 9.9 | 7.7 | 9.6 | 2.2 | 194,029 |
| Colombia | 18.6 | 2.7 | 15.0 | 6.4 | 3.0 | 7.2 | 5.5 | 3.4 | 9.7 | 10.4 | 15.0 | 3.1 | 6,295 |
| France | 25.6 | 0.7 | 13.7 | 4.2 | 1.4 | 8.0 | 1.4 | 3.9 | 5.8 | 9.2 | 20.1 | 6.0 | 8,232 |
| Germany | 24.2 | 1.6 | 7.6 | 4.0 | 2.0 | 8.7 | 0.3 | 3.8 | 7.9 | 13.1 | 21.0 | 5.8 | 9,347 |
| Hong Kong | 28.5 | 1.3 | 7.2 | 7.0 | 3.6 | 3.9 | 1.3 | 5.8 | 7.0 | 15.0 | 16.4 | 3.0 | 8,032 |
| India | 14.1 | 0.6 | 36.7 | 1.3 | 4.8 | 0.7 | 0.1 | 21.7 | 11.4 | 3.2 | 4.3 | 1.1 | 100,270 |
| Indonesia | 29.0 | 2.5 | 19.0 | 8.9 | 2.9 | 3.2 | 1.0 | 4.8 | 5.7 | 8.6 | 12.1 | 2.3 | 7,131 |
| Iran | 4.1 | 0.7 | 58.4 | 4.5 | 2.2 | 1.2 | 0.8 | 9.5 | 9.1 | 4.3 | 4.3 | 0.9 | 6,982 |
| Japan | 19.2 | 2.6 | 4.6 | 7.2 | 3.1 | 6.5 | 12.1 | 2.8 | 5.7 | 13.5 | 18.5 | 4.2 | 19,966 |
| Malaysia | 18.5 | 2.4 | 27.0 | 3.5 | 3.1 | 1.9 | 0.2 | 8.1 | 13.4 | 8.6 | 10.4 | 2.9 | 6,743 |
| Mexico | 22.2 | 3.1 | 17.0 | 6.8 | 3.7 | 3.4 | 2.6 | 3.9 | 6.4 | 8.8 | 16.8 | 5.3 | 13,893 |
| Nepal | 20.9 | 0.6 | 17.8 | 1.5 | 8.7 | 0.7 | 0.1 | 11.6 | 19.2 | 5.4 | 10.4 | 3.1 | 9,621 |
| Nigeria | 16.3 | 1.3 | 22.7 | 1.7 | 14.3 | 3.2 | 0.4 | 7.4 | 12.5 | 7.3 | 9.4 | 3.5 | 7,028 |
| Pakistan | 19.8 | 2.4 | 24.7 | 2.4 | 4.0 | 1.8 | 0.1 | 9.0 | 7.8 | 11.6 | 11.1 | 5.3 | 4,600 |
| Russia | 29.4 | 1.9 | 6.9 | 6.4 | 3.1 | 5.8 | 2.1 | 6.8 | 12.1 | 10.9 | 11.4 | 3.2 | 4,805 |
| Saudi Arabia | 15.9 | 2.0 | 18.4 | 1.4 | 4.7 | 1.0 | 36.3 | 6.7 | 3.0 | 2.6 | 6.2 | 1.8 | 34,139 |
| South Korea | 16.8 | 3.2 | 12.2 | 11.1 | 4.9 | 5.3 | 4.3 | 5.1 | 7.8 | 11.5 | 14.6 | 3.2 | 72,295 |
| Taiwan | 21.3 | 4.7 | 17.0 | 11.6 | 3.8 | 2.4 | 3.6 | 6.2 | 10.6 | 6.8 | 10.4 | 1.6 | 23,250 |
| Thailand | 21.1 | 2.4 | 18.0 | 6.7 | 5.4 | 2.4 | 3.5 | 7.5 | 8.3 | 7.2 | 15.4 | 2.1 | 7,626 |
| Turkey | 15.2 | 4.2 | 25.1 | 3.9 | 0.7 | 3.3 | 4.1 | 9.7 | 8.8 | 14.4 | 8.8 | 1.8 | 11,973 |
| United Kingdom | 17.8 | 3.2 | 4.9 | 6.6 | 3.4 | 7.9 | 0.2 | 2.5 | 7.1 | 16.8 | 24.1 | 5.5 | 9,186 |
| Venezuela | 25.6 | 2.6 | 15.5 | 7.7 | 3.2 | 2.1 | 10.4 | 2.9 | 4.8 | 7.0 | 14.3 | 3.9 | 6,281 |
| Vietnam | 39.0 | 1.1 | 9.6 | 2.9 | 4.5 | 1.3 | 2.9 | 7.1 | 6.8 | 4.5 | 10.5 | 9.8 | 15,572 |

SOURCE: "Fields of Study of Students from Selected Places of Origin, 2011/12," in *Open Doors Report on International Educational Exchange,* Institute of International Education, 2012, http://www.iie.org/opendoors (accessed March 12, 2013)

**TABLE 3.22**

## Summary of immigrant and nonimmigrant visa ineligibilities, fiscal year 2012

[By grounds for refusal under the Immigration and Nationality Act. Fiscal year 2012 data is preliminary and subject to change. Any changes would not be statistically significant.]

| Grounds for refusal under the Immigration and Nationality Act | | Immigrant | | Nonimmigrant | |
|---|---|---|---|---|---|
| | | Ineligibility finding[a] | Ineligibility overcome[b] | Ineligibility finding[a] | Ineligibility overcome[b] |
| 212(a)(1)(A)(i) | Communicable disease | 421 | 507 | 14 | 3 |
| 212(a)(1)(A)(ii) | Immigrant lacking required vaccinations | 1,566 | 1,519 | — | — |
| 212(a)(1)(A)(iii) | Physical or mental disorder | 186 | 73 | 417 | 55 |
| 212(a)(1)(A)(iv) | Drug abuser or addict | 1,523 | 0 | 112 | 13 |
| 212(a)(2)(A)(i)(I) | Crime involving moral turpitude | 1,331 | 328 | 6,647 | 2,580 |
| 212(a)(2)(A)(i)(II) | Controlled substance violators | 557 | 78 | 4,155 | 1,619 |
| 212(a)(2)(B) | Multiple criminal convictions | 85 | 5 | 376 | 107 |
| 212(a)(2)(C)(i) | Illicit trafficker in any controlled substance | 432 | 0 | 2,833 | 585 |
| 212(a)(2)(C)(ii) | Spouse, son, or daughter who benefited from illicit activities of trafficker | 23 | 1 | 658 | 42 |
| 212(a)(2)(D)(i) | Prostitution (within 10 years) | 20 | 17 | 35 | 3 |
| 212(a)(2)(D)(ii) | Procuring (within 10 years) | 4 | 2 | 35 | 8 |
| 212(a)(2)(D)(iii) | Unlawful commercialized vice | 0 | 0 | 5 | 1 |
| 212(a)(2)(E) | Asserted immunity to avoid prosecution | 0 | 0 | 1 | 0 |
| 212(a)(2)(G) | Foreign government officials who have engaged in violations of religious freedom | 0 | 0 | 0 | 0 |
| 212(a)(2)(H) | Significant traffickers in persons | 1 | 0 | 4 | 0 |
| 212(a)(2)(I) | Money laundering | 1 | 0 | 20 | 7 |
| 212(a)(3)(A)(i) | Espionage, sabotage, technology transfer, etc. | 11 | 0 | 249 | 8 |
| 212(a)(3)(A)(ii) | Other unlawful activity | 223 | 0 | 73 | 7 |
| 212(a)(3)(A)(iii) | Act to overthrow U.S. government | 0 | 0 | 0 | 0 |
| 212(a)(3)(B) | Terrorist activities | 76 | 0 | 814 | 470 |
| 212(a)(3)(C) | Foreign policy | 0 | 0 | 0 | 0 |
| 212(a)(3)(D) | Immigrant membership in totalitarian party | 19 | 8 | — | — |
| 212(a)(3)(E)(i) | Participants in Nazi persecutions | 0 | 0 | 0 | 0 |
| 212(a)(3)(E)(ii) | Participants in genocide | 0 | 0 | 0 | 0 |
| 212(a)(3)(E)(iii) | Commission of acts of torture or extrajudicial killings | 0 | 0 | 6 | 2 |
| 212(a)(3)(F) | Association with terrorist organizations | 0 | 0 | 0 | 0 |
| 212(a)(3)(G) | Recruitment or use of child soldiers | 0 | 0 | 5 | 2 |
| 212(a)(4) | Public charge | 4,901 | 5,218 | 261 | 19 |
| 212(a)(5)(A) | Labor certification (immigrants only) | 11,386 | 1,386 | — | — |
| 212(a)(5)(B) | Unqualified physician (immigrants only) | 0 | 0 | — | — |
| 212(a)(5)(C) | Uncertified foreign health-care workers | 2 | 0 | 0 | 0 |
| 212(a)(6)(B) | Failure to attend removal proceedings | 172 | 0 | 10 | 2 |
| 212(a)(6)(C)(i) | Misrepresentation | 7,436 | 1,737 | 12,754 | 3,390 |
| 212(a)(6)(C)(ii) | Falsely claiming citizenship | 687 | 0 | 1,592 | 386 |
| 212(a)(6)(E) | Smugglers | 3,634 | 1,424 | 3,052 | 856 |
| 212(a)(6)(F) | Subject of civil penalty (under INA 274C) | 0 | 0 | 0 | 0 |
| 212(a)(6)(G) | Student visa abusers | 1 | 0 | 10 | 4 |
| 212(a)(7)(B) | Documentation requirement for nonimmigrants | — | — | 63 | 46 |
| 212(a)(8)(A) | Immigrant permanently ineligible for citizenship | 0 | 0 | — | — |
| 212(a)(8)(B) | Draft evader | 1 | 0 | 13 | 8 |
| 212(a)(9)(A)(i) | Ordered removed upon arrival | 903 | 326 | 668 | 66 |
| 212(a)(9)(A)(i) | Ordered removed upon arrival—multiple removals | 103 | 16 | 39 | 9 |
| 212(a)(9)(A)(i) | Ordered removed upon arrival—convicted aggravated felony | 20 | 0 | 17 | 5 |
| 212(a)(9)(A)(ii) | Ordered removed or departed while removal order outstanding | 1,631 | 700 | 594 | 107 |
| 212(a)(9)(A)(ii) | Ordered removed or departed while removal order outstanding—multiple removals | 188 | 35 | 95 | 18 |
| 212(a)(9)(A)(ii) | Ordered removed or departed while removal order outstanding—convicted aggravated felony | 96 | 5 | 71 | 13 |
| 212(a)(9)(B)(i)(I) | Unlawfully present 181–364 days (within 3 years) | 440 | 285 | 778 | 99 |
| 212(a)(9)(B)(i)(II) | Unlawfully present 365 or more days (within 10 years) | 27,524 | 21,673 | 13,954 | 969 |
| 212(a)(9)(C) | Unlawfully present after previous immigration violations | 2,964 | 0 | 2,653 | 304 |
| 212(a)(10)(A) | Practicing polygamist (immigrants only) | 44 | 6 | — | — |
| 212(a)(10)(C)(i) | International child abductor | 0 | 0 | 5 | 1 |
| 212(a)(10)(C)(ii) | Aliens supporting abductors and relatives of abductors | 0 | 0 | 0 | 0 |
| 212(a)(10)(D) | Unlawful voter | 1 | 0 | 0 | 0 |
| 212(a)(10)(E) | Former U.S. citizen who renounced citizenship to avoid taxation | 0 | 0 | 0 | 0 |
| 212(e) | Certain former exchange visitors | 26 | 9 | 10 | 5 |
| 212(f) | Presidential proclamation | 2 | 0 | 70 | 5 |
| 214(b) | Failure to establish entitlement to nonimmigrant status | — | — | 1,308,983 | 16,563 |
| 221(g) | Application does not comply with provisions of INA or regulations issued pursuant thereto | 303,166 | 197,489 | 806,773 | 724,217 |
| 222(g)(2) | Alien in illegal status, required to apply for new nonimmigrant visa in country of alien's nationality | — | — | 106 | 7 |
| Sec. 103 Pub. Law 105–227 | Disclosure/trafficking of confidential U.S. business information | 0 | 0 | 0 | 0 |

**TABLE 3.22**

**Summary of immigrant and nonimmigrant visa ineligibilities, fiscal year 2012** [CONTINUED]

[By grounds for refusal under the Immigration and Nationality Act. Fiscal year 2012 data is preliminary and subject to change. Any changes would not be statistically significant.]

| Grounds for refusal under the Immigration and Nationality Act | | Immigrant | | Nonimmigrant | |
|---|---|---|---|---|---|
| | | Ineligibility finding[a] | Ineligibility overcome[b] | Ineligibility finding[a] | Ineligibility overcome[b] |
| Sec. 401 Pub. Law 104–114 | Helms-Burton refusal | 0 | 0 | 0 | 0 |
| Sec. 402 Pub. Law 104–114 | Conversion of confiscated U.S. property for gain | 0 | 0 | 1 | 0 |
| Sec. 306 Pub. Law 107–173 | Inadmissible alien from a country that is a state sponsor of terrorism | 0 | 0 | 155 | 7 |
| | **Total grounds of ineligibility:** | **371,807** | **232,847** | **2,169,186** | **752,618** |
| | **Number of applications:**[a] | **311,835** | **215,321** | **2,132,149** | **749,257** |

Note: The figures at the end of this table show totals of applications refused and refusals overcome. The total of applications refused does not necessarily reflect the number of persons refused during the year. One applicant can apply and be found ineligible more than one time in a fiscal year.
[a]The total grounds of ineligibility may exceed the number of applications refused because one applicant may be found ineligible under more than one section of the Immigration and Nationality Act.
[b]The total of ineligibilities overcome may not necessarily represent the same visa applicants found ineligible and recorded in the total of ineligibility findings. A visa may be refused in one fiscal year and the refusal overcome in a subsequent fiscal year. Each action will be separately recorded as part of the appropriate statistical report for the year in which it occurred. A refusal can be overcome by evidence that the ineligibilty does not apply, by approval of a waiver, or by other relief as provided by law.

SOURCE: "Table XX. Immigrant and Nonimmigrant Visa Ineligibilities (by Grounds for Refusal under the Immigration and Nationality Act), Fiscal Year 2012," in *Report of the Visa Office 2012*, U.S. Department of State, Bureau of Consular Affairs, 2012, http://www.travel.state.gov/pdf/ FY12AnnualReport-TableXX .pdf (accessed March 6, 2013)

**FIGURE 3.17**

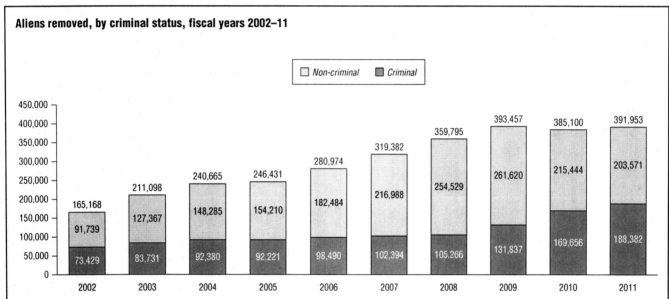

**Aliens removed, by criminal status, fiscal years 2002–11**

SOURCE: Adapted from "Table 41. Aliens Removed by Criminal Status and Region and Country of Nationality: Fiscal Years 2002 to 2011," in *2011 Yearbook of Immigration Statistics*, U.S. Department of Homeland Security, Office of Policy, Office of Immigration Statistics, September 2012, http://www .dhs.gov/sites/default/files/publications/immigration-statistics/yearbook/2011/ois_yb_2011.pdf (accessed March 6, 2013)

Most removal proceedings involve a hearing before an immigration judge, which can result in removal or adjustment to a legal status, such as granting asylum. Removal proceedings can also involve fines or imprisonment. The IIRIRA also empowers immigration officers to order an individual's removal without a hearing or review through a process called expedited removal. This process applies to cases involving fraud, misrepresentation, or the lack of proper documents. Returns are not based on an order of removal; the individual is offered the option to leave the country. Most such voluntary departures involve undocumented people who have been apprehended by the U.S. Border Patrol.

According to the OIS, in *2011 Yearbook of Immigration Statistics*, 391,953 aliens were removed from the United States in FY 2011, 188,382 for criminal reasons and 203,571 for noncriminal reasons. (See Figure 3.17.) Such removals had risen dramatically since 2002, when only 165,168 aliens were removed.

# CHAPTER 4
# THE WORLDWIDE REFUGEE CHALLENGE

## WHO IS A REFUGEE?

Every year millions of people around the world are displaced by war, famine, civil unrest, and political turmoil. Others are forced to flee their country to escape the risk of death and torture at the hands of persecutors on account of race, religion, nationality, membership in a particular social group, or political opinion. These refugees, as such persecuted and displaced people are called, are granted special consideration among immigration authorities in the United States and in other countries. Considerable effort is made among those in the international community, led by the Office of the United Nations High Commissioner for Refugees (UNHCR), to respond to refugee crises as they arise.

The United States works with other governmental, international, and private organizations to provide food, health care, and shelter to millions of refugees throughout the world. Resettlement in another country, including the United States, is considered for refugees in urgent need of protection, refugees for whom other long-term solutions are not feasible, and refugees able to join close family members. The United States gives priority to the safe, voluntary return of refugees to their homelands. This policy, recognized in the Refugee Act of 1980, is also the preference of the UNHCR.

## Legally Admitting Refugees

Before World War II (1939–1945) the U.S. government had no arrangements for admitting people seeking refuge. The only way oppressed people were able to enter the United States was through regular immigration procedures.

After World War II refugees were admitted through special legislation that was passed by Congress. The Displaced Persons Act of 1948, which admitted 400,000 East Europeans who had been displaced by the war, was the first U.S. refugee legislation. The Immigration and Nationality Act (INA) of 1952 did not specifically mention refugees, but

it did allow the U.S. attorney general parole authority (the authority to grant temporary admission) when dealing with oppressed people. Other legislation—the Refugee Relief Act of 1953, the Fair Share Refugee Act of 1960, and the Indochinese Refugee Act of 1977—responded to particular world events and admitted specific groups.

Refugees were legally recognized for the first time in the Immigration and Nationality Act Amendments of 1965 with a preference category that was reserved for refugees from the Middle East or from countries ruled by a communist government.

## Refugee Act of 1980

The Refugee Act of 1980 established a geographically and politically neutral adjudication standard for refugee status. The act redefined the term *refugee* as:

> (A) any person who is outside any country of such person's nationality or, in the case of a person having no nationality, is outside any country in which such person last habitually resided, and who is unable or unwilling to return to, and is unable or unwilling to avail himself or herself of the protection of, that country because of persecution or a well-founded fear of persecution on account of race, religion, nationality, membership in a particular social group, or political opinion, or (B) in such circumstances as the President after appropriate consultation … may specify, any person who is within the country of such person's nationality or, in the case of a person having no nationality, within the country in which such person is habitually residing, and who is persecuted or who has a well-founded fear of persecution on account of race, religion, nationality, membership in a particular social group, or political opinion.

The Refugee Act of 1980 required the president, at the beginning of each fiscal year, to determine the number of refugees to be admitted without consideration of any overall immigrant quota. The 1980 law also regulated U.S. asylum policy.

**REFUGEES AND ASYLEES.** The Refugee Act of 1980 made a distinction between refugees and asylees. A refugee is someone who applies for protection while outside the United States; an asylee is someone who is already in the United States when he or she applies for protection.

## The Application Process

The U.S. Refugee Admissions Program (USRAP) is responsible for processing applications to enter the United States as a refugee. In "The United States Refugee Admissions Program (USRAP): Consultation & Worldwide Processing Priorities" (April 8, 2013, http://www.uscis.gov/), the U.S. Citizenship and Immigration Services (USCIS) describes USRAP as "an interagency effort involving a number of governmental and non-governmental partners both overseas and in the United States." The U.S. Department of State's Bureau of Population, Refugees, and Migration (PRM) plays an important role, as does the USCIS, other elements of the U.S. Department of Homeland Security (DHS), various nongovernmental organizations (NGOs), and the UNHCR.

The United States processes applications for refugee and asylum status based on three priority categories. Priority One applicants are those individuals and their immediate families who are referred to USRAP by the UNHCR, a U.S. embassy, or a prominent NGO. Members of groups of special humanitarian concern are considered Priority Two applicants, and family members of refugees who have already been admitted to the United States are considered Priority Three applicants. Due to a difficulty in determining the authenticity of family relationships on Priority Three applications, USRAP suspended the processing of those applications in 2008.

PRM officials conduct prescreening interviews of applicants and assist in the completion of paperwork to be submitted to the USCIS. Applicants are then interviewed by the USCIS, and if the agency determines that they are eligible for resettlement in the United States, applicants must submit to medical examinations. Those granted refugee status are then provided with assistance in traveling to the United States, obtaining housing and employment, and other services. They may enter and leave the United States thereafter by applying for a refugee travel document, and as discussed in Chapter 3, they may apply for a green card one year from the date of their entry into the United States.

## Material Support Denials

The 2001 Patriot Act and the 2005 REAL ID Act prohibit granting entrance to the United States to anyone who has given material support (money or other support) to terrorists or terrorist organizations. In "The 'Material Support' Problem: An Uncertain Future for Thousands of Refugees and Asylum Seekers" (*Bender's Immigration Bulletin*, vol. 10, December 15, 2005), Melanie Nezer of the Hebrew Immigrant Aid Society in Washington, D.C., argues that people who had been "coerced under extreme duress to make payments to armed groups on the State Department's list of foreign terrorist organizations" are being denied admission to the United States as refugees. Nezer cites as an example Colombian refugees who gave money to the Autodefensas Unidas de Colombia (United Self-Defense Forces of Colombia), the Fuerzas Armadas Revolucionarias de Colombia (Revolutionary Armed Forces of Colombia), or the Ejército de Liberación Nacional (National Liberation Army). Payments to these groups were made under the threat of torture or death to self or a loved one. Making such payments became a necessity of survival for many Colombians. Nezer contends that refugees who provide nonvoluntary material support should not be denied admission to the United States.

## REFUGEES

According to the UNHCR, in *Asylum Trends 2012: Levels and Trends in Industrialized Countries* (March 21, 2013, http://www.unhcr.org/5149b81e9.html), the 44 industrialized countries called on most often to accept refugees fielded an estimated 479,300 asylum applications in 2012. This was the second-highest number of applications in a decade; only in 2003, when 505,000 refugees applied for asylum, were there more asylum seekers in the developed world. Afghanistan was the top source country of asylum seekers, with 36,600 claims, followed by Syria (24,800), Serbia and Kosovo (24,300), China (24,100), and Pakistan (23,200). European countries received 355,500 applications for asylum, and 103,900 refugees applied for protection in North America. Smaller numbers of refugees sought asylum in Australia and New Zealand (16,100) and Japan and South Korea (3,700). The United States received 83,400 asylum applications, more than any other country, followed by Germany (64,500), France (54,900), Sweden (43,900), and the United Kingdom (27,400).

### Admissions to the United States

As Figure 4.1 shows, refugee admissions to the United States have declined since the 1990s, peaking at roughly 122,000 refugee arrivals in 1990 before falling to a low of 25,000 in 2002. This decline is partly due to changes in security procedures after the September 11, 2001, terrorist attacks against the United States and tighter admission requirements resulting from the Patriot Act. Admissions were on the rise by the end of that decade, however, returning to pre-2001 levels.

Admissions ceilings for refugees are, in keeping with the Refugee Act of 1980, established by the president prior to each fiscal year (FY). The ceiling increased from 70,000 in FY 2007 to 80,000 in FY 2008, where it remained through FY 2011. (See Table 4.1.) The president also sets ceilings for particular regions of the world, based on world events. Between FYs 2009 and 2011 these allocations remained roughly steady, with the most

FIGURE 4.1

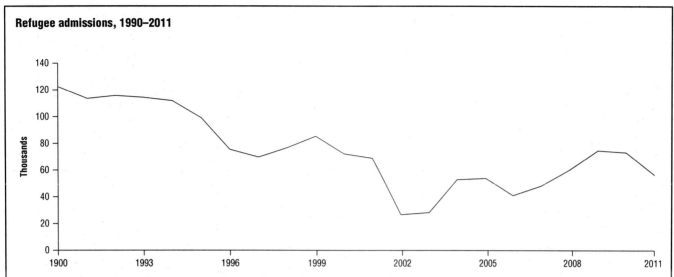

**Refugee admissions, 1990–2011**

SOURCE: Daniel C. Martin and James E. Yankay, "Figure 1. Refugee Admissions to the United States: 1990 to 2011," in *Refugees and Asylees: 2011*, U.S. Department of Homeland Security, Office of Immigration Statistics, May 2012, http://www.dhs.gov/xlibrary/assets/statistics/publications/ois_rfa_fr_2011 .pdf (accessed March 6, 2013)

---

**TABLE 4.1**

**Refugee admissions ceilings, fiscal years 2009–11**

| | Ceiling | | |
|---|---|---|---|
| Region | 2011 | 2010 | 2009 |
| **Total** | **80,000** | **80,000** | **80,000** |
| Africa | 15,000 | 15,500 | 12,000 |
| East Asia | 19,000 | 18,000 | 20,500 |
| Europe/Central Asia | 2,000 | 2,500 | 2,500 |
| Latin America/Caribbean | 5,500 | 5,500 | 5,500 |
| Near East/South Asia | 35,500 | 38,000 | 39,500 |
| Unallocated reserve | 3,000 | 500 | 0 |

Note: Ceiling numbers reflect revisions made each fiscal year.

SOURCE: Daniel C. Martin and James E. Yankay, "Table 1. Refugee Admissions Ceilings: 2009 to 2011," in *Refugees and Asylees: 2011*, U.S. Department of Homeland Security, Office of Immigration Statistics, May 2012, http://www.dhs.gov/xlibrary/assets/statistics/publications/ois_rfa_fr_2011.pdf (accessed March 6, 2013)

---

**TABLE 4.2**

**Refugee arrivals by category of admission, fiscal years 2009–11**

| Category of admission | 2011 | | 2010 | | 2009 | |
|---|---|---|---|---|---|---|
| | Number | Percent | Number | Percent | Number | Percent |
| **Total** | **56,384** | **100.0** | **73,293** | **100.0** | **74,602** | **100.0** |
| Principal applicant | 25,075 | 44.5 | 32,251 | 44.0 | 32,511 | 43.6 |
| Dependents | 31,309 | 55.5 | 41,042 | 56.0 | 42,091 | 56.4 |
| Spouse | 9,751 | 17.3 | 12,835 | 17.5 | 13,440 | 18.0 |
| Child | 21,558 | 38.2 | 28,207 | 38.5 | 28,651 | 38.4 |

SOURCE: Daniel C. Martin and James E. Yankay, "Table 2. Refugee Arrivals by Category of Admission: Fiscal Years 2009 to 2011," in *Refugees and Asylees: 2011*, U.S. Department of Homeland Security, Office of Immigration Statistics, May 2012, http://www.dhs.gov/xlibrary/assets/statistics/publications/ois_rfa_fr_2011.pdf (accessed March 6, 2013)

---

refugee admissions allotted to the Near East/South Asia region, largely to account for refugees from Iraq (where instability following the U.S.-led invasion in 2003 generated large numbers of refugees) and Bhutan (where one of the world's most severe refugee crises had begun in 1991 and remained ongoing as of 2013). In FY 2011 the Near East/South Asia region accounted for 44.4% (35,500) of the total refugee ceiling, followed by East Asia (23.8%, or 19,000), Africa (18.8%, or 15,000), Latin America and the Caribbean (6.9%, or 5,500), and Europe/ Central Asia (2.5%, or 2,000). Another 3,000 admissions were unallocated, or set aside to be used in any region where the need should arise. Although the number of refugees admitted each year are limited by these ceilings, the number admitted as refugees does not count against the overall limits on legal immigration.

A total of 56,384 refugees were admitted to the United States during fiscal year FY 2011. (See Table 4.2.) Of this total, there were 25,075 principal applicants, 9,751 spouses of principal applicants, and 21,558 children of principal applicants. The leading countries of origin for refugees were Burma (Myanmar), with 16,972 refugee admissions (30.1% of the total); Bhutan, with 14,999 admissions (26.6%); and Iraq, with 9,388 (16.7%). (See Table 4.3.) Texas accepted 5,627 refugees in FY 2011, 10% of the national total and more than any other state. (See Table 4.4.) California was second with 4,987 (8.8%) refugees, followed by New York (3,529, or 6.3%), Pennsylvania (2,972, or 5.3%), and Florida (2,906, or 5.2%). With the exception of Pennsylvania, refugee admissions in FY 2011 were down from FY 2009 in each of the top-10 recipient states.

Table 4.5 provides a portrait of the group of refugees admitted to the United States by age, gender, and marital status between FYs 2009 and 2011. The relative distribution

**TABLE 4.3**

**Refugee arrivals by country of nationality, fiscal years 2009–11**

[Ranked by 2011 country of nationality]

| Country of nationality | 2011 Number | 2011 Percent | 2010 Number | 2010 Percent | 2009 Number | 2009 Percent |
|---|---|---|---|---|---|---|
| Total | 56,384 | 100.0 | 73,293 | 100.0 | 74,602 | 100.0 |
| Burma | 16,972 | 30.1 | 16,693 | 22.8 | 18,202 | 24.4 |
| Bhutan | 14,999 | 26.6 | 12,363 | 16.9 | 13,452 | 18.0 |
| Iraq | 9,388 | 16.7 | 18,016 | 24.6 | 18,838 | 25.3 |
| Somalia | 3,161 | 5.6 | 4,884 | 6.7 | 4,189 | 5.6 |
| Cuba | 2,920 | 5.2 | 4,818 | 6.6 | 4,800 | 6.4 |
| Eritrea | 2,032 | 3.6 | 2,570 | 3.5 | 1,571 | 2.1 |
| Iran | 2,032 | 3.6 | 3,543 | 4.8 | 5,381 | 7.2 |
| Congo, Democratic Republic | 977 | 1.7 | 3,174 | 4.3 | 1,135 | 1.5 |
| Ethiopia | 560 | 1.0 | 668 | 0.9 | 321 | 0.4 |
| Afghanistan | 428 | 0.8 | 515 | 0.7 | 349 | 0.5 |
| All other countries, including unknown | 2,915 | 5.2 | 6,049 | 8.3 | 6,364 | 8.5 |

SOURCE: Daniel C. Martin and James E. Yankay, "Table 3. Refugee Arrivals by Country of Nationality: Fiscal Years 2009 to 2011," in *Refugees and Asylees: 2011*, U.S. Department of Homeland Security, Office of Immigration Statistics, May 2012, http://www.dhs.gov/xlibrary/assets/statistics/publications/ois_rfa_fr_2011.pdf (accessed March 6, 2013)

**TABLE 4.4**

**Refugee arrivals by state of residence, fiscal years 2009–11**

[Ranked by 2011 state of residence]

| State of residence | 2011 Number | 2011 Percent | 2010 Number | 2010 Percent | 2009 Number | 2009 Percent |
|---|---|---|---|---|---|---|
| Total | 56,384 | 100.0 | 73,293 | 100.0 | 74,602 | 100.0 |
| Texas | 5,627 | 10.0 | 7,918 | 10.8 | 8,195 | 11.0 |
| California | 4,987 | 8.8 | 8,577 | 11.7 | 11,274 | 15.1 |
| New York | 3,529 | 6.3 | 4,559 | 6.2 | 4,411 | 5.9 |
| Pennsylvania | 2,972 | 5.3 | 2,632 | 3.6 | 2,155 | 2.9 |
| Florida | 2,906 | 5.2 | 4,216 | 5.8 | 4,193 | 5.6 |
| Georgia | 2,636 | 4.7 | 3,224 | 4.4 | 3,270 | 4.4 |
| Michigan | 2,588 | 4.6 | 3,188 | 4.3 | 3,500 | 4.7 |
| Arizona | 2,168 | 3.8 | 3,400 | 4.6 | 4,312 | 5.8 |
| Washington | 2,137 | 3.8 | 3,004 | 4.1 | 2,581 | 3.5 |
| North Carolina | 2,120 | 3.8 | 2,342 | 3.2 | 2,235 | 3.0 |
| Other | 24,714 | 43.8 | 30,233 | 41.2 | 28,476 | 38.2 |

SOURCE: Daniel C. Martin and James E. Yankay, "Table 5. Refugee Arrivals by State of Residence: Fiscal Years 2009 to 2011," in *Refugees and Asylees: 2011*, U.S. Department of Homeland Security, Office of Immigration Statistics, May 2012, http://www.dhs.gov/xlibrary/assets/statistics/publications/ois_rfa_fr_2011.pdf (accessed March 6, 2013)

among age groups remained roughly consistent, with children under the age of 18 years accounting for more than one-third of all refugees admitted in each of the three fiscal years. The gender balance and the balance between married and single refugees remained similarly consistent between FYs 2009 and 2011. In FY 2011, 52.2% of admitted refugees were male and 47.8% were female. A majority of refugees (55.6%) were single, while 39.2% were married and 5.3% were either separated, divorced, widowed, or of unknown marital status.

## ASYLUM SEEKERS IN THE UNITED STATES

The difference between asylees and refugees, according to U.S. immigration law, is a difference in terminology.

In common usage, refugees are people who are displaced from their home countries due to war, persecution, or other causes discussed in this chapter and who therefore often seek asylum in a country where they will be safe from the threats that forced them to leave. An asylee, then, is simply a refugee who has found asylum. According to U.S. immigration law, however, a refugee is a displaced individual seeking entry to the United States from outside the country, whereas an asylee is a displaced individual who is already in the United States and who is seeking the legal right to remain in the country.

Asylees sometimes enter the United States as tourists and then apply for asylum. Others jump ship in a maritime port of entry. Still others may enter under other

**TABLE 4.5**

**Refugee arrivals by age, gender, and marital status, fiscal years 2009–11**

| Characteristic | 2011 | | 2010 | | 2009 | |
|---|---|---|---|---|---|---|
| | Number | Percent | Number | Percent | Number | Percent |
| **Age** | | | | | | |
| **Total** | **56,384** | **100.0** | **73,293** | **100.0** | **74,602** | **100.0** |
| 0 to 17 years | 19,232 | 34.1 | 25,373 | 34.6 | 25,185 | 33.8 |
| 18 to 24 years | 9,588 | 17.0 | 11,853 | 16.2 | 11,747 | 15.7 |
| 25 to 34 years | 11,802 | 20.9 | 14,954 | 20.4 | 14,842 | 19.9 |
| 35 to 44 years | 7,124 | 12.6 | 9,587 | 13.1 | 10,082 | 13.5 |
| 45 to 54 years | 4,230 | 7.5 | 5,727 | 7.8 | 5,971 | 8.0 |
| 55 to 64 years | 2,438 | 4.3 | 3,218 | 4.4 | 3,649 | 4.9 |
| 65 years and over | 1,970 | 3.5 | 2,581 | 3.5 | 3,126 | 4.2 |
| **Gender** | | | | | | |
| **Total** | **56,384** | **100.0** | **73,293** | **100.0** | **74,602** | **100.0** |
| Male | 29,436 | 52.2 | 38,624 | 52.7 | 38,491 | 51.6 |
| Female | 26,948 | 47.8 | 34,669 | 47.3 | 36,111 | 48.4 |
| **Marital status** | | | | | | |
| **Total** | **56,384** | **100.0** | **73,293** | **100.0** | **74,602** | **100.0** |
| Married | 22,095 | 39.2 | 28,567 | 39.0 | 29,770 | 39.9 |
| Single | 31,324 | 55.6 | 41,022 | 56.0 | 40,798 | 54.7 |
| Other* | 2,965 | 5.3 | 3,704 | 5.1 | 4,034 | 5.4 |

*Includes persons who were divorced, separated, divorced, widowed, or unknown marital status.

SOURCE: Daniel C. Martin and James E. Yankay, "Table 4. Refugee Arrivals by Age, Gender, and Marital Status: Fiscal Years 2009 to 2011," in *Refugees and Asylees: 2011*, U.S. Department of Homeland Security, Office of Immigration Statistics, May 2012, http://www.dhs.gov/xlibrary/assets/statistics/publications/ois_rfa_fr_2011.pdf (accessed March 6, 2013)

nonimmigrant visa status groups, such as foreign students or temporary workers, and then apply to remain on as asylees. Like a refugee applying for entrance into the country, an asylee seeks the protection of the United States because of persecution or a well-founded fear of persecution. Any foreign-born person physically present in the United States or at a port of entry can request asylum. It is irrelevant whether the person is a legal or illegal immigrant. Like refugees, asylum applicants do not count against the worldwide annual U.S. limitation of immigrants.

**Filing Claims**

Asylum seekers must apply for asylum within one year from the date of their last arrival in the United States. If the application is filed past the one-year mark, asylum seekers must show changed circumstances that materially affect their eligibility or extraordinary circumstances that delayed filing. They must also show that they filed within a reasonable amount of time given these circumstances.

An applicant who is ruled ineligible for asylum status and who is not allowed to remain in the United States under another visa status becomes subject to removal proceedings. An applicant who is ruled ineligible for asylum but who is eligible to remain in the United States under another visa status will revert to that prior status for as long as it is valid. Those applicants who are granted asylum status are eligible to work in the United States and to obtain assistance in finding employment. They are

also able to participate in social assistance programs and acquire a Social Security card.

The DHS identifies three main types of asylum claims: affirmative, defensive, and follow-to-join. Aliens in the United States can apply for asylum by filing an Application for Asylum (Form I-589) with the USCIS. Initiating this process is called an affirmative asylum claim. Aliens who have been placed in removal proceedings and who are in immigration court can request asylum through the Executive Office of Immigration Review. This last-resort effort is called a defensive asylum claim. Follow-to-join asylum status is available to the spouses and children of individuals who have been granted asylum. These derivative asylum applicants do not have to demonstrate that they will be persecuted if not granted asylum because their claims are derived from the application of someone who has already done so. If follow-to-join petitioners are outside the United States at the time that their applications are approved, they are granted asylum status upon entry. If they are inside the United States, they are granted asylum status upon approval of their application.

**How Many Are Admitted?**

Figure 4.2 shows the trends in affirmative and defensive asylum admissions between 1990 and 2011. The total volume of both types of asylum admissions during the early 1990s was less than 10,000. Defensive asylum admissions increased steadily from less than 3,000 in 1994 to a high of about 14,000 in 2006. Affirmative asylum admissions rose dramatically from about 4,000

**FIGURE 4.2**

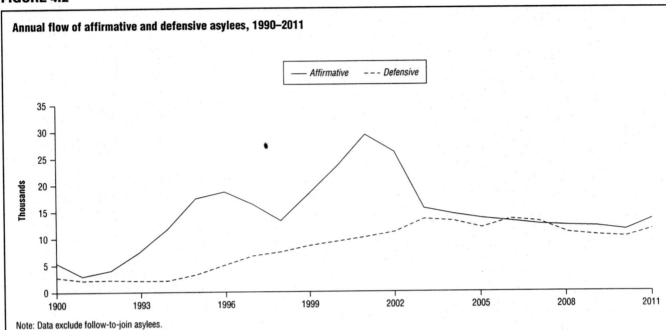

Annual flow of affirmative and defensive asylees, 1990–2011

Note: Data exclude follow-to-join asylees.

SOURCE: Daniel C. Martin and James E. Yankay, "Figure 2. Annual Flow of Affirmative and Defensive Asylees: 1990 to 2011" in *Refugees and Asylees: 2011*, U.S. Department of Homeland Security, Office of Immigration Statistics, May 2012, http://www.dhs.gov/xlibrary/assets/statistics/publications/ois_rfa_fr_2011.pdf (accessed March 6, 2013)

**TABLE 4.6**

Affirmative asylees by country of nationality, fiscal years 2009–11

[Ranked by 2011 country of nationality]

| Country of nationality | 2011 | | 2010 | | 2009 | |
|---|---|---|---|---|---|---|
| | Number | Percent | Number | Percent | Number | Percent |
| Total | 13,484 | 100.0 | 11,187 | 100.0 | 11,921 | 100.0 |
| China, People's Republic | 3,901 | 28.9 | 2,882 | 25.8 | 2,710 | 22.7 |
| Venezuela | 902 | 6.7 | 467 | 4.2 | 393 | 3.3 |
| Haiti | 822 | 6.1 | 666 | 6.0 | 596 | 5.0 |
| Egypt | 754 | 5.6 | 315 | 2.8 | 308 | 2.6 |
| Ethiopia | 571 | 4.2 | 679 | 6.1 | 701 | 5.9 |
| Russia | 469 | 3.5 | 389 | 3.5 | 364 | 3.1 |
| Nepal | 426 | 3.2 | 408 | 3.6 | 493 | 4.1 |
| Iran | 367 | 2.7 | 398 | 3.6 | 257 | 2.2 |
| Colombia | 325 | 2.4 | 358 | 3.2 | 637 | 5.3 |
| Guatemala | 285 | 2.1 | 298 | 2.7 | 349 | 2.9 |
| All other countries, including unknown | 4,662 | 34.6 | 4,327 | 38.7 | 5,113 | 42.9 |

Note: Data exclude follow-to-join asylees.

SOURCE: Daniel C. Martin and James E. Yankay, "Table 7. Affirmative Asylees by Country of Nationality: Fiscal Years 2009 to 2011," in *Refugees and Asylees: 2011*, U.S. Department of Homeland Security, Office of Immigration Statistics, May 2012, http://www.dhs.gov/xlibrary/assets/statistics/publications/ois_rfa_fr_2011.pdf (accessed March 6, 2013)

in 1991 to a peak of more than 28,000 in 2001, after which date they fell precipitously. Since 2003 roughly equal numbers of affirmative and defensive asylees have been admitted to the United States annually. (Follow-to-join asylees were not part of DHS statistics until 2011.)

In FY 2011, 13,484 individuals were granted asylum status affirmatively, 11,504 were granted asylum status defensively, and 9,550 were granted follow-to-join asylum status, for a total of 34,538 asylees admitted.

(See Table 4.6, Table 4.7, and Table 4.8.) China was by far the leading country of origin for all three types of asylum admissions in FY 2011. That year 3,901 Chinese nationals were granted affirmative asylum, accounting for 28.9% of all successful applicants in that category. The country of origin for the second-highest number of successful affirmative asylum claimants was Venezuela, with 902 admissions (6.7%). Chinese representation among defensive asylum admissions was even more disproportionate in FY 2011, when 4,700, or 40.9% of all

TABLE 4.7

**Defensive asylees by country of nationality, fiscal years 2009–11**

[Ranked by 2011 country of nationality]

| Country of nationality | 2011 | | 2010 | | 2009 | |
|---|---|---|---|---|---|---|
| | Number | Percent | Number | Percent | Number | Percent |
| Total | 11,504 | 100.0 | 9,869 | 100.0 | 10,298 | 100.0 |
| China, People's Republic | 4,700 | 40.9 | 3,796 | 38.5 | 3,449 | 33.5 |
| Ethiopia | 505 | 4.4 | 407 | 4.1 | 410 | 4.0 |
| Eritrea | 481 | 4.2 | 179 | 1.8 | 198 | 1.9 |
| Nepal | 323 | 2.8 | 230 | 2.3 | 172 | 1.7 |
| Egypt | 274 | 2.4 | 216 | 2.2 | 174 | 1.7 |
| India | 262 | 2.3 | 241 | 2.4 | 263 | 2.6 |
| Soviet Union, former | 248 | 2.2 | 176 | 1.8 | 154 | 1.5 |
| Colombia | 213 | 1.9 | 234 | 2.4 | 368 | 3.6 |
| Somalia | 213 | 1.9 | 208 | 2.1 | 168 | 1.6 |
| Venezuela | 205 | 1.8 | 181 | 1.8 | 192 | 1.9 |
| All other countries, including unknown | 4,080 | 35.5 | 4,001 | 40.5 | 4,750 | 46.1 |

Note: Data exclude follow-to-join asylees.

SOURCE: Daniel C. Martin and James E. Yankay, "Table 8. Defensive Asylees by Country of Nationality: Fiscal Years 2009 to 2011," in *Refugees and Asylees: 2011*, U.S. Department of Homeland Security, Office of Immigration Statistics, May 2012, http://www.dhs.gov/xlibrary/assets/statistics/publications/ois_rfa_fr_2011.pdf (accessed March 6, 2013)

**TABLE 4.8**

**Follow-to-join asylees by country of nationality, fiscal year 2011**

| Country of nationality | 2011 | |
|---|---|---|
| | Number | Percent |
| Total | 9,550 | 100.0 |
| China, People's Republic | 3,770 | 39.5 |
| Nepal | 1,053 | 11.0 |
| Haiti | 1,020 | 10.7 |
| Ethiopia | 548 | 5.7 |
| Cameroon | 403 | 4.2 |
| India | 163 | 1.7 |
| Eritrea | 138 | 1.4 |
| Egypt | 137 | 1.4 |
| Guinea | 136 | 1.4 |
| Kenya | 133 | 1.4 |
| All other countries, including unknown | 2,049 | 21.5 |

SOURCE: Daniel C. Martin and James E. Yankay, "Table 9. Follow-to-Join Asylee Travel Documents Issued by Country of Nationality: Fiscal Year 2011," in *Refugees and Asylees: 2011*, U.S. Department of Homeland Security, Office of Immigration Statistics, May 2012, http://www.dhs.gov/xlibrary/assets/statistics/publications/ois_rfa_fr_2011.pdf (accessed March 6, 2013)

defensive asylum admissions, were of Chinese origin. Ethiopia generated the second-highest number of defensive asylum admissions, with 505 (4.4%). Similarly, 3,770 Chinese nationals were granted follow-to-join asylee status in FY 2011, representing 39.5% of the total admitted in the category. Nepal (1,053, or 11%) and Haiti (1,020, or 10.7%) were the countries of origin for the next-largest groups of follow-to-join asylees.

## Controversy Surrounding Asylees

Critics charge that many people seek asylum in the United States to avoid dismal economic conditions in their home country rather than for the reasons specified by U.S. law: to escape political or religious persecution or because of a well-founded fear of physical harm or death. Such critics suggest that asylee status is often simply an avenue for unauthorized immigrants to obtain work authorization and access to social services.

Under the INA and subsequent legislation, however, a person can be granted asylum only if he or she establishes a well-founded fear of persecution on account of one of five protected grounds: race, religion, nationality, political opinion, or membership in a particular social group. A particular social group has members who share an unchangeable characteristic, such as race, gender, past experience, or kinship ties. Some people argue that the definition for "a particular social group" should be broad and that the intent of the law is to provide a catchall to include all the types of persecution that can occur. Others take a narrow view, seeing the law as a means of identifying and protecting individuals from known forms of harm, not in anticipation of future types of abuse.

Meanwhile, many reports in the press and among advocacy organizations suggest that the power to define asylum status rests with the individual adjudicators within the federal government and in immigration courts, leading to a high degree of variability in the criteria used to accept or reject petitions for asylum. For example, Amnesty International notes in "Violence against Women Information" (2013, http://www.amnestyusa.org/our-work/issues/women-s-rights/violence-against-women/violence-against-women-information) that some asylum adjudicators in the United States do not recognize gender-based violence as a valid claim for asylum protection. Additionally, Nina Bernstein reports in "In New York Immigration Court, Asylum Roulette" (NYTimes.com, October 8, 2006) that there are significant disparities among judges' decisions on asylum cases. Bernstein observes, for example, that in the same courthouse, one judge approved the petitions of 90% of asylum seekers while another judge just down the hall approved only 9%. These disparities are particularly worrisome to human rights advocates given that, as Bernstein writes, "the wrong decision can be a death sentence." Bernstein acknowledges the challenges faced by immigration judges required to mediate between "an intricate web of laws, changing conditions in distant lands, and a mix of false and truthful testimony in 227 tongues vulnerable to an interpreter's mistake as small as pronouncing 'rebels' like 'robbers.'"

In 2008 the U.S. Government Accountability Office conducted a study of immigration courts and judges. The resulting report, *U.S. Asylum System: Significant Variation Existed in Asylum Outcomes across Immigration Courts and Judges* (September 2008, http://www.gao.gov/new.items/d08940.pdf), states:

> The likelihood of being granted asylum differed for affirmative and defensive cases and varied depending on the immigration court in which the case was heard. Overall, the grant rate for affirmative cases (37 percent) was significantly higher than the grant rate for defensive cases (26 percent). The affirmative asylum grant rate ranged from 6 percent in Atlanta to 54 percent in New York City. The grant rate for defensive cases ranged from 7 percent in Atlanta to 35 percent in San Francisco and New York City. ... Even when immigration courts are relatively close to one another geographically, there were sometimes large differences in asylum decisions for a particular nationality and sometimes not. For example, the grant rate for affirmative asylum cases in New York and Newark was identical or similar for Chinese, El Salvadoran, and Nigerian applicants. In contrast, the grant rate for affirmative applicants from Colombia, Indonesia, and Peru was more than 2.5 times higher in New York than in nearby Newark. ... The likelihood of being granted asylum differed considerably across immigration courts, even after we statistically controlled simultaneously for the effects of a number of factors.

Another source of controversy surrounding the adjudication of asylum claims is the use of expedited removal proceedings. Under the provisions of the Illegal Immigration Reform and Immigrant Responsibility Act of 1996, any foreign national subject to expedited removal because of fraud, misrepresentation, or a lack of valid documents must be questioned by an immigration officer regarding the fear of being persecuted at home. Individuals who express such a fear are detained until an asylum officer can determine the credibility of the fear. Those whose fears are deemed credible are referred to an immigration judge for a final determination and are generally released until their case is heard. In some instances, however, asylum seekers are detained while their cases are pending. If the fear is deemed not credible either by an immigration officer or a judge, the alien is refused admission and removed.

Critics charge that the expedited removal process denies asylum seekers a fair chance to fully present their claims, places unprecedented authority in the hands of asylum officers, is conducted so quickly that mistakes are inevitable, limits asylum seekers' right to review a deportation order, and results in the wrongful expulsion of individuals with legitimate fears of persecution. Those who are deported under the expedited removal process are barred from returning to the United States for five years.

## VICTIMS OF TRAFFICKING AND VIOLENCE

Slavery has long been outlawed in the developed world, but it remains alarmingly widespread in the form of human trafficking. Traffickers often coerce victims into moving far from their homes with promises of good jobs, then force them to work for little or nothing, sometimes as prostitutes, and often under threat of death or extreme brutality. Although the victims of human trafficking frequently work in plain sight in the United States and elsewhere, the conditions allowing traffickers to maintain power over them are hidden. Accurate estimates of the number of victims are accordingly difficult to establish, but the U.S. government devotes substantial resources to combating the problem. As part of this effort, federal immigration law provides for the admission of trafficking victims on the same terms as refugees, and it provides immigration benefits to those who cooperate with investigations into trafficking.

Trafficking victims were made eligible for federal benefits and services through the Trafficking Victims Protection Act (TVPA) of 2000, which also made provisions for the prosecution of traffickers and for prevention efforts in the countries where the crime often originates. The Trafficking Victims Protection Reauthorization Act of 2003 strengthened the law by mandating informational awareness campaigns and creating a new civil action provision that allows victims to sue their traffickers in federal district court. It also required the U.S. attorney general to give an annual report to Congress on the results of U.S. government activities to combat trafficking. Reauthorization bills in 2005 and 2008 further expanded these laws.

The TVPA designates the U.S. Department of Health and Human Services (HHS) as the agency responsible for helping victims of human trafficking become eligible to receive benefits and services so they may rebuild their lives safely in the United States. Furthermore, the TVPA authorizes certification of adult victims to receive certain federally funded or federally administered benefits and services, such as cash assistance, medical care, food stamps, and housing. Though not required to be certified by the HHS, minors who are determined to be victims of severe forms of trafficking receive letters of eligibility for the same types of services.

**TABLE 4.9**

**TABLE 4.10**

**Certifications and letters of eligibility issued, fiscal years 2001–11**

| Fiscal year | Number of eligibility letters issued to children | Number of certification letters issued to adults | Total letters issued |
|---|---|---|---|
| 2001 | 4 | 194 | 198 |
| 2002 | 18 | 81 | 99 |
| 2003 | 6 | 145 | 151 |
| 2004 | 16 | 147 | 163 |
| 2005 | 34 | 197 | 231 |
| 2006 | 20 | 214 | 234 |
| 2007 | 33 | 270 | 303 |
| 2008 | 31 | 286 | 317 |
| 2009 | 50 | 330 | 380 |
| 2010 | 92 | 449 | 541 |
| 2011 | 101 | 463 | 564 |
| **Total** | **405** | **2,776** | **3,181** |

SOURCE: "Certifications and Letters of Eligibility," in *Attorney General's Annual Report to Congress and Assessment of U.S. Government Activities to Combat Trafficking in Persons, Fiscal Year 2011*, U.S. Department of Justice, January 2013, http://www.justice.gov/ag/annualreports/agreporthuman trafficking2011.pdf (accessed March 6, 2013)

**Top-10 countries of origin of adult trafficking victims who received certification letters, fiscal year 2011**

| Country of origin | Number of adult victims who received certification letters | Percentage of total* |
|---|---|---|
| Philippines | 119 | 26 |
| Mexico | 86 | 19 |
| Thailand | 34 | 7 |
| India | 28 | 6 |
| Honduras | 24 | 5 |
| Indonesia | 21 | 5 |
| Guatemala | 17 | 4 |
| El Salvador | 14 | 3 |
| Republic of South Korea | 10 | 2 |
| Peru | 10 | 2 |

*Percentages are rounded to closest whole number.

SOURCE: "The following chart depicts the top ten countries of origin of adult victims who received Certification Letters in FY 2011," in *Attorney General's Annual Report to Congress and Assessment of U.S. Government Activities to Combat Trafficking in Persons, Fiscal Year 2011*, U.S. Department of Justice, January 2013, http://www.justice.gov/ag/annualreports/agreporthumantrafficking2011.pdf (accessed March 6, 2013)

The U.S. attorney general states in *Attorney General's Annual Report to Congress and Assessment of U.S. Government Activities to Combat Trafficking in Persons, Fiscal Year 2011* (January 2013, http://www.justice.gov/ag/annual reports/agreporthumantrafficking2011.pdf) that the number of certification letters issued has consistently risen in the years since TVPA's passage. In FY 2001 the HHS issued four eligibility letters to children and 194 certification letters to adults, for a total of 198. (See Table 4.9.) In FY 2005, 34 letters were issued to children and 197 to adults, for a total of 231; and in FY 2011, 101 letters were issued to children and 463 to adults, for a total of 564.

The most common country of origin for certified adult victims of trafficking in FY 2011 was the Philippines, which accounted for 119 (26% of the total) certification letters. (See Table 4.10.) Mexico also had a high total of 86 (19%) certification letters. Other top countries of origin for certified trafficking victims were Thailand (7% of the total number of certifications), India (6%), Honduras (5%), and Indonesia (5%).

Trafficking victims in the United States are eligible for Continued Presence (CP), T, and U nonimmigrant visas. A CP visa authorizes the victim to remain in the United States for one year as a potential witness in the investigation and prosecution of traffickers, with extensions available as needed for ongoing criminal cases. T and U visa status are also available to certain trafficking victims who are cooperating with investigators or whose removal from the United States would result in extreme hardship. Both T and U nonimmigrant visas are valid for four years. Law enforcement authorities can grant extensions of T and U visas as needed for the investigation and prosecution of crimes. Both T and U visa holders are eligible for green cards, and the USCIS is obligated to extend the T and U status during the green-card application process.

The U.S. attorney general reports that there were 324 requests for CP visas in FY 2011. (See Table 4.11.) By the end of that fiscal year 283 requests had been authorized, two were denied, 15 were withdrawn, and 24 were still in process. The requesting victims came from 41 countries, with the highest number of victims coming from Thailand, the Philippines, and Mexico; and the U.S. cities from which the most requests originated were Honolulu, Hawaii; Miami, Florida; and New Orleans, Louisiana. The USCIS approved 1,279 T visas for trafficking victims and their family members in FY 2011, by far the largest number since the inception of the T visa program. (See Table 4.12.) By comparison, only 26 T visas were approved in FY 2002, the program's first year. The number rose to 544 in FY 2007 and 796 in FY 2010, the previous high. The number of U visas issued (which are available to victims of crimes other than trafficking) was also on the rise between FYs 2009 and 2011. (See Table 4.13.) Although there was a statutory cap of 10,000 on the number of U visas issued to victims and their families, eligible applications above that number were conditionally accepted and placed on a waiting list for the following year's available U visas. In FY 2009 the number of approved applicants was 8,663, fewer than were available under the statutory cap, but in both FY 2010 and FY 2011 the number of eligible applicants exceeded the statutory cap. In FY 2010, 19,388 U visas were either approved or conditionally approved. In FY 2011, 17,690 U visas were either approved or conditionally approved. Large numbers of applicants were denied U visas during these years, as well: 6,923 in FY 2010 and 4,574 in FY 2011.

**TABLE 4.11**

**Requests for Continued Presence (CP) visas, fiscal years (FY) 2006–11**

| FY | 2006 | 2007 | 2008 | 2009 | 2010 | 2011 |
|---|---|---|---|---|---|---|
| **Total requests for continued presence** | **117** | **125** | **239** | **301** | **198** | **324** |
| Number authorized | 112 | 122 | 225 | 299 | 186 | 283* |
| Number Withdrawn | 5 | 3 | 14 | 2 | 0 | 15 |
| Extensions authorized | 20 | 5 | 101 | 148 | 288 | 355 |
| Countries of origin represented | 24 | 24 | 31 | 35 | 32 | 41 |
| Countries with the highest number of requests | Mexico, El Salvador, and South Korea | Mexico, El Salvador, and China | Mexico, Philippines, and South Korea | Thailand, Philippines, Haiti, and Mexico | Thailand, Mexico, Honduras, and Philippines | Thailand, Philippines, and Mexico, |
| U.S. cities with the highest number of requests | Houston, Newark, and New York | Los Angeles, Newark, Houston, and New York | Miami, Newark, Atlanta, San Francisco, and Los Angeles | Honolulu, Chicago, Miami, and Tampa | Chicago, Honolulu, New York City, and Tampa | Honolulu, Miami, and New Orleans |

*The difference between the number of Continued Presence (CP) cases received (324) and number awarded (283) in fiscal year 2011 correlates to processing at the end of the reporting year and does not reflect denials. A total of two CP cases were denied during the reporting period.

SOURCE: "Requests for Continued Presence in Fiscal Years 2006–2011," in *Attorney General's Annual Report to Congress and Assessment of U.S. Government Activities to Combat Trafficking in Persons, Fiscal Year 2011*, U.S. Department of Justice, January 2013, http://www.justice.gov/ag/annualreports/agreporthumantrafficking2011.pdf (accessed March 6, 2013)

**TABLE 4.12**

**Applications for T nonimmigrant status, fiscal years 2002–11**

| Fiscal year | Victims | | | Family of victims | | | Totals | | |
|---|---|---|---|---|---|---|---|---|---|
| | Applied | Approved* | Denied* | Applied | Approved* | Denied* | Applied | Approved* | Denied* |
| 2002 | 163 | 17 | 12 | 234 | 9 | 4 | 397 | 26 | 16 |
| 2003 | 750 | 283 | 51 | 274 | 51 | 8 | 1,024 | 334 | 59 |
| 2004 | 566 | 163 | 344 | 86 | 106 | 11 | 652 | 269 | 355 |
| 2005 | 379 | 113 | 321 | 34 | 73 | 21 | 413 | 186 | 342 |
| 2006 | 384 | 212 | 127 | 19 | 95 | 45 | 403 | 307 | 172 |
| 2007 | 269 | 287 | 106 | 24 | 257 | 64 | 293 | 544 | 170 |
| 2008 | 408 | 243 | 78 | 118 | 228 | 40 | 526 | 471 | 118 |
| 2009 | 475 | 313 | 77 | 235 | 273 | 54 | 710 | 586 | 131 |
| 2010 | 574 | 447 | 138 | 463 | 349 | 105 | 1,037 | 796 | 241 |
| 2011 | 967 | 557 | 223 | 795 | 722 | 137 | 1,762 | 1,279 | 360 |

*Some approvals and denials are from prior fiscal year filings.

SOURCE: "Applications for T Visas," in *Attorney General's Annual Report to Congress and Assessment of U.S. Government Activities to Combat Trafficking in Persons, Fiscal Year 2011*, U.S. Department of Justice, January 2013, http://www.justice.gov/ag/annualreports/agreporthumantrafficking2011.pdf (accessed March 6, 2013)

**TABLE 4.13**

**Applications for U nonimmigrant status, fiscal years 2009–11**

| Fiscal year | Victims | | | Family of victims | | | Totals | | |
|---|---|---|---|---|---|---|---|---|---|
| | Applied | Approved* | Denied* | Applied | Approved* | Denied* | Applied | Approved* | Denied* |
| 2009 | 6,835 | 5,825 | 688 | 4,102 | 2,838 | 158 | 10,937 | 8,663 | 846 |
| 2010 | 10,742 | 10,073 | 4,347 | 6,418 | 9,315 | 2,576 | 17,160 | 19,388 | 6,923 |
| 2011 | 16,768 | 10,088 | 2,929 | 10,033 | 7,602 | 1,645 | 26,801 | 17,690 | 4,574 |

*Some approvals and denials are from prior fiscal year filings.

SOURCE: "Applications for U Visas," in *Attorney General's Annual Report to Congress and Assessment of U.S. Government Activities to Combat Trafficking in Persons, Fiscal Year 2011*, U.S. Department of Justice, January 2013, http://www.justice.gov/ag/annualreports/agreporthumantrafficking2011.pdf (accessed April 16, 2013)

## Monitoring Foreign Governments

The TVPA requires the State Department to monitor the efforts of foreign governments to eliminate trafficking. The State Department identifies governments in full compliance with the TVPA (Tier One); governments not in compliance with minimum standards but that are making progress toward compliance (Tier Two); governments that are not in compliance with the TVPA and have a demonstrated problem with human trafficking, but that are taking action to reduce trafficking (Tier Two Watch List); and governments that have not taken serious action to stop human trafficking (Tier Three). There were 17 countries listed as Tier Three in 2012. (See Table 4.14.) According to the State Department, in *Trafficking in Persons Report* (June 2012, http://www.state.gov/j/tip/rls/tiprpt/2012/), there were 7,206 prosecutions and 4,239 convictions of alleged traffickers worldwide in 2011.

Further efforts to combat human trafficking include the State Department post of ambassador-at-large to monitor and combat trafficking in people. President Barack Obama (1961–) nominated Luis C. de Baca for the post in March 2009. A former attorney in the U.S. Department of Justice and counsel to the U.S. House of Representatives Committee on the Judiciary, C. de Baca was confirmed and appointed in May 2011.

## REFUGEE ADJUSTMENT TO LIFE IN THE UNITED STATES

The PRM explains in *FY 2012 Summary of Major Activities* (November 6, 2012, http://www.state.gov/documents/organization/202560.pdf) that the U.S. government expected to spend nearly $1.9 billion in FY 2012 to help process and resettle refugees. (See Figure 4.3.) The bulk of this budget ($1.5 billion) supported overseas assistance, much of it used by the UNHCR and other diplomatic organizations. Meanwhile, the costs associated with refugee admissions to the United States totaled $329.5 million.

The State Department makes funds available for the transportation of refugees to resettle in the United States. The cost of transportation is provided to refugees in the form of a loan. Beginning six months after their arrival, refugees become responsible for repaying these loans. NGOs recruit church groups and volunteers from local communities to provide a variety of services and to contribute clothing and household furnishings to meet the needs of arriving refugees. They also become mentors and friends of the refugees by providing orientation to community services, offering supportive services such as tutoring children after school, and teaching families how to shop and handle other essential functions of living in the community.

Mutual assistance associations, many of which have national networks, provide opportunities for refugees to meet their countrymen who are already settled in the United States. These associations also help refugees connect with their ethnic culture through holiday and religious celebrations.

### Benefits to Assist Transition

Ongoing benefits for the newly arrived refugees include transitional cash assistance, health benefits, and a wide variety of social services, which are provided through grants from the HHS's Office of Refugee Resettlement. English-language training is a basic service that is offered to all refugees. The primary focus is preparation for employment through skills training, job development, orientation to the workplace, and job counseling. Early employment leads not only to economic self-sufficiency for the family but also helps establish the family in its new country and community. Special attention is paid to ensure that women have equal access to training and services that lead to job placement. Other services include family strengthening, youth and elderly services, adjustment counseling, and mental health services.

### Support for Elderly and Disabled Refugees

Refugees who are elderly or disabled receive benefits from the Social Security Administration, the same as U.S. citizens. However, changes by Congress during the late 1990s limit the eligibility of noncitizens to their first seven years in the United States. Time limits for noncitizens do not apply once they become U.S. citizens. The refugee program offers citizenship classes to assist refugees who want to study for the citizenship test.

### Unaccompanied Children

According to Lavinia Limon of the U.S. Committee for Refugees and Immigrants, in "Influx of Unaccompanied Migrant Children a Tragedy that Requires Congressional Action" (TexasObserver.org, June 14, 2012), an estimated 14,000 unaccompanied immigrant youth came to the United States in 2012—an 86% increase in the numbers of unaccompanied immigrant youth who had been arriving annually in previous years. Many children who immigrate on their own are fleeing gang violence, domestic abuse, poverty, or human trafficking. They want to be united with friends or family. The majority of these children fight for the right to stay in this country, but most go through immigration proceedings without speaking with an attorney.

Children who do not have parents in the United States and who are granted asylum are eligible for the Specialized Refugee Foster Care Program. This program is coordinated by the Lutheran Immigration and Refugee Service and the U.S. Conference of Catholic Bishops. Benefits include financial support for housing, food, clothing, and other necessities; case management by a social worker; medical care; independent living skills training; education and English as a second language; tutoring and mentoring; job skills training and career counseling; mental health services; ongoing family tracing; cultural activities and recreation; special education where needed; and legal assistance.

### Victims of Torture

The International Rehabilitation Council for Torture Victims estimates in "Asylum Seekers, Refugees and

**TABLE 4.14**

**Tier placement of countries, 2012**

| Country | Tier | Country | Tier | Country | Tier |
|---|---|---|---|---|---|
| Afghanistan | 2WL | Georgia | 1 | Niger | 2WL |
| Albania | 2 | Germany | 1 | Nigeria | 2 |
| Algeria | 3 | Ghana | 2 | Norway | 1 |
| Angola | 2WL | Greece | 2 | Oman | 2 |
| Antigua & Barbuda | 2 | Guatemala | 2 | Pakistan | 2 |
| Argentina | 2 | Guinea | 2 | Palau | 2 |
| Armenia | 2 | Guinea-Bissau | 2WL | Panama | 2 |
| Aruba | 2 | Guyana | 2 | Papua New Guinea | 3 |
| Australia | 1 | Haiti | 2WL | Paraguay | 2 |
| Austria | 1 | Honduras | 2 | Peru | 2 |
| Azerbaijan | 2WL | Hong Kong | 2 | Philippines | 2 |
| The Bahamas | 2WL | Hungary | 2 | Poland | 1 |
| Bahrain | 2WL | Iceland | 1 | Portugal | 2 |
| Bangladesh | 2 | India | 2 | Qatar | 2 |
| Barbados | 2WL | Indonesia | 2 | Romania | 2 |
| Belarus | 2WL | Iran | 3 | Russia | 2WL |
| Belgium | 1 | Iraq | 2WL | Rwanda | 2 |
| Belize | 2 | Ireland | 1 | St. Lucia | 2 |
| Benin | 2 | Israel | 1 | St. Vincent & The Gren. | 2 |
| Bolivia | 2 | Italy | 1 | Saudi Arabia | 3 |
| Bosnia & Herzegovina | 2 | Jamaica | 2WL | Senegal | 2WL |
| Botswana | 2 | Japan | 2 | Serbia | 2 |
| Brazil | 2 | Jordan | 2 | Seychelles | 2WL |
| Brunei | 2 | Kazakhstan | 2 | Sierra Leone | 2WL |
| Bulgaria | 2 | Kenya | 2WL | Singapore | 2 |
| Burkina Faso | 2 | Kiribati | 2 | Slovak Republic | 1 |
| Burma | 2WL | Korea, North | 3 | Slovenia | 1 |
| Burundi | 2WL | Korea, South | 1 | Solomon Islands | 2 |
| Cambodia | 2 | Kosovo | 2 | South Africa | 2 |
| Cameroon | 2 | Kuwait | 3 | South Sudan | 2WL |
| Canada | 1 | Kyrgyz Republic | 2 | Spain | 1 |
| Cape Verde | 2 | Laos | 2 | Sri Lanka | 2 |
| Central African Rep. | 3 | Latvia | 2 | Sudan | 3 |
| Chad | 2WL | Lebanon | 2WL | Suriname | 2WL |
| Chile | 2 | Lesotho | 2 | Swaziland | 2 |
| China (PRC) | 2WL | Liberia | 2WL | Sweden | 1 |
| Colombia | 1 | Libya | 3 | Switzerland | 2 |
| Comoros | 2WL | Lithuania | 1 | Syria | 3 |
| Congo (DRC) | 3 | Luxembourg | 1 | Taiwan | 1 |
| Congo, Republic of | 2WL | Macau | 2WL | Tajikistan | 2 |
| Costa Rica | 2 | Macedonia | 1 | Tanzania | 2 |
| Côte D'Ivoire | 2 | Madagascar | 3 | Thailand | 2WL |
| Croatia | 1 | Malawi | 2WL | Timor-Leste | 2 |
| Cuba | 3 | Malaysia | 2WL | Togo | 2 |
| Curacao | 2 | Maldives | 2WL | Tonga | 2 |
| Cyprus | 2WL | Mali | 2 | Trinidad & Tobago | 2 |
| Czech Republic | 1 | Malta | 2 | Tunisia | 2 |
| Denmark | 1 | Marshall Islands | 2 | Turkey | 2 |
| Djibouti | 2WL | Mauritania | 2WL | Turkmenistan | 2WL |
| Dominican Republic | 2 | Mauritius | 1 | Uganda | 2 |
| Ecuador | 2WL | Mexico | 2 | Ukraine | 2 |
| Egypt | 2 | Micronesia | 2WL | United Arab Emirates | 2 |
| El Salvador | 2 | Moldova | 2 | United Kingdom | 1 |
| Equatorial Guinea | 3 | Mongolia | 2 | United States of America | 1 |
| Eritrea | 3 | Montenegro | 2 | Uruguay | 2 |
| Estonia | 2 | Morocco | 2 | Uzbekistan | 2WL |
| Ethiopia | 2 | Mozambique | 2 | Venezuela | 2WL |
| Fiji | 2 | Namibia | 2WL | Vietnam | 2 |
| Finland | 1 | Nepal | 2 | Yemen | 3 |
| France | 1 | Netherlands | 1 | Zambia | 2 |
| Gabon | 2 | New Zealand | 1 | Zimbabwe | 3 |
| The Gambia | 2WL | Nicaragua | 1 | Somalia | Special case |

Notes: Tier 1 (1): Countries whose governments fully comply with the Trafficking Victims Protection Act's (TVPA) minimum standards.
Tier 2 (2): Countries whose governments do not fully comply with the TVPA's minimum standards, but are making significant efforts to bring themselves into compliance with those standards. Tier 2 Watch List (2WL): Countries whose governments do not fully comply with the TVPA's minimum standards, but are making significant efforts to bring themselves into compliance with those standards, AND: a) the absolute number of victims of severe forms of trafficking is very significant or is significantly increasing; b) there is a failure to provide evidence of increasing efforts to combat severe forms of trafficking in persons from the previous year; or, c) the determination that a country is making significant efforts to bring themselves into compliance with minimum standards was based on commitments by the country to take additional future steps over the next year.
Tier 3 (3): Countries whose governments do not fully comply with the minimum standards and are not making significant efforts to do so.

SOURCE: "Tier Placements," in *Trafficking in Persons Report*, U.S. Department of State, Office to Monitor Trafficking in Persons, June 2012, http://www.state.gov/documents/organization/192587.pdf (accessed March 6, 2013)

FIGURE 4.3

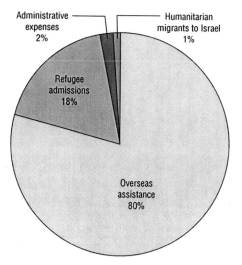

**Summary of refugee assistance major activities, fiscal year 2012**

| | |
|---|---|
| Overseas assistance | $1,484,692,174 |
| Refugee admissions | $329,528,030 |
| Administrative expenses | $31,782,333 |
| Humanitarian migrants to Israel | $20,000,000 |
| **Total** | **$1,866,002,537** |

Administrative expenses 2%

Humanitarian migrants to Israel 1%

Refugee admissions 18%

Overseas assistance 80%

Major activities include:
• Migration and Refugee Assistance (MRA)
• Emergency Refugee and Migration Assistance (ERMA)
• Overseas Contingency Operations (OCO)
• Economic Support Fund (ESF)
• Global HIV/AIDS initiative

SOURCE: "Bureau of Population, Refugees, and Migration FY 2012 Summary of Major Activities," in *FY 2012 Summary of Major Activities*, U.S. Department of State, Bureau of Population, Refugees, and Migration, November 6, 2012, http://www.state.gov/documents/organization/202560.pdf (accessed March 7, 2013)

Internally Displaced Persons" (2012, http://www.irct.org/our-work/current-focus-areas/asylum-seekers–refugees-and-internally-displace-persons.aspx) that between 4% and 35% of refugees worldwide are likely victims of torture. A nontrivial portion of the overall refugee and asylee population in the United States at any given time, then, is likely to be suffering the aftereffects of torture.

The term *torture*, as defined by U.S. code, refers to acts specifically intended to cause severe physical or mental pain or suffering when these acts are committed by representatives of the law against those in their custody or under their control. The Torture Victims Relief Act (TVRA) of 1998 provides funding to a variety of programs to support refugees, asylees, and asylum seekers who have been victims of torture. As used in the TVRA, the definition of torture explicitly includes the use of rape and other forms of sexual violence. Services available to torture victims under the 1998 law include physical and psychological rehabilitation, social and legal services, research and training for health care providers, and training programs for those who help with the rehabilitation of victims. The Office of Refugee Resettlement notes in "Services for Survivors of Torture Grants" (http://www.acf.hhs.gov/programs/orr/resource/services-for-survivors-of-torture-grants) that as of October 2012, 31 programs nationwide were supported by $10.9 million in TVRA funding.

# CHAPTER 5
# ILLEGAL IMMIGRATION

## BARRIERS TO LEGAL IMMIGRATION

As the preceding chapters make clear, significant constraints regulate the legal immigration process. A foreign national who would like to live in the United States must typically either be a close family member of a U.S. citizen, have a pending contract with an employer who is certified to hire foreign workers, or belong to one of the small groups of people eligible for special visa categories. Even a foreign national who qualifies for immigrant or nonimmigrant visas in one of these ways might have to wait years while pursuing the appropriate documentation to enter the country legally. Meanwhile, even jobs paying the minimum wage or less in the United States offer incomes significantly larger than jobs in impoverished countries. These competing pressures mean that unauthorized entry into the United States is often an attractive option for those foreign nationals intent on escaping poverty. Many unauthorized immigrants who enter the United States accept high risk and sometimes great expense for a chance to work, and their families often follow.

### Waiting Time for Legal Entry Documents

The annual limit on the number of U.S. employment-based legal admissions is well below the number that is requested by potential immigrants seeking employment. Compete America, an organization that advocates reform of U.S. immigration policy to attract highly educated foreign workers, notes in "America's Innovation Edge at Risk" (February 4, 2011, http://www.competeamerica.org/sites/default/files/files/Innovation%20at%20Risk%202011%20FINAL.pdf) that new employer-sponsored skilled workers and professionals can wait up to nine years for green cards, and that temporary H-1B visas have arbitrarily small caps that can be exhausted within days in certain years.

As of March 2013 the employment-based visa applications of priority workers from around the world were being evaluated in a timely manner. (See Table 5.1.) However, the supply of qualified foreign workers perennially exceeds the available temporary and permanent work visas. Holders of advanced degrees such as doctorates, as well as highly skilled workers likely to make a positive economic contribution to U.S. companies and the national economy, can expect to wait years for a work visa even after they have found an employer who wants to hire them. In March 2013, for example, the State Department was issuing visas only to Chinese nationals in the 2nd preference category ("advanced degree holders and persons of exceptional ability") if their applications had been received before February 15, 2008—more than five years earlier. Workers from India in the same class of applicants had been waiting even longer. In March 2013 the State Department was considering 2nd-preference applications from India that had been received before September 1, 2004.

The wait for family-based visas could be exceptionally long, as well. The foreign-born spouses and minor children of U.S. citizens, as the highest priority category among all visa applicants, never have to wait for entry into the country. Other family members of citizens are treated very differently under immigration law, however, as are all family members (even spouses and minor children) of green-card holders who are not yet citizens. As of March 2013, for example, if an unmarried adult child of a U.S. citizen was from Mexico, he or she would have been waiting since at least January 15, 1993 (over 20 years), for a family-sponsored visa to be approved. (See Table 5.2.) Likewise, green-card holders who were not citizens could expect to spend years apart from their families while they worked in the United States. As of March 2013, the State Department was processing visa applications in this category dating from November 2010.

Stuart Anderson of the National Foundation for American Policy (NFAP) outlines the predicament of skilled foreign workers and their families in the policy brief "Waiting and More Waiting: America's Family and Employment-Based

TABLE 5.1

**Employment-based visa application backlog, as of March 2013**

[In March 2013, the U.S. State Department was issuing employment-based visas for applications received before the dates listed below]

| | China | India | Mexico | Philippines | All other countries |
|---|---|---|---|---|---|
| 1st preference: Priority workers | Current applications | Current applications | Current applications | Current applications | Current applications |
| 2nd preference: Advanced degree holders and persons of exceptional ability | Feb. 15, 2008 | Sep. 1, 2004 | Current applications | Current applications | Current applications |
| 3rd preference: Skilled workers and professionals | Jan. 22, 2007 | Nov. 22, 2002 | May 1, 2007 | Sep. 1, 2006 | May 1, 2007 |
| 3rd preference: Other workers | July 1, 2003 | Nov. 22, 2002 | May 1, 2007 | Sep. 1, 2006 | May 1, 2007 |

SOURCE: Adapted from "Employment-Based Preferences," in *Visa Bulletin for March 2013*, vol. IX, no. 54, U.S. Department of State, Bureau of Consular Affairs, February 8, 2013, http://www.travel.state.gov/visa/bulletin/bulletin_5885.html (accessed March 7, 2013)

TABLE 5.2

**Family-sponsored visa application backlog, as of March 2013**

[In March 2013, the U.S. State Department was issuing family-sponsored visas for applications received before the dates listed below]

| | China | India | Mexico | Philippines | All other countries |
|---|---|---|---|---|---|
| 1st preference: Unmarried adult children of U.S. citizens | Feb. 15, 2006 | Feb. 15, 2006 | July 22, 1993 | Oct. 15, 1998 | Feb. 15, 2006 |
| 2nd preference A: Spouses and minor children of permanent residents | Nov. 22, 2010 | Nov. 22, 2010 | Nov. 15, 2010 | Nov. 22, 2010 | Nov. 20, 2010 |
| 2nd preference B: Unmarried adult children of permanent residents | Mar. 1, 2005 | Mar. 1, 2005 | Jan. 15, 1993 | June 8, 2002 | Mar. 1, 2005 |
| 3rd preference: Married adult children of U.S. citizens | July 15, 2002 | July 15, 2002 | Mar. 15, 1993 | Sep. 15, 1992 | July 15, 2002 |
| 4th preference: Siblings of U.S. citizens | Apr. 22, 2001 | Apr. 22, 2001 | Aug. 15, 1993 | July 15, 1989 | Apr. 22, 2001 |

SOURCE: Adapted from "Family-Sponsored Preferences," in *Visa Bulletin for March 2013*, vol. IX, no. 54, U.S. Department of State, Bureau of Consular Affairs, February 8, 2013, http://www.travel.state.gov/visa/bulletin/bulletin_5885.html (accessed March 7, 2013)

Immigration System" (October 2011, http://www.nfap.com/pdf/WAITING_NFAP_Policy_Brief_October_2011.pdf):

> Today, the most distinguishing characteristic of innovative and adaptive immigrants is an ability to wait a long time. That is because America's system for both family-sponsored and employment-based immigration is saddled with backlogs that force individuals and their American sponsors to wait many years—potentially decades—before obtaining a green card.... A highly skilled Indian national sponsored today for an employment-based immigrant visa in the 3rd preference [skilled workers and professionals] could wait potentially 70 years to receive a green card. The 70-year wait is derived from calculating that there exists a backlog of 210,000 or more Indians in the most common skilled employment-based category (the 3rd preference or EB-3) and dividing that by the approximately 2,800 Indian professionals who receive permanent residence in the category each year under the law.

Because of the long waits, many difficult scenarios arise. For example, a parent might learn that a spouse's recent death invalidates immigration applications for their adult children, forcing the children to reapply and wait an additional six to 19 years. Family members may receive their visas after many years in the backlog, only to learn that their children can no longer emigrate with them because they are older than 21 years and must now apply separately as adults or under the lower-priority categories allotted to adult children.

## ESTIMATES OF THE UNAUTHORIZED IMMIGRANT POPULATION

An unauthorized immigrant is a person who is not a U.S. citizen and who is in the United States in violation of U.S. immigration laws. Other terms commonly used to refer to this population include "undocumented immigrants," "illegal immigrants," and "illegal aliens," although some immigrants and their advocates consider the latter terms offensive, maintaining that equating these individuals' legal violations with their identities unfairly stigmatizes them.

An unauthorized immigrant can be one of the following:

• A person who enters the United States without a visa, often between land ports of entry

• A person who enters the United States using fraudulent documentation

• A person who enters the United States legally with a temporary visa and then stays beyond the time allowed (an act often called a nonimmigrant overstay or a visa overstay)

• A legal permanent resident who commits a crime after entry, becomes subject to an order of deportation, but fails to depart

Because unauthorized immigrants do not readily identify themselves out of fear of deportation, it is

FIGURE 5.1

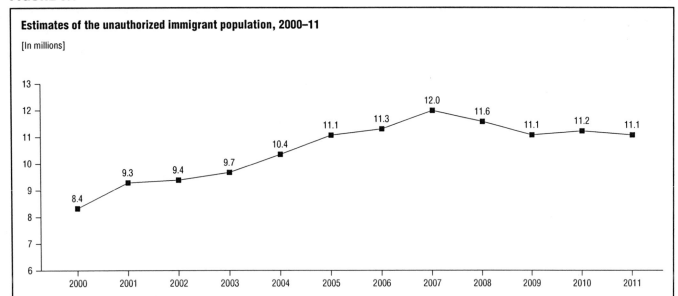

**Estimates of the unauthorized immigrant population, 2000–11**

[In millions]

SOURCE: Jeffery Passel and D'Vera Cohn, "Estimates of the U.S. Unauthorized Immigrant Population, 2000–2011," in *Unauthorized Immigrants: 11.1 Million in 2011*, Pew Hispanic Center, December 6, 2012, http://www.pewhispanic.org/2012/12/06/unauthorized-immigrants-11-1-million-in-2011/ (accessed March 7, 2013)

difficult to estimate their numbers accurately. The population further varies between the winter and summer months based on the number of people in agricultural work. However, widely respected estimates of the unauthorized immigrant population are generated each year by the Pew Hispanic Center. In December 2012 the center released its figures for 2011, estimating the unauthorized immigrant population at 11.1 million, down from a prerecession peak of 12 million. (See Figure 5.1.) In *Estimates of the Unauthorized Immigrant Population Residing in the United States: January 2011* (March 2012, http://www.dhs.gov/xlibrary/assets/statistics/publications/ois_ill_pe_2011.pdf), the Office of Immigration Statistics (OIS), a part of the Department of Homeland Security (DHS), arrived at a similar estimate of the unauthorized immigrant population in 2011, at 11.5 million.

Declines in the unauthorized immigration population, which coincided with the onset of the Great Recession in 2008, were the first such decreases in more than two decades. As the OIS notes, an estimated two to four million unauthorized immigrants were in the United States in 1980, and that number had increased to an estimated 8.5 million in 2000. Both the DHS and the Pew Hispanic Center suggest that the unauthorized immigrant population peaked in 2007. The fastest growth of the unauthorized immigrant population occurred in the years 1995 to 2004. Of the 11.5 unauthorized immigrants that the OIS estimated to be in the country in 2011, well over half (6.4 million) were believed to have entered between 1995 and 2004. (See Table 5.3.) Another 30% (nearly 3.6 million) were believed to have entered the United States between 1980 and 1995, and 14% (1.6 million) between 2005 and 2010.

**TABLE 5.3**

**Period of entry of the estimated unauthorized immigrant population, January 2011**

| Period of entry | Estimated population January 2011 | |
| --- | --- | --- |
| | Number | Percent |
| **All years** | **11,510,000** | **100** |
| 2005–2010 | 1,580,000 | 14 |
| 2000–2004 | 3,330,000 | 29 |
| 1995–1999 | 3,030,000 | 26 |
| 1990–1994 | 1,650,000 | 14 |
| 1985–1989 | 1,070,000 | 9 |
| 1980–1984 | 850,000 | 7 |

Note: Detail may not sum to totals because of rounding.

SOURCE: Michael Hoefer, Nancy Rytina, and Bryan Baker, "Table 1. Period of Entry of the Unauthorized Immigrant Population: January 2011," in *Estimates of the Unauthorized Immigrant Population Residing in the United States: January 2011*, U.S. Department of Homeland Security, Office of Immigration Statistics, March 2012, http://www.dhs.gov/xlibrary/assets/statistics/publications/ois_ill_pe_2011.pdf (accessed March 8, 2013)

According to OIS estimates, approximately 59% (6.8 million) of the unauthorized immigrants present in the United States in 2011 were born in Mexico. (See Table 5.4.) Between 2000 and 2011 the Mexican-born portion of the unauthorized population increased by an annual average of 190,000 people. The Central American countries El Salvador, Guatemala, and Honduras were the other leading source nations for illegal immigration in 2011, together accounting for 1.6 million (14%) of the total unauthorized population. China, Ecuador, India, Korea, the Philippines, and Vietnam each contributed approximately 2% of the total 2011 unauthorized population.

California, which shares a border with Mexico and has a large and varied economy, has long been home to

**TABLE 5.4**

**Country of birth of the estimated unauthorized immigrant population, 2000 and 2011**

| Country of birth | Estimated population in January | | Percent of total | | Percent change | Average annual change |
|---|---|---|---|---|---|---|
| | 2011 | 2000 | 2011 | 2000 | 2000 to 2011 | 2000 to 2011 |
| **All countries** | 11,510,000 | 8,460,000 | 100 | 100 | 36 | 280,000 |
| Mexico | 6,800,000 | 4,680,000 | 59 | 55 | 45 | 190,000 |
| El Salvador | 660,000 | 430,000 | 6 | 5 | 55 | 20,000 |
| Guatemala | 520,000 | 290,000 | 5 | 3 | 82 | 20,000 |
| Honduras | 380,000 | 160,000 | 3 | 2 | 132 | 20,000 |
| China | 280,000 | 190,000 | 2 | 2 | 43 | 10,000 |
| Philippines | 270,000 | 200,000 | 2 | 2 | 35 | 10,000 |
| India | 240,000 | 120,000 | 2 | 1 | 94 | 10,000 |
| Korea | 230,000 | 180,000 | 2 | 2 | 31 | — |
| Ecuador | 210,000 | 110,000 | 2 | 1 | 83 | 10,000 |
| Vietnam | 170,000 | 160,000 | 2 | 2 | 10 | — |
| Other countries | 1,750,000 | 1,940,000 | 15 | 23 | −10 | (20,000) |

—Represents less than 5,000.
Note: Detail may not sum to totals because of rounding.

SOURCE: Michael Hoefer, Nancy Rytina, and Bryan Baker, "Table 3. Country of Birth of the Unauthorized Immigrant Population: January 2011 and 2000," in *Estimates of the Unauthorized Immigrant Population Residing in the United States: January 2011*, U.S. Department of Homeland Security, Office of Immigration Statistics, March 2012, http://www.dhs.gov/xlibrary/assets/statistics/publications/ois_ill_pe_2011.pdf (accessed March 8, 2013)

**TABLE 5.5**

**State of residence of the unauthorized immigrant population, 2000 and 2011**

| State of residence | Estimated population in January | | Percent of total | | Percent change | Average annual change |
|---|---|---|---|---|---|---|
| | 2011 | 2000 | 2011 | 2000 | 2000 to 2011 | 2000 to 2011 |
| **All states** | 11,510,000 | 8,460,000 | 100 | 100 | 36 | 280,000 |
| California | 2,830,000 | 2,510,000 | 25 | 30 | 12 | 30,000 |
| Texas | 1,790,000 | 1,090,000 | 16 | 13 | 64 | 60,000 |
| Florida | 740,000 | 800,000 | 6 | 9 | −8 | (10,000) |
| New York | 630,000 | 540,000 | 6 | 6 | 18 | 10,000 |
| Illinois | 550,000 | 440,000 | 5 | 5 | 26 | 10,000 |
| Georgia | 440,000 | 220,000 | 4 | 3 | 95 | 20,000 |
| New Jersey | 420,000 | 350,000 | 4 | 4 | 19 | 10,000 |
| North Carolina | 400,000 | 260,000 | 3 | 3 | 53 | 10,000 |
| Arizona | 360,000 | 330,000 | 3 | 4 | 9 | — |
| Washington | 260,000 | 170,000 | 2 | 2 | 51 | 10,000 |
| Other states | 3,100,000 | 1,750,000 | 27 | 21 | 77 | 120,000 |

—Represents less than 5,000.
Note: Detail may not sum to totals because of rounding.

SOURCE: Michael Hoefer, Nancy Rytina, and Bryan Baker, "Table 4. State of Residence of the Unauthorized Immigrant Population: January 2011 and 2000," in *Estimates of the Unauthorized Immigrant Population Residing in the United States: January 2011*, U.S. Department of Homeland Security, Office of Immigration Statistics, March 2012, http://www.dhs.gov/xlibrary/assets/statistics/publications/ois_ill_pe_2011.pdf (accessed March 8, 2013)

more immigrants, both legal and unauthorized, than any other U.S. state. The state remained home to more unauthorized immigrants than any other in 2011, with 2.8 million, or 25% of the total. (See Table 5.5.) California's share of the unauthorized population declined between 2000 and 2011, however, whereas that of Texas and other states grew. An estimated 700,000 unauthorized immigrants settled in Texas during this period, bringing the state's share of the total unauthorized population to 16%.

Large portions of the unauthorized population continued to live in other populous states that had traditionally drawn immigrant arrivals, such as Florida,

Illinois, and New York, but outside of Texas, much of the growth between 2000 and 2011 in the unauthorized population happened in states not historically known for attracting immigrants. Washington's unauthorized population grew by an estimated 51% in these years, North Carolina's by 53%, and Georgia's by 95%.

**Decline in Immigration from Mexico**

The decrease in the population of unauthorized immigrants in the years 2007 to 2011 is primarily attributable to a standstill in illegal border crossings from Mexico. As Jeffrey Passel, D'Vera Cohn, and Ana Gonzalez-Barrera of the Pew Hispanic Center note in

*Net Migration from Mexico Falls to Zero—and Perhaps Less* (April 23, 2012, http://www.pewhispanic.org/files/2012/04/Mexican-migrants-report_final.pdf), by 2011 the unprecedented flow of immigrants from Mexico to the United States over the preceding 40 years had slowed and then stopped. In the period 2005 to 2010 as many people moved from the United States to Mexico as from Mexico to the United States.

This phenomenon was likely caused by a convergence of factors. First, there was a decrease in demand for workers during the Great Recession that began in late 2007 and particularly hit the housing construction industry (in which large numbers of unauthorized immigrants are typically employed). Additionally, the heightened border security that was initiated after the terrorist attacks in the United States on September 11, 2001 (9/11), and that became more focused with the 2003 establishment of the DHS had made border crossings far more difficult by the time the recession began. National security concerns and anti-immigrant political pressures had also led to increasing numbers of deportations. The increase in deportation began under the administration of President George W. Bush (1946–) and accelerated under President Barack Obama (1961–). Finally, demographers pointed to the falling birthrate in Mexico, which had begun to relieve some of the pressure that had driven so many in that country to leave home in the preceding decades. In 1960, the Pew authors point out, the average Mexican woman had 7.3 children. By 2009 the Mexican fertility rate was 2.4 children per woman, only slightly higher than that among U.S. women (2). Together with Mexico's economic growth during that same period, the falling fertility suggested that in the future Mexicans would be better able to find opportunities for personal and professional advancement in their home country.

As Figure 5.2 shows, the period 2005 to 2010 saw a striking reversal of the U.S.-Mexico net migration trends of the late 1990s. Between 1995 and 2000, an estimated 2.9 million Mexican-born individuals moved to the United States, most of them without legal authorization, compared with an estimated 670,000 people who moved from the United States to Mexico. Between 2005 and 2010, by contrast, net migration between United States and Mexico was essentially zero: 1.4 million Mexicans moved to the United States, and 1.4 million people moved from the United States to Mexico. Most of those who left the United States for Mexico are believed to have made the move voluntarily, but the Pew authors estimate that somewhere between 5% and 35% of returnees were deported.

Figure 5.3 shows the trend in the annual number of immigrants from Mexico. As mentioned previously, the years of peak migration from Mexico to the United States came in the period 1995 to 2004, when at least 500,000

FIGURE 5.2

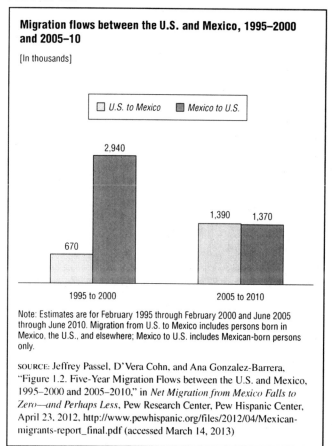

**Migration flows between the U.S. and Mexico, 1995–2000 and 2005–10**

[In thousands]

☐ U.S. to Mexico  ■ Mexico to U.S.

Note: Estimates are for February 1995 through February 2000 and June 2005 through June 2010. Migration from U.S. to Mexico includes persons born in Mexico, the U.S., and elsewhere; Mexico to U.S. includes Mexican-born persons only.

SOURCE: Jeffrey Passel, D'Vera Cohn, and Ana Gonzalez-Barrera, "Figure 1.2. Five-Year Migration Flows between the U.S. and Mexico, 1995–2000 and 2005–2010," in *Net Migration from Mexico Falls to Zero—and Perhaps Less*, Pew Research Center, Pew Hispanic Center, April 23, 2012, http://www.pewhispanic.org/files/2012/04/Mexican-migrants-report_final.pdf (accessed March 14, 2013)

Mexican-born individuals are believed to have settled in the United States annually. Immigration from Mexico peaked in 1999 at 770,000; by 2010 the number had fallen to 140,000, the majority of whom were legally authorized to stay in the United States either temporarily or permanently.

**Children of Unauthorized Immigrants**

The 14th Amendment of the U.S. Constitution states, "All persons born or naturalized in the United States, and subject to the jurisdiction thereof, are citizens of the United States and of the State wherein they reside." The original intent of the amendment was to give freed slaves U.S. citizenship, but it has been interpreted to give children born in the United States "birthright citizenship"—even those born to parents who are in the country illegally.

As Paul Taylor et al. of the Pew Hispanic Center observe in *Unauthorized Immigrants: Length of Residency, Patterns of Parenthood* (December 1, 2011, http://www.pewhispanic.org/files/2011/12/Unauthorized-Characteristics.pdf), unauthorized immigrant adults were more likely than adult U.S. natives or legal immigrants to be parents of minor children in 2010. (See Figure 5.4.) In that year an estimated 46% of adult unauthorized immigrants had minor children, compared with 38% of legal immigrant adults and 29% of the native-born

## FIGURE 5.3

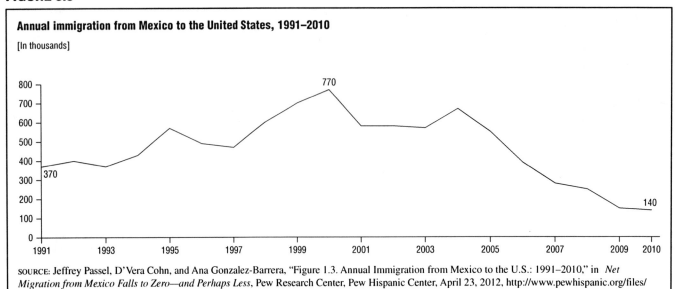

**Annual immigration from Mexico to the United States, 1991–2010**

[In thousands]

SOURCE: Jeffrey Passel, D'Vera Cohn, and Ana Gonzalez-Barrera, "Figure 1.3. Annual Immigration from Mexico to the U.S.: 1991–2010," in *Net Migration from Mexico Falls to Zero—and Perhaps Less*, Pew Research Center, Pew Hispanic Center, April 23, 2012, http://www.pewhispanic.org/files/2012/04/Mexican-migrants-report_final.pdf (accessed March 14, 2013)

## FIGURE 5.4

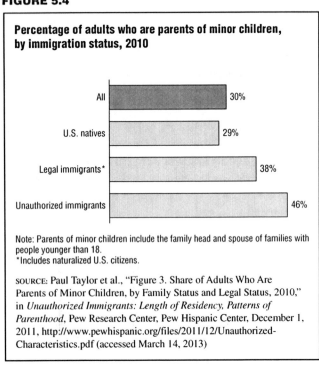

**Percentage of adults who are parents of minor children, by immigration status, 2010**

Note: Parents of minor children include the family head and spouse of families with people younger than 18.
*Includes naturalized U.S. citizens.

SOURCE: Paul Taylor et al., "Figure 3. Share of Adults Who Are Parents of Minor Children, by Family Status and Legal Status, 2010," in *Unauthorized Immigrants: Length of Residency, Patterns of Parenthood*, Pew Research Center, Pew Hispanic Center, December 1, 2011, http://www.pewhispanic.org/files/2011/12/Unauthorized-Characteristics.pdf (accessed March 14, 2013)

adult population. This disparity was primarily a function of the relative youth of the unauthorized adult population, according to the Pew researchers. The median age of U.S. native-born adults was 46.5 years, and the median age of legal immigrant adults was 46.1 years, whereas the median age for unauthorized immigrant adults was 36.2 years. Therefore, unauthorized immigrant adults were more likely to be in their childbearing years, and in cases where unauthorized immigrant adults already had children, those children were more likely to be minors.

The Pew authors note that in 2010 there were approximately 1 million unauthorized immigrants who were children—who, in other words, were not born in the United States—as well as a much larger group of children, 4.5 million, who were both born in the United States and had at least one parent who was an unauthorized immigrant. This represented a doubling, since 2000, of the population of U.S.-born children with at least one unauthorized immigrant parent.

Birthright citizenship became one of the flashpoints in the debates surrounding immigration reform in the years 2010 to 2013. Although most legal experts considered the 14th Amendment's guarantee of birthright citizenship a settled constitutional issue, a number of lawmakers at the state and national levels sought to deny citizenship to the children of unauthorized immigrants. Beginning in 2011, legislators in states including Arizona, Georgia, Oklahoma, Pennsylvania, and South Carolina introduced bills that would require parents to prove their legal immigration status before their children would be granted U.S. birth certificates. Although civil rights groups warned that such legislation was inhumane and inflammatory, the opposition to birthright citizenship reached the national political arena in the following years. In March 2013, as Paul C. Barton reports in "Birthright Citizenship Contested on Capitol Hill" (March 30, 2013, http://www.usatoday.com/story/news/politics/2013/03/30/birthright-citizenship-constitution/2036095/), Republicans in both the U.S. House and Senate introduced bills that would redefine the 14th Amendment so as to exclude the children of unauthorized immigrants from the guarantee of birthright citizenship.

Such challenges to the precedent of birthright citizenship had little chance of passing Congress, given the opposition of Democrats, who controlled both the Senate and the presidency at the time. Even were such bills to become law, it was doubtful that such a law could take effect, since the intended change to the law required a constitutional amendment altering the 14th Amendment. Amending the Constitution is a rare occurrence and is significantly more difficult than passing ordinary legislation.

Meanwhile, the Obama administration provided significant legal protections to certain unauthorized immigrants who had been brought to the United States as children and thus did not qualify for birthright citizenship. As discussed in Chapter 2, the long-running attempt to pass various versions of the Development, Relief, and Education for Alien Minors (DREAM) Act, which would offer a path to citizenship to many unauthorized immigrants brought to the United States as children, finally yielded fruit in 2012, as a result not of legislation but through a directive issued by the DHS. As Secretary of Homeland Security Janet Napolitano (1957–) announced in June 2012, certain people under the age of 30 years who had been brought to the United States illegally by their parents would be eligible for so-called deferred action, or relief from deportation. Generally speaking, an unauthorized immigrant brought to the United States at the age of 15 years or younger could apply for deferred action so long as he or she had been continuously in the United States for five years as of the date of the announcement; was in school, a high school graduate, or an honorably discharged veteran of the U.S. military; and neither had significant criminal convictions nor posed a threat to national security or public safety. Deferred action status lasted for two years, at the end of which recipients could apply for renewal. Recipients were also eligible for work authorization in the United States.

According to the Pew Hispanic Center, an estimated 1.7 million unauthorized immigrants were likely eligible for deferred action. (See Figure 2.3 in Chapter 2.) U.S. Citizenship and Immigration Services (USCIS) began processing deferred action applications in August 2012, and by mid-March of 2013, 453,589 applications had been approved and only 15,941 rejected. (See Table 5.6.) Among applicants for deferred action, 338,334 (72.1%) were born in Mexico. (See Table 5.7.) The other top countries of origin for applicants were El Salvador, with 18,449 (4%) applicants; Honduras, with 12,183 (2.6%), and Guatemala, with 11,395 (2.4%). The top states of residence for applicants were California, with 128,412 (27.3%) applicants; and Texas, with 73,258 (15.6%). Florida, Illinois, and New York were each home to more than 20,000 applicants.

## FEDERAL RESPONSE TO ILLEGAL IMMIGRATION

As illegal immigration from Mexico and Central America increased through the 1990s and the early years of the following decade, and as comprehensive immigration reform such as the proposals embodied by the DREAM Act foundered in Congress, federal immigration policy focused intently on the enforcement of laws intended to restrict the flow of unauthorized immigrants. As Doris Meissner et al. of the Migration Policy Institute report in *Immigration Enforcement in the United States: The Rise of a Formidable Machinery* (January 2013, http://www.migrationpolicy.org/pubs/enforcementpillars .pdf), immigration policy in the post-9/11 era has focused on six areas of enforcement: border security,

**TABLE 5.6**

**Deferred Action for Childhood Arrivals applications processed, August 2012–March 2013**

| | Month* | | | | | | | | Cumulative totals |
|---|---|---|---|---|---|---|---|---|---|
| | Aug | Sept | Oct | Nov | Dec | Jan | Feb | Mar | |
| **Intake** | | | | | | | | | |
| Accepted | 36,601 | 104,910 | 113,494 | 77,280 | 45,705 | 31,173 | 28,278 | 16,148 | 453,589 |
| Rejected | 1,263 | 3,676 | 3,719 | 2,477 | 1,626 | 1,281 | 1,269 | 630 | 15,941 |
| Total received | 37,864 | 108,586 | 117,213 | 79,757 | 47,331 | 32,454 | 29,547 | 16,778 | 469,530 |
| Average requests/day | 2,913 | 5,715 | 5,328 | 3,988 | 2,367 | 1,545 | 1,555 | 1,678 | 3,261 |
| **Biometrics** | | | | | | | | | |
| Scheduled | 18,616 | 105,439 | 98,430 | 87,037 | 42,062 | 42,678 | 30,128 | 17,651 | 442,041 |
| **Case review** | | | | | | | | | |
| Under review | 0 | 29,552 | 105,648 | 147,577 | 152,155 | 131,744 | 108,214 | 100,060 | — |
| Approved | 0 | 1,707 | 26,908 | 47,954 | 49,358 | 50,218 | 45,631 | 23,717 | 245,493 |

*August data from August 15–August 30, 2012.
September data from September 1–September 30, 2012.
October data from October 1–October 31, 2012.
November data from November 1–November 30, 2012.
December data from December 1–December 31, 2012.
January data from January 1–January 31, 2013.
February data from February 1–February 28, 2013.
March data from March 1–March 14, 2013.

SOURCE: Adapted from "Deferred Action for Childhood Arrivals Process," in *Data on Individual Applications and Petitions*, U.S. Department of Homeland Security, U.S. Citizenship and Immigration Services, March 15, 2013, http://www.uscis.gov/USCIS/Resources/Reports%20and%20Studies/Immigration%20 Forms%20Data/All%20Form%20Types/DACA/daca-13-3-15.pdf (accessed April 2, 2013)

TABLE 5.7

**Top countries of origin and states of residence for deferred action applicants, August 2012–March 2013**

| Top 10 countries of origin | Received to date |
|---|---|
| Mexico | 338,334 |
| El Salvador | 18,449 |
| Honduras | 12,183 |
| Guatemala | 11,395 |
| Peru | 6,495 |
| South Korea | 5,599 |
| Brazil | 5,487 |
| Colombia | 4,875 |
| Ecuador | 4,733 |
| Philippines | 3,241 |
| **Top 10 states of residence** | |
| California | 128,412 |
| Texas | 73,258 |
| New York | 25,735 |
| Illinois | 23,602 |
| Florida | 20,245 |
| North Carolina | 16,554 |
| Arizona | 16,009 |
| Georgia | 14,861 |
| New Jersey | 14,050 |
| Colorado | 9,658 |

Note: Data represents period August 15, 2012–March 14, 2013.

SOURCE: Adapted from "Deferred Action for Childhood Arrivals Process," in *Data on Individual Applications and Petitions*, U.S. Department of Homeland Security, U.S. Citizenship and Immigration Services, March 15, 2013, http://www.uscis.gov/USCIS/Resources/Reports%20and%20Studies/Immigration%20Forms%20Data/All%20Form%20Types/DACA/daca-13-3-15.pdf (accessed April 2, 2013)

FIGURE 5.5

**U.S. border patrol apprehensions, 1970–2010**

SOURCE: Lesley Sapp, "Figure 1. U.S. Border Patrol Apprehensions: 1970 to 2010," in *Apprehensions by the U.S. Border Patrol: 2005–2010*, U.S. Department of Homeland Security, Office of Immigration Statistics, July 2011, http://www.dhs.gov/xlibrary/assets/statistics/publications/ois-apprehensions-fs-2005-2010.pdf (accessed April 2, 2013)

visa controls and the screening of travelers, data-system improvements, workplace enforcement, the pursuit of unauthorized immigrants via the criminal justice system, and the removal of noncitizens.

Resources devoted to securing the southwest border of the United States increased dramatically following the creation of the DHS in 2003. As Meissner et al. note, the number of agents in the U.S. Border Patrol, a part of U.S. Customs and Border Protection (CBP), doubled in size between 2005 and 2012, reaching 21,370 as of fiscal year (FY) 2012. The number of border apprehensions, meanwhile, peaked in 2000, at 1.7 million. By 2005 the number of border apprehensions stood at 1.2 million, and by 2010 at 463,000, the lowest number since the early 1970s. (See Figure 5.5.) These declines have been attributed in part to the success of the CBP's deterrence efforts, as well as to the slowing of immigration from Mexico discussed earlier in this chapter.

Demands for increased border security following 9/11 also led to enhancements of the visa screening process that allowed for heightened scrutiny of nonimmigrant visitors and workers. After an initial dramatic drop in nonimmigrant visas, especially those issued to visitors from countries with large populations of Muslims, by 2011 nonimmigrant entries had returned to pre-2001 levels. Additionally, the DHS developed an electronic screening system, U.S. Visitor and Immigrant Status Indicator Technology (US-VISIT), which allows agents to check noncitizens against immigration, criminal, and terrorist databases.

The DHS has also devoted substantial resources to the expansion, upgrading, and interconnection of the information systems used by various executive and law enforcement agencies. The interconnection of databases and computer systems allows for the coordination of antiterrorist, criminal justice, and immigration enforcement efforts at the federal level. Immigration officials are thus armed with much more information than in earlier decades, and they can use this information in making decisions regarding the issuance of visas, border apprehensions, and other activities that affect the movements of unauthorized immigrants.

Although the Immigration Reform and Control Act (IRCA) of 1986 obligated employers to determine the immigration status of employees, enforcement of this part of the act has generally been unsuccessful. One way in which the DHS has sought to remedy this failure is the development of the E-Verify system. As of 2012 fewer than 10% of all employers used E-Verify, but participation rates had been steadily increasing in the preceding years, partly as a result of a growing number of state laws making it mandatory for employers to use the system. As Figure 2.2 in Chapter 2 shows, 20.2 million cases were processed in the E-Verify system in 2012, resulting in confirmations that employees were authorized to work in the United States 98.7% of the time.

Between 2006 and 2009, the Bush administration changed the focus on workplace enforcement to target workers rather than employers, undertaking large-scale raids of suspected businesses and arresting scores of unauthorized workers. These raids were extremely unpopular among immigrants regardless of their legal status, and the Obama administration de-emphasized them, returning the focus of workplace enforcement to employer sanctions. Between January 2009 and January 2013, U.S. Immigrations and Customs Enforcement (ICE) audited more than 8,000 employers and leveled almost $90 million in fines for workplace violations of immigration law.

Additionally, cooperation has increased between federal, state, and local law enforcement agencies on immigration issues. This trend has been advanced by a number of federal programs aimed at the removal of noncitizens arrested or convicted of criminal offenses. According to Meissner et al., the period between FY 2004 and FY 2011 saw the funding for such programs increase from $23 million to $690 million. One result of this development was that an increasing share of those deported by DHS—half or more in some years—had criminal convictions.

This coordinated approach between the criminal justice and immigration systems is supplemented by an ongoing, broader emphasis on the deportation of unauthorized immigrants and other noncitizens. Deportation reached record levels in FY 2012, when ICE removed 409,849 noncitizens, 55% of whom were convicted criminals. (See Figure 5.6.)

**FIGURE 5.6**

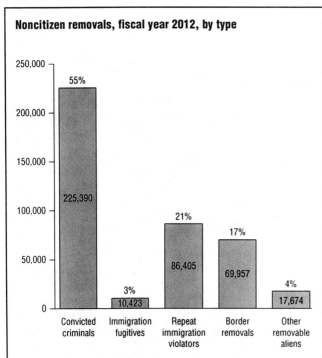

Noncitizen removals, fiscal year 2012, by type

SOURCE: "FY2012 Removals by Priorities," in *Removal Statistics*, U.S. Department of Homeland Security, U.S. Immigration and Customs Enforcement, 2013, http://www.ice.gov/removal-statistics/ (accessed April 2, 2013)

## STATE AND REGIONAL RESPONSES TO ILLEGAL IMMIGRATION

The US/Mexico Border Counties Coalition, a policy group involving representatives of the 24 U.S. counties that border Mexico, commissioned a 2006 report evaluating the economic conditions in its member counties. (See Figure 5.7.) Dennis L. Soden et al. frame the report, *At the Cross Roads: US/Mexico Border Counties in Transition* (March 2006, http://www.bordercounties.org/index.asp?Type=B_BASIC& SEC={62E35327-57C7-4978-A39A-36A8E00387B6}), with the question, "If the 24 southwest border counties were a 51st state, how would they compare to the other 50 states?"

Between 1990 and 2004 the 24 U.S. border counties collectively experienced a 29.3% growth rate. By 2006 there were 6.7 million residents. The border counties were home to 5% of the foreign-born residents of the United States, and nearly 72% of the foreign-born people living in the border counties were from Mexico. If the 24 border counties made up the 51st state, Soden et al. conclude, then that state would rank second in the percentage of population under the age of 18 years, second in unemployment, fourth in military employment, 12th in incidence of the acquired immunodeficiency syndrome (AIDS), 13th in population, 16th in violent crime, and 29th in total federal government expenditures. (See Table 5.8.)

Some of the stresses placed on these counties result from the many unauthorized immigrants that flow through them. Local governments in border counties bear many costs associated with investigating, jailing, and prosecuting unauthorized immigrants either for immigration violations or for criminal acts. As illustrated by the above statistics, the population and needs of these counties significantly outweigh the federal funding they receive. Indeed, border states have not been consistently reimbursed by the federal government, according to the coalition, even though the federal government reserves the exclusive power to enforce immigration law. Other residents of border states and of states that have seen large increases in immigrant numbers complain that unauthorized immigrants take advantage of social services that should be reserved for legal residents, and that they are therefore a drain on state budgets. Still others angered by illegal immigration lament the cultural changes brought about by rising numbers of Spanish-speaking residents.

In spite of the federal government's deployment of ever-larger resources to border-security initiatives, and despite its removals of ever-larger numbers of unauthorized immigrants in the years since 9/11, the perception exists that the federal government is not committed to preventing illegal immigration. Therefore, populist anger over illegal immigration, whether based on real economic arguments or not, has since the late 1990s been increasingly channeled into state legislative action. Based on the assumption that

FIGURE 5.7

**U.S. counties bordering Mexico**

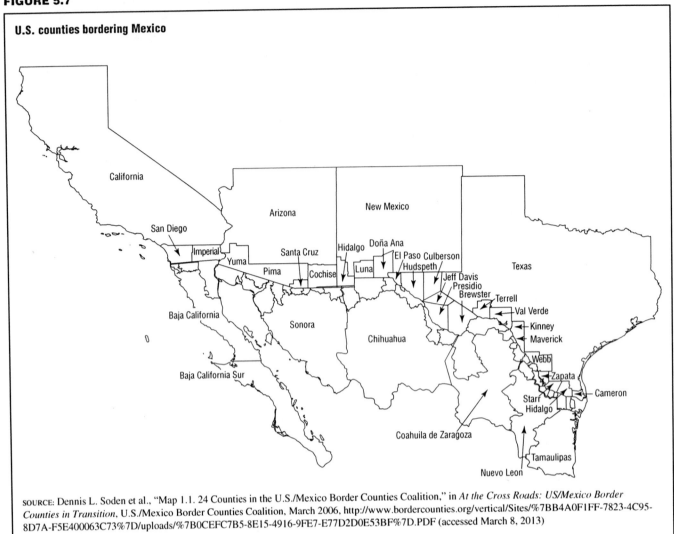

SOURCE: Dennis L. Soden et al., "Map 1.1. 24 Counties in the U.S./Mexico Border Counties Coalition," in *At the Cross Roads: US/Mexico Border Counties in Transition*, U.S./Mexico Border Counties Coalition, March 2006, http://www.bordercounties.org/vertical/Sites/%7BB4A0F1FF-7823-4C95-8D7A-F5E400063C73%7D/uploads/%7B0CEFC7B5-8E15-4916-9FE7-E77D2D0E53BF%7D.PDF (accessed March 8, 2013)

the states must step in to secure their own borders and protect resources from overuse by unauthorized immigrants, state laws have tested the limits of the federal government's power and remade the terms of the immigration debate.

## Arizona's Leading Role

Arizona's immigration enforcement laws that were passed in April 2010 stirred national debate; as discussed in Chapter 2, however, the state had a decade-long history of enforcement actions against unauthorized immigrants. Arizona's successful implementation of restrictions on unauthorized immigrants was emulated by many other state legislatures beginning in the middle years of that decade. (See Table 2.2 and Table 2.3 in Chapter 2.) An Arizona law called Proposition 200 in 2004 effectively banned undocumented immigrants from applying for public benefits and required government employees to report those suspected of immigration violations to the authorities, and a 2007 law mandated the use of E-Verify and provided for the suspension and revocation of the business licenses of Arizona employers who knowingly employ unauthorized immigrants. The Arizona law that went furthest in its attempt to deter illegal immigration was SB1070 (2010), also discussed in Chapter 2, which famously obligated law enforcement officers to check the immigration status of anyone they suspected, during a routine traffic stop or other type of interaction, of being unauthorized.

Although much of SB1070 was ruled unconstitutional by the U.S. Supreme Court in May 2012, the "show me your papers" provision requiring law enforcement officers to verify the immigration status of those they stopped was upheld. Meanwhile, between the time SB1070 passed in 2010 and the Supreme Court ruling, numerous other state legislatures passed laws modeled on the Arizona law. Among the most aggressive of these laws were those passed in Alabama, Georgia, Indiana, South Carolina, and Utah in 2011, each of which were, like Arizona's law, challenged by the U.S. Justice Department.

**TABLE 5.8**

## If the 24 U.S. counties bordering Mexico were the 51st state, how would they compare to the rest of the nation?

1st in federal crimes, primarily due to drug and immigration arrests by federal agencies
2nd in incidence of tuberculosis
2nd in percentage of population under age 18
2nd in unemployment (5th with San Diego County included)
3rd in deaths due to hepatitis
3rd in concentration of Hispanics
4th in military employment
5th in diabetes-related deaths
7th in incidence of adult diabetes
10th in employment of federal civilians
12th in government and government enterprise employment
12th in incidence of AIDS
13th in population
16th in violent crime
22nd in allocation of federal highway planning and construction expenditures
22nd in home ownership
29th in receipt of total federal government expenditures
37th in low birth weight babies
39th in infant mortality
42nd in percent of teen pregnancy
45th in home affordability (37th with San Diego County included)
46th in percentage of adults with four-year college degree (27th with San Diego County included)
50th in insurance coverage for adults and children
51st in percent of population that has completed high school (50th with San Diego)
51st in per capita income (40th with San Diego County included)
51st in number of health care professionals

Note: San Diego County is a major metropolitan area and an anomaly to the other 23 border counties in many respects.

SOURCE: Adapted from Dennis L. Soden et al., "One Page Report Highlights," in *At the Cross Roads: US/Mexico Border Counties in Transition*, U.S./Mexico Border Counties Coalition, March 2006, http://www.bordercounties.org/vertical/Sites/%7BB4A0F1FF-7823-4C95-8D7A-F5E400063C73%7D/uploads/%7B01CF6553-9553-4457-BA23-50B41E06536B%7D.PDF (accessed March 8, 2013)

---

The Alabama immigration law won national attention for being even more extreme than Arizona's in its attempt to make life for unauthorized immigrants difficult. Among its most controversial provisions was a requirement for school officials to determine the immigration status of children registered for public education, the introduction of criminal penalties for any immigrant who failed to carry documents establishing his or her legal right to residency in the United States, and a measure declaring invalid all contracts with unauthorized immigrants. The Alabama law also shared with the Georgia law a provision making it illegal to transport or harbor certain immigrants. Each of the above provisions in the Alabama law, as well as the provision common to the Alabama and Georgia law, was struck down by a federal appeals court in August 2012.

Provisions in the state laws that required individuals to prove their documented status, however, appeared safe from judicial intervention following the Supreme Court ruling in the Arizona case. The American Civil Liberties Union and other advocacy groups continued to challenge the state laws on other constitutional grounds in 2012 and 2013.

## OTHER FEDERAL MEASURES TO PREVENT UNAUTHORIZED IMMIGRATION

### Secure Fence Act of 2006

The United States began using barrier fencing during the 1990s to deter illegal entry and drug smuggling, particularly to prevent vehicle entry. In *Border Security: Barriers along the U.S. International Border* (March 16, 2009, http://www.fas.org/sgp/crs/homesec/RL33659.pdf), Chad C. Haddal, Yule Kim, and Michael John Garcia of the Congressional Research Service note that the 14-mile (22.5-km) fence at San Diego, California, the nation's busiest border port of entry, was the first to be constructed. It was strengthened by increased Border Patrol staffing. However, Haddal, Kim, and Garcia indicate that increased enforcement in San Diego had "little impact on overall apprehensions" of illegal entrants because the border barrier simply shifted illegal traffic to more remote areas. An unintended consequence of this shift in migration paths was an increase in migrant deaths in the desert.

According to Haddal, Kim, and Garcia, the Border Patrol's San Diego sector of the international border with Mexico extends about 66 miles (106 km) from the Pacific Ocean and encompasses 7,000 square miles (18,100 square km) of territory. This sector is located north of Tecate and Tijuana, Mexico, and does not contain any natural barriers that deter unauthorized migrants and smugglers from passing through. The primary San Diego fence covers the first 14 miles (22.5 km), starting from the Pacific Ocean, and was constructed of 10-foot-high (3-m-high) welded steel. The operations in San Diego are labeled "Operation Gatekeeper" and employ a three-tiered fence system that was first conceived at Sandia Laboratory in Albuquerque, New Mexico, to detect intruders early and delay them as long as possible. It channels border crossers to geographic locations such as Tucson and Yuma in Arizona, San Diego, and other sector stations.

In a further effort to close the porous southwestern border, President Bush signed the Secure Fence Act of 2006, which authorized the construction of hundreds of miles of additional fencing along the U.S.-Mexican border and added more vehicle barriers, checkpoints, and lighting to help prevent people from entering the country illegally. Haddal, Kim, and Garcia explain that the Secure Fence Act required the DHS to fence five additional stretches: the 20 miles (32.2 km) around Tecate; from Calexico, California, to Douglas, Arizona; from Columbus, New Mexico, to El Paso, Texas; from Del Rio to Eagle Pass, Texas; and from Laredo to Brownsville, Texas. The 370-mile (595.5-km) portion of the U.S.-Mexican border between Calexico and Douglas is a "priority area," and the act required the DHS to install an "interlocking surveillance camera system."

To get the fence built, the U.S. attorney general and the secretary of homeland security waived the National Environmental Policy Act of 1969 and the Endangered Species Act of 1973, to the extent the attorney general determined necessary to ensure expeditious construction of the barriers that were authorized to be constructed. This resulted in many lawsuits from environmental advocacy groups, which slowed down the actual construction of the fence.

The act also authorized the DHS to increase the use of advanced technology such as cameras, satellites, and unmanned aerial vehicles to reinforce infrastructure at the border. This authorization led to the development of a virtual fence network called the Secure Border Initiative Network. Furthermore, the secretary of homeland security was directed to conduct a study on the construction of a state-of-the-art barrier system along the U.S.-Canadian border. Amid reports of cost overruns and ineffectiveness, the Secure Border Initiative Network was discontinued in 2011. As of February 2012, the CBP had completed 352 miles of pedestrian fencing and 299 miles of vehicle fencing.

## Visa Waiver Program

As of 2013, citizens or nationals of 37 countries participated in the Visa Waiver Program (VWP) overseen by the U.S. State Department. The program allows individuals from the authorized countries to enter the United States on a passport issued by their country of citizenship, without the need for any additional visa. Representatives of the foreign press, radio, film, or other information media cannot use the visa waiver when traveling for professional pursuits.

The Enhanced Border Security and Visa Entry Reform Act of 2002, as amended, sought to address security threats under the VWP program. Congress mandated that machine-readable, biometric passports be required for all VWP travelers, and that children no longer be able to travel on their parents' passports. This change required VWP countries to certify that they had programs in place to issue their citizens machine-readable passports that incorporated biometric identifiers and complied with standards established by the International Civil Aviation Organization.

The new passports are identified by an international e-passport logo on the cover and contain a secure contactless chip with the passport holder's biographic information and a biometric identifier. Biometric data are measurable physical characteristics or personal behavioral traits that are used to recognize the identity or verify the claimed identity of an enrollee. Among the features that can be measured are the face, fingerprints, hand geometry, handwriting, irises, retinas, and voice. The size of the passport and photograph and the arrangement of the data fields have to be exact to be read by an optical character reader.

## Tracking Security Risks

The National Security Entry-Exit Registration System was launched in 2003 to track nonimmigrant visitors coming from designated countries and others who meet a combination of intelligence-based criteria that identify them as potential security risks. State Department offices in foreign countries identify such people when issuing visas. These individuals are required to register on arrival at a port of entry, to participate in an interview with USCIS before being allowed into the country, and to report any change of address, employment, or educational institution while in the country. They are also required to register on departure and are restricted to using certain designated ports of entry/departure. This system focuses on only the preidentified security risk visitors.

## BORDERS ON THE WATER

The U.S. Coast Guard (USCG) is responsible for preventing unauthorized people from entering the United States by water. The USCG reports in "USCG Migrant Interdictions" (March 2013, http://www.uscg.mil/hq/cg5/cg531/AMIO/FlowStats/currentstats.asp) that it intercepted 2,955 illegal entry attempts in FY 2012. (See Table 5.9.) Most noncitizens attempting to enter the country illegally by water came from Central America and the Caribbean, particularly Cuba (1,275), Haiti (977), and the Dominican Republic (456), which together accounted for 91.6% of all interdictions in that year.

Before FY 2009 the numbers of migrants from Cuba who annually sought to enter the United States by water had been much higher. (See Table 5.9.) In 1994 the United States made an informal agreement with Cuba. This U.S.-Cuba Immigration Accord (http://www.state.gov/www/regions/wha/cuba/fs_000828_migration_accord.html) focused on Cuban migrants seeking to enter the United States. In a related agreement (informally called "wet-foot, dry-foot"), Cuban migrants intercepted at sea by the USCG would be returned to Cuba. Migrants who presented a "well-founded fear of persecution" would be sent to another country for asylum. Cuba agreed not to persecute returning migrants. Cuban migrants who made it to U.S. soil would be allowed to stay. After one year they would be eligible to apply for legal residence.

However, although some Cuban migrants continue to attempt entry into the United States, the promise of economic reforms under President Raul Castro (1931–), who took over responsibilities to lead the country in 2008, seems to have stemmed the flow of refugees in FYs 2009 and 2010. After 2,868 Cubans were intercepted in FY 2007, the numbers dropped to 2,216 in FY 2008,

TABLE 5.9

**U.S. Coast Guard alien interdictions, by country of origin, fiscal years 2000–12**

| Fiscal year | Haiti | Dominican Republic | People's Republic of China | Cuba | Mexico | Ecuador | Other | Total |
|---|---|---|---|---|---|---|---|---|
| 2012 | 977 | 456 | 23 | 1,275 | 79 | 7 | 138 | 2,955 |
| 2011 | 1,137 | 222 | 11 | 985 | 68 | 1 | 50 | 2,474 |
| 2010 | 1,377 | 140 | 0 | 422 | 61 | 0 | 88 | 2,088 |
| 2009 | 1,782 | 727 | 35 | 799 | 77 | 6 | 41 | 3,467 |
| 2008 | 1,583 | 688 | 1 | 2,216 | 47 | 220 | 65 | 4,825 |
| 2007 | 1,610 | 1,469 | 73 | 2,868 | 26 | 125 | 167 | 6,338 |
| 2006 | 1,198 | 3,011 | 31 | 2,810 | 52 | 693 | 91 | 7,886 |
| 2005 | 1,850 | 3,612 | 32 | 2,712 | 55 | 1,149 | 45 | 9,455 |
| 2004 | 3,229 | 5,014 | 68 | 1,225 | 86 | 1,189 | 88 | 10,899 |
| 2003 | 2,013 | 1,748 | 15 | 1,555 | 0 | 703 | 34 | 6,068 |
| 2002 | 1,486 | 177 | 80 | 666 | 32 | 1,608 | 55 | 4,104 |
| 2001 | 1,391 | 659 | 53 | 777 | 17 | 1,020 | 31 | 3,948 |
| 2000 | 1,113 | 499 | 261 | 1,000 | 49 | 1,244 | 44 | 4,210 |

SOURCE: Adapted from "U.S. Coast Guard Migrant Interdictions," in *Alien Migrant Interdiction*, U.S. Coast Guard, March 2013, http://www.uscg.mil/hq/cg5/cg531/AMIO/FlowStats/currentstats.asp (accessed March 8, 2013)

799 in FY 2009, and 422 in FY 2010, before rising again in FYs 2011 and 2012. (See Table 5.9.) The lack of economic opportunity in the United States resulting from the Great Recession perhaps played a role in the decreased numbers of Cuban migrants, as well.

## THE NORTHERN BORDER

According to the International Boundary Commission (http://www.internationalboundarycommission.org/boundary.html), the U.S.-Canadian border is the longest undefended border in the world. Unlike the U.S.-Mexican border that is actively patrolled by CBP agents to prevent illegal immigration and drug trafficking, most of the U.S.-Canadian border is open. It crosses through mountainous terrain and heavily forested areas and 13 U.S. states. (See Table 5.10.) Significant portions cross remote prairie farmland through Alaska, the Great Lakes, the St. Lawrence River, and forests and mountains in the American and Canadian Rockies. The border also runs through the middle of the Akwesasne Nation and even divides some communities in Vermont and Quebec.

Despite its seemingly low-level threat to U.S. security—especially when compared with the U.S.-Mexican border—the U.S.-Canadian border attracted attention at the start of the 21st century and beyond with some incidents of concern. In late 1999 Ahmed Ressam (1967–), an al-Qaeda terrorist who became known as the Millennium Bomber, was captured during his entry into the United States on a Canadian ferry near Seattle, Washington, with explosives he planned to use to bomb Los Angeles International Airport on New Year's Eve of that year. In 2006 U.S. and Canadian authorities discovered a human trafficking ring that was smuggling illegal immigrants into the United States through Canada. Incidents such as these led to calls for increased security at the U.S.-Canadian border, such as those outlined in the report "Enhanced DHS Oversight and Assessment of Inter-

TABLE 5.10

**Length of U.S.-Canada land and water boundaries by state**

[In descending order in miles]

| State | Boundary length |
|---|---|
| Alaska | 1,538 |
| Michigan | 721 |
| Maine | 611 |
| Minnesota | 547 |
| Montana | 545 |
| New York | 445 |
| Washington | 427 |
| North Dakota | 310 |
| Ohio | 146 |
| Vermont | 90 |
| New Hampshire | 58 |
| Idaho | 45 |
| Pennsylvania | 42 |
| **Total** | **5,525** |

SOURCE: Janice Cheryl Beaver, "Table 1. Length of U.S.-Canada Land and Water Boundary by State," in *U.S. International Borders: Brief Facts*, Congressional Research Service, November 9, 2006, http://www.fas.org/sgp/crs/misc/RS21729.pdf (accessed March 8, 2013)

agency Coordination Is Needed for the Northern Border" (December 2010, http://www.gao.gov/highlights/d1197high.pdf), issued by the Government Accountability Office (GAO). The GAO notes that only 32 miles (51.5 km) of the nearly 4,000-mile (6,400-km) border "had reached an acceptable level of security" in FY 2010.

In June 2012 Secretary of Homeland Security Napolitano announced the official U.S. Northern Border Strategy, the primary goals of which are the deterrence and prevention of terrorism and other crimes such as smuggling, trafficking, and illegal immigration; the protection and encouragement of those involved in legal trade, travel, and immigration; and the provision of resources to communities affected by terrorist attacks and other catastrophic events.

## ILLEGAL IMMIGRATION AND CRIME

In *Information on Certain Illegal Aliens Arrested in the United States* (April 2005, http://www.gao.gov/new.items/d05646r.pdf), the GAO studied 55,322 unauthorized immigrants who had been incarcerated in federal and state prison or local jail during FY 2003. Among the findings presented are the number of arrests, the types of crimes committed, and the location of the crimes. The GAO indicates that "[the imprisoned illegal immigrants] were arrested at least a total of 459,614 times, averaging about 8 offenses per individual. Ninety-seven percent had more than 1 arrest. About 38 percent had between 2 and 5 arrests, 32 percent had between 6 and 10 arrests, and 26 percent had over 11 arrests. Eighty-one percent of all arrests occurred after 1990." The GAO also notes that not all arrests were prosecuted; of those that were prosecuted, not all led to a conviction.

The GAO further reports that the total number of alleged criminal offenses covered in the arrests numbered 691,890. Drugs (24%) topped the list of offenses, followed by immigration violations (21%), traffic violations (8%), assault (7%), obstruction of justice (7%), burglary (6%), larceny/theft (5%), and fraud, forgery, and counterfeiting (4%). Weapons violations and motor vehicle theft registered 3% apiece, and robbery, sex offenses, and stolen property numbered 2% each. Murder was cited in only 1% of the offenses. The state with the most arrests of illegal immigrants was California (58%), followed by Texas (14%) and Arizona (8%).

The GAO, however, does not compare the arrest rates of foreign-born people to those of native-born people. In spite of having the most arrests of illegal immigrants, California—a state with a large immigrant population—experiences rates indicating that immigrants do not pose a larger crime threat than native-born citizens. Kristen F. Butcher, Anne Morrison Piehl, and Jay Liao of the Public Policy Institute of California state in "Crime, Corrections, and California: What Does Immigration Have to Do with It?" (*California Counts: Population Trends and Profiles*, vol. 9, no. 3, February 2008) that "the foreign-born, who make up about 35 percent of the adult population in California, constitute only about 17 percent of the adult prison population. Thus, immigrants are underrepresented in California prisons compared to their representation in the overall population. In fact, U.S.-born adult men are incarcerated at a rate over two-and-a-half times greater than that of foreign-born men." In addition, the incarceration rate for foreign-born individuals for violent crimes was 161 per 100,000 in 2005, whereas the incarceration rate for native-born individuals for violent crimes was much higher, at 259 per 100,000.

Butcher, Piehl, and Liao acknowledge, however, that their "data do not reveal the precise [legal or illegal] immigration status of the foreign-born." Nonetheless, because data exist for naturalized citizens and noncitizens—and illegal immigrants are noncitizens—the researchers are able "to provide some insight into whether institutionalization rates for illegal immigrants are likely to be higher than they are for the foreign-born overall." Butcher, Piehl, and Liao conclude that "institutionalization rates for noncitizens are dramatically lower than for the U.S.-born, as were the rates for the foreign-born overall. Indeed, U.S.-born institutionalization rates are almost 10 times higher."

Additionally, statistics released by ICE suggest that the DHS has been increasingly successful at apprehending those unauthorized immigrants who are involved in criminal behaviors. As Figure 5.6 shows, cooperation between immigration and criminal-justice agencies has driven a large share of the number of noncitizens removed from the U.S. annually.

# CHAPTER 6

# THE COSTS AND BENEFITS OF IMMIGRATION

The arrival of tens of millions of immigrants in the years since 1970 has transformed the United States profoundly. The cultural aspects of that change—the mixing of traditions, cuisines, languages, religions, modes of expression, and family norms—are evident on the streets, in the workplaces, in the schools, and in the homes of many American cities and small towns. The impact of immigrants on the national economy is less visible but a matter of enormous importance. Nevertheless, for a number of reasons, consensus as to the costs and benefits of immigration has remained elusive.

Some reasons for the failure to reach a consensus on the costs and benefits of immigration to the economy relate to the nature of economic study. A detailed understanding of the issue requires specialized economic knowledge, but many of the most vocal commentators on immigration are not economists. Furthermore, the size and complexity of immigrants' impact on the economy make calculations difficult even for specialists, so the results of most studies are often less conclusive than the political feelings surrounding the debate. The political stances on the issue are often driven by beliefs and values that are not easily reducible to data, and these beliefs and values themselves often affect what data are collected and publicized because the officials in charge of policy and data-gathering are themselves not necessarily neutral on the issues.

Accordingly, some policy analysts and public figures contend that immigrants take jobs from workers born in the United States and are a drain on public coffers due to a disproportionate use of welfare and other services. Other analysts and politicians argue that immigrants not only contribute considerable sums of money to public reserves but that they are also a crucial driver of economic activity, helping to offset a low native-born birthrate and an aging population so that they bring net increases in revenue to public programs. Contrary to longstanding assumptions regarding competition for jobs between unauthorized immigrants and the native born, an increasing number of economic studies have begun to indicate that the impact of immigrants on the labor market is a net positive not only for the economy as a whole but for native-born workers.

## IMMIGRANTS AND SOCIAL SERVICES

No simple answer exists to the question of how much immigration—both legal and illegal—costs federal, state, and local governments. Some policy analysts on the conservative side of the political spectrum, including those at the Heritage Foundation and the Center for Immigration Studies (CIS), have consistently argued that immigrants, regardless of their legal status, cost taxpayers more in government services than they contribute. Meanwhile, liberal analysts, including those at the Center for American Progress (CAP), argue that the Heritage and CIS data are flawed and that they are designed to reach predetermined conclusions rooted more in cultural anxiety than economic reality.

Among the most prominent studies arguing that immigrants contribute less money to government coffers than they enjoy in the form of services is the 2007 Heritage Foundation paper *The Fiscal Cost of Low-Skill Immigrants to the U.S. Taxpayer* (May 2007, http://www.heritage.org/Research/Reports/2007/05/The-Fiscal-Cost-of-Low-Skill-Immigrants-to-the-US-Taxpayer), written by Robert Rector and Christine Kim. Rector and Kim argue that low-skilled immigrant households (defined as households headed by immigrants without high school diplomas) cost U.S. taxpayers $89.1 billion per year. The researchers estimate that there were 4.5 million low-skilled immigrant households in the United States in 2004 and that the 15.9 million people living in these households represented about 5% of the U.S. population.

Rector and Kim maintain that each low-skilled immigrant household received $10,428 in means-tested benefits (welfare) and $4,891 in direct benefits (mainly Social Security and Medicare) in fiscal year (FY) 2004.

FIGURE 6.1

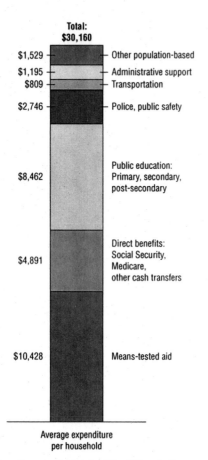

Government expenditures for immediate benefits and services for households headed by immigrants without a high school diploma, fiscal year 2004

Total:
$30,160

$1,529 — Other population-based
$1,195 — Administrative support
$809 — Transportation

$2,746 — Police, public safety

$8,462 — Public education: Primary, secondary, post-secondary

$4,891 — Direct benefits: Social Security, Medicare, other cash transfers

$10,428 — Means-tested aid

Average expenditure per household

SOURCE: Robert Rector and Christine Kim, "Chart 2. Government Expenditures for Immediate Benefits and Services for Households Headed by Immigrants without a High School Diploma," in *The Fiscal Cost of Low-Skill Immigrants to the U.S. Taxpayer*, The Heritage Foundation, 2007, http://www.heritage.org/Research/Reports/2007/05/The-Fiscal-Cost-of-Low-Skill-Immigrants-to-the-US-Taxpayer (accessed March 8, 2013)

FIGURE 6.2

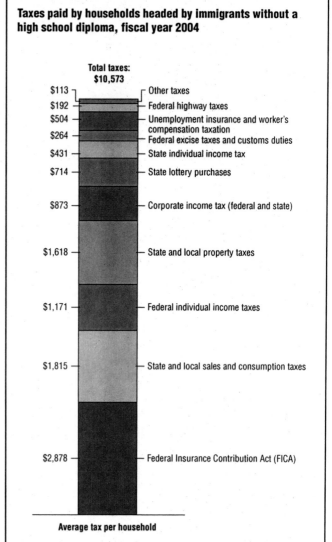

Taxes paid by households headed by immigrants without a high school diploma, fiscal year 2004

Total taxes:
$10,573

$113 — Other taxes
$192 — Federal highway taxes
$504 — Unemployment insurance and worker's compensation taxation
$264 — Federal excise taxes and customs duties
$431 — State individual income tax
$714 — State lottery purchases

$873 — Corporate income tax (federal and state)

$1,618 — State and local property taxes

$1,171 — Federal individual income taxes

$1,815 — State and local sales and consumption taxes

$2,878 — Federal Insurance Contribution Act (FICA)

Average tax per household

SOURCE: Robert Rector and Christine Kim, "Chart 3. Taxes Paid by Households Headed by Immigrants without a High School Diploma," in *The Fiscal Cost of Low-Skill Immigrants to the U.S. Taxpayer*, The Heritage Foundation, 2007, http://www.heritage.org/Research/Reports/2007/05/The-Fiscal-Cost-of-Low-Skill-Immigrants-to-the-US-Taxpayer (accessed March 8, 2013)

(See Figure 6.1.) These benefits plus the costs of education and population-based services totaled $30,160 per household. Figure 6.2 details the authors' calculations of the taxes paid by these low-skilled immigrant households. Federal, state, and local taxes paid totaled $10,573 per household in FY 2004. As a result, each low-skilled immigrant household passed on $19,588 in annual costs to federal, state, and local governments. (See Figure 6.3.)

Rector and Kim argue, "The fiscal cost of low-skill immigrants will be increased in the future by government policies that increase: the number of low-skill immigrants, the immigrants' length of stay in the United States, or the access of low-skill immigrants to government benefits. Conversely, fiscal costs will be reduced by policies that decrease these variables."

Steven A. Camarota of the CIS largely supports this view. In the report *Immigrants in the United States, 2010: A Profile of America's Foreign-Born Population* (August 2012, http://www.cis.org/sites/cis.org/files/articles/2012/immigrants-in-the-united-states-2012.pdf), Camarota maintains that because many immigrants are lacking in education, the primary predictor of success in the United States, their financial status lags behind that of the native-born population and exerts a drag on the government.

According to Camarota, analysts once believed immigrants spent 12 to 14 years working before they closed the economic gap with U.S. natives, but current research indicates that even after 20 years in the United States many immigrants still lag behind native-born Americans in important economic indicators. Figure 6.4 shows that the

FIGURE 6.3

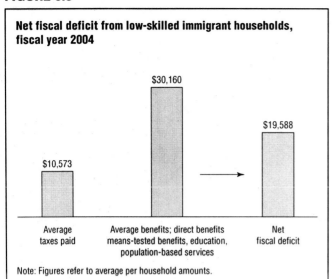

**Net fiscal deficit from low-skilled immigrant households, fiscal year 2004**

Note: Figures refer to average per household amounts.

SOURCE: Robert Rector and Christine Kim, "Chart 5. Dropout Households Receive More Than Three Dollars in Benefits for Every Dollar Paid in Taxes," in *The Fiscal Cost of Low-Skill Immigrants to the U.S. Taxpayer*, The Heritage Foundation, 2007, http://www.heritage.org/Research/Reports/2007/05/The-Fiscal-Cost-of-Low-Skill-Immigrants-to-the-US-Taxpayer (accessed March 8, 2013)

longer immigrants remain in the United States, the less likely they are to live near or below the poverty line, be among the lowest-earning American workers, and use welfare. The figure also shows the dramatic increase in home ownership rates between immigrants who have been in the United States for less than five years and immigrants who have been in the United States for 20 or more years. However, even immigrants who have been in the United States for 20 years lag significantly behind natives in all of the above categories.

Table 6.1 shows the percentages of immigrants and their U.S.-born children living in or near poverty in 2011, according to their country of origin. Although immigrants in general were more likely to live in or near poverty than those born in the United States, immigrants from Mexico and Central America were particularly likely to be poor, according to Camarota. Almost half (47.6%) of all immigrants and their U.S.-born children lived in or near poverty, compared with 31.1% of the native-born population. Immigrants from countries such as India (15.5%), the Philippines (20.1%), the United Kingdom (21.4%), Germany (22.4%), Japan (25%), and Poland (30.5%) were less likely to be poor than native-born Americans (31.1%), whereas immigrants from Mexico (67.8%), Guatemala (66.9%), and Honduras (66.3%) were more than twice as likely to be poor as natives.

**FIGURE 6.4**

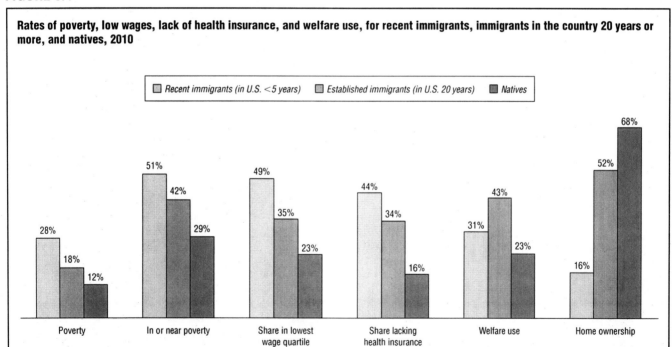

**Rates of poverty, low wages, lack of health insurance, and welfare use, for recent immigrants, immigrants in the country 20 years or more, and natives, 2010**

Data from: Except for home ownership, all figures are from a Center for Immigration Studies analysis of the March 2011 Current Population Survey public-use file. Home ownership is based on Center for Immigration Studies analysis of the 2010 American Community Survey public-use file. Poverty and health insurance figures are for adults only. Quartile figures are for average weekly wages in 2010 for adults who indicated that they were employed full time and year-round. Welfare use and home ownership are based on the nativity of the household head. Welfare programs include food stamps, WIC (Women, Infants, and Children), school lunches, TANF (Temporary Assistance for Needy Families), SSI (Social Security Income), housing assistance, and Medicaid.

SOURCE: Steven A. Camarota, "Figure 5. Immigrants make significant progress the longer they reside in the U.S., but even established immigrants still lag well behind natives," in *Immigrants in the United States: A Profile of America's Foreign-Born Population*, Center for Immigration Studies, August 2012, http://www.cis.org/articles/2012/immigrants-in-the-united-states-2012.pdf (accessed March 8, 2013)

**TABLE 6.1**

**Rates of poverty and near poverty by immigrants and their U.S.-born children, by country of birth, 2010**

| Country | Poverty | | In or near poverty[a] | |
| --- | --- | --- | --- | --- |
| | Immigrants | Immigrants and their U.S.-born children[b] | Immigrants | Immigrants and their U.S.-born children[b] |
| Mexico | 30.1% | 34.8% | 62.9% | 67.8% |
| Honduras | 32.7% | 34.0% | 66.4% | 66.3% |
| Guatemala | 28.5% | 31.4% | 63.2% | 66.9% |
| Dominican Republic | 21.2% | 25.7% | 49.0% | 54.8% |
| Haiti | 23.7% | 25.2% | 49.5% | 49.5% |
| Cuba | 22.9% | 24.3% | 48.7% | 49.4% |
| Ecuador | 19.2% | 22.6% | 43.0% | 46.7% |
| El Salvador | 20.3% | 22.0% | 53.2% | 56.7% |
| Laos | 13.8% | 18.0% | 32.7% | 44.0% |
| Vietnam | 17.4% | 17.6% | 37.6% | 38.3% |
| Colombia | 14.9% | 16.0% | 31.0% | 33.6% |
| Jamaica | 12.2% | 16.0% | 33.5% | 37.1% |
| Iran | 16.2% | 15.2% | 32.7% | 32.8% |
| USSR/Russia | 12.5% | 12.9% | 12.8% | 30.7% |
| China | 14.0% | 13.6% | 33.4% | 30.8% |
| Peru | 10.1% | 13.6% | 32.4% | 36.4% |
| Pakistan | 11.0% | 11.9% | 30.6% | 32.9% |
| Korea | 9.7% | 11.1% | 23.8% | 24.8% |
| Japan | 12.1% | 10.1% | 26.2% | 25.0% |
| Canada | 9.1% | 8.0% | 19.4% | 18.1% |
| Poland | 7.2% | 7.5% | 32.1% | 30.5% |
| United Kingdom | 5.6% | 7.2% | 16.9% | 21.4% |
| Germany | 6.7% | 6.8% | 23.7% | 22.4% |
| India | 6.7% | 6.2% | 15.4% | 15.5% |
| Philippines | 5.3% | 5.5% | 19.4% | 20.1% |
| Middle East | 27.6% | 28.2% | 45.1% | 47.9% |
| Central America (Excludes Mexico) | 25.2% | 26.8% | 56.8% | 59.1% |
| Sub-Saharan Africa | 22.9% | 24.6% | 42.9% | 46.2% |
| Caribbean | 19.4% | 22.0% | 43.4% | 46.2% |
| South America | 14.5% | 16.0% | 34.6% | 37.1% |
| East Asia | 12.4% | 12.8% | 30.0% | 30.6% |
| Europe | 9.5% | 10.1% | 27.6% | 27.8% |
| South Asia | 8.9% | 8.9% | 20.2% | 21.1% |
| **All immigrants** | **19.9%** | **23.0%** | **43.6%** | **47.6%** |
| Hispanic | 26.9% | 31.2% | 57.2% | 62.2% |
| Black | 20.5% | 23.3% | 41.7% | 45.1% |
| Asian | 11.8% | 12.0% | 27.9% | 28.6% |
| White | 13.1% | 14.0% | 31.1% | 32.1% |

| | Poverty | In or near poverty |
| --- | --- | --- |
| **All natives[c]** | **13.5%** | **31.1%** |
| Hispanic | 21.5% | 46.4% |
| Black | 27.8% | 51.9% |
| Asian | 11.8% | 25.2% |
| White | 9.7% | 25.2% |
| Children of immigrants (<18) | 32.1% | 59.2% |
| Children of natives (<18) | 19.2% | 39.3% |
| All persons | 15.1% | 33.9% |

Data from: Center for Immigration Studies analysis of the March 2011 Current Population Survey (CPS) public-use file. Figures for blacks, Asians, and whites are for those who chose only one race. Hispanics can be of any race and are excluded from other categories. Official government poverty statistics do not include unrelated individuals under age 15 (mostly foster children) and they are therefore not included in this table.
[a]Near-poverty is defined as less than 200 percent of the poverty threshold.
[b]Includes U.S.-born children under age 18 of immigrant fathers.
[c]Excludes U.S.-born children under age 18 of immigrant fathers.

SOURCE: Steven A. Camarota, "Table 10. Poverty and Near Poverty," in *Immigrants in the United States: A Profile of America's Foreign-Born Population*, Center for Immigration Studies, August 2012, http://www.cis.org/articles/2012/immigrants-in-the-united-states-2012.pdf (accessed March 8, 2013)

In "Immigrants Are Makers, Not Takers" (February 8, 2013, http://www.americanprogress.org/issues/immigration/news/2013/02/08/52377/immigrants-are-makers-not-takers/), Marshall Fitz, Philip E. Wolgin, and Patrick Oakford of the CAP maintain, by contrast, that once appropriate statistical controls have been applied to the Census data used by Heritage and the CIS, immigrants are not significantly more likely than natives to exert a burden on government. Figure 6.5, for example, shows that at 200% of poverty, no substantial difference exists between the welfare participation rates of immigrants and those born in the United States; and it further shows that there is no substantial disparity between immigrants as a whole and Hispanic immigrants. Although it is true that

FIGURE 6.5

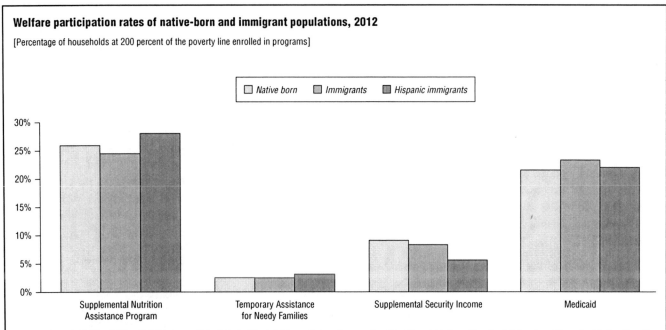

**Welfare participation rates of native-born and immigrant populations, 2012**

[Percentage of households at 200 percent of the poverty line enrolled in programs]

SOURCE: Marshall Fitz, Philip E. Wolgin, and Patrick Oakford, "Figure 2. Immigrants Are Not More Likely to Use Social Services Than the Native Born," in *Immigrants Are Makers, Not Takers*, Center for American Progress, February 8, 2013, http://www.americanprogress.org/issues/immigration/news/2013/02/08/52377/immigrants-are-makers-not-takers/ (accessed March 11, 2013). This material was created by the Center for American Progress (www.americanprogress.org).

immigrants, especially those from Mexico and Central America, are disproportionately likely to live in poverty, it is also true that the immigrant population has many obstacles to overcome on the way to prosperity, whereas many in the native-born population have fewer such obstacles. Comparing the welfare-participation rates without controlling for income levels, then, "is akin to comparing the welfare-participation rates of a highly developed country to that of an underdeveloped country." Providing data based on this sort of comparison, in the view of the CAP and others, inappropriately compares immigrants in poverty to all other Americans, rather than comparing immigrants in poverty to natives in poverty and immigrants with higher incomes to natives with higher incomes.

Similarly, although the Heritage Foundation authors maintain that low-skilled immigrants receive far more in Social Security benefits than they pay into the system, the CAP authors argue that this contention is based on a misleading use of data, whereby the amount paid into the system by immigrants is slighted and the amount of benefits received is overestimated. Fitz, Wolgin, and Oakford note that the average immigrant retiree receives a smaller annual Social Security benefit than the average native. (See Figure 6.6.) As of 2012, according to the CAP authors, naturalized immigrants received 7% less in benefits than natives, and noncitizen immigrants received 16% less than natives.

Paul N. Van de Water of the Center on Budget and Policy Priorities indicates in "Immigration and Social Security" (November 20, 2008, http://www.cbpp.org/11-20-08socsec.pdf) that, far from burdening U.S. safety net programs, increases in immigration generally improve the finances of the Social Security and Medicare trust funds. The immigrant workforce is younger than the native

**FIGURE 6.6**

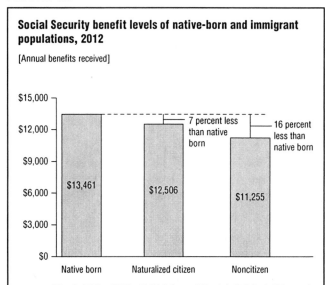

**Social Security benefit levels of native-born and immigrant populations, 2012**

[Annual benefits received]

SOURCE: Marshall Fitz, Philip E. Wolgin, and Patrick Oakford, "Figure 1. Immigrants Receive Less in Social Security Benefits Than the Native Born," in *Immigrants Are Makers, Not Takers*, Center for American Progress, February 8, 2013, http://www.americanprogress.org/issues/immigration/news/2013/02/08/52377/immigrants-are-makers-not-takers/ (accessed March 11, 2013). This material was created by the Center for American Progress (www.americanprogress.org).

workforce, so as a group, immigrants tend to pay into the system for more years (as workers) before they collect benefits. According to Van de Water, the trustees of the Social Security and Medicare trust funds estimate that an increase in net immigration of 300,000 people per year would eliminate about one-tenth of Social Security's 75-year deficit.

Van de Water notes that even undocumented workers are good for Social Security. These workers' earnings are unlikely to be reported for tax purposes and therefore rarely result in future Social Security benefit payments (since payments into the system, as well as benefits paid out of the system, are based on income tax payments). As a result, Van de Water explains, "undocumented immigrants improved Social Security's cash flow by an estimated $12 billion in 2007."

Although much of the debate surrounding the costs of immigration centers on those who have entered the United States illegally, almost all government benefits at the federal level are unavailable to unauthorized immigrants. State and local governments, however, are required to provide certain services without regard to immigration status. In *The Impact of Unauthorized Immigrants on the Budgets of State and Local Governments* (December 2007, http://www .cbo.gov/tpdocs/87xx/doc8711/12-6-Immigration.pdf) the Congressional Budget Office (CBO) explains that the bulk of state and local spending on immigrants is related to education, health care, and law enforcement. After reviewing 29 reports that attempted to determine how the budgets of state and local governments are affected by unauthorized immigrants, the CBO concludes:

- State and local governments have limited options for "avoiding or minimizing" the cost of providing services to unauthorized immigrants.

- The amount that is spent on unauthorized immigrants is minimal when compared with the total cost of providing such services to all residents.

- Tax revenues generated by unauthorized immigrants are not sufficient to offset the cost of services provided.

- Federal aid to state and local governments does not fully offset the cost of these services to unauthorized immigrants.

## ENFORCEMENT COSTS
### At the Federal Level

As discussed in Chapter 5, immigration policy at the federal level has for many years focused almost exclusively on enforcement. Those federal agencies charged with securing the border and apprehending unauthorized immigrants inside the United States grew dramatically during the 1990s and the following decade, with a particular acceleration of funding levels occurring in the years after the terrorist attacks of

September 11, 2001 (9/11). Enforcement is generally believed to have done comparatively little to slow the numbers of unauthorized immigrants arriving from Mexico, and indeed, increases in funding corresponded with rapid increases in the population of unauthorized immigrants. Flows of unauthorized immigrants began to slow dramatically as a result of the Great Recession that began in 2007 and subsided in 2009, however, which reduced prospects for employment and thus decreased the allure of illegal entry. As Figure 5.1 in Chapter 5 shows, the unauthorized immigrant population grew by approximately 3.6 million between 2000 and 2007, before it declined and then stabilized during and after the Great Recession. Although the population of unauthorized immigrants had ceased to grow by 2008, funding levels for immigration enforcement continued to increase rapidly.

As Figure 6.7 shows, a large proportion of the FY 2013 budget of the Department of Homeland Security (DHS) was devoted specifically to agencies dealing with immigration enforcement. The largest agency within DHS by budget allocation was U.S. Customs and Border Protection (CBP), which received 21% of the total $59 billion department budget. U.S. Immigration and Customs Enforcement (ICE), the other primary federal immigration enforcement agency, was allotted 10% of the total DHS budget. U.S. Citizenship and Immigration Services (USCIS), the agency through which all legal immigration occurs, was allotted 5% of the DHS budget.

Figure 6.8 shows the growth in the CBP and ICE budgets in the years 2003 to 2009. After 2003, the year that the DHS was established with a budget of $6 billion, CBP's budget grew steadily, reaching $7.8 billion by 2006 and almost doubling by 2009, when the agency was allotted a budget of $11.3 billion. Much of this growth came in the form of increased numbers of officers in the U.S. Border Patrol. As Figure 6.9 shows, the number of agents patrolling the southwest border with Mexico—the entry point for the overwhelming majority of unauthorized immigrants—grew from 9,840 in 2003 to 17,415 in 2009. The ICE budget almost doubled between 2003 and 2009, growing from $3.26 billion to $5.93 billion. (See Figure 6.8.) The cost per apprehension of each unauthorized immigrant grew accordingly, from $1,626 in 2003 to $3,102 in 2008. (See Figure 6.10.)

### At the State and Local Levels

In a report commissioned by the U.S.-Mexico Border Counties Coalition, *Undocumented Immigrants in U.S.-Mexico Border Counties: The Costs of Law Enforcement and Criminal Justice Services* (September 2007, http:// www.bordercounties.org/vertical/sites/%7BB4A0F1FF-7823-4C95-8D7A-F5E400063C73%7D/uploads/%7B6 90801CA-CEE6-413C-AC8B-A00DA765D96E%7D .PDF), Tanis J. Salant of the University of Arizona notes that in cases involving illegal immigration, a disproportionate

FIGURE 6.7

**Department of Homeland Security budget by organization, fiscal year 2013**

[$59,032,346,000]

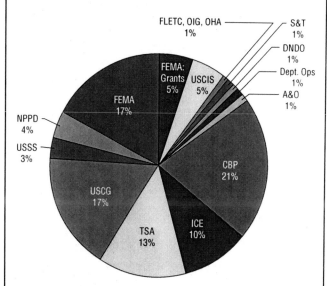

Notes: Departmental Operations is comprised of the Office of the Secretary & Executive Management, DHS Headquarters Consolidation, the Office of the Undersecretary for Management, the Office of the Chief Financial Officer, and the Office of the Chief Information Officer.

A&O = Analysis and Operations.
CBP = U.S. Customs & Border Protection.
Dept. Ops = Departmental Operations.
DHS = Department of Homeland Security.
DNDO = Domestic Nuclear Detection Office.
FEMA = Federal Emergency Management Agency.
FLETC = Federal Law Enforcement Training Center.
ICE = U.S. Immigration & Customs Enforcement.
NPPD = National Protection and Programs Directorate.
OHA = Office of Health Affairs.
OIG = Office of the Inspector General.
S&T = Science & Technology Directorate.
TSA = Transportation Security Administration.
USCG = U.S. Coast Guard.
USCIS = U.S. Citizenship and Immigration Services.
USSS = U.S. Secret Service.

SOURCE: "FY 2013 Percent of Total Budget Authority by Organization," in *FY 2013 Budget in Brief*, U.S. Department of Homeland Security. 2012, http://www.dhs.gov/xlibrary/assets/mgmt/dhs-budget-in-brief-fy2013.pdf (accessed March 11, 2013)

share of the law enforcement burden falls on the southwest border counties. Between 1999 and 2006, according to Salant, "the 24 counties along the U.S.-Mexico border spent a cumulative $1.23 billion on services to process criminal undocumented immigrants through the law enforcement and criminal justice system.... These are staggering costs considering the rural nature and poverty level of most of these border counties." Outside of border counties, as well, the burden for incarcerating and prosecuting unauthorized immigrants falls heavily on local and state governments.

Under the State Criminal Alien Assistance Program (SCAAP) of the U.S. Department of Justice, states and localities are partially reimbursed for law enforcement costs related to unauthorized immigrants. The program was created

in 1995, with the intent of reimbursing state prisons and county jails that detained unauthorized immigrants who had committed a felony or two misdemeanors. As the National Conference of State Legislatures (NCSL) notes in "The State Criminal Alien Assistance Program (SCAAP)" (April 2013, http://www.ncsl.org/issues-research/immig/state-criminal-alien-assistance-program.aspx), funding for SCAAP ranged from $130 million in 1995 to $565 million in 2002, before settling at a level of approximately $400 million between 2006 and 2009. SCAAP funding fell to $330 million in 2010, and continued to fall during FYs 2011 through 2013, from $273 million in 2011 to $238 million in 2013.

In 2011, according to the NCSL, the reimbursement rate under the SCAAP program was 23% of total costs submitted by state and local authorities. State and local authorities therefore claimed to have spent nearly $12 billion to house unauthorized immigrants in jails and prisons in 2011. In addition to the 77% of that figure that they paid out of their own coffers, they also likely incurred numerous other expenses related to illegal immigration, such as those associated with the courts, the juvenile justice system, and the probation system. There were no federal reimbursement programs accounting for such costs.

## EDUCATION COSTS

In *Plyler v. Doe* (457 U.S. 202 [1982]), the U.S. Supreme Court overturned a Texas law allowing local school systems to deny public education to children who had entered the country illegally. In its 5–4 ruling, the court maintained that the Texas law violated the 14th Amendment and that public schools have an obligation to educate all children regardless of their immigration status. Because of this, and because extra resources are often necessary to educate children whose first language is not English, educational spending by state and local governments represents by far the largest outlay of funds needed to accommodate the large immigrant population in the United States.

However, no consensus exists as to the price tag for educating the children of immigrants across the United States. As the CBO notes in *Impact of Unauthorized Immigrants on the Budgets of State and Local Governments*, a number of factors make it difficult to estimate the aggregate level of state and local spending on immigrants and to compare spending in one state or locality with spending in another. Among these factors are inconsistent data sources across state and local jurisdictions, the wide variance in funding mechanisms and tax collections among different states and municipalities, and the disproportionate concentration of immigrants in certain states and cities, which makes statistical sampling difficult at the national level. Most studies, as the CBO reports, have focused on the effect of unauthorized immigrants and their children on state educational budgets.

## FIGURE 6.8

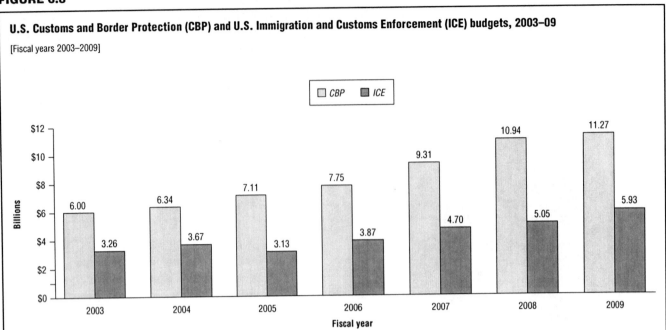

**U.S. Customs and Border Protection (CBP) and U.S. Immigration and Customs Enforcement (ICE) budgets, 2003–09**

[Fiscal years 2003–2009]

SOURCE: Raúl Hinojosa-Ojeda, "Figure 4. CBP and ICE Budgets, Fiscal Years 2003–2009," in *Raising the Floor for American Workers: The Economic Benefits of Comprehensive Immigration Reform*, Center for American Progress, January 2010, http://www.americanprogress.org/wp-content/uploads/2012/09/immigrationeconreport3.pdf (accessed March 11, 2013). This material was created by the Center for American Progress (www.americanprogress.org).

## FIGURE 6.9

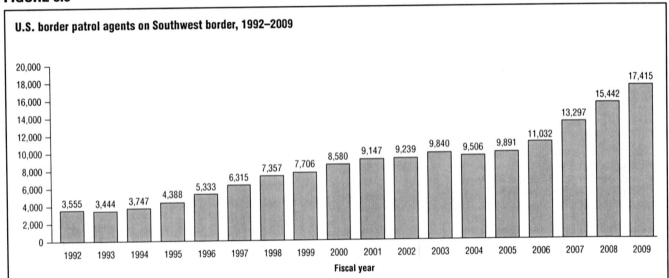

**U.S. border patrol agents on Southwest border, 1992–2009**

SOURCE: Raúl Hinojosa-Ojeda, "Figure 3. U.S. Border Patrol Agents Stationed along Southwest Border," *Raising the Floor for American Workers: The Economic Benefits of Comprehensive Immigration Reform*, Center for American Progress, January 2010, http://www.americanprogress.org/wp-content/uploads/2012/09/immigrationeconreport3.pdf (accessed April 15, 2013). This material was created by the Center for American Progress (www.americanprogress.org).

Among the state-level data cited by the CBO are studies focusing on education spending in Minnesota and New Mexico during the 2003–04 school year. In that year, state and local governments in Minnesota spent an estimated $79 million to $118 million on education for children who were unauthorized immigrants, as well as approximately $39 million on education for children with birthright citizenship whose parents were unauthorized. The combined amount spent to educate unauthorized immigrants and the children of unauthorized immigrants that year represented less than 3% of the $8 billion in state and local funds spent on public education. Minnesota, however, was experiencing rapid increases in its immigrant population at the time, which can create

**FIGURE 6.10**

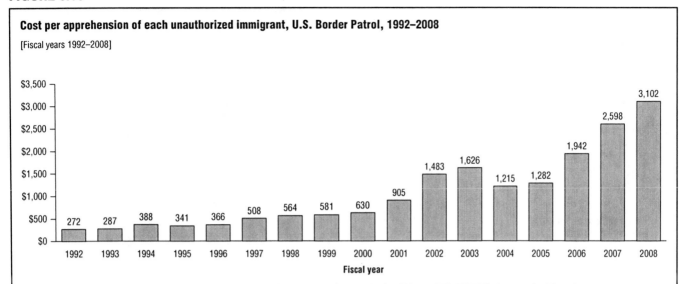

**Cost per apprehension of each unauthorized immigrant, U.S. Border Patrol, 1992–2008**

[Fiscal years 1992–2008]

SOURCE: Raúl Hinojosa-Ojeda, "Figure 2. Cost per Apprehension, U.S. Border Patrol, Fiscal Years 1992–2008," in *Raising the Floor for American Workers: The Economic Benefits of Comprehensive Immigration Reform*, Center for American Progress, January 2010, http://www.americanprogress.org/wp-content/uploads/2012/09/immigrationeconreport3.pdf (accessed March 11, 2013). This material was created by the Center for American Progress (www.americanprogress.org).

significant budgetary strain even when the overall spending amount concerned is comparatively small. Between 2000 and 2004, the state's total immigrant student population grew from approximately 9,000 to approximately 16,000. Of the 16,000 immigrant students, between 9,400 and 14,000 were believed to be unauthorized.

The New Mexico study painted a similar portrait of state-level educational spending. In 2003–04 New Mexico had approximately 9,200 unauthorized immigrant students, on whom state and local governments spent an estimated $67 million. This represented approximately 2% of the $3 billion in state and local funds spent on public education.

In addition to being required to educate children regardless of their immigration status, state school systems are required to make accommodations for students whose English-language proficiency is limited. As Table 6.2 shows, approximately 57 million of 285.8 million U.S. residents over the age of five years spoke a language other than English at home in 2009. Approximately 35.5 million (62%) of these individuals spoke Spanish; Chinese, spoken by 2.6 million people over the age of five years, was the second-most-common household language other than English.

Under the terms of the Elementary and Secondary Education Act of 1965, as amended numerous times in subsequent decades, school districts receive federal funds to create and maintain programs to meet the needs of children with limited English proficiency. The U.S. Department of Education provides grants to states according to the numbers of English learners (ELs) in their schools. "Supporting English Learners" (April 10, 2013, http://www2.ed.gov/about/over view/budget/budget14/crosscuttingissues/englishlearners.pdf) indicates that

the Department of Education requested $732 million to fund these grants in FY 2014. Other funding for ELs in public schools came from a variety of other Department of Education programs, such as the Race to the Top assessment program, which included specific considerations for ELs along with the broader testing mandates it imposed on schools to ensure educational quality. Because ELs were the fastest-growing major student population in the United States as of 2013, the Department of Education placed a high priority on addressing their educational needs. As Table 6.3 shows, approximately 4.7 million public-school students, or 9.7% of the total enrollment of just over 48 million, took part in EL programs during 2009–10. ELs constituted 14.3% of the student population in cities, 8.3% in the suburbs, 6.8% in towns, and 3.6% in rural areas.

## THE FISCAL BENEFITS OF IMMIGRATION

One of the most persistent beliefs about the effect of immigrants on the national economy is that they create an oversupply in the labor market, taking jobs that would otherwise go to native-born workers and depressing wages due to their willingness to work under trying conditions for low pay. Most economists understand the effect of immigrants on the U.S. economy to be far more complex, and increasingly, researchers have found evidence suggesting that immigrants create net positive effects on the economy as a whole and even on the wages of the native born.

### The Benefits of Specialization in the Workforce

In 2007 the Council of Economic Advisers to President George W. Bush (1946–) released "Immigration's Economic

## TABLE 6.2

**Languages spoken at home, 2009**

[The American Community Survey universe includes the household population and the population living in institutions, college dormitories, and other group quarters. Based on a sample and subject to sampling variability.]

| Language | Number |
|---|---|
| **Total population 5 years old and over** | **285,797,349** |
| Speak only English | 228,699,523 |
| Spanish or Spanish Creole | 35,468,501 |
| French (including Patois, Cajun) | 1,305,503 |
| French Creole | 659,053 |
| Italian | 753,992 |
| Portuguese or Portuguese Creole | 731,282 |
| German | 1,109,216 |
| Yiddish | 148,155 |
| Other West Germanic languages | 271,227 |
| Scandinavian languages | 126,337 |
| Greek | 325,747 |
| Russian | 881,723 |
| Polish | 593,598 |
| Serbo-Croatian | 269,333 |
| Other Slavic languages | 298,094 |
| Armenian | 242,836 |
| Persian | 396,769 |
| Gujarathi | 341,404 |
| Hindi | 560,983 |
| Urdu | 355,964 |
| Other Indic languages | 668,596 |
| Other Indo-European languages | 455,483 |
| Chinese | 2,600,150 |
| Japanese | 445,471 |
| Korean | 1,039,021 |
| Mon-Khmer, Cambodian | 202,033 |
| Hmong | 193,179 |
| Thai | 152,679 |
| Laotian | 146,297 |
| Vietnamese | 1,251,468 |
| Other Asian languages | 783,140 |
| Tagalog | 1,513,734 |
| Other Pacific Island languages | 371,653 |
| Navajo | 169,009 |
| Other Native North American languages | 196,372 |
| Hungarian | 90,612 |
| Arabic | 845,396 |
| Hebrew | 221,593 |
| African languages | 777,553 |
| Other and unspecified languages | 134,670 |

SOURCE: "Table 53. Languages Spoken at Home: 2009," in *Statistical Abstract of the United States: 2012*, U.S. Census Bureau, 2011, http://www.census.gov/compendia/statab/2012/tables/12s0053.pdf (accessed March 11, 2013)

## TABLE 6.3

**English language learners in public schools, school year 2009–10**

| Locale | Total public school enrollment | ELL enrollment | Percent ELL enrollment |
|---|---|---|---|
| **Total** | **48,023,353** | **4,658,504** | **9.7** |
| City | 14,728,569 | 2,230,902 | 14.3 |
| Large | 7,520,317 | 1,331,503 | 17.7 |
| Midsize | 3,476,763 | 488,732 | 14.1 |
| Small | 3,731,489 | 410,667 | 11.0 |
| Suburban | 17,948,070 | 1,710,003 | 8.3 |
| Large | 15,503,775 | 1,527,763 | 9.9 |
| Midsize | 1,525,844 | 112,352 | 7.4 |
| Small | 918,451 | 69,888 | 7.6 |
| Town | 5,794,191 | 365,182 | 6.8 |
| Fringe | 868,821 | 77,121 | 8.9 |
| Distant | 2,992,047 | 176,716 | 5.9 |
| Remote | 1,933,323 | 111,345 | 5.8 |
| Rural | 9,551,976 | 352,356 | 3.6 |
| Fringe | 5,141,851 | 228,438 | 4.4 |
| Distant | 3,286,339 | 81,690 | 2.5 |
| Remote | 1,123,786 | 42,228 | 3.8 |

ELL = English language learners.
Note: Total ELL enrollment does not include data inputed for Vermont in 2009–2010.

SOURCE: Susan Aud et al., "Table A-8-2. Number of Public School Students and Number and Percentage of Public School Students Who Were English Language Learners (ELLs), by Locale: School Year 2009–2010," in *The Condition of Education 2012*, U.S. Department of Education, National Center for Education Statistics, May 2012, http://nces.ed.gov/pubs2012/2012045.pdf (accessed March 11, 2013)

3. Skilled immigrants are likely to be especially beneficial to natives. In addition to contributions to innovation, they have a significant positive fiscal impact.

Lazear and Marron noted that immigrants participate in the workforce at higher rates than natives and come to the United States specifically to work hard in the interest of improving their fortunes and those of their children. Immigrants at the time the report was issued constituted 15% of all workers and were an especially central part of the workforce in occupations including construction, food services, and health care. They also noted that immigrants were especially important in the realms of scientific research and entrepreneurship: approximately 40% of scientists with doctoral degrees who were then working in the United States were foreign born, and immigrants were approximately 40% more likely to be entrepreneurs than were natives. Additionally, Lazear and Marron sought to debunk common concerns about immigrants, noting that their rates of assimilation into U.S. culture, including rates of English-speaking, were extremely high; that they were much less likely to be criminals than their native-born counterparts; that they had a slight positive effect on the solvency of Social Security and Medicare, the two biggest entitlement programs in the United States; and that in the aggregate, they were likely to have a net positive impact on government budgets.

In addressing the widely held belief that immigrants depress wages for American workers, Lazear and Marron noted that in addition to enlarging the overall size of the labor force, immigrants changed the relative supplies of

Impact" (June 2007, http://georgewbush-whitehouse.archives.gov/cea/cea_immigration_062007.html), a report summarizing the effects of their studies on immigrants' roles in the U.S. economy. The primary authors of the report, Edward P. Lazear, the council chairman, and Donald B. Marron, a council member, are highly regarded mainstream economists rather than immigration advocates or opponents. They issued three "key findings":

1. On average, U.S. natives benefit from immigration. Immigrants tend to complement (not substitute for) natives, raising natives' productivity and income.

2. Careful studies of the long-run fiscal effects of immigration conclude that it is likely to have a modest, positive influence.

different types of economic factors. In other words, native-born workers and immigrants both group in varying percentages into the categories of unskilled labor, skilled labor, and capital (the money and resources necessary to hire workers, make products, and pursue business); but the two groups' tendencies to fall into one category or the other are markedly different. "U.S. natives tend to benefit from immigration," the authors write, "precisely because immigrants are not exactly like natives in terms of their productive characteristics and factor endowments."

As an example of how this works in practice, Lazear and Marron point to the construction industry, noting that the large supply of foreign-born unskilled workers allows native-born contractors and skilled craftspeople to undertake more projects than they would be capable of pursuing if the pool of unskilled laborers was smaller. Immigrants thus increase overall economic productivity, leading to more money and other resources to be divided among immigrants (in the form of wages) and natives (in the form of wages but also capital).

Lazear and Marron note that one group of native-born workers likely misses out on the aggregate economic benefits produced by unskilled immigrant workers in the labor force: natives without high school diplomas. Studies have shown that increasing numbers of unskilled immigrant workers in the labor force have a small negative effect on the wages of unskilled native-born workers. To this problem the authors respond, "The difficulties faced by high school dropouts are a serious policy concern, but it is safe to conclude that immigration is not a central cause of those difficulties, nor is reducing immigration a well-targeted way to help these low-wage natives."

### The Projected Benefits of Immigration Reform

Some economists further project that significant positive effects would be generated by immigration reform that addresses two key drags on economic productivity: the costs associated with illegal immigration and the shortage of visas for highly skilled temporary and permanent workers. Those who have legal authorization to work in the United States are far more likely to earn more money than unauthorized workers and to advance in their occupations; thus, they are more likely to contribute more than unauthorized workers to total economic output and to government coffers. Making work visas available based on U.S. employers' demand for workers, meanwhile, would allow those employers to select from among the most qualified job applicants in the world. Such workers are almost universally acknowledged to have a highly positive impact on the U.S. economy and to pay more in taxes than they receive in government benefits.

In a study commissioned by the CAP, *Raising the Floor for American Workers: The Economic Benefits of*

*Comprehensive Immigration Reform* (September 2012, http://www.americanprogress.org/wp-content/uploads/2012/09/immigrationeconreport3.pdf), the economist Raúl Hinojosa-Ojeda concludes that the "enforcement-only" policy that has been the status quo in U.S. immigration law since 1986 represents an economically unsound approach. The astronomical growth in federal resources devoted to immigration enforcement did little to stop the flow of unauthorized immigrants during the 1990s and the following decade. Instead, illegal immigration flows have historically been determined largely by economic opportunity in the United States, combined with a lack of economic opportunity in Mexico and Central America. As the U.S. economy grew during the 1990s and beyond, record numbers of immigrants entered the country by any available means, even as border security was tightened and illegal crossings became extremely dangerous. As the Great Recession began and jobs in the United States became scarce, these immigration flows came to a standstill.

Hinojosa-Ojeda cites studies indicating that during periods of economic opportunity in the United States, 92% to 98% of unauthorized immigrants who are turned back at the border or deported keep attempting to enter the United States until they do so successfully. Rigorous attempts at securing the border have not prevented or even measurably slowed rates of illegal immigration, but these attempts have resulted in an estimated 5,607 migrant deaths and an increase in business for smugglers who charge migrants for transporting them across the border. Ironically, given that tightened border security is intended to keep immigrants out of the United States, another unintended consequence of "enforcement-only" policy is that unauthorized immigrants who do successfully enter the country have an especially strong incentive to stay. Whereas less arduous border crossing conditions would have allowed them to come and go from their home country as economic conditions warranted, current conditions make it more likely that they will attempt to stay in the United States permanently.

Meanwhile, Hinojosa-Ojeda suggests, the focus on immigration enforcement, by making it increasingly difficult for unauthorized immigrants to work, places downward pressure on wages. Unauthorized immigrants have to choose those jobs most likely to allow them to avoid deportation, rather than jobs offering competitive wages or humane working conditions. Unscrupulous employers, in a climate dictated by the constant threat of deportation, are well-positioned to take advantage of those without work authorization. These depressed wage levels affect not only unauthorized workers but unskilled native-born workers, as well.

Pointing to studies of those unauthorized immigrants who gained legal residency and a path to citizenship under the terms of the 1986 Immigration Reform and Control Act (IRCA), Hinojosa-Ojeda predicts that a similar offer of legalization to current unauthorized immigrants would empower workers and exert upward pressure on wages. In a landmark study, *Characteristics and Labor Market Behavior of the Legalized Population Following Five Years of Legalization* (1996), the U.S. Department of Labor found that on average, the unauthorized immigrants offered legal residency under the terms of IRCA saw their incomes rise by 15.1% in the first five years after legalization. Using this and other studies of those who received legal status under IRCA, Hinojosa-Ojeda models three different scenarios for future immigration law and projects the economic consequences of each. In Hinojosa-Ojeda's words, those three scenarios are:

1. Comprehensive immigration reform: Create a pathway to legal status for unauthorized immigrants already living in the United States, and establish new, flexible legal limits on permanent and temporary immigration that respond to changes in U.S. labor demand in the future.

2. A program for temporary workers only: Develop a new temporary-worker program for currently unauthorized immigrants and future immigrants that does not include a pathway to permanent status for unauthorized immigrants or more flexible legal limits on permanent immigration in the future.

3. Mass deportation: Expel all unauthorized immigrants from the United States and effectively seal the U.S.-Mexico border to future immigration. This is not a realistic scenario, but it is useful for comparison purposes.

Hinojosa-Ojeda projects that the first scenario, comprehensive immigration reform, would result in a cumulative increase in gross domestic product (GDP, or the sum total of all economic output in the country in a given year) of $1.5 trillion in the 10 years following reform. (See Figure 6.11.) Scenario two, in which a program is created allowing temporary work authorization but no path to permanent residency, would also have a net positive economic effect, resulting in a cumulative GDP increase of $792 billion over 10 years. Scenario three, by contrast, would result in a cumulative GDP loss of $2.6 billion over 10 years. This scenario would, according to Hinojosa-Ojeda, result in increased wages for unskilled native-born workers, while having no positive effect on other native workers and causing substantial job losses in the aggregate. As Figure 6.12 shows, Hinojosa-Ojeda's model predicts that the increases in economic output under the first two reform scenarios would be spread widely across industries, with industries employing large numbers of unauthorized immigrants, such as garments, textiles, and ferrous metals experiencing the largest increases in output. Likewise, the mass deportation scenario would inflict sharp losses across many economic sectors.

Hinojosa-Ojeda's study is limited to a consideration of the effect of extending legal permanent resident (LPR) status

**FIGURE 6.11**

Cumulative change in U.S. gross domestic product under different immigration policy scenarios, 2009–19 (projected)

SOURCE: Raúl Hinojosa-Ojeda, "Figure 7. Cumulative Change in U.S. G.D.P. under Different Scenarios, over 10 Years," in *Raising the Floor for American Workers: The Economic Benefits of Comprehensive Immigration Reform*, Center for American Progress, January 2010, http://www.americanprogress.org/wp-content/uploads/2012/09/immigrationeconreport3.pdf (accessed March 11, 2013). This material was created by the Center for American Progress (www.americanprogress.org).

to the U.S. unauthorized immigrant population, but other observers point out that offering this population a path to full citizenship would possibly have an even larger positive impact on the economy. Although the 1996 Labor Department study of IRCA beneficiaries did not follow the subjects through to their acquisition of citizenship (which was available to them under the law), Census Bureau surveys offer unmistakable evidence that naturalized citizens are by far the most economically productive group of immigrants. As Figure 3.8 in Chapter 3 shows, naturalized immigrant families had a median income of $61,333 in 2010, almost as high as the median income of the native-born population ($63,231) and far higher than that of foreign-born noncitizens ($39,542). Naturalized citizens were, furthermore, far less likely to live below the poverty level than were foreign-born noncitizens, and they were less likely to live below the poverty level than native-born citizens. In 2010, 10.8% of naturalized citizens lived below the poverty line, compared with 13.6% of natives and 25.1% of foreign-born noncitizens.

In *The Economic Effects of Granting Legal Status and Citizenship to Undocumented Immigrants* (March 2013, http://www.americanprogress.org/wp-content/uploads/2013/03/EconomicEffectsCitizenship-1.pdf), Robert Lynch and Patrick Oakford of the CAP use Census Bureau, Department of Labor, and other data to construct projections of the economic effects of granting full citizenship to the estimated 11 million unauthorized immigrants who were in the

**FIGURE 6.12**

## Annual impact of different immigration policy scenarios on individual economic sectors

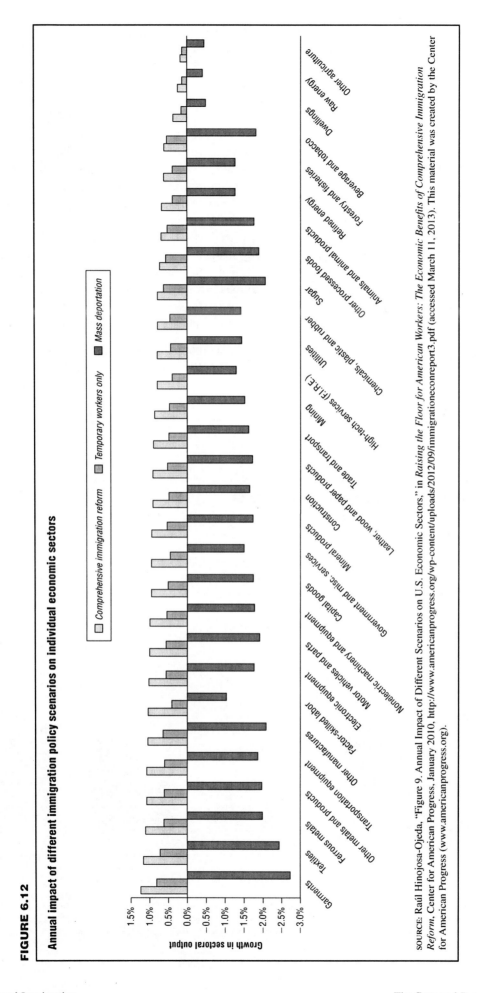

SOURCE: Raúl Hinojosa-Ojeda, "Figure 9. Annual Impact of Different Scenarios on U.S. Economic Sectors," in *Raising the Floor for American Workers: The Economic Benefits of Comprehensive Immigration Reform*, Center for American Progress, January 2010, http://www.americanprogress.org/wp-content/uploads/2012/09/immigrationeconreport3.pdf (accessed March 11, 2013). This material was created by the Center for American Progress (www.americanprogress.org).

United States as of 2013. They offer four possible scenarios representing a range of policy options for immigration reform:

1. No reform

2. Undocumented immigrants acquire legal status in 2013 but no citizenship within 10 years

3. Undocumented immigrants acquire legal status in 2013 and citizenship in five years

4. Undocumented immigrants acquire legal status and citizenship in 2013

As Figure 6.13 shows, Lynch and Oakford project significant increases in GDP, incomes for all Americans, tax receipts at the state and federal levels, the earnings of the unauthorized immigrants themselves, and the average number of jobs added to the economy each year. Because the gains would increase over time, according to the authors, the scenario offering citizenship to unauthorized immigrants immediately would result in the largest gains.

## Other Benefits of Immigration

Estimating the costs and benefits of immigration on the U.S. economy in terms of GDP, tax receipts, government spending, and the labor market is extremely complicated, and the results are subject to wide variations. Even more difficult to quantify are the many additional contributions that immigrants make to American social and cultural life that produce economic gains indirectly. For example, the presence of a wide variety of ethnic foods in New York City or Los Angeles is a significant part of what attracts visitors and new residents to those cities, creating a great deal of economic activity that might not otherwise exist. Likewise, it is inarguable that many Americans, whether native or foreign born, feel more stimulated and/or more welcome in a place characterized by ethnic and cultural diversity, and that they make a wide range of personal and economic commitments to such communities. Although it seems obvious that such factors influence the economic fortunes of cities, states, and of the United States in general, the economic value of such factors is not easily isolated.

Some researchers have nevertheless found strong correlations between levels of cultural diversity and economic growth in U.S. cities. In "The Economic Value of Cultural Diversity: Evidence from U.S. Cities" (September 2004, http://www.international.ucla.edu/cms/files/ottaviano_peri _nber.pdf), the economists Gianmarco I. P. Ottaviano and

**FIGURE 6.13**

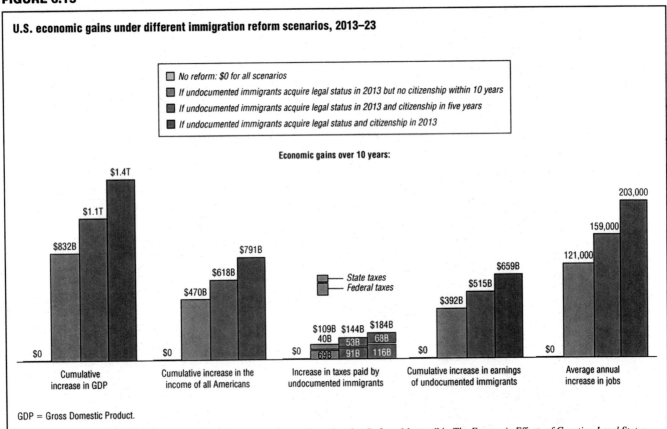

U.S. economic gains under different immigration reform scenarios, 2013–23

Economic gains over 10 years:

GDP = Gross Domestic Product.

SOURCE: Robert Lynch and Patrick Oakford, "The Nature and Timing of Immigration Reform Matters," in *The Economic Effects of Granting Legal Status and Citizenship to Undocumented Immigrants*, Center for American Progress, March 20, 2013, http://www.americanprogress.org/wp-content/uploads/2013/03/EconomicEffectsCitizenship-1.pdf (accessed April 2, 2013). This material was created by the Center for American Progress (www .americanprogress.org).

Giovanni Peri identify the impact of cultural diversity on the economies of 160 U.S. metropolitan areas in the years 1970 to 1990. Seeking to answer the questions, "What is there in cultural diversity for the U.S.-born people? Do they benefit or lose from the presence of the foreign born? How do we measure such benefits or costs?" the researchers created a diversity index based on the likelihood that of any two people in a city, one is foreign born, and they studied wages and rents in these cities. They found unmistakable evidence that, all other things being equal, "U.S.-born workers living in cities with higher cultural diversity are paid, on average, higher wages and pay higher rents than those living in cities with lower cultural diversity." They additionally controlled for a number of other possible variables, including the possibility that cities might become more diverse because economic growth attracts immigrants (which would mean that the presence of immigrants was an effect rather than a cause of economic growth), and they found that the correlation not only persists after factoring in these controls but that its persistence is so strong that it points toward the clear likelihood that higher levels of cultural diversity cause higher wages and rents.

At the national level, researchers have also found correlations between countries' success at integrating immigrants and their levels of economic productivity. Since 2004 the British Council (a nongovernmental group committed to advancing cultural relations between the United Kingdom and other countries) and the Migration Policy Group (a Brussels-based nongovernmental organization not to be confused with the Migration Policy Institute mentioned elsewhere in this book) have been refining a joint project called the Migration Integration Policy Index (MIPEX). MIPEX has evolved into an interactive tool (http://www.mipex.eu/) for calculating various countries' success at integrating immigrants according to 148 indicators. The indicators include questions related to how difficult it is for immigrants to acquire legal status, to find authorized employment, and to keep their families intact; how accessible such amenities as education and professional development are to immigrants; and what degree of political liberty and electoral participation are extended to immigrants.

As the social scientist Richard Florida writes in "The Melting Pot That Isn't: Why America Needs Better Integration" (April 19, 2011, http://www.theatlantic.com/business/archive/2011/04/the-melting-pot-that-isnt-why-america-needs-better-immigration/72048/), as of 2011 the U.S. MIPEX ranking was ninth among the 31 developed countries studied. The countries most successful at integrating immigrants, according to MIPEX, were Sweden, Portugal, and Canada. Comparing MIPEX scores with other measures related to "economic output, innovation, entrepreneurship, and the broader happiness of nations," Florida and his colleague Charlotta Mellander found that nations that do the best job of integrating immigrants also tend to perform best on those other indexes. "Nations that welcome the best and most diverse talent win," Florida writes, "while those that close their borders to it fall further and further behind. The ability not just to attract immigrants but to integrate and effectively harness their skills is a key axis of global economic success, now and even more so in the future."

# CHAPTER 7
# THE IMPACT OF IMMIGRATION ON THE UNITED STATES IN THE 21ST CENTURY

## WHAT WILL THE UNITED STATES LOOK LIKE IN 2060?

In December 2012 the U.S. Census Bureau released another in its regular series of population projections for the coming decades. The 2012 projections, the first to be based on the results of the 2010 census, maintain that in the period from 2012 to 2060, the U.S. population will become older and more diverse. Even though net migration into the United States was expected to slow during this period, the effects of the preceding decades' immigration boom had already laid the groundwork for enormous demographic change. Thomas L. Mesenbourg, the acting director of the Census Bureau, notes in the press release "U.S. Census Bureau Projections Show a Slower Growing, Older, More Diverse Nation a Half Century from Now" (December 12, 2012, https://www.census.gov/newsroom/releases/archives/population/cb12-243.html) that continuing immigration along with the flourishing of second- and third-generation immigrants means that over the course of the next five decades "the U.S. will become a plurality nation, where the non-Hispanic white population remains the largest single group, but no group is in the majority."

Table 7.1 shows the predicted numerical changes in population, the rate of change, and the components of the changes between 2015 and 2060. The aging of the baby boom generation (people born between 1946 and 1964) was expected to be a key factor in the rate of population increase during this period. Baby boomers constitute an unprecedentedly large generation and are the beneficiaries of medical and technological advances that have extended the average life span considerably relative to previous generations. The size of the elderly population, together with slowly increasing numbers of births and slightly larger annual increases in new immigrant arrivals, is expected to result in an annual population growth of 0.77% through 2019. The annual rate of population growth is then expected to decline steadily as the natural rate of population increase (the difference between the number of births and the number of deaths) slows dramatically with the aging and deaths of baby boomers. The annual number of deaths is projected to grow faster than the annual number of births in subsequent decades, and by the 2030s annual increases in immigration are projected to surpass the level of population increases brought about by natural means (births and deaths).

Total population growth is expected to slow between 2015 and 2060, but population growth projections will vary widely among different ethnic and racial groups. As Table 7.2 shows, growth of the non-Hispanic portion of the U.S. population is expected to decline steadily in each of the subsequent decades, from an increase of 5.8 million between 2015 and 2020 to an increase of only 1.9 million between 2055 and 2060. Meanwhile, growth of the Hispanic population is projected to accelerate, from an increase of 6.7 million between 2015 and 2020 to an increase of 8.5 million between 2055 and 2060. Growth of the Asian-American population is projected to remain steady, increasing at a rate approaching or slightly more than 2 million in each of the periods shown in Table 7.2. By 2060 Hispanics are projected to account for 30.6% of the total population, an increase of over 12.8 percentage points from 2015, and Asian-Americans are projected to account for 8.2% of the total population in 2060, an increase of approximately 2.9 percentage points from 2015. (See Table 7.3.)

As Table 7.4 demonstrates, this sweeping change, whereby Hispanics are expected to account for a rapidly increasing share of the total U.S. population and Asian-Americans for a measurably larger share than they previously constituted, is an effect of both immigration and the natural rate of increase among different demographic groups. The annual number of non-Hispanic white births is projected to decline, from 2.1 million in 2015 to 1.5 million in 2060, whereas the annual number of deaths for this group is projected to increase from 2 million in 2015 to a peak of

109

**TABLE 7.1**

## Population projections and components of population change, 2015–60

[Resident population as of July 1. Numbers in thousands.]

| Year | Population | Numeric change | Percent change | Natural increase | Vital events Births | Deaths | Net international migration* |
|------|-----------|---------------|---------------|-----------------|--------|--------|----------------------------|
| 2015 | 321,363 | 2,471 | 0.77 | 1,677 | 4,290 | 2,613 | 794 |
| 2016 | 323,849 | 2,486 | 0.77 | 1,669 | 4,312 | 2,643 | 817 |
| 2017 | 326,348 | 2,499 | 0.77 | 1,659 | 4,333 | 2,673 | 840 |
| 2018 | 328,857 | 2,510 | 0.77 | 1,647 | 4,351 | 2,704 | 863 |
| 2019 | 331,375 | 2,517 | 0.77 | 1,631 | 4,367 | 2,736 | 886 |
| 2020 | 333,896 | 2,521 | 0.76 | 1,612 | 4,380 | 2,768 | 909 |
| 2021 | 336,416 | 2,520 | 0.75 | 1,588 | 4,390 | 2,803 | 932 |
| 2022 | 338,930 | 2,515 | 0.75 | 1,559 | 4,398 | 2,839 | 955 |
| 2023 | 341,436 | 2,506 | 0.74 | 1,527 | 4,404 | 2,877 | 978 |
| 2024 | 343,929 | 2,493 | 0.73 | 1,492 | 4,409 | 2,917 | 1,001 |
| 2025 | 346,407 | 2,478 | 0.72 | 1,453 | 4,413 | 2,959 | 1,024 |
| 2026 | 348,867 | 2,459 | 0.71 | 1,412 | 4,416 | 3,004 | 1,047 |
| 2027 | 351,304 | 2,438 | 0.70 | 1,367 | 4,419 | 3,052 | 1,070 |
| 2028 | 353,718 | 2,414 | 0.69 | 1,320 | 4,422 | 3,102 | 1,093 |
| 2029 | 356,107 | 2,389 | 0.68 | 1,272 | 4,426 | 3,154 | 1,116 |
| 2030 | 358,471 | 2,364 | 0.66 | 1,225 | 4,433 | 3,208 | 1,139 |
| 2031 | 360,792 | 2,321 | 0.65 | 1,178 | 4,443 | 3,265 | 1,143 |
| 2032 | 363,070 | 2,278 | 0.63 | 1,132 | 4,456 | 3,324 | 1,146 |
| 2033 | 365,307 | 2,237 | 0.62 | 1,087 | 4,470 | 3,383 | 1,149 |
| 2034 | 367,503 | 2,197 | 0.60 | 1,044 | 4,487 | 3,443 | 1,153 |
| 2035 | 369,662 | 2,159 | 0.59 | 1,002 | 4,505 | 3,503 | 1,156 |
| 2036 | 371,788 | 2,126 | 0.58 | 966 | 4,525 | 3,559 | 1,160 |
| 2037 | 373,883 | 2,095 | 0.56 | 932 | 4,545 | 3,613 | 1,163 |
| 2038 | 375,950 | 2,067 | 0.55 | 900 | 4,567 | 3,666 | 1,167 |
| 2039 | 377,993 | 2,043 | 0.54 | 873 | 4,589 | 3,717 | 1,171 |
| 2040 | 380,016 | 2,022 | 0.53 | 848 | 4,612 | 3,765 | 1,174 |
| 2041 | 382,021 | 2,005 | 0.53 | 827 | 4,636 | 3,809 | 1,178 |
| 2042 | 384,012 | 1,991 | 0.52 | 809 | 4,660 | 3,851 | 1,182 |
| 2043 | 385,992 | 1,980 | 0.52 | 795 | 4,684 | 3,889 | 1,185 |
| 2044 | 387,965 | 1,973 | 0.51 | 785 | 4,707 | 3,922 | 1,188 |
| 2045 | 389,934 | 1,969 | 0.51 | 778 | 4,729 | 3,951 | 1,191 |
| 2046 | 391,902 | 1,968 | 0.50 | 774 | 4,750 | 3,976 | 1,194 |
| 2047 | 393,869 | 1,967 | 0.50 | 770 | 4,769 | 3,999 | 1,197 |
| 2048 | 395,841 | 1,971 | 0.50 | 772 | 4,788 | 4,016 | 1,199 |
| 2049 | 397,818 | 1,977 | 0.50 | 776 | 4,804 | 4,029 | 1,202 |
| 2050 | 399,803 | 1,985 | 0.50 | 781 | 4,820 | 4,038 | 1,204 |
| 2051 | 401,796 | 1,993 | 0.50 | 787 | 4,834 | 4,047 | 1,206 |
| 2052 | 403,798 | 2,002 | 0.50 | 794 | 4,846 | 4,052 | 1,208 |
| 2053 | 405,811 | 2,013 | 0.50 | 804 | 4,858 | 4,055 | 1,209 |
| 2054 | 407,835 | 2,024 | 0.50 | 814 | 4,869 | 4,055 | 1,211 |
| 2055 | 409,873 | 2,037 | 0.50 | 825 | 4,879 | 4,054 | 1,212 |
| 2056 | 411,923 | 2,051 | 0.50 | 838 | 4,889 | 4,051 | 1,213 |
| 2057 | 413,989 | 2,065 | 0.50 | 852 | 4,899 | 4,048 | 1,214 |
| 2058 | 416,068 | 2,079 | 0.50 | 865 | 4,909 | 4,044 | 1,214 |
| 2059 | 418,161 | 2,093 | 0.50 | 879 | 4,920 | 4,041 | 1,215 |
| 2060 | 420,268 | 2,106 | 0.50 | 891 | 4,930 | 4,039 | 1,215 |

*Net international migration includes the international migration of both native and foreign-born populations. Specifically, it includes: (a) the net international migration of the foreign born, (b) the net international migration of the native born, and (c) the net migration between the United States and Puerto Rico.

Note: Data on population change and components of change refer to events occurring between July 1 of the preceding year and June 30 of the indicated year.

SOURCE: "Table 1. Projections of the Population and Components of Change for the United States: 2015 to 2060," in *2012 National Population Projections: Summary Tables*, U.S. Census Bureau, December 2012, http://www.census.gov/population/projections/data/national/2012/summarytables.html (accessed March 15, 2013)

approximately 2.6 million in 2040 and 2050, before declining again slightly to 2.4 million by 2060. Meanwhile, although Hispanic death rates are projected to rise in approximate proportion to non-Hispanic death rates, annual births among Hispanics are expected to increase substantially, from 1.2 million in 2015 to 2 million in 2060. Additionally, Hispanics are expected to continue to account for a large share of net international immigrants. Births among the Asian-American population are expected to grow enough to maintain net natural increases, at the same time that

immigration from Asia is expected to remain steady. Between 2015 and 2060, increases in the Asian-American population via immigration are expected to range from between 252,000 to 302,000 annually.

## THE CHANGING GEOGRAPHY OF IMMIGRATION

The changes brought about by immigration have historically been concentrated in large-population states with major metropolitan centers, such as California,

**TABLE 7.2**

**Population projections by race and Hispanic origin, 2015–60**

[Numbers in thousands.]

| Race and Hispanic origin | Numeric change in resident population as of July 1 | | | | | | | | |
|---|---|---|---|---|---|---|---|---|---|
| | 2015–2020 | 2020–2025 | 2025–2030 | 2030–2035 | 2035–2040 | 2040–2045 | 2045–2050 | 2050–2055 | 2055–2060 |
| **Total population** | **12,533** | **12,511** | **12,064** | **11,191** | **10,354** | **9,918** | **9,869** | **10,070** | **10,395** |
| One race | 11,135 | 10,973 | 10,377 | 9,340 | 8,319 | 7,694 | 7,465 | 7,504 | 7,667 |
| White | 6,621 | 6,415 | 5,843 | 4,889 | 3,945 | 3,360 | 3,161 | 3,223 | 3,405 |
| Black | 2,278 | 2,254 | 2,182 | 2,102 | 2,064 | 2,062 | 2,079 | 2,109 | 2,160 |
| AIAN | 286 | 285 | 276 | 265 | 253 | 243 | 231 | 219 | 208 |
| Asian | 1,875 | 1,946 | 2,003 | 2,016 | 1,989 | 1,960 | 1,928 | 1,887 | 1,835 |
| NHPI | 75 | 74 | 71 | 70 | 68 | 67 | 67 | 65 | 61 |
| Two or more races | 1,398 | 1,539 | 1,686 | 1,851 | 2,034 | 2,225 | 2,404 | 2,566 | 2,728 |
| *Race alone or in combination:* * | | | | | | | | | |
| White | 7,927 | 7,860 | 7,433 | 6,639 | 5,877 | 5,479 | 5,456 | 5,679 | 6,020 |
| Black | 3,092 | 3,174 | 3,215 | 3,260 | 3,363 | 3,509 | 3,666 | 3,829 | 4,013 |
| AIAN | 521 | 525 | 519 | 506 | 497 | 491 | 485 | 478 | 470 |
| Asian | 2,377 | 2,494 | 2,604 | 2,677 | 2,717 | 2,752 | 2,779 | 2,793 | 2,796 |
| NHPI | 165 | 171 | 174 | 179 | 187 | 196 | 204 | 210 | 214 |
| **Not Hispanic** | **5,823** | **5,323** | **4,382** | **3,187** | **2,137** | **1,535** | **1,397** | **1,558** | **1,858** |
| One race | 4,749 | 4,146 | 3,108 | 1,804 | 632 | −99 | −357 | −299 | −98 |
| White | 864 | 244 | −740 | −1,931 | −2,999 | −3,666 | −3,887 | −3,803 | −3,580 |
| Black | 1,926 | 1,884 | 1,792 | 1,689 | 1,628 | 1,607 | 1,612 | 1,636 | 1,678 |
| AIAN | 104 | 95 | 81 | 68 | 56 | 49 | 42 | 37 | 32 |
| Asian | 1,805 | 1,872 | 1,926 | 1,935 | 1,902 | 1,868 | 1,834 | 1,789 | 1,734 |
| NHPI | 51 | 50 | 48 | 46 | 43 | 43 | 42 | 41 | 39 |
| Two or more races | 1,075 | 1,175 | 1,275 | 1,383 | 1,505 | 1,633 | 1,754 | 1,858 | 1,955 |
| *Race alone or in combination:* * | | | | | | | | | |
| White | 1,874 | 1,354 | 468 | −617 | −1,562 | −2,101 | −2,203 | −2,016 | −1,696 |
| Black | 2,567 | 2,608 | 2,596 | 2,581 | 2,620 | 2,706 | 2,811 | 2,924 | 3,055 |
| AIAN | 234 | 225 | 206 | 184 | 168 | 159 | 155 | 152 | 146 |
| Asian | 2,210 | 2,312 | 2,402 | 2,450 | 2,464 | 2,471 | 2,474 | 2,463 | 2,437 |
| NHPI | 113 | 115 | 115 | 115 | 116 | 120 | 124 | 125 | 125 |
| **Hispanic** | **6,709** | **7,189** | **7,682** | **8,004** | **8,217** | **8,383** | **8,473** | **8,510** | **8,538** |
| One race | 6,386 | 6,826 | 7,270 | 7,536 | 7,687 | 7,793 | 7,822 | 7,802 | 7,765 |
| White | 5,757 | 6,171 | 6,583 | 6,821 | 6,943 | 7,026 | 7,048 | 7,026 | 6,985 |
| Black | 353 | 370 | 390 | 413 | 436 | 455 | 467 | 474 | 480 |
| AIAN | 183 | 189 | 195 | 197 | 197 | 194 | 189 | 182 | 176 |
| Asian | 71 | 73 | 77 | 81 | 87 | 92 | 95 | 97 | 101 |
| NHPI | 24 | 23 | 24 | 24 | 25 | 25 | 24 | 23 | 22 |
| Two or more races | 323 | 363 | 412 | 468 | 530 | 591 | 650 | 708 | 773 |
| *Race alone or in combination:* * | | | | | | | | | |
| White | 6,053 | 6,506 | 6,965 | 7,256 | 7,438 | 7,581 | 7,659 | 7,694 | 7,717 |
| Black | 524 | 566 | 619 | 679 | 742 | 804 | 855 | 905 | 958 |
| AIAN | 287 | 300 | 313 | 322 | 328 | 332 | 331 | 327 | 322 |
| Asian | 167 | 182 | 202 | 227 | 253 | 281 | 305 | 330 | 359 |
| NHPI | 52 | 55 | 60 | 64 | 70 | 76 | 81 | 85 | 89 |

| Race and Hispanic origin | Percent change in resident population as of July 1 | | | | | | | | |
|---|---|---|---|---|---|---|---|---|---|
| | 2015–2020 | 2020–2025 | 2025–2030 | 2030–2035 | 2035–2040 | 2040–2045 | 2045–2050 | 2050–2055 | 2055–2060 |
| **Total population** | **3.90** | **3.75** | **3.48** | **3.12** | **2.80** | **2.61** | **2.53** | **2.52** | **2.54** |
| One race | 3.56 | 3.38 | 3.10 | 2.70 | 2.34 | 2.12 | 2.01 | 1.98 | 1.99 |
| White | 2.66 | 2.51 | 2.23 | 1.83 | 1.45 | 1.22 | 1.13 | 1.14 | 1.19 |
| Black | 5.36 | 5.03 | 4.64 | 4.27 | 4.02 | 3.86 | 3.75 | 3.66 | 3.62 |
| AIAN | 7.08 | 6.59 | 5.98 | 5.42 | 4.91 | 4.49 | 4.09 | 3.72 | 3.41 |
| Asian | 11.02 | 10.31 | 9.62 | 8.83 | 8.00 | 7.30 | 6.69 | 6.14 | 5.63 |
| NHPI | 10.01 | 8.98 | 7.91 | 7.22 | 6.54 | 6.05 | 5.71 | 5.24 | 4.67 |
| Two or more races | 16.83 | 15.86 | 15.00 | 14.32 | 13.76 | 13.23 | 12.63 | 11.97 | 11.36 |
| *Race alone or in combination:* * | | | | | | | | | |
| White | 3.10 | 2.98 | 2.73 | 2.38 | 2.06 | 1.88 | 1.84 | 1.88 | 1.95 |
| Black | 6.69 | 6.43 | 6.12 | 5.85 | 5.70 | 5.63 | 5.57 | 5.51 | 5.47 |
| AIAN | 7.81 | 7.30 | 6.72 | 6.14 | 5.68 | 5.31 | 4.98 | 4.68 | 4.39 |
| Asian | 11.88 | 11.14 | 10.47 | 9.74 | 9.01 | 8.37 | 7.80 | 7.27 | 6.79 |
| NHPI | 11.03 | 10.30 | 9.50 | 8.92 | 8.56 | 8.26 | 7.94 | 7.58 | 7.18 |
| **Not Hispanic** | **2.20** | **1.97** | **1.59** | **1.14** | **0.76** | **0.54** | **0.49** | **0.54** | **0.64** |

Florida, Illinois, New Jersey, New York, and Texas. These states remain home to the largest immigrant populations in the United States, but since the 1990s rapid growth of the immigrant population in other states has changed the nature of the public discussion of immigra-

tion. As Figure 7.1 shows, states not known for their ethnic and cultural diversity, such as Colorado, Idaho, Minnesota, and Nebraska, have seen their immigrant populations increase by 200% or more since 1990, as have southern states including Alabama, Arkansas,

**TABLE 7.2**

**Population projections by race and Hispanic origin, 2015–60** [CONTINUED]

[Numbers in thousands.]

| Race and Hispanic origin | Percent change in resident population as of July 1 | | | | | | | | |
|---|---|---|---|---|---|---|---|---|---|
| | 2015–2020 | 2020–2025 | 2025–2030 | 2030–2035 | 2035–2040 | 2040–2045 | 2045–2050 | 2050–2055 | 2055–2060 |
| One race | 1.84 | 1.58 | 1.17 | 0.67 | 0.23 | −0.04 | −0.13 | −0.11 | −0.04 |
| White | 0.44 | 0.12 | −0.37 | −0.97 | −1.52 | −1.89 | −2.04 | −2.04 | −1.96 |
| Black | 4.83 | 4.51 | 4.10 | 3.72 | 3.45 | 3.30 | 3.20 | 3.15 | 3.13 |
| AIAN | 4.38 | 3.83 | 3.14 | 2.56 | 2.06 | 1.76 | 1.48 | 1.29 | 1.10 |
| Asian | 10.98 | 10.26 | 9.57 | 8.78 | 7.93 | 7.22 | 6.61 | 6.05 | 5.53 |
| NHPI | 9.31 | 8.35 | 7.40 | 6.60 | 5.79 | 5.47 | 5.07 | 4.71 | 4.28 |
| Two or more races | 16.23 | 15.26 | 14.37 | 13.63 | 13.05 | 12.53 | 11.96 | 11.31 | 10.69 |
| *Race alone or in combination:** | | | | | | | | | |
| White | 0.92 | 0.66 | 0.23 | −0.30 | −0.75 | −1.02 | −1.08 | −1.00 | −0.85 |
| Black | 6.00 | 5.75 | 5.41 | 5.10 | 4.93 | 4.85 | 4.81 | 4.77 | 4.76 |
| AIAN | 5.46 | 4.98 | 4.34 | 3.72 | 3.27 | 3.00 | 2.84 | 2.71 | 2.53 |
| Asian | 11.65 | 10.92 | 10.23 | 9.46 | 8.69 | 8.02 | 7.44 | 6.89 | 6.38 |
| NHPI | 9.98 | 9.24 | 8.46 | 7.80 | 7.30 | 7.03 | 6.79 | 6.41 | 6.02 |
| **Hispanic** | **11.75** | **11.27** | **10.82** | **10.18** | **9.48** | **8.84** | **8.21** | **7.62** | **7.10** |
| One race | 11.53 | 11.05 | 10.60 | 9.93 | 9.22 | 8.55 | 7.91 | 7.31 | 6.78 |
| White | 11.45 | 11.01 | 10.58 | 9.92 | 9.18 | 8.51 | 7.87 | 7.27 | 6.74 |
| Black | 13.17 | 12.20 | 11.46 | 10.89 | 10.36 | 9.80 | 9.16 | 8.52 | 7.95 |
| AIAN | 10.99 | 10.23 | 9.57 | 8.83 | 8.11 | 7.39 | 6.70 | 6.05 | 5.52 |
| Asian | 12.50 | 11.42 | 10.81 | 10.27 | 10.00 | 9.61 | 9.06 | 8.48 | 8.14 |
| NHPI | 11.94 | 10.22 | 9.68 | 8.82 | 8.45 | 7.79 | 6.94 | 6.22 | 5.60 |
| Two or more races | 19.19 | 18.10 | 17.39 | 16.83 | 16.31 | 15.64 | 14.87 | 14.10 | 13.50 |
| *Race alone or in combination:** | | | | | | | | | |
| White | 11.69 | 11.25 | 10.83 | 10.18 | 9.47 | 8.82 | 8.19 | 7.60 | 7.08 |
| Black | 15.22 | 14.27 | 13.66 | 13.18 | 12.73 | 12.23 | 11.59 | 11.00 | 10.49 |
| AIAN | 12.01 | 11.21 | 10.52 | 9.79 | 9.08 | 8.43 | 7.75 | 7.11 | 6.53 |
| Asian | 16.03 | 15.05 | 14.52 | 14.25 | 13.90 | 13.56 | 12.96 | 12.41 | 12.01 |
| NHPI | 14.29 | 13.22 | 12.74 | 12.05 | 11.76 | 11.43 | 10.93 | 10.34 | 9.81 |

*'In combination' means in combination with one or more other races. For numeric change, the sum of the five race groups adds to more than the total because individuals may report more than one race.

Note: Hispanic origin is considered an ethnicity, not a race. Hispanics may be of any race. Black = black or African American. AIAN = American Indian and Alaska Native. NHPI = Native Hawaiian and other Pacific Islander.

SOURCE: "Table 7. Projected Change in Population Size by Race and Hispanic Origin for the United States: 2015 to 2060," in *2012 National Population Projections: Summary Tables*, U.S. Census Bureau, December 2012, http://www.census.gov/population/projections/data/national/2012/summarytables.html (accessed March 15, 2013)

Georgia, Kentucky, North Carolina, South Carolina, and Tennessee. Similarly, Table 7.5 shows that although the Hispanic population—by far the largest portion of the U.S. immigrant population—remained concentrated, as of 2011, in the same 10 states that had boasted the largest Hispanic populations in 2000, the bulk of the growth in the Hispanic population from 2000 to 2011 came in other states.

Most of these new immigrant destinations had far smaller immigrant populations than states such as California, New York, and Texas, but they were also, in many cases, states with comparatively small populations overall. The rapid growth in immigrant arrivals, then, had a particularly noticeable impact, and these changes often provoked anxiety. Some of these new immigrant destinations were towns that had not witnessed the arrival of new immigrants since the early 20th century. Common fears regarding economic competition, crime, the rise of foreign-language speaking and instruction, and rising demand for social services led in some cases to the proposal of restrictive legislation at the local and state levels, as discussed in Chapters 2 and 5.

Miriam Jordan reports in "Heartland Draws Hispanics to Help Revive Small Towns" (WSJ.com, November 8, 2012) on the growing numbers of Hispanic immigrants who have left immigrant-rich parts of the western United States for the more sparsely populated midwestern and southern states. These immigrants settled in out-of-the-way small towns, Jordan relates, because of the combination of good jobs, lower housing costs, and safe neighborhoods. According to Jordan, the 2010 census found that the Hispanic population in the Midwest grew by 49% between 2000 and 2010, contributing much of the overall population growth in the region (which was only 4%). The states of Indiana (82%), Iowa (82%), Nebraska (77%), and Minnesota (74.5%) saw particularly high growth in their Hispanic populations between 2000 and 2010.

Some of the localities subject to rapid influxes of Hispanic residents responded by passing ordinances meant to deter undocumented immigrants from settling, and cultural and economic anxieties were common. Additionally, the rapid growth of Hispanic populations, which tend to vote heavily Democratic in state and national elections, threatened to upset the balance of political

TABLE 7.3

**Percentage distribution of projected population by race and Hispanic origin, 2015–60**

[Percent of total resident population as of July 1]

| Race and Hispanic origin | 2015 | 2020 | 2025 | 2030 | 2035 | 2040 | 2045 | 2050 | 2055 | 2060 |
|---|---|---|---|---|---|---|---|---|---|---|
| **Total population** | **100.00** | **100.00** | **100.00** | **100.00** | **100.00** | **100.00** | **100.00** | **100.00** | **100.00** | **100.00** |
| One race | 97.42 | 97.09 | 96.75 | 96.39 | 96.00 | 95.58 | 95.12 | 94.64 | 94.14 | 93.64 |
| White | 77.40 | 76.47 | 75.56 | 74.65 | 73.71 | 72.74 | 71.76 | 70.77 | 69.82 | 68.91 |
| Black | 13.23 | 13.42 | 13.59 | 13.74 | 13.89 | 14.06 | 14.23 | 14.40 | 14.56 | 14.71 |
| AIAN | 1.26 | 1.30 | 1.33 | 1.36 | 1.39 | 1.42 | 1.45 | 1.47 | 1.49 | 1.50 |
| Asian | 5.29 | 5.66 | 6.01 | 6.37 | 6.72 | 7.06 | 7.39 | 7.69 | 7.96 | 8.20 |
| NHPI | 0.23 | 0.25 | 0.26 | 0.27 | 0.28 | 0.29 | 0.30 | 0.31 | 0.32 | 0.33 |
| Two or more races | 2.58 | 2.91 | 3.25 | 3.61 | 4.00 | 4.42 | 4.88 | 5.36 | 5.86 | 6.36 |
| *Race alone or in combination:** | | | | | | | | | | |
| White | 79.69 | 79.07 | 78.48 | 77.92 | 77.35 | 76.79 | 76.24 | 75.73 | 75.25 | 74.82 |
| Black | 14.39 | 14.78 | 15.16 | 15.55 | 15.96 | 16.41 | 16.89 | 17.39 | 17.90 | 18.41 |
| AIAN | 2.08 | 2.15 | 2.23 | 2.30 | 2.37 | 2.43 | 2.50 | 2.56 | 2.61 | 2.66 |
| Asian | 6.23 | 6.70 | 7.18 | 7.67 | 8.16 | 8.65 | 9.14 | 9.61 | 10.05 | 10.47 |
| NHPI | 0.47 | 0.50 | 0.53 | 0.56 | 0.59 | 0.62 | 0.66 | 0.69 | 0.73 | 0.76 |
| **Not Hispanic** | 82.24 | 80.90 | 79.51 | 78.06 | 76.56 | 75.03 | 73.52 | 72.05 | 70.66 | 69.36 |
| One race | 80.18 | 78.59 | 76.95 | 75.23 | 73.44 | 71.60 | 69.76 | 67.95 | 66.20 | 64.54 |
| White | 61.75 | 59.69 | 57.61 | 55.46 | 53.26 | 51.02 | 48.78 | 46.61 | 44.53 | 42.58 |
| Black | 12.40 | 12.51 | 12.60 | 12.68 | 12.75 | 12.83 | 12.92 | 13.00 | 13.08 | 13.16 |
| AIAN | 0.74 | 0.74 | 0.74 | 0.74 | 0.74 | 0.73 | 0.73 | 0.72 | 0.71 | 0.70 |
| Asian | 5.12 | 5.46 | 5.81 | 6.15 | 6.49 | 6.81 | 7.12 | 7.40 | 7.65 | 7.88 |
| NHPI | 0.17 | 0.18 | 0.19 | 0.19 | 0.20 | 0.21 | 0.21 | 0.22 | 0.22 | 0.23 |
| Two or more races | 2.06 | 2.31 | 2.56 | 2.83 | 3.12 | 3.43 | 3.76 | 4.11 | 4.46 | 4.82 |
| *Race alone or in combination:** | | | | | | | | | | |
| White | 63.58 | 61.75 | 59.91 | 58.03 | 56.10 | 54.16 | 52.25 | 50.41 | 48.68 | 47.07 |
| Black | 13.32 | 13.59 | 13.85 | 14.11 | 14.38 | 14.68 | 15.00 | 15.33 | 15.67 | 16.01 |
| AIAN | 1.33 | 1.35 | 1.37 | 1.38 | 1.39 | 1.39 | 1.40 | 1.40 | 1.41 | 1.41 |
| Asian | 5.90 | 6.34 | 6.78 | 7.22 | 7.67 | 8.11 | 8.53 | 8.94 | 9.32 | 9.67 |
| NHPI | 0.35 | 0.37 | 0.39 | 0.41 | 0.43 | 0.45 | 0.47 | 0.49 | 0.51 | 0.52 |
| **Hispanic** | 17.76 | 19.10 | 20.49 | 21.94 | 23.44 | 24.97 | 26.48 | 27.95 | 29.34 | 30.64 |
| One race | 17.24 | 18.50 | 19.80 | 21.17 | 22.56 | 23.97 | 25.36 | 26.69 | 27.94 | 29.10 |
| White | 15.64 | 16.78 | 17.96 | 19.19 | 20.45 | 21.72 | 22.97 | 24.17 | 25.29 | 26.33 |
| Black | 0.83 | 0.91 | 0.98 | 1.06 | 1.14 | 1.22 | 1.31 | 1.39 | 1.47 | 1.55 |
| AIAN | 0.52 | 0.55 | 0.59 | 0.62 | 0.66 | 0.69 | 0.72 | 0.75 | 0.78 | 0.80 |
| Asian | 0.18 | 0.19 | 0.21 | 0.22 | 0.24 | 0.25 | 0.27 | 0.29 | 0.30 | 0.32 |
| NHPI | 0.06 | 0.07 | 0.07 | 0.08 | 0.08 | 0.08 | 0.09 | 0.09 | 0.10 | 0.10 |
| Two or more races | 0.52 | 0.60 | 0.68 | 0.78 | 0.88 | 0.99 | 1.12 | 1.26 | 1.40 | 1.55 |
| *Race alone or in combination:** | | | | | | | | | | |
| White | 16.11 | 17.32 | 18.57 | 19.89 | 21.25 | 22.63 | 24.00 | 25.32 | 26.58 | 27.75 |
| Black | 1.07 | 1.19 | 1.31 | 1.44 | 1.58 | 1.73 | 1.89 | 2.06 | 2.23 | 2.40 |
| AIAN | 0.74 | 0.80 | 0.86 | 0.92 | 0.98 | 1.04 | 1.10 | 1.15 | 1.20 | 1.25 |
| Asian | 0.32 | 0.36 | 0.40 | 0.44 | 0.49 | 0.55 | 0.60 | 0.67 | 0.73 | 0.80 |
| NHPI | 0.11 | 0.12 | 0.14 | 0.15 | 0.16 | 0.17 | 0.19 | 0.21 | 0.22 | 0.24 |

*'In combination' means in combination with one or more other races.
NHPI = Native Hawaiian and other Pacific Islander.
Note: Hispanic origin is considered an ethnicity, not a race. Hispanics may be of any race. Black = black or African American. AIAN = American Indian and Alaska Native.

SOURCE: "Table 6. Percent Distribution of the Projected Population by Race and Hispanic Origin for the United States: 2015 to 2060," in *2012 National Population Projections: Summary Tables*, U.S. Census Bureau, December 2012, http://www.census.gov/population/projections/data/national/2012/summarytables.html (accessed March 15, 2013)

power in the small towns of the Midwest and the Southeast, many of which were Republican strongholds.

Nevertheless, the positive economic effects of this population growth were evident. Jordan describes the effect of Hispanic population growth on Ottumwa, Iowa, a small town with a population of about 30,000:

> Ottumwa had fallen on hard times before Latinos arrived. Once a bustling railroad hub, it had lost thousands of jobs as the railroads closed many routes and a large meatpacking plant shut down.

> Latinos ... now account for 11% of the town's population, according to the census. Storefronts that were boarded up on Main Street are occupied by Latino-

owned groceries and restaurants. ... Taxable property valuation reached $700 million last year, almost double the 2000 value, thanks to Hispanic home buyers.

In "Can Immigration Save Small-Town America? Hispanic Boomtowns and the Uneasy Path to Renewal" (*Annals of the American Academy of Political and Social Science*, vol. 641, no. 1, May 2012), Patrick J. Carr, Daniel T. Lichter, and Maria J. Kefalas tell a similar story, while further assessing the significance of the wave of Hispanic migration to small towns. The researchers note that the overwhelming movement of the American population to metropolitan areas in the late 20th and early 21st centuries had left many small towns in the Midwest on the brink of

**TABLE 7.4**

**Projected components of population change by race and Hispanic origin, 2015–60**

[Numbers in thousands]

| Component, race, and Hispanic origin | 2015 | 2020 | 2030 | 2040 | 2050 | 2060 |
|---|---|---|---|---|---|---|
| **Natural increase** | **1,677** | **1,612** | **1,225** | **848** | **781** | **891** |
| One race | 1,423 | 1,332 | 890 | 441 | 303 | 348 |
|   White | 894 | 819 | 461 | 73 | −25 | 50 |
|   Black | 356 | 340 | 272 | 227 | 203 | 193 |
|   AIAN | 50 | 49 | 44 | 40 | 35 | 31 |
|   Asian | 112 | 112 | 103 | 93 | 82 | 67 |
|   NHPI | 11 | 11 | 9 | 9 | 9 | 7 |
| Two or more races | 254 | 280 | 335 | 407 | 478 | 543 |
| Non-Hispanic white alone | 92 | −9 | −422 | −854 | −966 | −886 |
| Hispanic | 960 | 994 | 1,072 | 1,150 | 1,192 | 1,216 |
| **Births** | **4,290** | **4,380** | **4,433** | **4,612** | **4,820** | **4,930** |
| One race | 4,013 | 4,073 | 4,061 | 4,155 | 4,275 | 4,304 |
|   White | 3,052 | 3,086 | 3,051 | 3,074 | 3,125 | 3,104 |
|   Black | 666 | 676 | 670 | 700 | 734 | 754 |
|   AIAN | 72 | 74 | 75 | 79 | 82 | 82 |
|   Asian | 209 | 224 | 250 | 286 | 318 | 345 |
|   NHPI | 14 | 14 | 14 | 16 | 17 | 18 |
| Two or more races | 277 | 307 | 372 | 458 | 544 | 626 |
| Non-Hispanic white alone | 2,076 | 2,046 | 1,865 | 1,727 | 1,638 | 1,497 |
| Hispanic | 1,151 | 1,227 | 1,407 | 1,618 | 1,803 | 1,970 |
| **Deaths** | **2,613** | **2,768** | **3,208** | **3,765** | **4,038** | **4,039** |
| One race | 2,590 | 2,741 | 3,171 | 3,714 | 3,972 | 3,956 |
|   White | 2,158 | 2,267 | 2,590 | 3,001 | 3,150 | 3,054 |
|   Black | 310 | 336 | 398 | 474 | 531 | 561 |
|   AIAN | 21 | 24 | 31 | 39 | 46 | 52 |
|   Asian | 97 | 111 | 147 | 193 | 236 | 279 |
|   NHPI | 3 | 3 | 5 | 7 | 9 | 10 |
| Two or more races | 23 | 27 | 37 | 51 | 66 | 83 |
| Non-Hispanic white alone | 1,984 | 2,055 | 2,287 | 2,581 | 2,604 | 2,383 |
| Hispanic | 191 | 233 | 336 | 467 | 611 | 754 |
| **Net international migration** | **794** | **909** | **1,139** | **1,174** | **1,204** | **1,215** |
| One race | 785 | 898 | 1,125 | 1,159 | 1,188 | 1,199 |
|   White | 427 | 501 | 650 | 657 | 658 | 645 |
|   Black | 95 | 116 | 158 | 185 | 215 | 243 |
|   AIAN | 7 | 8 | 10 | 10 | 10 | 10 |
|   Asian | 252 | 269 | 302 | 302 | 301 | 296 |
|   NHPI | 4 | 4 | 5 | 5 | 5 | 5 |
| Two or more races | 9 | 11 | 15 | 15 | 16 | 16 |
| Non-Hispanic white alone | 126 | 145 | 183 | 186 | 189 | 189 |
| Hispanic | 326 | 385 | 504 | 509 | 507 | 494 |

Black = black or African American. AIAN = American Indian and Alaska Native. NHPI = Native Hawaiian and other Pacific Islander.
Note: Data on population change and components of change refer to events occuring between July 1 of the preceding year and June 30 of the indicated year. Hispanic origin is considered an ethnicity, not a race. Hispanics may be of any race.

SOURCE: "Table 8. Projected Components of Change by Race and Hispanic Origin for the United States: 2015 to 2060," in *2012 National Population Projections: Summary Tables*, U.S. Census Bureau, December 2012, http://www.census.gov/population/projections/data/national/2012/summarytables.html (accessed March 15, 2013)

collapse: "Any demographic and economic effects have been exacerbated by who is leaving, namely, young adults of reproductive age and the most educated and talented. ... While young people have always left small towns, the exodus comes at a time when opportunities for those who stay have been severely reduced by consolidation in agriculture and the globalization of manufacturing. ... The net result is that the jobs remaining in nonmetro America are fewer and often pay less than they did even a decade ago."

A primary driver of the growth in the Hispanic population in these areas is the very consolidation of the agribusiness industry that played a role in undermining the career opportunities of many of the native-born residents of the Midwest. Many Hispanic immigrants have been drawn to these midwestern towns by the relocation of food-processing facilities away from cities. These slaughterhouses and meat-packing plants have relocated to rural areas to be closer to raw materials (beef, chicken, and pork) and because of lower labor costs, a result of lower costs of living and a lack of unions. These jobs pay less and are more dangerous than many of the manufacturing or agricultural jobs native-born residents in the Midwest had enjoyed in previous decades. Food-processing companies have actively courted Hispanic immigrants to work in their plants, and immigrants have arrived in large numbers.

Carr, Lichter, and Kefalas analyze the responses of two small middle America towns, Hazleton, Pennsylvania, and St. James, Minnesota, to the growth of their Hispanic

**FIGURE 7.1**

**States with the largest and fastest-growing immigrant populations, 1990–2009**

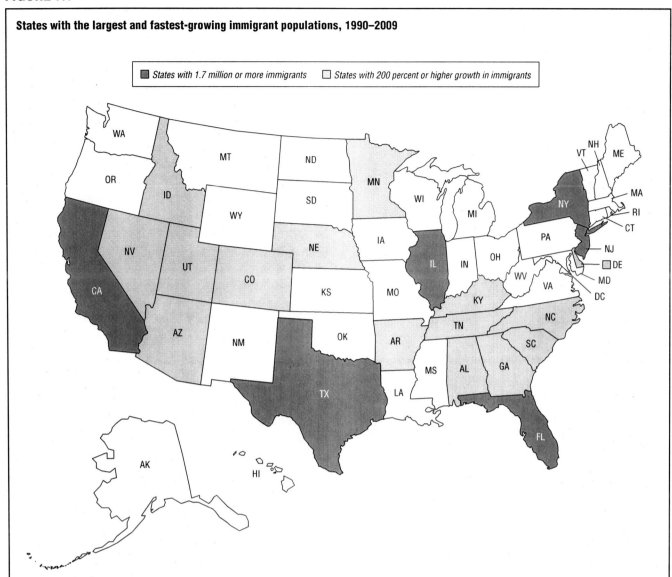

■ States with 1.7 million or more immigrants    ☐ States with 200 percent or higher growth in immigrants

SOURCE: "Figure 1. Immigration Spreads to New States, 1990–2009," in "The Facts on Immigration Today," Center for American Progress, July 6, 2012, http://www.americanprogress.org/wp-content/uploads/issues/2012/07/pdf/immigration_facts_final.pdf (accessed April 15, 2013). This material was created by the Center for American Progress (www.americanprogress.org).

populations. Prior to 2000 Hazleton, a town of around 25,000, had been losing population for seven decades because of deindustrialization. Over the course of the next decade, the town's Hispanic population grew rapidly, from 4.9% of the total population to 37.3%, and the town as a whole grew by approximately 2,000 residents, even though the death rate of its native-born population outpaced its birthrate. Anti-immigration activists such as the national television personality Lou Dobbs (1945–) pointed to Hazleton as symptomatic of the larger threat that immigration posed to the American way of life, and several local politicians made anti-immigrant rhetoric the cornerstone of their agendas, claiming that many of the new residents were illegal immigrants and that their arrival had driven crime rates higher. In fact, as Carr, Lichter, and Kefalas point out, although there were isolated instances of high-profile crimes allegedly committed by undocumented

immigrants, Hazleton's violent crime rate declined during the period of rapid Hispanic population growth. Nevertheless, Hazleton became a test case for restrictive immigration law, passing a local measure that became a model for other municipalities. Although the law caused widespread tension and attracted national media scrutiny, its effect on the growth of the Hispanic population was inconclusive at best. Meanwhile, Carr, Lichter, and Kefalas note, even those politicians who back the restrictive law acknowledge that Hispanic immigration has revitalized the town economically and greatly improved the fiscal health of local government.

Even though many observers point to Hazleton as emblematic of the complex response to immigration in the 21st century, Carr, Lichter, and Kefalas offer an alternative view of how immigration plays out in their

**Distribution of Hispanic population in top 10 states, 2000 and 2011**

[Top 10 states are listed in descending order of their share of the Hispanic population in 2011]

**Universe:** 2000 and 2011 Hispanic resident population

| | Percent 2011 | Percent 2000 | Change 2000–2011 |
|---|---|---|---|
| California | 27.7 | 31.0 | −3.4 |
| Texas | 18.9 | 18.9 | 0.0 |
| Florida | 8.4 | 7.6 | 0.8 |
| New York | 6.7 | 8.1 | −1.4 |
| Illinois | 4.0 | 4.3 | −0.3 |
| Arizona | 3.8 | 3.7 | 0.1 |
| New Jersey | 3.1 | 3.2 | −0.1 |
| Colorado | 2.1 | 2.1 | 0.0 |
| New Mexico | 1.9 | 2.2 | −0.3 |
| Georgia | 1.7 | 1.2 | 0.5 |
| Other states | 21.9 | 17.7 | 4.2 |
| **Total** | **100.0** | **100.0** | — |

SOURCE: Seth Motel and Eileen Patten, "Table 15. Distribution of Hispanics across States: 2000 and 2011," in *Statistical Portrait of Hispanics in the United States, 2011*, Pew Research Hispanic Center, February 15, 2013, http://www.pewhispanic.org/2013/02/15/statistical-portrait-of-hispanics-in-the-united-states-2011/#15 (accessed March 11, 2013)

analysis of the experience of St. James, Minnesota. Smaller than Hazleton, St. James, a town with 4,600 residents, saw more gradual growth in its immigrant population. Hispanics began coming to the area during the 1970s and 1980s, when they were recruited from south Texas by a local food-processing plant. Like Hazleton, St. James saw its fortunes become increasingly dependent on its immigrant population. During the mid-1990s a strategic planning group assembled by local leaders and composed entirely of white natives discovered, as part of their information-gathering process, that new arrivals to the town frequently felt excluded and uncomfortable. In response to this information, St. James began focusing on integrating its immigrant community through the newly formed Family Services Collaborative, which mediated the concerns of immigrants, school systems, and social services providers and generated numerous spin-off initiatives. Tensions remained between the new arrivals and the natives, and some of the residents interviewed by Carr, Lichter, and Kefalas expressed concern that the successes of the program could be easily reversed if, for example, local politicians were to begin exploiting native anxieties. As of May 2013, however, St. James had yet to pass any restrictive ordinances or other sanctions targeting its immigrant population.

## THE SITUATION IN MAJOR CITIES

Large U.S. metropolitan areas experience their own complex challenges as a result of immigration, but these challenges take very different forms from those in small towns, given the vast differences in scale and diversity of both the immigrant and native-born populations. Among U.S. metropolitan areas, New York City and Los Angeles County (which includes the city of Los Angeles as well as numerous adjacent cities and unincorporated areas) have long been on the front lines of immigration-related change. The foreign born constitute over one-third of the population in both New York City, which is home to nearly 8 million residents, and Los Angeles County, home to more than 10 million; and a large proportion of residents of both areas are second-generation immigrants (people born in the United States but who in many cases still strongly identify with their culture of origin), as well. Unlike in much of the rest of the United States, in these two areas non-Hispanic whites are a minority, accounting for approximately one-third of the population; and both areas have long histories as entry points for immigrants to the United States. Accordingly, the challenges brought by immigration relate more to the changing nature of the immigrant populations and the scale of the challenges than to straightforward resistance to or anxiety about immigration.

### New York City

Throughout its history New York City has been defined by a large and ever-changing immigrant population, and the city continues to attract large numbers of immigrants in the 21st century. According to the Census Bureau (2011, http://factfinder2.census.gov/faces/tableservices/jsf/pages/productview.xhtml?pid=ACS_11_1YR_NP01&prodType=narrative_profile), in 2011 the city was home to approximately 8.2 million people, of whom 3.1 million (37%) were foreign born. These numbers, along with the large number of second-generation immigrants in the city, make New York one of the most diverse cities in the world.

Although New York, like many other areas of the country, saw rapid increases in the size of its immigrant population in the latter decades of the 20th century and the beginning of the 21st, the composition of the city's immigrant population differed substantially from that of the country at large. Latin America was the leading region of origin among New York immigrants, as in the country at large, but only 186,298 (6%) of New York's 2011 immigrant population of 3.1 million had been born in Mexico, whereas almost 30% of the total U.S. foreign-born population came from Mexico. (See Table 7.6.) Instead, over half of New York's 1.6 million Latin American immigrants came from the Caribbean, including 380,160 individuals from the Dominican Republic. Dominicans represented the top nationality among the city's foreign-born population, at 12.4% of the whole. Chinese immigrants (including immigrants from Hong Kong and Taiwan) were the second-largest group, at 350,231, or 11.4% of the total. Other leading countries of origin among the city's immigrant population were Jamaica

## TABLE 7.6

### Immigrant population of New York City, by place of birth, 2011

| | New York City, New York |
|---|---|
| | Estimate |
| **Total** | **3,066,599** |
| **Europe** | **486,806** |
| Northern Europe | 53,100 |
| United Kingdom (inc. Crown Dependencies) | 34,134 |
| United Kingdom, excluding England and Scotland | 17,215 |
| England | 15,311 |
| Scotland | 1,608 |
| Ireland | 12,392 |
| Denmark | 858 |
| Norway | 1,462 |
| Sweden | 2,956 |
| Other Northern Europe | 1,298 |
| Western Europe | 46,255 |
| Austria | 3,837 |
| Belgium | 2,524 |
| France | 15,186 |
| Germany | 18,657 |
| Netherlands | 2,663 |
| Switzerland | 3,160 |
| Other Western Europe | 228 |
| Southern Europe | 86,241 |
| Greece | 22,915 |
| Italy | 49,075 |
| Portugal | 1,901 |
| Spain | 10,798 |
| Other Southern Europe | 1,552 |
| Eastern Europe | 299,588 |
| Albania | 15,992 |
| Belarus | 12,639 |
| Bulgaria | 4,261 |
| Croatia | 4,266 |
| Czechoslovakia (includes Czech Republic and Slovakia) | 6,272 |
| Hungary | 7,938 |
| Latvia | 3,352 |
| Lithuania | 2,050 |
| Macedonia | 2,810 |
| Moldova | 4,848 |
| Poland | 57,726 |
| Romania | 14,134 |
| Russia | 76,264 |
| Ukraine | 59,820 |
| Bosnia and Herzegovina | 1,717 |
| Yugoslavia | 11,441 |
| Serbia | 2,523 |
| Other Eastern Europe | 14,058 |
| Europe, n.e.c. | 1,622 |
| **Asia** | **843,321** |
| Eastern Asia | 441,656 |
| China | 350,231 |
| China, excluding Hong Kong and Taiwan | 292,035 |
| Hong Kong | 34,255 |
| Taiwan | 23,941 |
| Japan | 18,314 |
| Korea | 72,822 |
| Other Eastern Asia | 289 |
| South Central Asia | 240,480 |
| Afghanistan | 4,125 |
| Bangladesh | 74,692 |
| India | 76,493 |
| Iran | 6,860 |
| Kazakhstan | 1,892 |
| Nepal | 6,939 |
| Pakistan | 39,794 |
| Sri Lanka | 4,740 |
| Uzbekistan | 21,065 |
| Other South Central Asia | 3,880 |

### Immigrant population of New York City, by place of birth, 2011

[CONTINUED]

| | New York City, New York |
|---|---|
| | Estimate |
| South Eastern Asia | 93,960 |
| Cambodia | 2,978 |
| Indonesia | 5,043 |
| Laos | 396 |
| Malaysia | 7,103 |
| Burma | 5,323 |
| Philippines | 50,925 |
| Singapore | 2,521 |
| Thailand | 4,909 |
| Vietnam | 14,762 |
| Other South Eastern Asia | 0 |
| Western Asia | 64,249 |
| Iraq | 2,214 |
| Israel | 20,847 |
| Jordan | 1,442 |
| Kuwait | 236 |
| Lebanon | 5,495 |
| Saudi Arabia | 1,185 |
| Syria | 5,415 |
| Yemen | 7,427 |
| Turkey | 6,662 |
| Armenia | 2,698 |
| Other Western Asia | 10,628 |
| Asia, n.e.c. | 2,976 |
| **Africa** | **128,176** |
| Eastern Africa | 6,727 |
| Eritrea | 227 |
| Ethiopia | 2,619 |
| Kenya | 1,121 |
| Other Eastern Africa | 2,760 |
| Middle Africa | 3,174 |
| Cameroon | 945 |
| Other Middle Africa | 2,229 |
| Northern Africa | 26,939 |
| Egypt | 17,450 |
| Morocco | 6,308 |
| Sudan | 1,288 |
| Other Northern Africa | 1,893 |
| Southern Africa | 3,369 |
| South Africa | 3,009 |
| Other Southern Africa | 360 |
| Western Africa | 76,710 |
| Cape Verde | 0 |
| Ghana | 27,371 |
| Liberia | 3,861 |
| Nigeria | 17,163 |
| Sierra Leone | 4,116 |
| Other Western Africa | 24,199 |
| Africa, n.e.c. | 11,257 |
| **Oceania** | **6,271** |
| Australia and New Zealand subregion | 5,895 |
| Australia | 4,714 |
| Other Australian and New Zealand subregion | 1,181 |
| Fiji | 38 |
| Oceania, n.e.c. | 338 |
| **Americas** | **1,602,025** |
| Latin America | 1,580,462 |
| Caribbean | 845,000 |
| Bahamas | 1,273 |
| Barbados | 23,798 |
| Cuba | 17,687 |
| Dominica | 7,720 |
| Dominican Republic | 380,160 |
| Grenada | 17,613 |
| Haiti | 94,171 |
| Jamaica | 169,235 |
| St. Vincent and the Grenadines | 12,542 |
| Trinidad and Tobago | 87,635 |
| West Indies | 8,687 |

**TABLE 7.6**

Immigrant population of New York City, by place of birth, 2011

[CONTINUED]

| | New York City, New York |
|---|---|
| | **Estimate** |
| Other Caribbean | 24,479 |
| Central America | 311,319 |
|   Mexico | 186,298 |
|   Belize | 8,640 |
|   Costa Rica | 4,410 |
|   El Salvador | 32,903 |
|   Guatemala | 26,136 |
|   Honduras | 28,552 |
|   Nicaragua | 6,415 |
|   Panama | 16,096 |
|   Other Central America | 1,869 |
| South America | 424,143 |
|   Argentina | 11,165 |
|   Bolivia | 3,485 |
|   Brazil | 13,384 |
|   Chile | 4,453 |
|   Colombia | 65,678 |
|   Ecuador | 137,791 |
|   Guyana | 139,947 |
|   Peru | 31,849 |
|   Uruguay | 3,084 |
|   Venezuela | 8,162 |
|   Other South America | 5,145 |
| Northern America | 21,563 |
|   Canada | 21,070 |
|   Other Northern America | 493 |

n.e.c. = not elsewhere classified.
Notes: Estimates of urban and rural population, housing units, and characteristics reflect boundaries of urban areas defined based on Census 2000 data. Boundaries for urban areas have not been updated since Census 2000. As a result, data for urban and rural areas from the ACS do not necessarily reflect the results of ongoing urbanization.

SOURCE: "Place of Birth for the Foreign-Born Population: New York City, New York," in *American Community Survey 1-Year Estimates*, U.S. Census Bureau, 2011, http://factfinder2.census.gov/faces/nav/jsf/pages/searchresults.xhtml?refresh=t (accessed April 13, 2013)

(169,235), Guyana (139,947), Ecuador (137,791), Haiti (94,171), Trinidad and Tobago (87,635), India (76,493), Russia (76,264), Bangladesh (74,692), and Korea (72,822).

As Table 7.7 shows, nearly half (49.1%) of all New Yorkers over the age of five years spoke a language other than English at home, and 23.3% of New Yorkers over the age of five years spoke English less than "very well." A substantial percentage of natives (31.3%) spoke languages other than English at home, which is a measure of the large number of second-generation immigrants in the city. Meanwhile, over three-quarters (76.3%) of foreign-born residents spoke another language at home, and 49.2% of the total over age-five immigrant population spoke English less than very well, according to the Census Bureau. A large percentage of households in the city (15.1%) were classified as "linguistically isolated," a term the Census Bureau uses to describe households in which no adult speaks English very well.

The diversity of languages spoken by the city's immigrants presents municipal officials with a range of challenges regarding the delivery of services and the enforcement of human rights and fair business and labor practices. As Table 7.7 indicates, approximately 367,471 of the city's 2.1 million students were foreign born, and many second-generation immigrants also required language accommodation in the schools. Hospitals are required by state law to provide translation services to those who request them, but the task is greatly complicated by more than 100 languages spoken by the city's

**TABLE 7.7**

Native and immigrant populations of New York City, by school enrollment and language characteristics, 2011

| Subject | New York City, New York | | | | |
|---|---|---|---|---|---|
| | **Total** | **Native** | **Foreign born** | **Foreign born; naturalized citizen** | **Foreign born; not[a] U.S. citizen** |
| | **Estimate** | **Estimate** | **Estimate** | **Estimate** | **Estimate** |
| **Total population** | **8,244,910** | **5,178,311** | **3,066,599** | **1,569,672** | **1,496,927** |
| **School enrollment** | | | | | |
| Population 3 years and over enrolled in school | 2,074,477 | 1,707,006 | 367,471 | 134,380 | 233,091 |
| Nursery school, preschool | 6.0% | 7.1% | 1.2% | 0.8% | 1.5% |
| Elementary school (grades K–8) | 41.5% | 46.2% | 19.2% | 12.3% | 23.1% |
| High school (grades 9–12) | 20.1% | 20.0% | 20.7% | 14.6% | 24.3% |
| College or graduate school | 32.4% | 26.7% | 58.8% | 72.3% | 51.1% |
| **Language spoken at home and ability to speak English** | | | | | |
| Population 5 years and over | 7,710,510 | 4,658,254 | 3,052,256 | 1,567,503 | 1,484,753 |
| English only | 50.9% | 68.7% | 23.7% | 28.3% | 18.9% |
|   Language other than English | 49.1% | 31.3% | 76.3% | 71.7% | 81.1% |
|   Speak English less than "very well" | 23.3% | 6.3% | 49.2% | 40.9% | 58.0% |
| **Selected characteristics** | | | | | |
| Linguistically isolated households | 15.1% | 3.8% | 29.9% | 25.0% | 37.6% |

Note: Estimates of urban and rural population, housing units, and characteristics reflect boundaries of urban areas defined based on Census 2000 data. Boundaries for urban areas have not been updated since Census 2000. As a result, data for urban and rural areas from the American Community Survey (ACS) do not necessarily reflect the results of ongoing urbanization.

SOURCE: Adapted from "Selected Characteristics of the Native and Foreign-Born Populations: New York City, New York," in *2011 American Community Survey 1-Year Estimates*, U.S. Census Bureau, 2011, http://factfinder2.census.gov/faces/nav/jsf/pages/searchresults.xhtml?refresh=t (accessed April 13, 2013)

residents. To address language barriers, the city's Commission on Human Rights prints educational literature about human rights laws and discrimination in Arabic, Chinese, Creole, French, Korean, Polish, Russian, Spanish, and Urdu. In July 2008 Mayor Michael Bloomberg (1942–) issued Executive Order 120 (http://72.34.53.249/~thenyic/sites/default/files/exe_order_120.pdf), which, to ensure equal access to public services, directed all city agencies to provide language services to all New Yorkers for whom English was not their primary language.

Immigrants face challenges beyond language barriers in adjusting to the culture of their new country. They can become victims of discrimination and exploitation because they do not understand U.S. laws and standards. Immigrants often do not seek help because they feel unwelcome outside their own community or, based on experiences in their homeland, do not trust government officials. New York City attempts to address these problems through a variety of channels, including agencies such as the Mayor's Office of Immigrant Affairs (2013, http://www.nyc.gov/html/imm/html/about/about.shtml), which "promotes the well-being of immigrant communities by recommending policies and programs that facilitate successful integration of immigrant New Yorkers into the civic, economic, and cultural life of the City." Additionally, the Commission on Human Rights offers extensive education programs for immigrants regarding fair housing—the right of people to housing opportunity without regard to their age, familial status, religion, or sex (according to federal law) or to their citizenship status, lawful occupation, marital status, or sexual orientation (according to the New York City Human Rights Law). The Neighborhood Human Rights Program works to foster positive relations among residents of diverse racial, ethnic, and religious backgrounds. It offers mediation and conflict resolution services through community service centers.

## Los Angeles County

According to the Census Bureau (2011, http://factfinder2.census.gov/faces/tableservices/jsf/pages/productview.xhtml?pid=ACS_11_1YR_NP01&prodType=narrative_profile), Los Angeles County, whose total population was 9.9 million in 2011, was home to an immigrant population of approximately 3.5 million. As with New York City, a majority of Los Angeles's foreign-born population consisted of arrivals from Latin America (2 million, or 58.4%) and Asia (1.2 million, or 34%). (See Table 7.8.) In contrast to New York, however, a majority of Los Angeles County's population of Latin American immigrants were from Mexico. Mexican immigrants accounted for almost 40% of the county's foreign-born population. In fact, were Los Angeles County's Mexician-born population a city, it would have been among the 10 largest cities in the United States in 2011, with 1.4 million people. Other leading Latin

**TABLE 7.8**

**Immigrant population of Los Angeles County, by place of birth, 2011**

| | Los Angeles County, California |
| --- | --- |
| | Estimate |
| **Total** | **3,474,561** |
| **Europe** | **169,929** |
| Northern Europe | 37,846 |
| United Kingdom (inc. Crown Dependencies) | 27,414 |
| United Kingdom, excluding England and Scotland | 9,770 |
| England | 15,543 |
| Scotland | 2,101 |
| Ireland | 4,204 |
| Denmark | 1,716 |
| Norway | 580 |
| Sweden | 2,713 |
| Other Northern Europe | 1,219 |
| Western Europe | 35,710 |
| Austria | 2,695 |
| Belgium | 1,029 |
| France | 7,896 |
| Germany | 17,737 |
| Netherlands | 4,014 |
| Switzerland | 2,339 |
| Other Western Europe | 0 |
| Southern Europe | 20,974 |
| Greece | 5,408 |
| Italy | 7,858 |
| Portugal | 2,742 |
| Spain | 4,457 |
| Other Southern Europe | 509 |
| Eastern Europe | 75,232 |
| Albania | 565 |
| Belarus | 2,054 |
| Bulgaria | 2,596 |
| Croatia | 2,657 |
| Czechoslovakia (includes Czech Republic and Slovakia) | 3,176 |
| Hungary | 4,372 |
| Latvia | 1,061 |
| Lithuania | 1,765 |
| Macedonia | 68 |
| Moldova | 1,421 |
| Poland | 5,955 |
| Romania | 7,656 |
| Russia | 21,465 |
| Ukraine | 14,019 |
| Bosnia and Herzegovina | 124 |
| Yugoslavia | 2,934 |
| Serbia | 787 |
| Other Eastern Europe | 3,344 |
| Europe, n.e.c. | 167 |
| **Asia** | **1,180,465** |
| Eastern Asia | 444,558 |
| China | 250,623 |
| China, excluding Hong Kong and Taiwan | 159,192 |
| Hong Kong | 26,783 |
| Taiwan | 64,648 |
| Japan | 36,253 |
| Korea | 155,890 |
| Other Eastern Asia | 1,792 |
| South Central Asia | 194,798 |
| Afghanistan | 2,720 |
| Bangladesh | 6,189 |
| India | 53,165 |
| Iran | 111,629 |
| Kazakhstan | 371 |
| Nepal | 1,499 |
| Pakistan | 10,971 |
| Sri Lanka | 5,448 |
| Uzbekistan | 1,679 |
| Other South Central Asia | 1,127 |

| | Los Angeles County, California |
| --- | --- |
| | Estimate |
| South Eastern Asia | 409,640 |
| Cambodia | 24,862 |
| Indonesia | 12,776 |
| Laos | 3,037 |
| Malaysia | 3,417 |
| Burma | 6,939 |
| Philippines | 236,246 |
| Singapore | 2,224 |
| Thailand | 23,016 |
| Vietnam | 97,123 |
| Other South Eastern Asia | 0 |
| Western Asia | 130,178 |
| Iraq | 5,560 |
| Israel | 14,597 |
| Jordan | 2,381 |
| Kuwait | 521 |
| Lebanon | 16,588 |
| Saudi Arabia | 2,878 |
| Syria | 11,654 |
| Yemen | 252 |
| Turkey | 4,958 |
| Armenia | 62,645 |
| Other Western Asia | 8,144 |
| Asia, n.e.c. | 1,291 |
| **Africa** | **55,269** |
| Eastern Africa | 12,389 |
| Eritrea | 942 |
| Ethiopia | 4,527 |
| Kenya | 2,903 |
| Other Eastern Africa | 4,017 |
| Middle Africa | 2,384 |
| Cameroon | 1,452 |
| Other Middle Africa | 932 |
| Northern Africa | 17,147 |
| Egypt | 12,235 |
| Morocco | 2,979 |
| Sudan | 452 |
| Other Northern Africa | 1,481 |
| Southern Africa | 5,023 |
| South Africa | 5,023 |
| Other Southern Africa | 0 |
| Western Africa | 15,117 |
| Cape Verde | 0 |
| Ghana | 996 |
| Liberia | 969 |
| Nigeria | 11,112 |
| Sierra Leone | 835 |
| Other Western Africa | 1,205 |
| Africa, n.e.c. | 3,209 |
| **Oceania** | **13,175** |
| Australia and New Zealand subregion | 8,397 |
| Australia | 6,100 |
| Other Australian and New Zealand subregion | 2,297 |
| Fiji | 2,170 |
| Oceania, n.e.c. | 2,608 |
| **Americas** | **2,055,723** |
| Latin America | 2,029,249 |
| Caribbean | 31,111 |
| Bahamas | 191 |
| Barbados | 490 |
| Cuba | 17,145 |
| Dominica | 248 |
| Dominican Republic | 1,414 |
| Grenada | 453 |
| Haiti | 951 |
| Jamaica | 5,914 |
| St. Vincent and the Grenadines | 189 |
| Trinidad and Tobago | 3,756 |
| West Indies | 217 |
| Other Caribbean | 143 |

| | Los Angeles County, California |
| --- | --- |
| | Estimate |
| Central America | 1,905,446 |
| Mexico | 1,375,706 |
| Belize | 12,663 |
| Costa Rica | 6,151 |
| El Salvador | 266,889 |
| Guatemala | 176,003 |
| Honduras | 32,459 |
| Nicaragua | 30,958 |
| Panama | 2,568 |
| Other Central America | 2,049 |
| South America | 92,692 |
| Argentina | 13,208 |
| Bolivia | 3,657 |
| Brazil | 7,126 |
| Chile | 5,832 |
| Colombia | 12,988 |
| Ecuador | 14,568 |
| Guyana | 1,341 |
| Peru | 26,677 |
| Uruguay | 1,827 |
| Venezuela | 3,165 |
| Other South America | 2,303 |
| Northern America | 26,474 |
| Canada | 26,439 |
| Other Northern America | 35 |

n.e.c. = not elsewhere classified.
Notes: Estimates of urban and rural population, housing units, and characteristics reflect boundaries of urban areas defined based on Census 2000 data. Boundaries for urban areas have not been updated since Census 2000. As a result, data for urban and rural areas from the American Community Survey (ACS) do not necessarily reflect the results of ongoing urbanization.

SOURCE: "Place of Birth for the Foreign-Born Population: Los Angeles County, California," in *2011 American Community Survey 1-Year Estimates*, U.S. Census Bureau, 2011, http://factfinder2.census.gov/faces/nav/jsf/pages/searchresults.xhtml?refresh=t (accessed April 13, 2013)

American countries of origin were El Salvador (266,889) and Guatemala (176,003).

In 2011 the number of Asian immigrants in Los Angeles County (1.2 million) was more than that of New York City (843,321), and the county's Asian-born population was distributed more widely among countries of origin. (See Table 7.8 and Table 7.6.) There were 250,623 immigrants from China (including those from Hong Kong and Taiwan), 236,246 from the Philippines, 155,890 from Korea, 111,629 from Iran, and 97,123 from Vietnam. (See Table 7.8.)

As with New York City, language barriers play a major role in the dispensation of municipal services and protection in Los Angeles County. Over half (57%) of the 9.2 million Los Angeles County residents over the age of five years spoke a language other than English at home, and 26.4% spoke English less than very well. (See Table 7.9.) Among the 5.8 million natives over the age of five years, 35.7% spoke a language other than English at home, again likely pointing to a large second-generation immigrant population. An overwhelming majority (92.4%) of the 3.5 million immigrants over the age of five years

TABLE 7.9

**Native and immigrant populations of Los Angeles County, by school enrollment and language characteristics, 2011**

| Subject | Los Angeles County, California | | | | |
| --- | --- | --- | --- | --- | --- |
| | Total | Native | Foreign born | Foreign born; naturalized citizen | Foreign born; not a U.S. citizen |
| | Estimate | Estimate | Estimate | Estimate | Estimate |
| **Total population** | 9,889,056 | 6,414,495 | 3,474,561 | 1,630,868 | 1,843,693 |
| **School enrollment** | | | | | |
| Population 3 years and over enrolled in school | 2,789,629 | 2,421,142 | 368,487 | 118,511 | 249,976 |
| Nursery school, preschool | 5.7% | 6.4% | 1.3% | 0.5% | 1.6% |
| Elementary school (grades K–8) | 41.6% | 45.0% | 19.1% | 8.3% | 24.2% |
| High school (grades 9–12) | 21.9% | 22.0% | 21.1% | 12.6% | 25.2% |
| College or graduate school | 30.8% | 26.5% | 58.5% | 78.5% | 49.0% |
| **Language spoken at home and ability to speak English** | | | | | |
| Population 5 years and over | 9,240,851 | 5,779,257 | 3,461,594 | 1,628,371 | 1,833,223 |
| English only | 43.0% | 64.3% | 7.6% | 10.1% | 5.5% |
| Language other than English | 57.0% | 35.7% | 92.4% | 89.9% | 94.5% |
| Speak English less than "very well" | 26.4% | 5.1% | 61.9% | 52.0% | 70.6% |
| **Selected characteristics** | | | | | |
| Linguistically isolated households | 14.1% | 1.3% | 31.1% | 25.4% | 38.4% |

Estimates of urban and rural population, housing units, and characteristics reflect boundaries of urban areas defined based on Census 2000 data. Boundaries for urban areas have not been updated since Census 2000. As a result, data for urban and rural areas from the American Community Survey (ACS) do not necessarily reflect the results of ongoing urbanization.

SOURCE: Adapted from "Selected Characteristics of the Native and Foreign-Born Populations: Los Angeles County, California," in *2011 American Community Survey 1-Year Estimates*, U.S. Census Bureau, 2011, http://factfinder2.census.gov/faces/nav/jsf/pages/searchresults.xhtml?refresh=t (accessed April 13, 2013)

spoke a language other than English at home, and 61.9% of Los Angeles County immigrants spoke English less than very well. An estimated 31.1% of the immigrant population and an estimated 14.1% of the total population were classified as linguistically isolated.

Michael Fix et al. of the Migration Policy Institute assess the challenges posed to Los Angeles County by its large immigrant population in *Los Angeles on the Leading Edge: Immigrant Integration Indicators and Their Policy Implications* (April 2008, http://www.migrationpolicy.org/pubs/nciip_los_angeles_on_the_leading_edge.pdf). Among other issues affecting the integration of Los Angeles County's immigrants in 2008, the researchers identify the following:

- Over 40% of all students in Los Angeles schools were English learners (ELs). The great majority were U.S. citizens, and the number of EL students—almost 330,000—was three times higher than the next highest district in the nation.

- Almost half (46%) of the Los Angeles County workforce was foreign born, a share three times higher than the United States as a whole.

- One-third of Los Angeles adults were ELs, a number that rose from 1.7 million to 2.3 million between 1990 and 2006.

- With 40% of adult immigrants lacking a high school diploma, and 43% of California's recent Latin American immigrants who entered after the age of 25 years with a bachelor's degree or higher employed in unskilled jobs, workforce incorporation and economic

mobility questions loomed large for both low- and high-skilled immigrants.

Fix et al. note that Los Angeles County has seen its immigrant population mature significantly since the 1980s. In 1980, 57% of the county's immigrants were new arrivals (immigrants who arrived in the United States within the previous 10 years), but by 2000 only 36% were. The percentage of the foreign born in Los Angeles County who were naturalized citizens had risen from 9% in 1990 to 16% in 2006, and second-generation immigrants were rapidly beginning to outnumber first-generation immigrants. Thus, Los Angeles County's immigrant population was significantly more empowered than the U.S. immigrant population as a whole, and it was poised to shape the future of the immigration debate by exerting its growing political clout in elections. As the researchers note, however, voting among immigrants will likely not be enough to address Los Angeles County's challenges; successful integration of the immigrant population requires more widespread legislative and municipal commitment to the issue, as well.

## IMMIGRANTS' CONTRIBUTIONS TO THE U.S. ECONOMY

### Entrepreneurs

In October 2012 Vivek Wadhwa, AnnaLee Saxenian, and F. Daniel Siciliano of the Kauffman Foundation released *Then and Now: America's New Immigrant Entrepreneurs, Part VII* (http://www.kauffman.org/uploadedFiles/Then _and_now_americas_new_immigrant_entrepreneurs.pdf), the latest in a series of research reports assessing the role of immigrant entrepreneurs in the U.S. economy. The first such report, written by Saxenian and issued in 1999, provided the first in-depth analysis of the effect that highly skilled immigrants had on innovation and economic output in Silicon Valley (the Northern California region famous for producing many of the world's leading high-tech companies). In the first report, Saxenian found that one-third of the Silicon Valley workforce consisted of immigrants and that one-quarter of technology companies in the region (which were responsible for a combined $16.8 billion in annual sales and over 58,000 jobs) were operated by either Indian or Chinese immigrants.

Building on Saxenian's research, a subsequent study *America's New Immigrant Entrepreneurs* (http://people.ischool.berkeley.edu/~anno/Papers/Americas_new_immigrant_entrepreneurs_I.pdf), written by Wadhwa et al., was released in January 2007. The researchers of that report found that immigrant contributions to the tech industry in Silicon Valley had accelerated since the release of Saxenian's report. Specifically, Wadhwa et al. determined that 52.4% of all technology start-ups in Silicon Valley between 1995 and 2005 had at least one key founder who was an immigrant. They also extended their focus to consider immigrant entrepreneurs' contributions to the national economy, finding that 25.3% of all U.S. engineering and technology companies started between 1995 and 2005 had at least one immigrant among its founders. In 2005 alone, these companies collectively employed approximately 450,000 people and generated an estimated $52 billion in sales.

The Kauffman Foundation commissioned another 2007 report that focused on the backlog of high-skilled immigrants who had applied for legal permanent resident (LPR) status. The researchers of that report, observing the years-long waits for LPR status imposed on many high-skilled immigrant applicants, predicted a reverse brain drain whereby immigration restrictions caused many of the world's most talented technology professionals to leave the United States after exhausting student or temporary visas. Wadhwa, Saxenian, and Siciliano's 2012 report was designed to assess whether this prediction had come true in subsequent years.

Wadhwa, Saxenian, and Siciliano find conclusive evidence that the predictions issued in 2007 had been borne out. They determine that the percentage of engineering and technology companies founded by immigrants had fallen from 25.3% in 2005 to 24.3% in 2012. Although the decline in immigrant ownership was small enough to fall within the study's margin of error, the 2012 number still demonstrated that the period of rapid growth in immigrant contributions to the tech industry had flattened out and perhaps been reversed. Even more suggestive of such a reversal are the researchers' findings

in Silicon Valley, where the proportion of immigrant-founded start-ups had fallen from 52.4% between 1995 and 2005 to 43.9% between 2006 and 2012.

**SOME NOTABLE IMMIGRANT ENTREPRENEURS.** The article "The World's Billionaires" (Forbes.com, March 2013) offers examples of immigrant entrepreneurs:

- Len Blavatnik (1957–) emigrated from Russia in 1978. After earning a master's degree in business administration at Harvard University, he founded the holding company Access Industries in 1986 and was partly responsible for the merger of the Russian oil company TNK-BP. He was worth $16 billion in 2013.

- Russian-born Sergey Brin (1973–) founded Google with partner Larry Page. They started the company in a garage after dropping out of graduate school in 1998; the company went public in 2004. In 2013 Brin was the world's 21st-richest man, with a fortune of $22.8 billion.

- The Australian-born media giant Rupert Murdoch (1931–) renounced his Australian citizenship and became a U.S. citizen in 1985 because of laws that restricted the ownership of American television stations to citizens. In 2013 his personal fortune was $11.2 billion.

- Pierre Omidyar (1967–) was born in France to Iranian immigrant parents. His family immigrated to the United States when he was six years old. He founded an online auction site that in 1997 was renamed eBay, of which he remains chairman. His personal wealth totaled $8.7 billion in 2013.

- George Soros (1930–) was born in Hungary and survived the World War II (1939–1945) German occupation of Budapest. He immigrated to the United States in 1945, founding Quantum Fund in 1969. In 2013 his personal fortune was worth $19.2 billion.

### Small Business Owners

Even though the contributions of immigrants in Silicon Valley and the tech industry at large have attracted substantial media coverage and begun to factor into policy discussions surrounding immigration reform, the contributions of smaller-scale immigrant entrepreneurs have drawn less attention. In *Immigrant Small Business Owners: A Significant and Growing Part of the Economy* (June 2012, http://fiscalpolicy.org/wp-content/uploads/2012/06/immigrant-small-business-owners-FPI-20120614.pdf), the Fiscal Policy Institute, a New York–based nonprofit economic and tax research group, provides the first comprehensive analysis of immigrant small business owners' contributions to the U.S. economy. The institute notes that of the 4.9 million small business owners (the Census Bureau defines a small business as a company with one to

100 workers) in the United States in 2010, 900,000 (18%) were immigrants. Immigrants, who accounted for approximately 13% of the U.S. population, were thus significantly overrepresented among small business owners. In 2007, the most recent year for which such data were available, immigrant-owned small businesses employed an estimated 4.7 million employees, which amounted to 30% of all private-sector employment, and generated an estimated $776 billion in sales. The most common types of immigrant-owned small businesses as of 2010 were grocery stores, physicians' offices, real estate firms, restaurants, and truck transportation services.

### Immigrants in the Labor Force

Immigrants' participation in the labor force is the underlying subject in most debates about the virtues and drawbacks of immigration in the United States. Sensitivity about the presence of the foreign born in the workforce becomes particularly acute at times of economic contraction and high unemployment such as that initiated by the Great Recession, which began in late 2007 and lasted through mid-2009. The recession's effects on employment remained pronounced well beyond its end, however, with unemployment remaining extremely high by historic standards well into the following decade.

As discussed in Chapter 6, many economists discount the widely held belief that immigrant competition depresses wages in the United States, and some economists suggest that immigration reform that offers legal work authorization to undocumented workers would be a boon for the U.S. economy while having little if any adverse effect on native-born workers. Even absent such reform, however, it is clear that immigrants are a crucial part of the U.S. labor force, and their roles in the labor force are expected to grow. As Table 7.10 shows, workforce participation among Asian-Americans and Hispanics increased rapidly between 1990 and 2010. The increases in these groups' numbers in the labor force far outpaced increases in the numbers of white and African-American workers during the same period. Although workforce growth overall was expected to be much slower from 2010 to 2020 as the aftereffects of the Great Recession continued to reverberate, growth in the numbers of Asian-American and Hispanic workers was expected to continue outpacing growth in the numbers of white and African-American workers.

Audrey Singer of the Brookings Institution provides in *Immigrant Workers in the U.S. Labor Force* (March 15, 2012, http://www.brookings.edu/research/papers/2012/03/15-immigrant-workers-singer) further analysis of the role of immigrants in the U.S. labor force. Between 1970 and 2010 the immigrant population expanded rapidly as a share of the total U.S. population, from 4.8% to 12.9%. (See Figure 7.2.) Even more rapid than this expansion, though, was the growth of immigrant workers as a share

of the overall labor force. In 1970 immigrants were only slightly overrepresented in the labor force, accounting for 4.8% of the population and 4.9% of the labor force; by 2010, however, when immigrants accounted for 12.9% of the total population, they accounted for 16.4% of the labor force. Certain industries were particularly dependent on immigrant workers. As Figure 7.3 illustrates, in 2010 immigrants made up 20% or more of the workforce in industries such as high-tech manufacturing, construction, food services, agriculture, management and administration, and warehousing. Immigrants accounted for more than 30% of workers in the accommodation industry (which chiefly consists of hotels and other lodgings), and they accounted for 49% of all workers employed in private households.

Not only were immigrants central to the functioning of numerous sectors of the economy, they were also projected to play an even bigger role in future economic growth. Singer notes that immigrants were overrepresented in a number of those industries that were among the fastest growing as of 2010. Of the 15 occupations projected to grow the fastest between 2010 and 2020, immigrants were overrepresented in seven. (See Figure 7.4.) These included a number of low-skilled occupations, such as iron and rebar workers in construction, over 60% of whom were immigrants in 2010, as well as home health aides (24%) and personal care aides (23%). Immigrants accounted for 41% of all interpreters and translators, one of the fastest-growing skilled professions in the United States. Singer indicates that each of these professions is expected to grow by at least 42% between 2010 and 2020, and immigrants are expected to remain disproportionately central to each.

## AMERICAN VIEWS ON IMMIGRATION

Concerns about immigration's effect on the United States were hardly uniform in the first decade of the 21st century. Republican voters and politicians tended to support restrictive immigration policies, whereas Democratic voters and politicians tended to focus more on integrating the existing immigrant population. Nevertheless, with the dovetailing of national security and immigration issues in the aftermath of the September 11, 2001, terrorist attacks against the United States, advocates of tightened border security and mass deportation had the upper hand in elections at the national level as well as in most Republican-leaning states. Although the proposed Development, Relief, and Education for Alien Minors (DREAM) Act enjoyed some support among Republicans and solid support among Democrats, resistance to any immigration reform that loosened restrictions on unauthorized immigration remained fierce throughout the administration of George W. Bush (1946–), a Republican. In 2007 President Bush backed a U.S. Senate bill that incorporated much of the DREAM Act and also strengthened border security, but the bill never came to a vote in Congress, largely because of resistance in his own party.

**TABLE 7.10**

**Civilian labor force, by race and ethnicity, 1990–2020**

[In thousands]

| Race, and ethnicity | Levels | | | | Change | | | Percent change | | | Percent distribution | | | | Annual growth rate (percent) | | |
|---|---|---|---|---|---|---|---|---|---|---|---|---|---|---|---|---|---|
| | 1990 | 2000 | 2010 | 2020 | 1990–2000 | 2000–10 | 2010–20 | 1990–2000 | 2000–10 | 2010–20 | 1990 | 2000 | 2010 | 2020 | 1990–2000 | 2000–10 | 2010–20 |
| **Race** | | | | | | | | | | | | | | | | | |
| White | 107,447 | 118,545 | 125,084 | 130,516 | 11,098 | 6,539 | 5,432 | 10.3 | 5.5 | 4.3 | 85.4 | 83.1 | 81.3 | 79.4 | 1.0 | 0.5 | 0.4 |
| Black | 13,740 | 16,397 | 17,862 | 19,676 | 2,657 | 1,465 | 1,814 | 19.3 | 8.9 | 10.2 | 10.9 | 11.5 | 11.6 | 12.0 | 1.8 | 0.9 | 1.0 |
| Asian | 4,653 | 6,270 | 7,248 | 9,430 | 1,617 | 978 | 2,182 | 34.8 | 15.6 | 30.1 | 3.7 | 4.4 | 4.7 | 5.7 | 3.0 | 1.5 | 2.7 |
| All other groups* | — | 1,371 | 3,694 | 4,738 | — | 2,323 | 1,044 | — | — | 28.3 | — | 1.0 | 2.4 | 2.9 | — | — | 2.5 |
| **Ethnicity** | | | | | | | | | | | | | | | | | |
| Hispanic origin | 10,720 | 16,689 | 22,748 | 30,493 | 5,969 | 6,059 | 7,745 | 55.7 | 36.3 | 34.0 | 8.5 | 11.7 | 14.8 | 18.6 | 4.5 | 3.1 | 3.0 |
| Other than Hispanic origin | 115,120 | 125,894 | 131,141 | 133,867 | 10,774 | 5,247 | 2,726 | 9.4 | 4.2 | 2.1 | 91.5 | 88.3 | 85.2 | 81.4 | 0.9 | 0.4 | 0.2 |
| White non-Hispanic | 97,818 | 102,729 | 103,947 | 102,371 | 4,911 | 1,218 | −1,576 | 5.0 | 1.2 | −1.5 | 77.7 | 72.0 | 67.5 | 62.3 | 0.5 | 0.1 | −0.2 |

*The "all other groups" category includes (1) those classified as being of multiple racial origin and (2) the race categories of (2a) American Indian and Alaska Native and (2b) Native Hawaiian and other Pacific Islanders. Dash indicates no data collected for category. Details may not sum to totals because of rounding.

SOURCE: Adapted from "Table 1. Civilian Labor Force, by Age, Sex, Race, and Ethnicity, 1990, 2000, 2010, and Projected 2020," in *Employment Projections—2010–2020*, U.S. Department of Labor, Bureau of Labor Statistics, February 1, 2012, http://www.bls.gov/news.release/pdf/ecopro.pdf (accessed March 15, 2013)

FIGURE 7.2

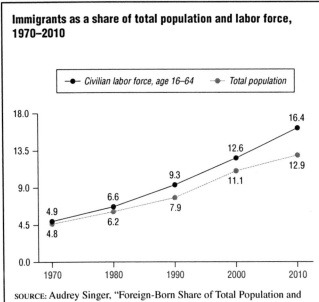

**Immigrants as a share of total population and labor force, 1970–2010**

Legend:
—●— Civilian labor force, age 16–64    ⋯●⋯ Total population

Civilian labor force values: 4.9 (1970), 6.6 (1980), 9.3 (1990), 12.6 (2000), 16.4 (2010)

Total population values: 4.8 (1970), 6.2 (1980), 7.9 (1990), 11.1 (2000), 12.9 (2010)

SOURCE: Audrey Singer, "Foreign-Born Share of Total Population and Labor Force, 1970–2010," in *Immigrant Workers in the U.S. Labor Force*, Brookings Institution, March 15, 2012, http://www.brookings.edu/research/papers/2012/03/15-immigrant-workers-singer (accessed March 15, 2013)

Barack Obama (1961–) won the presidency in 2008 with strong support from Hispanics and other minorities, and Republicans became more resolutely opposed to DREAM-style legislation in the years that followed. The passage of harsh immigration laws in Republican-controlled states such as Arizona and Alabama further polarized voters and pitted the governments of those states against the U.S. Department of Justice in numerous legal challenges during the Obama administration. In June 2012 President Obama signaled solidarity with the immigrant population by announcing the Deferred Action for Childhood Arrivals Program, which grants reprieves from deportation to unauthorized immigrants brought to the country as children. At the Democratic National Convention in September of that year, Benita Veliz, a so-called DREAMer (an undocumented immigrant who became eligible to stay in the country under the Deferred Action program), was among the keynote speakers. By contrast, President Obama's Republican opponent, Mitt Romney (1947–), ran on a platform that called for increasing attention to border security and strict opposition to creating any path to citizenship for unauthorized immigrants. Although Romney garnered a majority of the white vote nationally, he lost badly among Hispanics and other minorities, whose strong support for President Obama was considered integral to his reelection.

Following the election, many prominent Republicans noted the demographic predictions about the country's future racial and ethnic makeup and voiced concerns about the party's continued appeals to anti-immigrant sentiment. In what was widely perceived as an attempt to reach out to the country's growing Hispanic population, prominent Republicans such as Senator Marco Rubio (1971–; R-FL), a second-generation Cuban-American, began publicly attempting to move the party toward a compromise position on immigration reform. Added to strong Democratic backing of DREAM-style legislation, this new support among some Republicans created the first opening for a comprehensive immigration reform bill since President Bush's failed effort in 2007.

In 2013 the so-called Gang of Eight, a group of four Democratic and four Republican senators, crafted a new reform proposal that would create a path to citizenship for all undocumented immigrants who came to the country prior to December 31, 2011, raise limits on the number of high-skilled immigrants admitted under the H-1B visa program (which allows employers to temporarily employ foreign workers on a nonimmigrant basis in a specialty occupation), and create a new guest-worker program for admitting more low-skilled immigrants. The reform proposal would, however, tie these loosened restrictions to mandatory increases in border security and workplace enforcement.

Meanwhile, public opinion on the immigration issue remained hard to gauge, with pollsters extracting different portraits of the general public's views depending on how certain questions were asked. In "Majority of U.S. Citizens Say Illegal Immigrants Should Be Deported" (Reuters, February 20, 2013), Rachelle Younglai reports that according to a Reuters/Ipsos poll that was conducted in February 2013, a majority of Americans believed that most or all illegal immigrants should be deported. Of those polled, 23% thought that all illegal immigrants should be deported, while 30% believed that most illegal immigrants (with some exceptions) should be deported. Only 5% believed that all illegal immigrants should be allowed to stay in the United States. Younglai notes that "these results are in line with other polls in recent years, suggesting that people's views on immigration have not changed dramatically since the immigration debate reignited in Congress last month."

In contrast, a poll conducted by the Public Religion Research Institute (PRRI) in partnership with the Brookings Institution had a very different conclusion. In the press release "More Than 6-in-10 Americans Support a Path to Citizenship" (March 21, 2013, http://publicreligion.org/newsroom/2013/03/2013-religion-values-immigration-survey-release/), the PRRI indicates that 63% of Americans believed that illegal immigrants should be offered a path to citizenship and that support for a path to a citizenship was strong among Democrats (71%), Independents (64%), and Republicans (53%). Robert P. Jones, the chief executive officer of the PRRI, claimed, "Support for a path to citizenship for illegal immigrants who are already living in the United States is that rarest of rarities in our polarized political environment—a policy that enjoys majority support across partisan and religious lines."

## FIGURE 7.3

**Immigrant share of workforce in individual industries, 2010**

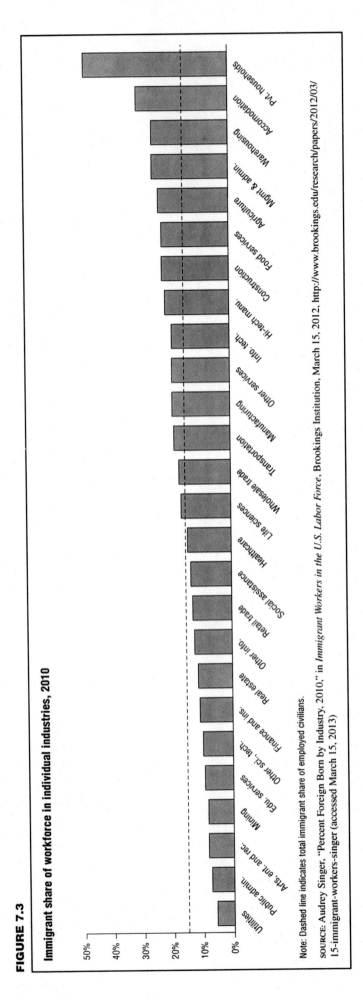

Note: Dashed line indicates total immigrant share of employed civilians.

SOURCE: Audrey Singer, "Percent Foreign Born by Industry, 2010," in *Immigrant Workers in the U.S. Labor Force,* Brookings Institution, March 15, 2012, http://www.brookings.edu/research/papers/2012/03/15-immigrant-workers-singer (accessed March 15, 2013)

**FIGURE 7.4**

**Immigrant share of workforce among occupations projected to grow fastest from 2010 to 2020**

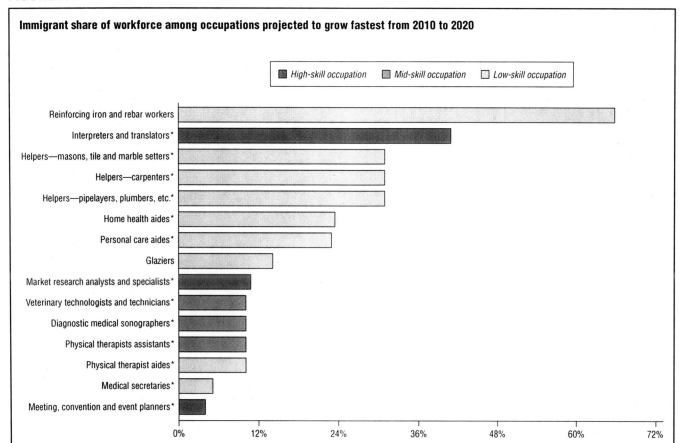

*For occupations marked with an asterisk, there is not a one-to-one match between Bureau of Labor Statistics (BLS) and Current Population Survey (CPS) data. CPS data, which was used to determine the share foreign-born, has less detailed occupational categories.
Note: Biomedical engineers and occupational therapy assistants were among the fifteen occupations projected to grow the fastest by BLS, but they are not included on this graph because the sample size for foreign-born workers in those occupations in the 2010 CPS was too small to produce a reliable estimate.

SOURCE: Audrey Singer, "Foreign-Born Share in 2010 of the Fifteen Fastest-Growing Occupations, 2010–2020," in *Immigrant Workers in the U.S. Labor Force*, Brookings Institution, March 15, 2012, http://www.brookings.edu/research/papers/2012/03/15-immigrant-workers-singer (accessed March 15, 2013)

## CHAPTER 8
# THE UNITED STATES NEEDS MORE TOLERANT IMMIGRATION LAWS

**TESTIMONY OF JOSE ANTONIO VARGAS, FOUNDER OF DEFINE AMERICAN, BEFORE THE COMMITTEE ON THE JUDICIARY, U.S. SENATE, HEARING ON "COMPREHENSIVE IMMIGRATION REFORM," FEBRUARY 13, 2013**

Thank you Chairman Leahy, Ranking Member Grassley, and distinguished members of this Committee.

I come to you as one of our country's 11 million undocumented immigrants, many of us Americans at heart, but without the right papers to show for it. Too often, we're treated as abstractions, faceless and nameless, subjects of debate rather than individuals with families, hopes, fears, and dreams.

I am in America because of the sacrifices of my family. My grandparents legally emigrated from the Philippines to Silicon Valley in the mid-1980s. A few years later, Grandpa Teofilo became a U.S. citizen and legally changed his name to Ted—after Ted Danson in "Cheers." Because grandparents cannot petition for their grandkids—and because my mother could not come to the United States—grandpa saved up money to get his only grandson, me, a passport and green card to come to America. My mother gave me up to give me a better life.

I arrived in Mountain View, Calif. on August 3, 1993. One of my earliest memories was singing the National Anthem as a 6th grader at Crittenden Middle School, believing the song had somehow something to do with me. I thought the first lines were, "Jose, can you see?"

Four years later, I applied for a driver's permit like any 16 year old. That was when I discovered that the green card that my grandpa gave me was fake.

But I wanted to work. I wanted to contribute to a country that is now my home. At age 17, I decided to be a journalist for a seemingly naive reason: if I am not supposed to be in America because I don't have the right kind of papers, what if my name—my byline—was on the paper? How can they say I don't exist if my name is in newspapers and magazines? I thought I could write my way into America.

As I built a successful career as a journalist—paying Social Security and state and federal taxes along the way—as fear and shame, as denial and pain, enveloped me—words became my salvation. I found solace in the words of the Rev. Martin Luther King, quoting St. Augustine: "An unjust law is no law at all."

Ultimately, it took me 12 years to come out as an undocumented American—because that is what I am, an American. But I am grateful to have been able to tell the truth. And in the past few years, more undocumented people, particularly young DREAMers, are coming out. Telling the truth about the America we experience.

We dream of a path to citizenship so we can actively participate in our American democracy.

We dream of not being separated from our families and our loved ones, regardless of sexual orientation, no matter our skill set. This government has deported more than 1.6 million people—fathers and mothers, sons and daughters—in the past four years.

We dream of contributing to the country we call our home.

In 21st century America, diversity is destiny. That I happen to be gay; that I speak Tagalog, my first language, and want to learn Spanish—that does not threaten my love for this country. How interconnected and integrated we are as Americans makes us stronger.

Sitting behind me today is my Filipino-American family—my grandma Leonila, whom I love very much; my Aunt Aida Rivera, who helped raise me; and my Uncle Conrad Salinas, who served, proudly, in the U.S. Navy for 20 years. They're all naturalized American citizens.

I belong in what is called a mixed-status family. I am the only one in my extended family of 25 Americans who is undocumented. When you inaccurately call me "illegal," you're not only dehumanizing me, you're offending them. No human being is illegal.

Also here is my Mountain View High School family—my support network of allies who encouraged and protected me since I was a teenager. After I told my high school principal and school superintendent that I was not planning to go to college because I could not apply for financial aid, Pat Hyland and Rich Fischer secured a private scholarship for me. The scholarship was funded by a man named Jim Strand. I am honored that Pat, Rich and Jim are all here today. Across the country, there are countless other Jim Strands, Pat Hylands, and Rich Fischers of all backgrounds who stand alongside their undocumented neighbors. They don't need to see pieces of paper—a passport or a green card—to treat us as human beings.

This is the truth about immigration in our America.

As this Congress decides on fair, humane reform, let us remember that immigration is not merely about borders. "Immigration is in our blood ... part of our founding story," writes Sen. Ted Kennedy, former chairman of this very Committee, in the introduction to President Kennedy's book, "A Nation of Immigrants." Immigration is about our future. Immigration is about all of us.

And before I take your questions, I have a few of my own:

What do you want to do with me?

What do you want to do with us?

How do you define "American"?

Thank you. (http://judiciary.senate.gov/pdf/2-13-13VargasTestimony.pdf)

## TESTIMONY OF VIVEK WADHWA, DIRECTOR OF RESEARCH AT DUKE UNIVERSITY'S PRATT SCHOOL OF ENGINEERING, BEFORE THE COMMITTEE ON THE JUDICIARY, U.S. HOUSE OF REPRESENTATIVES, HEARING ON "AMERICA'S IMMIGRATION SYSTEM: OPPORTUNITIES FOR LEGAL IMMIGRATION AND ENFORCEMENT OF LAWS AGAINST ILLEGAL IMMIGRATION," FEBRUARY 5, 2013

Chairman Bob Goodlatte and members of the Judiciary Committee, I want to thank you for the opportunity to submit my testimony and share my thoughts on the importance of immigration reform.

Being in Washington DC, it is very easy to be pessimistic. We worry about our competitiveness and wonder whether the future does indeed belong to China, as some people say. We fear that America will stop innovating and that its economy will stagnate; that we will be fighting for limited resources. We therefore debate whether there are shortages of engineers or a glut. In our dark moments, we try to raise trade barriers and keep foreigners out.

I am here to tell you that these fears are largely unfounded and that the future is ours to lose. America has a way of constantly reinventing itself and reaching new heights. This is what is happening now; America is in the midst of its next great rebound. Its scientists and entrepreneurs are setting the wheels in motion to solve humanity's grand challenges—in areas such as health, energy, food, education, water, and security. This will be the most innovative decade in human history—when we begin to go from worrying about shortages to worrying about how to share the abundance that we are create.

The decisions we make on immigration will either facilitate this rebound or trip up the entrepreneurs who are working to make it happen. Let me briefly explain the advances I am talking about so that you understand the increasing importance of a skilled workforce.

We have seen how computers are becoming more powerful year by year as prices drop. In the technology industry, this advance is known as Moore's Law. It's not just in computer hardware; the same exponential growth is happening in an assortment of other technologies.

Take the manufacturing industry. Advances in robotics, artificial intelligence, and 3D printing are dramatically reducing the costs of manufacturing and making it possible to create new types of products. These technologies are rapidly eroding China's cost advantage. It is very likely that, within a few years, we will reach the tipping point when it becomes cheaper to manufacture in the U.S. than in China. Note how fracking technology has rejuvenated America's oil industry. We are about to see an even greater rejuvenation in American manufacturing.

Advances in digital medicine and genomics are also transforming the health-care industry.

Inexpensive sensor-based devices are allowing us to start monitoring our health so that we can prevent disease and dramatically reduce health-care costs. Entrepreneurs are building iPhone apps that act like medical assistants and detect disease; smart pills that we swallow in order to monitor our internals; and body sensors that monitor heart, brain, and body activity. These new devices empower the patient to monitor and improve their own health. I am a heart patient, and carry an AliveCor heart monitor that can perform an instant EKG if I ever need it, for example.

Advances in DNA sequencing are opening up new possibilities for advancing health care. Full human-genome sequencing cost billions of dollars a decade ago. It now costs thousands of dollars, and will come to cost less than a blood test. Scientists and engineers are discovering the correlations between disease, lifestyle, and genome. In the future it will be possible for doctors to prescribe the most patient-appropriate medicines based on a person's DNA.

This is just the tip of the iceberg. There are similar advances happening in other fields where technology can be applied. Google is developing an Artificial Intelligence–based self-driving car that can change the face of cities by eliminating the need for parking spots, eliminate highway fatalities and traffic congestion, and dramatically reduce fuel consumption. New education technologies are changing the way we can teach and bring knowledge to the masses. Advances in nanotechnology are allowing us to develop new types of lighter and stronger materials such as carbon nanotubes, ceramic-matrix nanocomposites, and new carbon fibers.

All of these advances are being made by entrepreneurs working hand in hand with engineers, scientists, physicians, and researchers. Foreign-born workers are leading the charge in all of these fields.

In the era of exponential technologies that we are entering, education and skill matter more than ever. Small teams of people can do what was once possible only for governments and large corporations—solving grand problems. Diversity in background, in field of knowledge, and in thinking are great assets. We need the world's best and brightest more than ever before. Yet, as the research of my team at Stanford, Duke, and UC-Berkeley has shown, our visa policies are doing the opposite: chasing away this talent.

Our earlier research had determined that from 1995 to 2005—the time of the Internet boom—52% of Silicon Valley's startups were founded by people born abroad—people like me. When we updated our research recently, we found that this proportion had dropped to 44%. This was historically unprecedented.

Foreign students graduating from American colleges have difficulty in finding jobs because employers have difficulty in getting H1-B visas. Those graduates who are lucky enough to get a job and a visa and who decide to make the U.S. their permanent home find that it can take years—sometimes more than a decade—to get a green card. If they have ideas for building world-changing technologies and want to start a company, they are usually out of luck, because it is not usually possible for people on H1-B visas to work for the companies they might start.

The families of would-be immigrants are also held hostage to the visa-holder's immigration status. The spouses of H1-B workers are not allowed to work, and, depending on the state in which they live, they may not even be able to get a driver's license or open a bank account. They are forced to live as second-class citizens.

Not surprisingly, many are getting frustrated and returning home. We must stop this brain drain and do all we can to bring more engineers and scientists here. Contrary to what anti-immigrants groups say, these people expand the economy and create jobs for Americans.

In my book *The Immigrant Exodus*, I prescribed seven fixes to stem the tide and to attract the world's best and brightest to America:

1. Increase the numbers of green cards available to H-1B holders

2. Allow spouses of H-1B visa holders to work

3. Target immigration based on required skills

4. Allow H-1B Holders to change jobs without requiring sponsorship renewal

5. Extend the term of OPT for foreign students from one to four years

6. Institute the Startup Visa

7. Remove the country caps on green-card applications.

The bottom line is that Congress needs to double down and pass legislation which ensures that the supply of employment-based green cards matches the demands of a knowledge economy. Needless to say that at the same time, we need to improve U.S. education and ensure U.S. workers have the right skills and experience for the new era of technology and rapidly changing and competitive global economy.

As I concluded in my book, we need to do all this because a vibrant United States that opens its doors to skilled immigrants will provide a greater benefit to the rest of the world than a closed, shriveling United States because the rules by which the US practices the game of economic development, job formation and intellectual capital formation grow the global economic pie. And the ethos that drives America's entrepreneurs and inventors, and has driven US policy until very recently, is critically important for the continued development of the global economy. Not only will these entrepreneurs better the U.S., but they will better humanity, they will solve our Grand Challenges. (http://judiciary.house.gov/hearings/113th/02052013/Wadhwa%2002052013.pdf)

**STATEMENT OF JANET MURGUÍA, PRESIDENT AND CHIEF EXECUTIVE OFFICER OF THE NATIONAL COUNCIL OF LA RAZA, BEFORE THE COMMITTEE ON THE JUDICIARY, U.S. SENATE, HEARING ON "THE BORDER SECURITY, ECONOMIC OPPORTUNITY, AND IMMIGRATION MODERNIZATION ACT, S.744," APRIL 22, 2013**

Chairman Leahy and Ranking Member Grassley, thank you for holding this hearing on immigration reform legislation. I appreciate the opportunity to appear again before the Committee on this critically important issue to the Latino community.

I am the President and CEO of the National Council of La Raza (NCLR), the largest national Hispanic civil rights and advocacy organization in the United States, an American institution recognized in the book *Forces for Good* as one of the highest impact nonprofits in the nation. We represent some 300 Affiliates—local, community-based organizations in 41 states, the District of Columbia, and Puerto Rico—that provide education, health, housing, workforce development, and other services to millions of Americans and immigrants annually.

NCLR has a long legacy of engaging in immigration, evidenced through our work in the Hispanic community and in Washington, DC. We helped shape the Immigration Reform and Control Act of 1986, the Immigration Act of 1990 to preserve family-based immigration, and the Nicaraguan Adjustment and Central American Relief Act (NACARA). We also led four successful efforts to restore safety net systems that promote immigrant integration. We have worked with Presidents Ronald Reagan, George H. W. Bush, Bill Clinton, and George W. Bush to achieve the best results possible for our community and for the country. We know that working with both parties is the only way to get things done.

Fixing our broken immigration system is in the best interest of our country. That is why it is so important to acknowledge the work of the bipartisan group of senators who last week reached a critically important breakthrough in the push for immigration reform with the introduction of S. 744, the "Border Security, Economic Opportunity, and Immigration Modernization Act of 2013." The distinguished senators who worked on this bill have shown extraordinary perseverance, thoughtfulness and courage in their months-long effort to bring about a solution to a national concern too long neglected. Their unity and ability to work together to find common ground in the face of an increasingly polarized political atmosphere should be a model for addressing our country's challenges. Senate bill 744 is a significant milestone and presents a historic opportunity to deliver a common-sense solution for the country this year.

As I noted in my previous testimony, NCLR's principles for immigration reform are very clear that reform should (1) restore the rule of law by creating a roadmap to legalization and citizenship for the 11 million aspiring Americans, and include smart enforcement that improves safety, supports legal immigration channels, and prevents discrimination; (2) preserve the rule of law by creating workable legal immigration channels that reunite families, strengthen our economy, and protect workers' rights; and (3) strengthen the fabric of our society by adopting proactive measures that advance the successful integration of new immigrants. While Senate bill 744 is not

perfect, it has provisions that will give our country the tools to achieve a 21st Century immigration system—one that helps ensure immigration to the United States is orderly and legal, promotes economic growth, sustains our families, and protects workers and honest employers, if it is implemented in a way that is consistent with our nation's values.

**The Time Is Now**

There are three potent threads aligning that make this moment different and the opportunity for reform stronger: the moral, economic, and political imperatives for immigration reform.

• The moral imperative for reform has been made clear for years, with a wide ranging set of organizations raising awareness about the untold damage our broken immigration system has had on immigrants and families, a plight that found its most potent symbol recently in the courageous activism of DREAMers. And the magnitude of that devastation is much larger, as the lives and fate of immigrants are fundamentally interwoven with those of citizens and impacts how those who are deemed to be immigrants are treated.

• The economic imperative for reform has been gaining strength particularly in the last couple of years, with the consequences of deportation policies, state anti-immigrant laws, and an outdated legal immigration system, affecting more industries. Simultaneously, more and more studies show the economic benefit to our country of implementing legalization, promoting citizenship, and bringing in the best and brightest talent from around the globe.

• Election Day made the political imperative crystal clear. Adding to the strong participation by African American voters, according to the exit polls, Asian American and Pacific Islander voters were 3% of the electorate and Latinos were 10%. Latinos were decisive in Nevada, Colorado, and Florida, and an essential part of the winning coalition in places like Pennsylvania and Wisconsin, as were Asian American voters in Minnesota and Virginia.

These three imperatives, and the conditions that created them, have brought together the multi-sector voices and constituencies on the left and right of the debate necessary to help immigration reform become a reality. We understand that failure to achieve reform will mean a continued erosion of the family unit, working rights, community wellbeing, and civil rights protections that start with the vulnerable undocumented community and reverberate well beyond. For example, hundreds of thousands of U.S. citizens and lawful permanent residents have been separated from family members. This is untenable. We can do better, and have an opportunity to do so. The time to take action is now.

## A Roadmap to Citizenship

Our country places a high regard on the successful integration of immigrants into the socio-economic fabric of the nation. And we must remember that the American public puts a special premium on citizenship, because citizenship signifies fully embracing our country and accepting the contract that all of our ancestors at some point made: to be fully American. The American people want to see immigrants all in—not partially in, not in a special status, but in the same boat as everyone else.

We believe Senate bill 744 recognizes the importance of that process of integration, and seeks to strike a balance that can reflect our national principles and priorities. And it also recognizes the fact that, if we are serious about restoring the rule of law, it is essential that we acknowledge that no healthy society can tolerate the existence of a subclass of people outside the scope and protection of the law. Those living in the shadows are easily exploited by employers, thus lowering the wages and labor standards for all workers and undercutting businesses that play by the rules. They are afraid to report crimes that they may experience or witness, undermining public safety.

In addition, the lives of undocumented immigrants are inextricably linked with ours. Most of them are long-term U.S. residents; they work hard, pay taxes, and otherwise abide by our laws. They provide for U.S. citizen spouses and children; they are our fellow churchgoers and children's playmates. Some of them came to this country as children, and this is the only country they know and consider home. Many have contributed to the revitalization of the cities where they live, and are providing the services the aging Baby Boom generation requires.

The notion that we are going to hunt down and deport 11 million people is a fantasy, and one the American public neither buys nor supports. So the question then is, what do we do? The majority of Americans support an earned legalization with a roadmap to citizenship as an essential component of immigration reform—and Senate bill 744 offers that possibility.

It is a steep road, one that includes some conditions many civil rights and social justice organizations, including my own, have concerns about. But we are willing to give our support to Senate bill 744, as we pledge to improve it, because we know that the interests of our country are best served by creating that roadmap to legality and to citizenship for this population of immigrants, just like there was for every other group of immigrants before them. We know this roadmap can also help us prevent having a subclass of workers who are expected to support the rest of us in our pursuit of the American Dream without having access to it themselves.

With implementation in mind, we do want to express our concern to the Committee that the process of moving from unlawful status to potential citizenship may be too long and too costly for many who have been working and raising families in the U.S. It is also a significant concern that as these individuals move forward through the legalization process, they will not only be assessed multiple fees and fines, they will be required to pay taxes to fund critical services that ensure health, well-being and productivity without having access to them. As NCLR has testified, the ultimate goal of any public benefits system should be to provide the support that enables American families—including immigrant families—to become self-sustaining. However, the irony in the treatment of immigrants under S. 744 is that the rules in place may actually make it harder for them to do so.

The benefits to our country of allowing these immigrants to earn legalization are significant, both economically and socially. No longer could unscrupulous employers pit undocumented workers against other workers. Legalization is also the only way to reduce the ability of unscrupulous employers from exploiting them or threatening to deport them for reporting labor law violations, thereby endangering wages and working conditions for all workers.

And bringing stability through earned legality to this population would mean opportunity for deepening roots, as well as higher earnings and therefore higher tax revenue—which studies have estimated would add billions of dollars just in the next 10 years alone. Legalized immigrants would be able to invest and spend more as they would be able to work towards their dreams—starting a business, buying a home for their families, helping their children succeed.

In short, the legislation proposes a tough but reachable path for those who are willing to contribute and be vested in the future of our country. It should be noted that the success not just of the legalization program, but of reform itself, will be determined by how many undocumented immigrants who are law-abiding aside from their immigration status, are able to go through the process. If the legalization program is made more difficult, or imposes conditions designed to prevent people from applying, or provisions that exclude people with a legitimate claim, then reform will fail to achieve restoration of the rule of law, one of its fundamental goals.

## Family Unity

Keeping families together and strong is a core principle and a fundamental value of American life. In every religion, in every culture, in every wave of immigrants that have come to this country, the family unit has been critical both to the survival of immigrants in a strange land, and to their success in adapting and contributing to their newly adopted nation. It also promotes the economic stability of immigrants and their integration into our country, and we must continue our historic commitment to this idea.

We are glad that the bipartisan legislation seeks to address the unnecessary separation of families who are kept apart by extraordinarily long wait times for certain family visas. Millions of close family members of U.S. citizens and permanent residents are stuck waiting outside the U.S. for visas to become available; many wait for more than two decades. It is also important to remember that the family is not only a social unit, but a powerful economic engine. Close relatives are able to make vital contributions to the U.S. economy as productive workers and entrepreneurs. By clearing out the backlogs in the family and employment based categories and removing the limitation on the number of visas that are requested by legal permanent residents who apply for their spouses and minor children, the legislation would help promote the economic stability of immigrant families and their integration into our country.

Unfortunately, there are also provisions in the legislation that weaken our country's historic commitment to family unity. This proposal eliminates the ability of U.S. citizens to petition for their siblings and reduces the ability of U.S. citizens to petition for their adult married children who are more than 30 years old. Maintaining a commitment to "family values" requires the recognition that a rapidly changing society and economy requires an equally dynamic definition of family. Families in our country today come in all shapes and sizes and include not only siblings pooling their resources together to buy a home or start a business but also adult children taking care of their elderly parents. And it is ironic that same sex couples increasingly have been gaining appropriate recognition in our society, except in our immigration law.

## Future Flow of Workers

Unlike previous immigration reforms, which have tightened enforcement but failed to establish effective legal avenues that respond to the needs of our economy and protect the American workforce, this bill has a series of provisions offering the opportunity for future workers to eventually pursue legal permanent residency and then citizenship. This is the best way to prevent the nation from having another debate in the future about legalizing yet another group of workers who live and work unlawfully in the U.S. It is imperative that our legal immigration system keep pace with our economy and our changing society.

As such, the sponsors of the bipartisan senate bill took into account the needs of both our country and its workers, from the fields all the way to Silicon Valley, by providing multiple ways for immigrant workers to enter

the U.S. through safe and legal channels to meet legitimate workforce needs across sectors of our economy. The proposed legislation includes provisions that are complex and need further analysis. However, it appears it would create a 21st century process intended to be responsive to U.S. labor needs in a regulated, orderly fashion—while breaking precedent by providing labor rights and protections. We strongly believe that immigrant workers should have the same rights and responsibilities as other U.S. workers, including whistleblower protections and back-pay owed to them for their labor.

## Immigrant Integration

Americans hold immigrant integration in high regard and want to see immigrants pledge allegiance to our country. So we are very pleased to see that the bipartisan legislation also includes many measures designed to achieve the successful integration of immigrants into American society. Its provisions would help enhance social cohesion among neighbors and coworkers in communities across the United States. The legislation would prohibit the use of race and ethnicity in federal law enforcement activities and requires data collection and new regulations to ensure a prohibition of racial profiling is implemented effectively. It also establishes an Office of New Americans, a New Americans taskforce and includes additional initiatives to help immigrants learn English, American civics and integrate into local communities. From financial counseling to English and civics courses, there is a dramatic need for increased resources and collaboration across government agencies to achieve the full integration of immigrants. And immigrants want to learn English and make greater contributions to the nation—I know it, because my organization and our hundreds of Affiliates help immigrants on this journey every day of the week. We applaud the effort to strengthen that process. The sponsors of this legislation recognize that, as in the turn of the 20th century, the integration of immigrants needs to be accelerated by both the public and private sectors and it funds a public-private partnership to acquire the skills needed to work and integrate into the economic and social mainstream.

## Conclusion

I want to reiterate that Senate Bill 744 provides you an incredible opportunity to restore and preserve the rule of law, and to do so in a way that honors our country's values and strengthens our economy.

We acknowledge that compromises will have to be made by all parties. Significant concessions have already been made in this legislation, many that cut deeply into the interests of the Hispanic community. If each of us was looking at only individual pieces of this bill from our own parochial perspective, there is much we would be forced to oppose. But just as we are asking others to set aside some of their preferences to advance our nation's interests, we recognize that all of us have to accept some compromises to advance our common goal of producing a bill that reflects a strong, effective, and sustainable immigration policy for the 21st Century.

A bright line will soon emerge between those who seek to preserve a status quo, which serves no one except those who profit from a broken system, and those who are working in good faith to reach compromise and deliver a solution the country desperately needs. Put in stark terms, those who oppose progress are not just advocates for doing nothing, in essence, they are advocating for worse than nothing. Opponents of progress are supporting the continued existence of a subclass of 11 million people living outside the scope and protection of the law and an enforcement regime that separates families, turns a blind eye to racial profiling and the detention and even deportation of U.S. citizens and lawful residents. They would do nothing to address the growing gap between on the one hand, the family values of a 21st century society and the economic needs of a 21st Century economy and on the other, a legal immigration system that has remained unchanged for nearly three decades. They are opposing improved labor law enforcement, leveling the field for American workers, and laying the foundation for the accelerated integration of today's immigrants and those yet to arrive. In short, they offer the same feeble failed policies that may advance their political interests but don't produce real results, or they hold out for dystopian ends that cannot be achieved.

This bright line will be burnt indelibly in the minds of Latino voters. Those who created the game-changing moment for this debate in November, and the additional 14.4 million U.S. born and raised prospective Hispanic voters that will join the electorate between now and 2028. Our community will be engaged and watching closely to ensure that the legalization process is real, enforcement is accountable, and families and workers are protected. (http://judiciary.senate.gov/pdf/04-22-13Murguia Testimony.pdf)

## TESTIMONY OF GROVER NORQUIST, PRESIDENT OF AMERICANS FOR TAX REFORM, BEFORE THE COMMITTEE ON THE JUDICIARY, U.S. SENATE, HEARING ON "THE BORDER SECURITY, ECONOMIC OPPORTUNITY, AND IMMIGRATION MODERNIZATION ACT, S.744," APRIL 22, 2013

Chairman Leahy, Ranking Member Grassley, and Members of the Committee, my name is Grover Norquist, and I am President of Americans for Tax Reform (ATR). ATR is a nonprofit advocacy organization that promotes free market principles and a fiscally conservative approach to public policymaking.

Mr. Chairman, people are an asset, not a liability. America is the most immigrant-friendly country in the world, and we are the richest country in the world. This is not a coincidence. Those who would make us less immigrant-friendly would make us less successful, less prosperous, and less American.

Now, how do we evaluate the specific legislation before the Senate? The Border Security, Economic Opportunity, and Immigration Modernization Act of 2013's stated aim is to uphold America's tradition of strengthening its economy by maintaining its openness to immigrants.

### Dynamic Analysis: A Conservative Consensus

The consensus conservative, free market approach to evaluating any public policy change is to do so dynamically. Dynamic scoring takes into account both the costs and benefits of any policy change. Specific to immigration, providing a tough but fair pathway to legal status for America's undocumented population while facilitating an adequate future flow of legal immigrants will increase the size and productivity of our workforce and thus lead to accelerated economic growth for all Americans.

*Wall Street Journal* editorial board member Jason Riley made the case for dynamic scoring in his 2008 book:

> Supply siders have for decades been critical of the way federal agencies like the Congressional Budget Office and the Joint Committee on Taxation estimated, or "scored," the effects of tax cuts on revenue without figuring in their effects on the overall economy. And rightly so. Under static modeling, for instance, if a state doubles its cigarette tax, it will double its revenue from that tax. But that doesn't take into account, as a dynamic model would, the fact that the tax increase will affect behavior. Smokers, for example, may quit or smoke less. The tobacco taxes they previously paid would be lost to the state, offsetting some of the additional revenue anticipated by increasing the tax rate. Similarly, a tax cut might not result in a revenue reduction if it stimulates more economic activity.

Riley also provides a history of conservative policy organizations driving the center-right consensus on dynamic scoring:

> Along with other conservative outfits like the National Center for Policy Analysis and the Institute for Policy Innovation, [the Heritage Foundation] helped pioneer the use of dynamic analysis. Whether the issue was trade liberalization or tax policy, free-market conservatives regularly mocked economic studies that took into account only static impacts. "[No] matter how many times a 'static' analysis is disproved," Heritage Foundation president Ed Feulner once wrote, "Congress keeps doing business in the same wrongheaded way." When President Bush's 2007 budget proposal included a plan to create a Dynamic Analysis division inside the Treasury Department to assess how tax laws affect

economic activity, William Beach, Heritage's top numbers cruncher, praised the move. "Inside the Beltway, this type of work is called 'dynamic analysis,'" Beach wrote in *BusinessWeek*. "Outside the Beltway, this is called 'economics.'"

Indeed, any sound conservative evaluation of public policy changes must include an accounting of the legislation's costs and benefits. Conservatives do not consider tax cuts statically, because of behavioral changes that result when we incentivize work and investment. That dynamic increase in economic activity that takes place when the government loosens its grip on the private sector leads to more revenue than a static projection would suggest.

A number of conservative and free market organizations and leaders have added their voices to the debate, speaking to the importance of dynamic analysis.

Recently departed Heritage Foundation President Ed Feulner put forth a convincing argument about the flaws of static scoring:

Indeed, some lawmakers are fighting a proposal that would require them to take real-world considerations into account. They prefer to keep "scoring" each bill—estimating how it will affect the economy and the amount of taxes they take in—with the "static" model used by the store owner's friend. If, say, a 5 percent tax on something brings in $50 million, they assume a 10 percent tax will fetch $100 million.

Not surprisingly, this approach has caused lawmakers to come up with some wildly inaccurate assumptions over the years. Consider what happened with President Kennedy's tax cut. Many lawmakers were sure that, with the top marginal tax rate being slashed from 91 percent to 70 percent, tax revenues would plunge. Instead, the cut spurred economic growth. Between 1961 and 1968, tax revenues rose by one-third.

The same thing happened when President Reagan cut taxes in the early 1980s. Many lawmakers predicted financial ruin as the top rate plummeted from 70 percent to 28 percent. Again, they were wrong. Once the cuts were phased in, tax revenues soared. The amount of money the federal government was taking in through personal income taxes had increased 28 percent (adjusted for inflation) by 1989.

Yet no matter how many times a "static" analysis is disproved, Congress keeps doing business in the same wrong-headed way.

Newt Gingrich and Peter Ferrara criticized the static analyses of the Congressional Budget Office, Office of Management and Budget, and Joint Committee on Taxation thusly:

The methodologies used by analysts across the federal government to score the impact of legislation still do not take into account the dynamic, pro-growth effects of policy changes. They continue to use mostly static methodologies that assume no significant changes in

behavior in response to changes in incentives. The result of these antiquated scoring practices is that Congress is forced to discount any policy change that would increase economic growth or enhance efficiency in federal programs. Instead, Congress is constrained to consider legislation designed to meet a politically acceptable score from the CBO, even though experience demonstrates that the scoring will surely be erroneous—indeed, is effectively designed to be so.

Americans for Prosperity (AFP), the conservative advocacy group, argued:

CBO's current static scoring system fails to account for behavioral changes that individuals, households, and firms make in response to new economic policies. This makes tax increases look better and tax cuts look worse than they actually are . . .

Adjusting to dynamic scoring accounts for these (behavioral) changes and provides better cost estimates for Congress to weigh its decisions.

Other free market institutions such as the Club for Growth, FreedomWorks, the Cato Institute, and the National Taxpayers Union have been broadly supportive of dynamic scoring. This is a consensus issue in the center-right policy community.

### Dynamic Scoring Specific to the Immigration Debate

To score legislation dynamically we need to understand its impact on the economy first. The broad issue of dynamic scoring applies specifically to immigration reform because immigrants increase both the supply and demand sides of the economy. On the supply side, immigrants work and thereby increase economic production and the productivity of Americans. Because immigrants have different skills, they are complements rather than competitors to the vast majority of Americans. On the demand side, immigrants purchase and rent goods, services, and real estate produced by other Americans, thus incentivizing production.

Immigrants and Americans, in the face of such changes, do not respond statically. Both groups change their behavior in response to incentives, and it is incumbent upon us to measure the economic effects of these behavioral changes dynamically. For instance, immigrant incomes increase over time just as incomes increase during the working life of Americans. After the legalization of immigrants during the Reagan amnesty, their incomes rose by an average 15 percent just by gaining legal status. Those immigrants today are making much more than they did then and, as a result, paying more in taxes. In response to immigration, Americans also increase their investments in machines and capital to invest in a faster growing and productive workforce. Those are just two changes but they illustrate the magnitude of dynamic changes to the economy. Since both the supply and demand sides change in relation to each other, we have to use a dynamic scoring process to accurately estimate the broad effects.

The broader economic impacts are gigantic. A 2009 study prepared for the Cato Institute by economists Peter Dixon and Maureen Rimmer employed a dynamic economic model called USAGE to estimate the effects of changes in the U.S. economy due to an immigration policy change very similar to today's Senate legislation. It found that the incomes of U.S. households would increase by $180 billion a year. Increased legal immigration will add millions of consumers, workers, renters, and others who will make our economy larger by working with Americans to produce more of the goods and services we demand.

Another similar study commissioned by Cato and written by Professor Raul Hinojosa-Ojeda of UCLA employed a similar analysis using a dynamic model called the GMig2. The study found that an additional $1.5 trillion in GDP growth would occur ten years after immigration reform similar to the Senate's plan.

As a comparison, Professor Hinojosa-Ojeda ran a simulation on the GMig2 model whereby immigration reform was instead replaced by an effective enforcement-only policy that produced the mass removal of all illegal immigrants—a policy desired by immigration restrictionists. The result of that simulation was a $2.6 trillion decrease in estimated GDP growth over the same decade.

Most recently, American Action Forum President Douglas Holtz-Eakin, former Director of the Congressional Budget Office, authored a dynamic study on the economic impact of immigration reform. While not specifically related to the legislation before us today, Holtz-Eakin's study measures the costs and benefits of a "benchmark immigration reform," concluding that significantly increasing legal immigration would boost GDP growth by 0.9 points annually.

Holtz-Eakin's findings are primarily driven by immigration's impact on the size of the labor force. He writes:

> The mechanics of reform and the research literature suggest that immigration reform can raise the overall pace of population growth—indeed, in the absence of immigration, low birth-rates mean that the U.S. population will actually shrink. Because foreign-born individuals tend to have higher rates of labor force participation, this translates into an even more rapid pace of growth in the labor force. At historic rates of population growth, this immediately translates into more rapid overall growth in Gross Domestic Product.

Additionally, Holtz-Eakin cites the entrepreneurial vigor associated with immigrants as further evidence that more immigration will lead to higher rates of economic growth. This assertion is supplemented by the Kauffman Foundation, which found that immigrants in 2011 were twice as likely as native-born Americans to start a new business.

## Immigrants and Productivity Gains

To get a sense of how the productivity of today's undocumented workers might increase once they have earned legal status, imagine the converse. If your siblings or your children were denied the ability to have a driver's license and therefore fly on airplanes or drive themselves to and from work, how productive would they be? How would their income suffer? How many career opportunities would they be denied?

Allowing undocumented workers to move from job to job, travel easily and safely, search out and interview for different jobs in different sectors and locations would greatly increase their productivity, and they would become greater contributors to their own well-being and the wealth of our nation.

The majority of those undocumented immigrants currently here are low-skilled. Some argue that we should not be importing or legalizing this type of talent. But in reality, the U.S. economy demands an enormous number of low-skilled workers. They work in construction, retail, hospitality, food preparation, agriculture, manufacturing, and other industries. But the domestic labor supply is inadequate for these types of jobs. We need immigrant labor to fill demand for low-skill jobs.

For evidence of this, see the economic consequences of Georgia's House Bill 87, passed in 2011. Similar to harsh enforcement-first measures passed recently in Alabama and Arizona, HB 87 was intended to eliminate the supply of illegal immigrant labor in the state by imposing strict penalties on undocumented immigrants and the businesses that hired them.

The problem with HB 87 is that it worked. Undocumented immigrants fled the state in droves, and left a crippled agricultural industry behind them. Labor shortages led to $140 million in agricultural losses, with crops left unpicked and rotting in the fields. Georgia Gov. Nathan Deal even introduced a program for unemployed ex-convicts on probation to fill these vacant agriculture jobs. According to Georgia's Agriculture Commissioner, Gary Black, many of these new workers promptly quit because the jobs were too strenuous.

Increasing the supply of low-skilled immigrants doesn't only ensure that more vacant jobs are filled. It increases the overall productivity of the American economy by injecting talent that is complementary to the existing domestic labor supply. Immigrants are generally either lower-skilled or higher-skilled than most native-born workers. That means they aren't competing with Americans for the type of jobs they are qualified to do. Instead, they fill jobs that complement the existing American labor supply, raising productivity and wages across the board.

Think about this in the context of a restaurant. Immigrants, because of their low skills and lesser English speaking proficiency, work in non-communications jobs like dishwashing, cooking, bussing tables, and janitorial work. The Americans who filled these jobs in previous generations are now performing higher-paid jobs like waiting tables, hosting, and managing the restaurant. The availability of lower-skilled labor allows native-born Americans to work better jobs and earn more money.

By the same account, high-skilled immigrants are vital to America's dynamic economy. Similar to low-skilled immigrants, they rarely directly compete with native-born workers, but for different reasons. High-skilled labor is extremely entrepreneurial. They grow the economic pie by innovating and building new businesses. They directly create opportunity for Americans.

Immigrants or their children founded more than 40 percent of Fortune 500 companies. Those immigrant-founded Fortune 500s employ more than 10 million people worldwide, and have combined global revenues of $4.2 trillion.

## Baseless Criticism

Some people who choose to play politics with this issue have ignored dynamic analysis and instead considered only the inflated costs of reform. Errors found in pseudo-analysis by anti-immigration groups include:

• Exaggerating public benefit costs by citing household costs, rather than individual immigrant costs. By counting welfare costs on a household basis, critics including millions of native-born American spouses and children into their estimation. This is a misleading trick that inflates the true cost of public benefits for immigrants, and assumes native-born Americans are only public charges because of their association with their immigrant spouses or parents.

• Portraying impossible levels of welfare use. Putting aside the evidence that immigrants come to America to pursue economic opportunity, it is important to point out that leading criticisms of increased immigration predict levels of welfare use that are impossible under this bill. Most undocumented immigrants are barred from accepting public benefits, including Obamacare, for 13 years at the earliest. Those on a quicker path—agricultural workers and DREAMers—still must wait eight years. Yet prominent criticisms of the bill assume immediate adoption welfare benefits by those legalized.

• Assuming immigrant wages will remain stagnant throughout their lives. With legalization comes labor market flexibility and productivity gains, resulting in higher wages. After the 1986 Reagan amnesty, immigrant wages increased immediately after they became legal, sometimes by as much as 15 to 25 percent.

• Ignoring the costs of an enforcement-only approach. Professor Raul Hinojosa-Ojeda of UCLA using the GMig2, a dynamic bilateral labor flows model, to estimate the economic effects of a successful enforcement-only policy that mass removed of all illegal immigrants—a policy desired by immigration restrictionists. The result of that simulation was a $2.6 trillion decrease in estimated GDP growth over the same decade, decreasing tax revenues. Direct government costs of such a program are also enormous. Economist Rajeev Goyle estimated that deporting 11 million people would cost the government $206 billion over a five year period. More conservatively, Immigration and Customs Enforcement (ICE) assumed that the marginal immigrant costs $12,500 to deport which, assuming no increase in marginal costs, would cost the government approximately $140 billion to deport 11 million unauthorized immigrants.

• Conceding the size of the current welfare state, rather than working to reform it. Building a wall around the welfare state is a far more effective and economically beneficial policy than building a wall around the country. It is also politically possible.

There are groups that oppose growing the American economy via more immigration because of their extreme environmental and population control views, because they have a flawed Malthusian view of the economy, and because they don't understand free markets. Their failed arguments against immigration are also arguments against having children. These groups view people not as assets, but as liabilities. This is a fatally flawed argument, and completely inconsistent with conservative principles.

Some argue that the fiscal burden of America's entitlement programs make more immigration cost prohibitive. That is a false choice. That our entitlement systems are broken is not an argument for less immigration; it is an argument to fix our entitlement systems.

The legislation before us today puts at least 13 years between legal status and access to public benefits for most undocumented immigrants, mitigating the negative fiscal impacts of our bloated entitlement programs. Those who insist or imagine that this bill would impose trillions of dollars in new entitlement costs have not read the legislation, nor do they understand the current eligibility requirements.

Furthermore, immigrants come at the beginning of their working lives, which means they will have years to pay taxes and contribute to the economy before being eligible for entitlements. The American Community Survey estimates that the average age of immigrants who have come since the year 2000 is 31 while the average native-born American is 36 years old. Immigrants typically arrive in their mid-20s after their home countries pay for their education so they can begin to work and pay taxes in the U.S. immediately. By coming at such a young working age the government does not have to pay for their education but they could work around 40 years before being eligible for entitlements if they decide to stay.

Also, many low-skilled immigrants work for years in the U.S. before returning home with their savings as part of a phenomenon called circular migration. Forcing them to work in the illegal market means they will stay here longer than they otherwise would because if they did leave the U.S., there would be no guarantee they could come back later to make money if they had to. Allowing them to come legally or to legalize the ones here would reignite circular migration, allowing immigrants to plan on coming here for a few years to work and pay taxes and then returning home with their savings. Princeton Sociologist Doug Massey has observed that 20 percent to 30 percent of Mexican immigrants from 1965 to 1986 followed that pattern.

For almost all means-tested federal welfare programs, immigrants are substantially restricted access until they have had a green card for at least five years. Programs they are restricted from include: Medicaid, Supplemental Nutrition Assistance Program, Temporary Assistance for Needy Families, and Supplemental Security Income. The current legislation would construct even larger barriers to welfare, with a 10-year waiting period for most newly legalized immigrants to receive a green card, and then another 3 years until access to means-tested public benefits. That is a high wall around the welfare state.

### The Shining City on a Hill

Mr. Chairman, it is my belief that a position in favor of more legal immigration and a fair and humane path to citizenship for those undocumented immigrants already here is wholly consistent with the ideals of the center-right movement I have worked my entire life to help build. I believe that free markets lead to economic growth and prosperity for all. This includes free and flexible labor markets, which will benefit not only those who wish to come here to pursue the American Dream, but also those of us blessed enough to have been born in the United States of America.

I conclude with an excerpt from President Ronald Reagan's farewell address to the nation, in January of 1989:

> I've spoken of the shining city all my political life, but I don't know if I ever quite communicated what I saw when I said it. But in my mind it was a tall, proud city built on rocks stronger than oceans, wind-swept, God-blessed, and teeming with people of all kinds living in harmony and peace; a city with free ports that hummed with commerce and creativity. *And if there had to be city walls, the walls had doors and the doors were open to anyone with the will and the heart to get here.* (http://judiciary.senate.gov/pdf/04-22-13NorquistTestimony.pdf)

# CHAPTER 9
# THE UNITED STATES NEEDS TOUGHER IMMIGRATION LAWS

**TESTIMONY OF RAY TRANCHANT, DIRECTOR, ADVANCED TECHNOLOGY CENTER, TIDEWATER COMMUNITY COLLEGE, BEFORE THE SUBCOMMITTEE ON IMMIGRATION POLICY AND ENFORCEMENT, COMMITTEE ON THE JUDICIARY, U.S. HOUSE OF REPRESENTATIVES, HEARING ON "U.S. IMMIGRATION AND CUSTOMS ENFORCEMENT: PRIORITIES AND THE RULE OF LAW," OCTOBER 12, 2011**

As I can tell, the current positions on Illegal Immigration by the Obama Administration are:

- Amnesty with a secured border to slow down the flow,

- Promotion of the Dream act that somehow translates to 14th amendment rights for children,

- Amnesty with a path to citizenship that is undefined at this time.

This all sounds like a plan with no details; a "wish list" until another election. American leadership must either continue to enforce the laws that the current Executive Branch selectively ignores, or encourage a movement to change them. After all, laws are only as effective as our commitment to enforcement [of] them. How long can we wait?

Amnesty diminishes the allegiance of the immigrants who followed the legal process. It questions our approach to National Security, increases crime, promotes tax evasion, and has public health challenges. Currently, there are millions of people with no fingerprints on record, have false or no ID's, birth records, health records, visas or passports. This causes confusion and worry during a Great Recession.

During the Great Depression in 1932, more people left the country than immigrated. Hopefully history doesn't repeat itself!

It hurt the US when my hero, Ronald Reagan favored amnesty for Illegal Immigrants during the Cuban Boat Crisis of 1986. It caused all of the havoc that Castro intended in a much smaller scale than today. Fidel cleaned out the jails and allowed Cubans to board boats, encouraging them to leave in a risky attempt to gain a better life, just 90 miles away. After all, times were tough in Cuba.

There were a million immigrants in 1986, a number far less than the estimated 14 million illegals seeking amnesty today. Once we waived a magic wand, they were not required to speak English or even have knowledge of how our government works. Reagan's rationale then was covered under the 1980 Refugee Act; boat people were "refugees." He couldn't just let them die, and if they were sent back to Cuba, who knows what would have happened.

In the past few years, former President Fox of Mexico promoted a similar move, encouraging the Northern part of Mexico to "seek their fortune" by crossing the border. Today, President Calderon is more cooperative with the United States to stop the flow, but Narcoterrorism is his biggest challenge. Last year 3,000 Mexicans were murdered no more than 300 feet from the US border. It gravely affects the United States as well, not to mention a Border Patrol agent who was shot and killed during the past Christmas holiday.

These agents risk their lives daily protecting a broken system. I watch TV reality shows like "Border Wars" on National Geographic and am shocked at how undermanned they are. Can the United States Government do a better job securing the border? Sure it can.

For example, take Area 51 in Nevada. It is a very secure government site the size of a small State. I've seen it and it is impenetrable. Unwelcome visitors there will be stopped and arrested in the name of national security.

My parents were immigrants. They had to speak English (for safety reasons in the factories and coal mines), pass a citizenship test, stay out of trouble, have a public health and birth record to verify their age and lineage, pay taxes on all of their earnings, and had total buy-in to the "American Dream." People who "break in" and come illegally can't possibly have the same "buy in."

Immigration and Customs Enforcement (ICE) continues to prioritize enforcement of the laws by the hottest crisis of the moment. They are getting more support, deporting more criminals, but are still unable to keep on top of the numbers.

My late daughter Tessa and her friend Allison Kunhardt were killed in Virginia Beach by a repeat DUI offender, an Illegal with a fake driver's license. He was handed off many times and was not a priority call to ICE for deportation. Tessa has a Grandmother, Anita Carson from Chihuahua, Mexico. Her "Noni" was an immigrant who worked on B-17's during WWII in San Diego. She is appalled that migrants would get the same rights to citizenship by sneaking across the border. *The Hispanics I know generally are concerned about their America as well, and worry that the current administration focuses on potential Hispanic votes, and not about American Hispanic safety and prosperity.*

Once again, these and many more victims of crimes committed by illegal immigrants are lost in the justice system, sometimes invisible or waiting under a deportation order. There are many, many more stories like this. In Sanctuary Cities, ICE doesn't even get a call, which is another problem driven by politics. So how long will it be until America finds a fair solution? (http://judiciary.house.gov/hearings/pdf/Tranchant%2010122011.pdf)

## TESTIMONY OF MICHAEL W. CUTLER, SENIOR SPECIAL AGENT, U.S. IMMIGRATION AND NATURALIZATION SERVICE (RETIRED), BEFORE THE COMMITTEE ON THE JUDICIARY, U.S. SENATE, HEARING ON "BUILDING AN IMMIGRATION SYSTEM WORTHY OF AMERICAN VALUES," MARCH 20, 2013

Good afternoon Chairman Leahy, Senator Coons, Ranking Member Grassley, other members of the Judiciary Committee, fellow witnesses, ladies and gentlemen.

I greatly appreciate the opportunity to provide my perspectives at this important hearing concerning how America's immigration system be made reflective and worthy of American values. For me personally, immigration is the story of my own family and it has virtually been my life's work. As you may know, I was sworn in as an Immigration Inspector in October 1971 at the New York District Office of the former Immigration and Naturalization Service. Thus began my career with the INS that would span some 30 years. At the end of my career with the INS I was a Senior Special Agent assigned to the Organized Crime, Drug Enforcement Task Force.

My career provided me with a unique front row seat to the true importance of America's immigration laws to nearly every challenge and threat confronting America and Americans.

Rather than simply being a single issue, immigration is a *singular* issue that impacts everything from national security, criminal justice and community safety to the economy, unemployment, healthcare and public health, education and the environment to name the most prominent.

America's immigration laws were enacted to achieve two critical goals—protect innocent lives and protect the jobs of American workers.

A review of Title 8, United States Code, Section 1182 will make the purpose and intentions of our immigration laws clear. This section of the Immigration and Nationality Act enumerates the categories of aliens who are ineligible to enter the United States. Among these categories are aliens who have dangerous communicable diseases, suffer extreme mental illness and are prone to violence or are sex offenders. Criminals who have committed serious crimes are also excludible as are spies, terrorists, human rights violators and war criminals. Finally, aliens who would work in violation of law or become public charges are also deemed excludible.

It is vital to note that there is nothing in our immigration laws that would exclude aliens because of race, religion or ethnicity.

Our valiant members of the armed forces are charged with keeping our enemies as far from our borders as possible while the DHS [U.S. Department of Homeland Security] is charged with securing our borders from within. While mentioning our borders it is vital to understand that any state that has an international airport or has access to a seaport is as much a border state as are those states that are found along America's northern and southern borders.

We are constantly told that the immigration system is broken. What is never discussed is the fact that for decades the federal government has failed to effectively secure America's borders and enforce and administer the immigration laws. These failures convinced desperate people from around the world that the United States is not serious about it borders or its laws. This impression was further exacerbated by the Amnesty created by IRCA [Immigration Reform and Control Act] in 1986 which enabled more than 3.5 million illegal aliens to acquire lawful status and a pathway to United States citizenship.

This supposed one-time program that was to finally restore integrity to the immigration system was an abysmal failure. It could be argued that the failures to effectively enforce the immigration laws especially where the employer sanctions provisions of IRCA was concerned, to balance the amnesty provisions, provided a huge incentive for aliens to enter the United States in violation of America's borders and laws and consequently, the United States witnessed the largest influx of illegal aliens in history.

Respect for America's immigration laws have been further eroded by other factors such as the advocacy by the administration, and some Congressional leaders, for the creation of a program under the aegis of "Comprehensive Immigration Reform" that, if enacted, would provide unknown millions of illegal aliens, whose true identities and entry data are unverifiable, with pathways to citizenship. There are many reasons that programs such as these are problematic, but first and foremost is the undeniable fact that there is no way to determine the true identities of these aliens nor any way to verify how or when they entered the United States. This lack of integrity also plagues the program known as DACA (Deferred Action for Childhood Arrivals) that the administration created under the guise of "prosecutorial discretion" to provide illegal aliens who claim to have entered the United States as teenagers with temporary lawful status and employment authorization. It has been estimated that this program may ultimately provide between one million and two million such illegal aliens with official identity documents and employment authorization. The identity documents enable those to whom these documents are issued to obtain Social Security cards, driver's licenses and other such official identity documents even though it is virtually impossible to be certain of the true identities of the aliens to whom these documents are issued.

These are essentially the same aliens who would have been eligible for lawful status under the failed legislation known as the DREAM Act. As a former INS special agent I can tell you that there is no magical way to verify the information contained in the applications for participation in Comprehensive Immigration Reform or DACA is accurate or honest. The best chance to do this would be to conduct full field investigations—investigations that ICE and USCIS [U.S. Citizenship and Immigration Services] do not have the resources to conduct. Time and again the GAO [U.S. Government Accountability Office] and OIG [Office of Inspector General] have pointed to a lack of integrity to the immigration benefits program. Fraud undermines the immigration system and national security as well.

Here are two important excerpts from the 9/11 Commission Staff Report on Terrorist Travel.

First of all, here is the first paragraph from the preface of that report:

"It is perhaps obvious to state that terrorists cannot plan and carry out attacks in the United States if they are unable to enter the country. Yet prior to September 11, while there were efforts to enhance border security, no agency of the U.S. government thought of border security as a tool in the counterterrorism arsenal. Indeed, even after 19 hijackers demonstrated the relative ease of obtaining a U.S. visa and gaining admission into the United States, border security still is not considered a cornerstone of national security policy. We believe, for reasons we discuss in the following pages, that it must be made one."

Here is a paragraph under the title "Immigration Benefits" found on page 98:

"Terrorists in the 1990s, as well as the September 11 hijackers, needed to find a way to stay in or embed themselves in the United States if their operational plans were to come to fruition. As already discussed, this could be accomplished legally by marrying an American citizen, achieving temporary worker status, or applying for asylum after entering. In many cases, the act of filing for an immigration benefit sufficed to permit the alien to remain in the country until the petition was adjudicated. Terrorists were free to conduct surveillance, coordinate operations, obtain and receive funding, go to school and learn English, make contacts in the United States, acquire necessary materials, and execute an attack."

On December 7, 2012, the DHS OIG issued a report that was entitled:

"Improvements Needed for SAVE to Accurately Determine Immigration Status of Individuals Ordered Deported"

In conducting its investigation and preparing the report, the OIG examined the SAVE (Systematic Alien Verification for Entitlements) program. The results of the review were disconcerting, to say the least. The report noted that failures to update the data in the system could potentially affect the more than 800,000 individuals who have been ordered deported, removed, and excluded but who are still in the United States. That report went on to note that a random statistical sample test of individuals who had been ordered deported but still remained in the United States identified a 12 percent error rate in immigration status verification. In other words, these individuals had no status, but were erroneously identified as having lawful immigration status.

Adding this to the clearly stated policies of the administration which invoked "Prosecutorial Discretion" to not arrest or seek the removal of illegal aliens unless the aliens in question have been convicted of committing serious crimes.

Most recently the administration has engaged in a program to release thousands of illegal aliens from custody who have criminal histories. This program undermines any vestiges of integrity that the immigration law enforcement program might have had. I cannot imagine how a clearer message could be sent to people around the world that our nation is not only willing to ignore violations of law but reward violations of laws that were enacted to protect innocent lives and the jobs of American workers.

Meanwhile leaders of some cities and states openly demonstrate their disdain and contempt for our immigration laws by declaring that they have created "sanctuaries" for illegal aliens; yet the federal government refuses to take action against them.

Each of these actions, or lack of action, has served to encourage, induce, aid or abet aliens to violate our immigration laws. Sanctuary cities and states also serve to shield illegal aliens from detection by the federal government. It is important to note that this all represents violations of Title 8, United States Code, Section 1324 that addresses alien smuggling, harboring, inducing and, in general facilitating the entry of illegal aliens into the United States.

This would be wrong at any time but my concern is that today our nation is threatened by international terrorist organizations and transnational criminals from the four corners of our planet, and the pernicious gangs and criminal organizations that they often belong to.

Notwithstanding these threats and the fact that the American economy is hobbled by extraordinarily high unemployment and underemployment rates, the immigration component of these challenges has been ignored. Each month the United States lawfully admits tens of thousands of foreign workers who are authorized to work in the United States, while failures to effectively secure our borders and enforce the immigration laws from within the interior of the United States provides unfair competition for American workers desperate to find decent jobs. By not routinely enforcing the immigration laws and by its latest decision to release thousands of criminal aliens, the entire immigration system has come to lack integrity and fails to provide the deterrence against foreign nationals who would enter the United States intent on working illegally or, perhaps, with far more nefarious goals in mind.

Law enforcement is at its best when it creates a climate of deterrence to convince those who might be contemplating violating the law that such an effort is likely to be discovered and that if discovered, adverse consequences will result for the law violators. Current policies and statements by the administration, in my view, encourage aspiring illegal aliens around the world to head for the United States. In effect the starter's pistol

has been fired and for these folks, the finish line to this race is the border of the United States.

Back when I was an INS special agent I recall that Doris Meissner who was, at the time, the commissioner of the INS, said that the agency needed to be "customer oriented." Unfortunately, while I agree about the need to be customer oriented what Ms Meissner and too many politicians today seem to have forgotten is that the "customers" of the INS and of our government in general, are the citizens of the United States of America.

I look forward to your questions. (http://judiciary .senate.gov/pdf/3-20-13CutlerTestimony.pdf)

## TESTIMONY OF RUSSELL PEARCE, PRESIDENT OF BANAMNESTYNOW.COM, BEFORE THE SUBCOMMITTEE ON IMMIGRATION, REFUGEES, AND BORDER SECURITY, COMMITTEE ON THE JUDICIARY, U.S. SENATE, HEARING ON "EXAMINING THE CONSTITUTIONALITY AND PRUDENCE OF STATE AND LOCAL GOVERNMENTS ENFORCING IMMIGRATION LAW," APRIL 24, 2012

Good Morning. I'm Russell Pearce, the author of, and driving force behind [the controversial 2010 Arizona immigration law] the Support Our Law Enforcement and Safe Neighborhoods Act, known as "SB 1070," which is overwhelmingly supported by citizens across the nation.

Thank you, Chairman Schumer, for inviting me here today. It is an honor for me to appear before this Committee. As you well know, the illegal alien problem is a critical issue, not only in Arizona, but across the country. The adverse effects of illegal immigration ripple throughout our society.

In addressing this problem, we must begin by remembering that we are a nation of laws. We must have the courage—the fortitude—to enforce, with compassion but without apology, those laws that protect the integrity of our borders and the rights of our citizens from those who break our laws.

SB1070, in full accordance with federal law, removes the political handcuffs from state and local law enforcement. All law enforcement agencies have the legal authority, and a moral obligation, to uphold our laws, such as Sheriff Joe Arpaio, who is keeping his Oath and doing the job he was hired to do. His deputies were trained by ICE on how they want federal law enforced. And yet the Obama Justice Department continues to attack and threaten him.

The invasion of illegal aliens we face today—convicted felons, drug cartels, gang members, human traffickers and even terrorists—pose one of the greatest threats to our nation in terms of political, economic and national security. During the debate of SB1070, a rancher friend of mine, Rob Krentz, was murdered on the border by an illegal alien. I have attended funerals of many citizens and law enforcement officers murdered by illegal aliens. My own son, a Deputy Sheriff, was critically wounded in a gun battle with an illegal alien while serving a warrant. I have been in public service most of my life and I have seen the real costs and damage caused by the presence of illegal aliens in our country.

In Arizona alone, the annual cost of illegal immigration is approximately $2.6 billion and that is just to educate, medicate and incarcerate illegal aliens in Arizona. Nationally, the cost is in the tens of billions of dollars and the taxpayers foot the bill. And those numbers do not reflect the costs of crimes committed by those here illegally, or the jobs lost by legal residents. Government's failure to enforce our laws and secure our border is unforgivable and the total cost is staggering.

Had law enforcement enforced our immigration laws we would have averted 9/11. The terrorist attacks of September 11, 2001, underscored for all Americans the link between immigration law enforcement and terrorism. Four of the five leaders of the 9/11 attack were in violation of our immigration laws and had contact with law enforcement but were not arrested. Nineteen alien terrorists had been able to violate our immigration laws, overstay their visas or violate their Immigration statuses with impunity, and move freely within the Country without significant interference from federal or local law enforcement. The abuse of U.S. Immigration laws was instrumental in the deaths of nearly 3,000 people on that tragic day in America.

Yet, instead of addressing enforcing the law, the Obama administration does the opposite, by encouraging further law breaking. Under federal law, "Sanctuary Policies" plainly are illegal. But the Obama administration does not sue those cities that are openly in violation of federal law for having these illegal sanctuary policies. Instead, it chooses to sue Arizona for *enforcing* the law, *protecting* our citizens, *protecting* jobs for lawful residents, and *protecting* the taxpayers and the citizens of this Republic in attempting to secure our borders.

Contrary to the view of the Obama Justice Department, not every state action related to illegal aliens is preempted by federal law. America has a system of dual sovereignty. Only state laws that regulate immigration are preempted by federal law.

Almost 40 years ago, the Supreme Court made it clear that the mere fact aliens are the subject of a state statute does not render it a regulation of immigration. Only the determination of who should or should not be admitted into the country, and the conditions under which that person may remain, is the *regulation* of immigration.

During my eleven years in the Arizona State Legislature, I authored numerous legislative initiatives designed to protect the State of Arizona from the adverse effects of illegal immigration and most importantly, to uphold the rule of law. They include:

- Proposition 200 in 2004, which requires individuals to show identification at the polls prior to voting (passed by 57% of the voters);

- Proposition 100 in 2006, a State constitutional amendment to deny bond to any person unlawfully present in the United States who commits a serious crime in Arizona (passed by 78% of the voters, including 60% of Hispanics);

- Proposition 102, 2006, which states that a person unlawfully present in the United States who sues an American citizen cannot receive punitive damages (passed by 75% of the voters);

- In 2007, The "Legal Arizona Workers Act," prohibiting employers from hiring unauthorized workers and requiring use of federal E-Verify system to confirm employee eligibility (upheld by the Supreme Court in 2011 by a 5 to 3 vote).

I am also proud to say that each of these initiatives has become law and survived various legal challenges. In fact, the last time that I was in Washington, the Supreme Court upheld the Legal Arizona Workers Act against what I consider an unpatriotic challenge by the Chamber of Commerce and anti-rule of law challenge/attack by the Obama administration.

Because of these accomplishments, the citizens of Arizona are safer. According to the Phoenix Law Enforcement Association, the organization that represents the rank-and-file police officers in Phoenix:

> Since SB1070, Phoenix has experienced a 30-year low crime rate. 600 police vacancies, budget cuts, and old policing strategies didn't bring about these falling crime rates. SB1070 did. When hard-working rank-and-file Phoenix Police Officers were given access to the tool of SB1070, the deterrence factor this legislation brought about was clearly instrumental in our unprecedented drop in crime. And all of this without a single civil rights, racial profiling, or biased policing complaint. To ignore the positive impact of SB1070 in the City of Phoenix is to ignore the huge elephant in the middle of the room.

In other words, although city hall will not acknowledge the effect of my legislative initiatives on crime rates, the Phoenix Law Enforcement Association has no doubts: the various law enforcement provisions enacted by the Arizona State Legislature have worked.

Therefore, I am pleased to be here today to highlight for this Committee the importance of SB 1070 in combating rampant illegal immigration and upholding the rule of law.

Let me take a moment to reiterate why we are here today. We are here because the federal government has decided not to enforce the law. When I was at the Supreme Court in December 2010 listening to the oral arguments in the legal challenge to my E-Verify law, Justice Scalia commented that "nobody would [have thought] that ... the Federal Government would not enforce [immigration laws]. Of course, no one would have expected that." States, such as Arizona, have no choice but to take action to address the adverse effects of the federal government's failure to enforce the law.

Everyone knows that proactive state laws work. It is clear in Arizona. Neither the federal government nor the interest groups challenging the various laws around the country claim that these laws do not protect the public from additional lawlessness. Yet, they have taken unprecedented steps to prevent enforcement of state laws. Therefore, the only issue is whether a specific state law is "preempted" by some federal law.

And, importantly, as the Supreme Court has held, only the determination of who should or should not be admitted into the country, and the conditions under which that person may remain, is the regulation of immigration. Therefore, as long as states do not interfere with the federal government's enforcement activity, states indisputably have the authority to legislate in areas touching on immigration.

Again, let me be clear, SB 1070 does not regulate immigration. Instead, it utilizes Arizona's inherent "police powers" and regulates unlawfully present aliens consistent with the objectives of federal law. SB 1070 specifically authorizes and directs Arizona law enforcement officers to cooperate and communicate with federal officials regarding the enforcement of federal immigration law and imposes penalties under Arizona law for non-compliance with federal law. In other words, SB 1070 mirrors federal objectives while furthering entirely legitimate state goals.

A brief review of the actual provisions of SB 1070 at issue before the Supreme Court tomorrow demonstrates this point:

Section 2 of the law simply provides Arizona police officers with additional guidance as to how to interact with individuals who may not be lawfully present. It does nothing more than define a police officer's available discretion consistent with existing federal law to inquire about a person's immigration status. In addition, for Section 2 to even apply there must be a lawful stop, detention, or arrest and there must be reasonable suspicion that a person is an alien and is not lawfully present in the United States.

Section 3 simply reinforces federal law as it essentially makes it a state crime for unlawfully present aliens

in Arizona to violate federal registration laws. Under federal law, every alien who has been issued a registration document is required to carry that document on his or her person at all times. Therefore, Section 3 only creates state law penalties for failing to comply with federal law. Such a practice is common in other areas that the federal government regulates. In other words, an unlawfully present alien only violates Section 3 if he violates federal law.

Section 5 also reinforces federal law. Under federal law, it is unlawful to knowingly hire an illegal alien for employment. To assist employers in complying with this federal law, Section 5 was carefully crafted to ensure that only those who may lawfully work would apply for jobs. In other words, this provision does no more than protect the jobs of those who may lawfully work from those who are not eligible to work under federal law. And, with unemployment still at record levels, it is a critical function of state governments to protect available jobs for all legal workers.

And finally, Section 6 defines the existing warrantless arrest authority of Arizona law enforcement officers and is not preempted. It is undisputed under that law that state and local law enforcement officers have authority to enforce criminal provisions of federal immigration laws. Therefore, Section 6 simply makes clear that Arizona law enforcement officers have authority to arrest without a warrant individuals who have willfully failed or refused to depart after having been ordered to be removed by a federal immigration judge.

Contrary to what is reported in the press, it is only these simple and clear law enforcement measures that are before the Supreme Court tomorrow. This common sense law is fully within the authority of Arizona—and any other state—as it protects Arizona citizens from the effects of illegal immigration and upholds the rule of law. And protecting our citizens, I believe, is the highest duty of any public official.

Thank you and God bless you and may God continue to bless this Republic. (http://judiciary.senate.gov/pdf/12-4-24PearceTestimony.pdf)

### TESTIMONY OF PETER KIRSANOW, COMMISSIONER, U.S. COMMISSION ON CIVIL RIGHTS, BEFORE THE COMMITTEE ON THE JUDICIARY, U.S. SENATE, HEARING ON "THE HEARING ON COMPREHENSIVE IMMIGRATION REFORM LEGISLATION," APRIL 19, 2013

Chairman Leahy, Senator Grassley, Members of the Committee, I am Peter Kirsanow, a member of the U.S. Commission on Civil Rights, a former member of the National Labor Relations Board, and a partner in the labor and employment practice group of Benesch, Friedlander. I am appearing in my personal capacity.

The U.S. Commission on Civil Rights was established by the Civil Rights Act of 1957 to, among other things, examine matters related to discrimination and denials of equal protection. Because immigration often implicates issues of national origin and sometimes race discrimination, the Commission has conducted several hearings on various aspects of immigration, particularly illegal immigration. The most recent hearings occurred last August in Birmingham, Alabama, and in 2008—the latter specifically related to the effect of illegal immigration on the wages and employment opportunities of black Americans. The evidence adduced at the latter hearing showed that illegal immigration has a disproportionately negative effect on the wages and employment levels of blacks, particularly black males.

The briefing witnesses, well-regarded scholars from leading universities and independent groups, were ideologically diverse. All the witnesses acknowledged that illegal immigration has a negative impact on black employment, both in terms of employment opportunities and wages. The witnesses differed on the extent of that impact, but every witness agreed that illegal immigration has a discernible negative effect on black employment. For example, Professor Gordon Hanson's research showed that "Immigration ... accounts for about 40 percent of the 18 percentage point decline [from 1960–2000] in black employment rates." Professor Vernon Briggs wrote that illegal immigrants and blacks (who are disproportionately likely to be low-skilled) often find themselves in competition for the same jobs, and the huge number of illegal immigrants ensures that there is a continual surplus of low-skilled labor, thus preventing wages from rising. Professor Gerald Jaynes's research found that illegal immigrants had displaced U.S. citizens in industries that had traditionally employed large numbers of African-Americans, such as meatpacking.

Illegal immigration has a disparate impact on African-American men because these men are disproportionately represented in the low-skilled labor force. The Census Bureau released a new report on educational attainment after the Commission issued its report. This report, released in February 2012, found that 50.9 percent of native-born blacks had not continued their education beyond high school. The same report found that 75.5 percent of foreign-born Hispanics had not been educated beyond high school, although it does not disaggregate foreign-born Hispanics who are legal immigrants from those who are illegal immigrants. However, Professor Briggs estimated that illegal immigrants or former illegal immigrants who received amnesty constitute a third to over a half of the total foreign-born population. Foreign-born Hispanics who are in the United States illegally are disproportionately male. African-Americans who have not pursued education beyond high school are also disproportionately male. These poor educational attainment levels usually relegate both African-American men and illegal immigrant men to the same low-skilled labor market, where they must compete against each other for work.

The obvious question is whether there are sufficient jobs in the low-skilled labor market for both African-Americans and illegal immigrants. The answer is no. As Professor Briggs noted in his testimony to the Commission, "In February 2008 ... the national unemployment rate was 4.8 percent, but the unemployment rate for adults (over 25 years old) without a high school diploma was 7.3 percent." During 2007, "Black American adult workers without a high school diploma had an unemployment rate of 12.0 percent, and those with only a high school diploma had an unemployment rate of 7.3 percent." These statistics suggest both that there is an overall surplus of workers in the low-skilled labor market, and that African-Americans are particularly disfavored by employers. More recently, Professor George Borjas of Harvard wrote:

> Classifying workers by education level and age and comparing differences across groups over time shows that a 10 percent increase in the size of an education/age group due to the entry of immigrants (both legal and illegal) reduces the wage of native-born men in that group by 3.7 percent and the wage of all native-born workers by 2.5 percent. ... The same type of education/age comparison used to measure the wage impact shows that a 10 percent increase in the size of a skill group reduced the fraction of native-born blacks in that group holding a job by 5.1 percentage points.

Furthermore, these statistics reflect an economy that was not experiencing the persistent stagnation we are experiencing today. The country's economic woes have disproportionately harmed African-Americans, especially those with little education. In 2011, 24.6 percent of African-Americans without a high school diploma were unemployed, as were 15.5 percent of African-Americans with only a high school diploma. Two and half years into the economic recovery, African-Americans face particular difficulty obtaining employment. According to the Bureau of Labor Statistics, the seasonally adjusted January 2013 unemployment rate for all black Americans—not just those with few skills—was 13.8 percent, nearly twice the white unemployment rate of 7.0 percent. The economy has a glut of low-skilled workers, not a shortage.

Not only do illegal immigrants compete for jobs with African-Americans, but that competition drives down wages for the jobs that are available. Harvard professor George Borjas wrote:

> Illegal immigration reduces the wages of native workers by an estimated $99 to $118 billion a year. ... A theory-based framework predicts that the immigrants who entered the country from 1990 to 2010 reduced the average annual earnings of American workers by

$1,396 in the short run. Because immigration (legal and illegal) increased the supply of workers unevenly, the impact varies across skill groups, with high school dropouts being the most negatively affected group.

Immigration, both legal and illegal, resulted in a disproportionately large increase in the number of high school dropouts in the labor pool. This caused a drop in wages among the poorest and least-educated members of the workforce. As discussed above, these people are disproportionately likely to be African-American men. Furthermore, there is evidence that wages for these men have not just failed to increase as much as they would have in the absence of illegal immigration. Their real wages, the number of dollars they take home at the end of the week, have actually diminished. Julie Hotchkiss, a research economist and policy advisor at the Federal Reserve Bank of Atlanta, estimated that "as a result of this growth in the share of undocumented workers, the annual earnings of the average documented worker in Georgia in 2007 were 2.9 percent ($960) lower than they were in 2000. ... Annual earnings for the average documented worker in the leisure and hospitality sector in 2007 were 9.1 percent ($1,520) lower than they were in 2000." A $960 annual decrease may not seem like much to a lawyer or a doctor. But as President Obama noted in regard to the 2012 payroll tax cut extension, an extra $80 a month makes a big difference to many families: "It means $40 extra in their paycheck, and that $40 helps to pay the rent, the groceries, the rising cost of gas. ..."

The consequences of illegal immigration for black men and the black community in general are not limited to wages. In another study, Borjas found that lower wages and fewer jobs also correlate with an increase in the black incarceration rate.

Our study suggests that a 10% immigrant-induced increase in the supply of a particular skill group is associated with a reduction in the black wage of 2.5%, a reduction in the black employment rate of 5.9 percentage points, and an increase in the black institutionalization rate of 1.3%. Among white men, the same 10% increase in supply reduces the wage by 3.2%, but has much weaker employment and incarceration effects: a 2.1 percentage-point reduction in the employment rate and a 0.2 percentage-point increase in the incarceration rate. It seems, therefore, that black employment and incarceration rates are more sensitive to immigration rates than those of whites.

Both lower wages and incarceration likely contribute to one of the most serious problems facing the African-American community today: the dearth of intact nuclear families. The late senator Daniel Patrick Moynihan famously sounded the alarm about the disintegration of the black family during his tenure at the Department of Labor in the 1960s. It is one of the great tragedies of modern America that the disintegration of the African-American family has not abated. 72 percent of African-American children are born out of wedlock. It is now a truism that children born out of wedlock are far more likely to experience a host of negative outcomes than are children raised by their own biological, married parents.

Married men are more likely to be employed and to have higher earnings than unmarried men, although the relationship between marriage and economic success is complex. However, it is obvious that men who are unemployed or are incarcerated are far less appealing prospective spouses than men who hold down a steady job. Yet there are fewer and fewer jobs available—and at lower wages—for men in traditionally masculine industries. Giving amnesty to illegal immigrants would only exacerbate this problem facing low-skilled men, who are disproportionately African-American. The dearth of job opportunities gives these men less confidence in their ability to support a family, and gives women reason to fear that these prospective husbands will be only another mouth to feed.

Granting amnesty to illegal immigrants will only further harm African-American workers. Not only will the low-skilled labor market continue to experience a surplus of workers, making it difficult for African-Americans to find job opportunities, but African-Americans will be deprived of one of their few advantages in this market. Some states require private employers to use E-Verify to establish that their workers are in the country legally. This levels the playing field a bit for African-Americans. If illegal immigrants are granted legal status, this small advantage disappears.

Furthermore, recent history shows that granting amnesty to illegal immigrants will encourage more people to come to the United States illegally. The 1986 amnesty did not solve the illegal immigration problem. To the contrary, that amnesty established the precedent that if you come to America illegally, eventually you will obtain legal status. Thus, it is likely that if illegal immigrants are granted legal status, more people will come to America illegally and will further crowd African-American men (and other low-skilled men and women) out of the workforce.

Thank you again for inviting me to testify, and I look forward to your questions. (http://www.judiciary.senate.gov/pdf/04-19-13KirsanowTestimony.pdf)

## TESTIMONY OF MARK KRIKORIAN, EXECUTIVE DIRECTOR, CENTER FOR IMMIGRATION STUDIES, BEFORE THE COMMITTEE ON THE JUDICIARY, U.S. SENATE, HEARING ON "THE BORDER SECURITY, ECONOMIC OPPORTUNITY, AND IMMIGRATION MODERNIZATION ACT, S.744," APRIL 22, 2013

There may be circumstances under which an amnesty for certain illegal aliens would make sense. Given the pervasive and deliberate non-enforcement of the immigration laws for so many years, and the resulting large population of illegal aliens, one could make a case for clearing the decks, as it were, and making a fresh start. This would be a distasteful proposition, to be sure, given that virtually all illegal aliens are guilty of multiple felonies, among them identity theft, document fraud, tax evasion, and perjury. Nonetheless, for practical reasons conferring legal status on established, non-violent illegal aliens may well, at some point, be a policy option worth discussing.

But only *after* the problem that allowed the mass settlement of illegal aliens has been addressed.

S 744 takes the opposite approach. It legalizes the illegal population *before* the necessary tools are in place to avoid the development of yet another large illegal population. As such, it paves the way for yet more demands for amnesty a decade or so in the future, as those who entered in, say 2015, are so well-established by 2023 that we will be told that we have to permit them to stay as well.

What's more, the legalization provisions of the bill make widespread fraud very likely. Much has been made of the so-called triggers in Sec. 3 that would permit the Registered Provisional Immigrants (RPI) to receive permanent residence. Tying the green card to achievement of these benchmarks—which include an employment authorization system for all employers, biographical exit tracking at airports and seaports, and substantial completion of two border strategies—is presented as a guarantee that this scenario of serial amnesties would not happen. Unfortunately, those triggers are, in a very real sense, beside the point.

The other triggers mentioned in Sec. 3—those allowing the granting of the initial RPI status—are the submission by the Department of Homeland Security of two plans: A "Comprehensive Southern Border Security Strategy" and a "Southern Border Fencing Strategy." Since similar plans have been frequently offered over the years, this isn't much of a hurdle.

And yet it's the only hurdle that matters because receipt of Registered Provisional Immigrant status *is* the amnesty—that is to say, it represents the transformation of the illegal alien into a person who is lawfully admitted to the United States.

RPI status brings with it work authorization, a legitimate Social Security account, driver's license, travel documents—in effect, Green Card Lite. It is only the upgrade of this status to that of lawful permanent resident—Green Card Premium, if you will—that is on hold until the enforcement benchmarks are satisfied. But the political and bureaucratic incentives to press for the achievement of those enforcement benchmarks are blunted by the fact that the amnesty has already happened. With

people "out of the shadows" and no longer "undocumented," the urgency to meet enforcement deadlines would evaporate, especially in the face of determined opposition to enforcement by business and civil liberties groups.

To use an analogy, if you're flying to the West Coast, it doesn't ultimately matter whether you're in coach or first class—your destination is the same. By the same token, whether or not the beneficiary of the RPI amnesty is upgraded to a green card, the destination is the same—the ability to live and work in the United States. An upgrade from coach to first class may actually be more consequential than the upgrade from RPI to permanent residence; while the former results in wider seats and free drinks, all a green card offers that RPI status does not is the right to apply for citizenship, something most recipients of green cards from the IRCA amnesty had not done a quarter century after the enactment of the law.

And many of those who receive the RPI amnesty are likely to do so fraudulently. Reading Sec. 2101 harkens back to the 1986 Immigration Reform and Control Act's Special Agricultural Worker program, which the *New York Times* called "one of the most extensive immigration frauds ever perpetrated against the United States Government." The Justice Department's Office of Inspector General described it this way:

> To be eligible for adjustment of status under the SAW provisions, the applicant had to prove with documentation that he or she had worked in an agricultural enterprise in the United States for 90 days in each calendar year from 1984 through 1986, or for 90 days between May 1985 and May 1986. The evidence of having engaged in such work, INS employees believed, was often forged and sold to undocumented individuals seeking U.S. residency. *Given the crush of applications under the program and the relative fewer investigative resources, INS approved applications absent explicit proof that they were in fact fraudulent.*

("An Investigation of the Immigration and Naturalization Service's Citizenship USA Initiative," USDoJ OIG, July 2000, http://www.justice.gov/oig/special/0007/listpdf.htm, p. 72; emphasis added)

When Sec. 2101 of S 744 is considered in this light, the sources of fraud become apparent:

- If IRCA created a "crush" of applications when only 3 million people applied, what should we call the workload that DHS will face when triple the number of people—at least—apply for the RPI amnesty? The administrative capacity does not exist to handle this properly, which all but guarantees that most applications will be rubber-stamped by overwhelmed DHS staff.

- The bill says DHS "may interview," not "shall interview," applicants for the RPI amnesty. Given the aforementioned crush, it is unlikely many will be interviewed. In fact, the current DACA amnesty

(Deferred Action for Childhood Arrivals) is a good model for how the administration would manage S 744's amnesty provisions. DACA processing is almost entirely paper-based, with few interviews, resulting in the approval of 99.5 percent of applications. And yet the number of cases so far decided amounts to perhaps one-fiftieth the number likely to apply for the RPI amnesty.

- S 744 allows affidavits by non-relatives regarding the work or education history of RPI amnesty applicants. Fraudulent affidavits were common among IRCA applicants, with some small farmers claiming to have employed hundreds of illegal-alien farmworkers. The temptation to fraud will be great in any program giving away something as valuable as the RPI amnesty, but the ability to investigate fraudulent affidavits will be extremely limited given the millions of applicants. And there is no realistic level of fees or penalties that could raise enough money to hire enough staff to follow up on questionable affidavits. They will be approved, as in the 1980s, absent specific proof that they're fraudulent.

- The current bill also contains a confidentiality clause, prohibiting the use of any information provided by illegal alien applicants for other purposes. This means illegal aliens with little likelihood of approval are free to apply and try their luck, knowing that there's no downside, and a significant upside.

- As a corollary to this, there is no requirement that rejected applicants be immediately taken into custody and deported. In fact, the bill specifically says that failure to qualify does not require DHS to commence removal proceedings. Again, unqualified applicants would have nothing to lose in applying, in the hope that they could fall through the cracks and get approved, something certain to happen to a significant number of people.

- As an additional incentive to fraudulent applicants, S 744 provides de facto work authorization to those merely *applying* for the RPI amnesty, pending the adjudication of the application. Application alone also forestalls removal, making a frivolous application an attractive option for illegal aliens with no chance at amnesty.

We don't have to speculate about the consequences of such widespread fraud. Mahmoud "The Red" Abouhalima was an Egyptian illegal alien driving a cab in New York when he fraudulently—and successfully—applied for amnesty as a farmworker. This legal status allowed him to travel to Afghanistan for terrorist training, which he put to use in the first World Trade Center attack in 1993. A co-conspirator, Mohammed Salameh, also applied for the 1986 amnesty but was, remarkably, turned down. But since that amnesty, like the one in S 744, did not mandate the removal of failed applicants, Salameh was able to remain and assist in the 1993 bombing.

S 744 thus places amnesty before enforcement, and ensures an amnesty process that would reward fraud. A better approach would be to make the *initial* legalization dependent on the bill's enforcement provisions, rather than a future upgrade in status. The enforcement provisions themselves would have to be strengthened by requiring, for instance, biometric exit-tracking at all ports of entry, not just airports and seaports—as it already required in current law and as was recommended by the 9/11 Commission. Another trigger for initial legalization would have to be an explicit statement by Congress that states and localities are not preempted from enforcing civil immigration law.

And any future amnesty would need to be constructed differently. Not only should all lies, however small, be punished with criminal prosecution, but the amnesty might best be conducted piecemeal, rather than addressing millions of people effectively all at once. That is to say, candidates might be considered as they are apprehended for traffic stops or factory raids or what have you, with those who fail to qualify be removed.

Thank you for the opportunity to speak on this important matter and I look forward to any questions you might have. (http://judiciary.senate.gov/pdf/04-22-13KrikorianTestimony.pdf)

## APPENDIX I: FEDERAL PROTECTIONS AGAINST NATIONAL ORIGIN DISCRIMINATION—U.S. DEPARTMENT OF JUSTICE

# POTENTIAL DISCRIMINATION AGAINST IMMIGRANTS BASED ON NATIONAL ORIGIN

This brochure, which was issued in October 2000 and is reprinted virtually in its entirety below, is available on the U.S. Department of Justice website (http://www.justice.gov/crt/legalinfo/nordwg_brochure.php). The brochure is also published in Arabic, Cambodian, Chinese, Farsi, French, Haitian Creole, Hindi, Hmong, Korean, Laotian, Punjabi, Russian, Spanish, Tagalog, Urdu, and Vietnamese.

## INTRODUCTION

Federal laws prohibit discrimination based on a person's national origin, race, color, religion, disability, sex, and familial status. Laws prohibiting national origin discrimination make it illegal to discriminate because of a person's birthplace, ancestry, culture or language. This means people cannot be denied equal opportunity because they or their family are from another country, because they have a name or accent associated with a national origin group, because they participate in certain customs associated with a national origin group, or because they are married to or associate with people of a certain national origin.

The Department of Justice's Civil Rights Division is concerned that national origin discrimination may go unreported in the United States because victims of discrimination do not know their legal rights, or may be afraid to complain to the government. To address this problem, the Civil Rights Division has established a National Origin Working Group to help citizens and immigrants better understand and exercise their legal rights. ...

## CRIMINAL VIOLATIONS OF CIVIL RIGHTS

• A young man of South Asian descent is assaulted as he leaves a concert at a nightclub. The assailant, a member of a skinhead group, yells racial epithets as he beats the victim unconscious in the club's parking lot with fists and a pipe.

• At Ku Klux Klan meetings, a Klansman tells other members that Mexicans and Puerto Ricans should go "back where they came from." They burn a cross in the front yard of a young Hispanic couple in order to frighten them and force them to leave the neighborhood. Before burning the cross, the defendant displays a gun and gives one of his friends another gun in case the victims try to stop them.

• An American company recruits workers in a small Mexican town, promising them good work at high pay. The company smuggles the Mexicans to the United States in an empty tanker truck. When they finally arrive in the U.S., the workers are threatened, told that if they attempt to leave their factory they will be killed.

The Criminal Section of the Civil Rights Division prosecutes people who are accused of using force or violence to interfere with a person's federally protected rights because of that person's national origin. These rights include areas such as housing, employment, education, or use of public facilities. You can reach the Criminal Section at (202) 514-3204. ...

## DISABILITY RIGHTS

• An HMO that enrolls Medicaid patients tells a Mexican American woman with cerebral palsy to come back another day for an appointment while it provides immediate assistance to others.

This example may be a violation of federal laws that prohibit discrimination because of disability as well as laws that prohibit discrimination because of national origin. If you believe you have been discriminated against because you have a disability you may contact the Disability Rights Section at (800) 514-0301 (voice) or 800-514-0383 (TTY). ...

## EDUCATION

- A child has difficulty speaking English, but her school does not provide her with the necessary assistance to help her learn English and other subjects.

- A majority Haitian school does not offer honors classes. Other schools in the district that do not have many Haitian students offer both honors and advanced placement courses.

These examples may be violations of federal law, which prohibits discrimination in education because of a person's national origin. The Division's Educational Opportunities Section enforces these laws in elementary and secondary schools as well as public colleges and universities. The Education Section's work addresses discrimination in all aspects of education, including assignment of students to schools and classes, transportation of students, hiring and placement of faculty and administrators, distribution of school resources, and provision of educational programs that assist limited English speaking students in learning English.

To file a complaint or for more information, contact the Education Section at (202) 514-4092. ...

## EMPLOYMENT

- A transit worker's supervisor makes frequent racial epithets against the worker because his family is from Iran. Last week, the boss put up a fake sign on the bulletin board telling everyone not to trust the worker because he is a terrorist.

- A woman who immigrated from Russia applies for a job as an accountant. The employer turns her down because she speaks with an accent even though she is able to perform the job requirements.

- A food processing company requires applicants who appear or sound foreign to show work authorization documents before allowing them to complete an employment application while native born Caucasian applicants are not required to show any documents before completing employment applications. Moreover, the documents of the ethnic employees are more closely scrutinized and more often rejected than the same types of documents shown by native born Caucasian employees.

These examples may be violations of the law that prohibits discrimination against an employee or job applicant because of his or her national origin. This means an employer cannot discipline, harass, fire, refuse to hire or promote a person because of his or her national origin. If you believe an employer, labor organization or employment agency has discriminated against you because of your national origin, contact:

Equal Employment Opportunity Commission

(800) 669-4000

(Employers with 15 or more employees)

Office of Special Counsel

(800) 255-7688

(Employers with 4 to 14 employees)

Employment Litigation Section

(202) 514-3831

(State or local government employer with a pattern or practice of illegal discrimination)

In addition, an employer may violate federal law by requiring specific work authorization documents, such as a green card, or rejecting such documents only from applicants of certain national origins. For more information or to file a charge, contact the Division's Office of Special Counsel at the above . . . toll-free number.

## HOUSING

- A Native Hawaiian family is looking for an apartment. They are told by the rental agent that no apartments are available, even though apartments are available and are shown to white applicants.

- A realtor shows a Latino family houses only in Latino neighborhoods and refuses to show the family houses in white neighborhoods.

These examples may be violations of the federal Fair Housing Act. That law prohibits discrimination because of national origin, race, color, sex, religion, disability, or familial status (presence of children under 18) in housing. Individual complaints of discrimination may be reported to the Department of Housing and Urban Development (HUD) at (800) 669-9777. If you believe there is a pattern or practice of discrimination, contact the Division's Housing and Civil Enforcement Section at (202) 514-4713.

## LENDING

- A Latina woman is charged a higher interest rate and fees than white male customers who have similar financial histories and apply for the same type of loan.

This example may be a violation of federal laws that prohibit discrimination in lending because of national origin, race, color, sex, religion, disability and marital status or because any of a person's income comes from public assistance. If you believe you have been denied a loan because of your national origin or other protected reason, you may ask the lender for an explanation in writing of why your application was denied.

If the loan is for a home mortgage, home improvement, or other housing-related reasons, you may file a complaint with the Department of Housing and Urban Development at (800) 669-9777. If the loan is for purposes other than housing (such as a car loan), you may file a complaint either with the Division's Housing and Civil Enforcement Section or with the lender's regulatory agency. If your experience was part of a pattern or practice of discrimination you may also call the Housing and Civil Enforcement Section at (202) 514-4713, to obtain more information about your rights or to file a complaint.

## PUBLIC ACCOMMODATIONS

- In a restaurant, a group of Asian Americans waits for over an hour to be served, while white and Latino customers receive prompt service.

- Haitian American visitors to a hotel are told they must pay in cash rather than by credit card, are charged higher rates than other customers, and are not provided with the same amenities, such as towels and soap.

These examples may be violations of federal laws that prohibit discrimination because of national origin, race, color, or religion in places of public accommodation. Public accommodations include hotels, restaurants, and places of entertainment. If you believe you have been denied access to or equal enjoyment of a public accommodation where there is a pattern or practice of discrimination, contact the Housing and Civil Enforcement Section at (202) 514-4713. ...

## POLICE MISCONDUCT

- Police officers constantly pull over cars driven by Latinos, for certain traffic violations, but rarely pull over white drivers for the same violations.

- A police officer questioning a man of Vietnamese origin on the street gets angry when the man is unable to answer his questions because he does not speak English. The Officer arrests the man for disorderly conduct.

These examples may be violations of the Equal Protection Clause of the United States Constitution. They may also be violations of the Omnibus Crime Control and Safe Streets Act of 1968. That law prohibits discrimination because of national origin, race, color, religion, or sex by a police department that gets federal funds through the U.S. Department of Justice. They may also violate Title VI of the Civil Rights Act of 1964, which prohibits discrimination by law enforcement agencies that receive any federal financial assistance, including asset forfeiture property.

Complaints of individual discrimination can be filed with the Coordination and Review Section ... at 1-888-848-5306.

Complaints of individual discrimination may also be filed with the Office of Justice Programs ... at (202) 307-0690.

The Special Litigation Section investigates and litigates complaints that a police department has a pattern or practice of discriminating on the basis of national origin. To file a complaint, contact the Special Litigation Section at (202) 514-6255. ...

## CIVIL RIGHTS OF INSTITUTIONALIZED PERSONS

- A jail will not translate disciplinary hearings for detainees who do not speak English.

- A state's psychiatric hospital has no means of providing treatment for people who do not speak English.

These examples may be violations of the Equal Protection Clause of the United States Constitution. The Special Litigation Section enforces the constitutional rights of people held in state or local government institutions, such as prisons, jails, juvenile correctional facilities, mental health facilities, developmental disability or mental retardation facilities, and nursing homes. If you are a resident of any such facility and you believe there is a pattern or practice of discrimination based on your national origin, contact the Special Litigation Section at (202) 514-6255. ...

## FEDERALLY ASSISTED PROGRAMS

- A local social services agency does not provide information or job training in Korean even though one quarter of local residents speak only Korean.

- A hospital near the Texas/Mexico border dresses its security officers in clothes that look like INS uniforms to scare Latinos away from the emergency room. Latino patients are told to bring their own translators before they can see a doctor.

These examples may be violations of federal laws that prohibit discrimination because of national origin, race or color by recipients of federal funds. If you believe you have been discriminated against by a state or local government agency or an organization that receives funds from the federal government, you may file a complaint with the Division's Coordination and Review Section at (888) 848-5306. ... The Coordination and Review Section will refer the complaint to the federal funding agency that is primarily responsible for enforcing non-discrimination prohibitions applicable to its recipients.

## VOTING

- Despite requests from voters in a large Spanish-speaking community, election officials refuse to provide election materials, including registration forms and sample ballots, in Spanish or to allow Spanish speakers to bring translators into the voting booth.

- A polling official requires a dark-skinned voter, who speaks with a foreign accent and has an unfamiliar last name, to provide proof of American citizenship, but does not require proof of citizenship from white voters.

The election officials' conduct may violate the federal laws prohibiting voting discrimination. The Voting Rights Acts do not specifically prohibit national origin discrimination. However, provisions of the Acts make it illegal to limit or deny the right to vote of any citizen not only because of race or color, but also because of membership in a language minority group. In addition, the Acts also require in certain jurisdictions that election materials and assistance be provided in languages other than English.

Additionally, Section 208 of the Voting Rights Act allows voters, who need help because of blindness, disability or because they cannot read or write, to bring someone (other than an employer or union representative) to help. This means that a voter who needs help reading the ballot in English can bring a friend or family member to translate. In some places, election officials must provide information, such as voter registration and the ballot, in certain language(s) other than English. This can include interpreters to help voters vote.

If you believe that you have been discriminated against in voting or denied assistance in casting your ballot, you may contact the Division's Voting Section at (800) 253-3931. ...

When you call any of the offices listed in this brochure, the phone will be answered in English. If you need an interpreter, tell the operator what language you speak. The operator will put you on hold while an interpreter is found. Please do not hang up. Through a language interpreter service, we are equipped to assist callers in all languages.

Note: For persons with disabilities, this document will be available in large print, audio tape, computer disc, and Braille.

# APPENDIX II
# MAPS OF THE WORLD

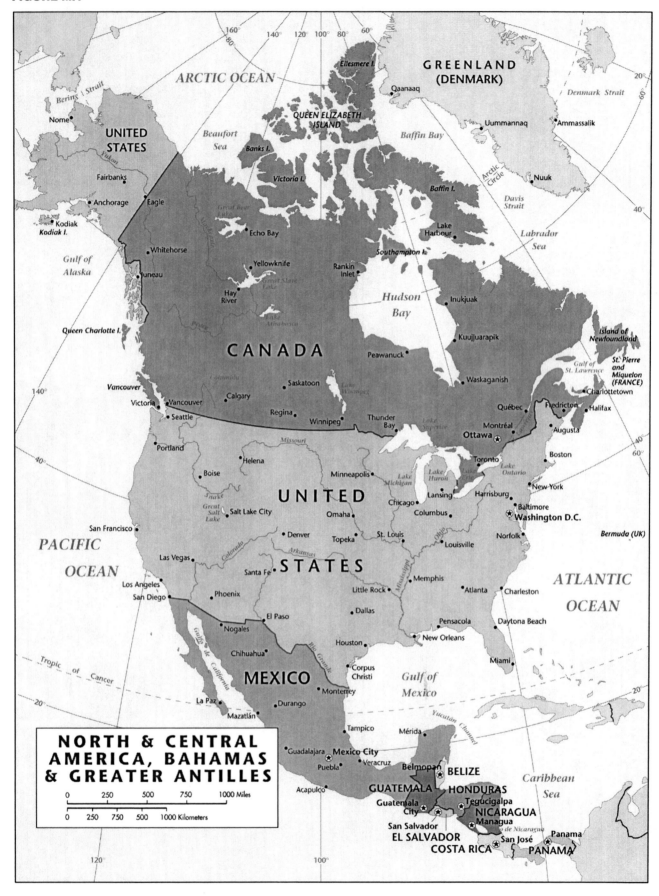

**NORTH & CENTRAL AMERICA, BAHAMAS & GREATER ANTILLES**

0    250    500    750    1000 Miles

0    250    750    500    1000 Kilometers

© *Maryland Cartographics*

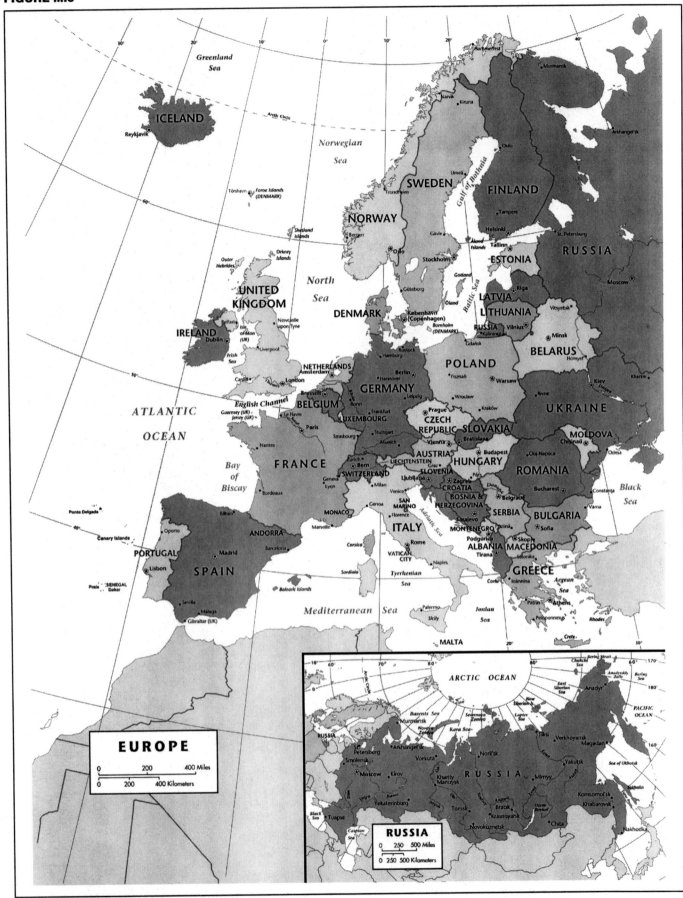

**EUROPE**

0        200        400 Miles

0        200        400 Kilometers

**RUSSIA**

0    250    500 Miles

0   250   500 Kilometers

© *Maryland Cartographics*

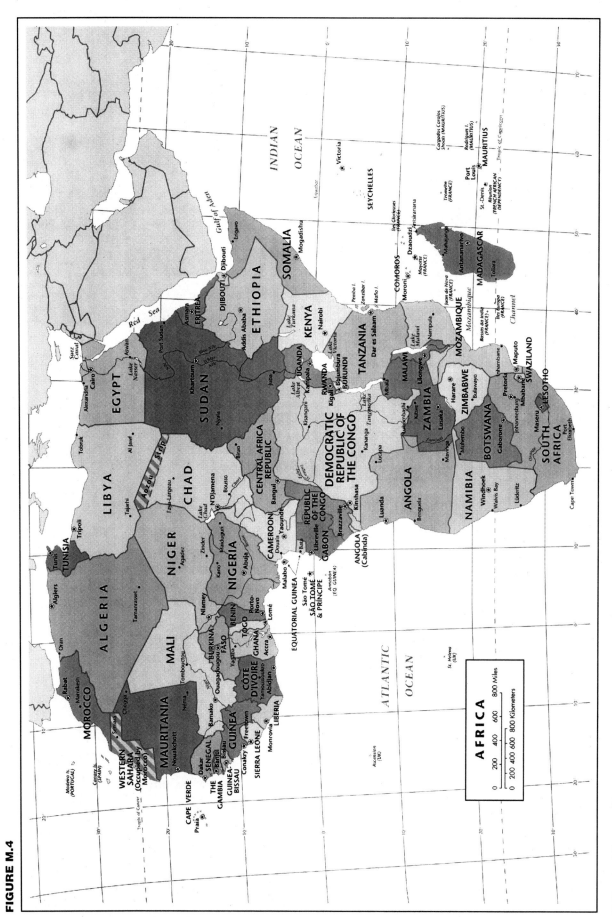

AFRICA

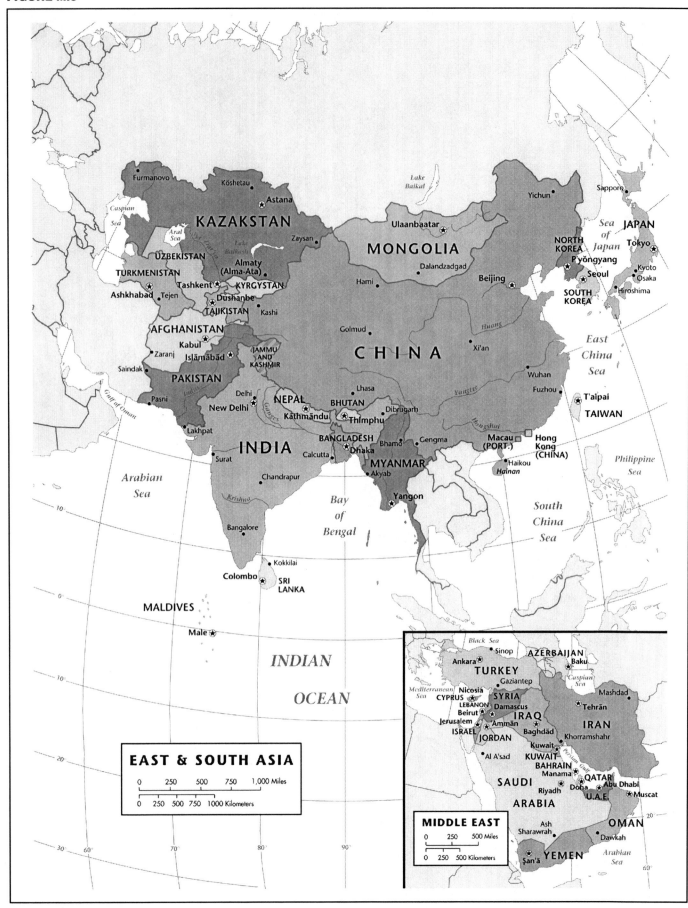

**EAST & SOUTH ASIA**

0   250   500   750   1,000 Miles

0   250   500   750   1000 Kilometers

**MIDDLE EAST**

0      250      500 Miles

0    250    500 Kilometers

© *Maryland Cartographics*

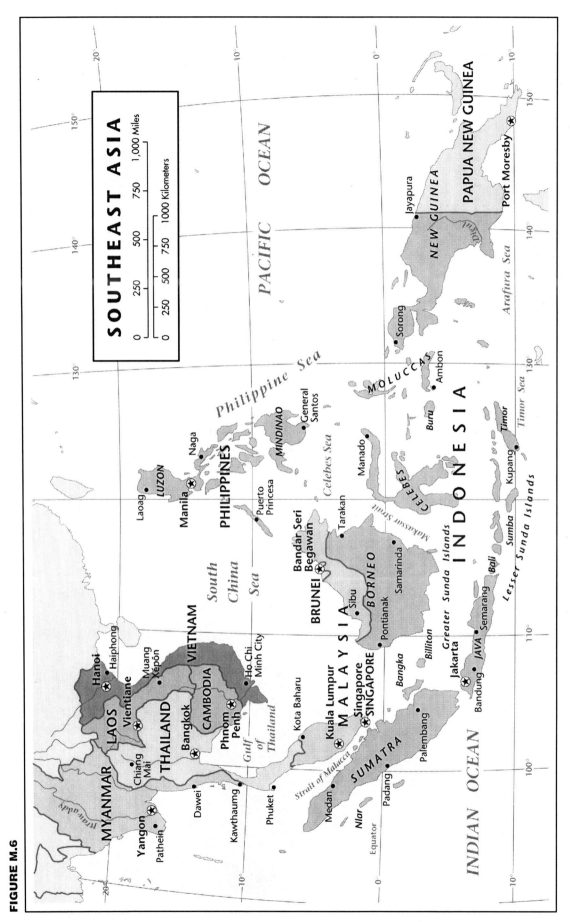

© *Maryland Cartographics*

**FIGURE M.7**

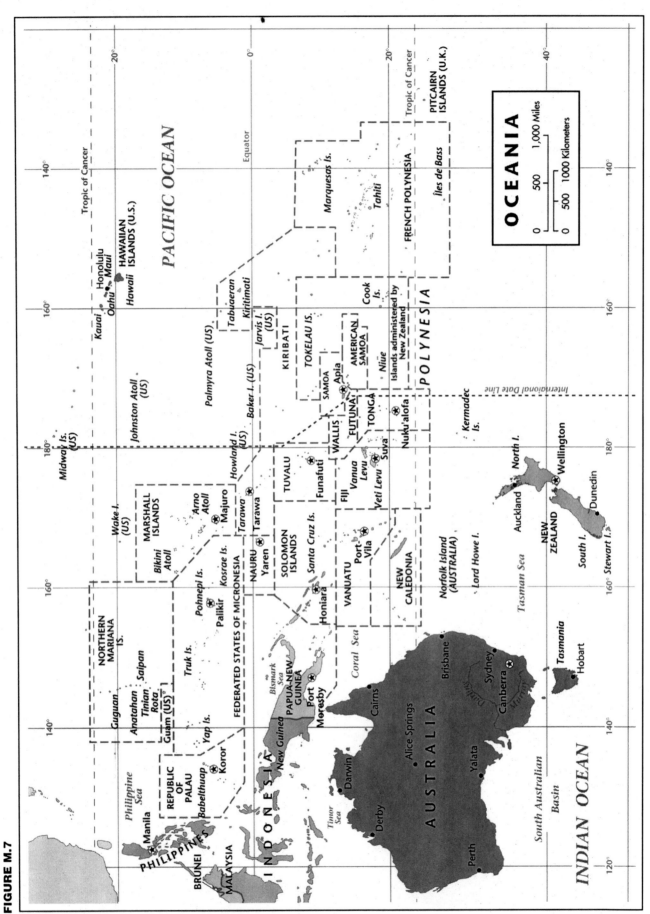

© Maryland Cartographics

# IMPORTANT NAMES
# AND ADDRESSES

**American Civil Liberties Union**
125 Broad St., 18th Floor
New York, NY 10004
(212) 549-2500
URL: http://www.aclu.org/

**American Immigration Lawyers
Association**
1331 G St. NW, Ste. 300
Washington, DC 20005-3142
(202) 507-7600
FAX: (202) 783-7853
URL: http://www.aila.org/

**Amnesty International USA**
Five Penn Plaza
New York, NY 10001
(212) 807-8400
FAX: (212) 627-1451
E-mail: aimember@aiusa.org
URL: http://www.amnestyusa.org/

**The Brookings Institution**
1775 Massachusetts Ave. NW
Washington, DC 20036
(202) 797-6000
E-mail: communications@brookings.edu
URL: http://www.brookings.edu/

**Cato Institute**
1000 Massachusetts Ave. NW
Washington, DC 20001-5403
(202) 842-0200
FAX: (202) 842-3490
URL: http://www.cato.org/

**Center for American Progress**
1333 H St. NW, 10th Floor
Washington, DC 20005
(202) 682-1611
URL: http://www.americanprogress.org/

**Center for Comparative Immigration
Studies**
**University of California, San Diego**
9500 Gilman Dr., Mail Code 0548
La Jolla, CA 92093-0548

(858) 822-4447
E-mail: ccis@ucsd.edu
URL: http://ccis.ucsd.edu/

**Center for Immigration Research
University of Houston**
450 Philip Hoffman Hall
Houston, TX 77204
(713) 743-3940
URL: http://www.class.uh.edu/cir/

**Center for Immigration
Studies**
1629 K St. NW, Ste. 600
Washington, DC 20006
(202) 466-8185
FAX: (202) 466-8076
URL: http://www.cis.org/

**Federation for American Immigration
Reform**
25 Massachusetts Ave. NW, Ste. 330
Washington, DC 20001
(202) 328-7004
1-877-627-3247
FAX: (202) 387-3447
URL: http://www.fairus.org/

**The Heritage Foundation**
214 Massachusetts Ave. NE
Washington, DC 20002-4999
(202) 546-4400
E-mail: info@heritage.org
URL: http://www.heritage.org/

**Human Rights Watch**
350 Fifth Ave., 34th Floor
New York, NY 10118-3299
(212) 290-4700
FAX: (212) 736-1300
E-mail: hrwpress@hrw.org
URL: http://www.hrw.org/

**Immigration History Research Center**
311 Elmer L. Andersen Library
222 21st Ave. S
Minneapolis, MN 55455

(612) 625-4800
FAX: (612) 626-0018
E-mail: ihrc@umn.edu
URL: http://www.ihrc.umn.edu/

**ImmigrationWorks USA**
737 Eighth St. SE, Ste. 201
Washington, DC 20003
(202) 506-4541
FAX: (202) 595-8962
E-mail: info@immigrationworksusa.org
URL: http://www.immigrationworksusa.org/

**Institute of International Education**
809 United Nations Plaza
New York, NY 10017
(212) 883-8200
FAX: (212) 984-5452
URL: http://www.iie.org/

**Lutheran Immigration and
Refugee Service**
700 Light St.
Baltimore, MD 21230
(410) 230-2700
FAX: (410) 230-2890
URL: http://www.lirs.org/

**Mexican American Legal Defense and
Education Fund**
634 S. Spring St., Ste. 1100
Los Angeles, CA 90014
(213) 629-2512
URL: http://www.maldef.org/

**Migration Policy Institute**
1400 16th St. NW, Ste. 300
Washington, DC 20036
(202) 266-1940
FAX: (202) 266-1900
E-mail: Communications@migrationpolicy.org
URL: http://www.migrationpolicy.org/

**National Conference of State
Legislatures**
444 N. Capitol St. NW, Ste. 515
Washington, DC 20001

(202) 624-5400
FAX: (202) 737-1069
URL: http://www.ncsl.org/

**National Council of
La Raza**
Raul Yzaguirre Bldg.
1126 16th St. NW, Ste. 600
Washington, DC 20036-4845
(202) 785-1670
FAX: (202) 776-1792
E-mail: comments@nclr.org
URL: http://www.nclr.org/

**National Foundation for
American Policy**
2111 Wilson Blvd., Ste. 700
Arlington, VA 22201
(703) 351-5042
URL: http://www.nfap.com/

**National Immigration
Forum**
50 F St. NW, Ste. 300
Washington, DC 20001
(202) 347-0040
FAX: (202) 347-0058
E-mail: info@immigrationforum.org
URL: http://www.immigrationforum.org/

**Office of Refugee Resettlement
Administration for Children and Families**
901 D St. SW
ORR/Eighth Floor
Washington, DC 20447
(202) 401-9246
FAX: (202) 401-4685
URL: http://www.acf.hhs.gov/programs/orr/

**Pew Hispanic Center**
1615 L St. NW, Ste. 700
Washington, DC 20036
(202) 419-4300
FAX: (202) 419-4349
E-mail: info@pewhispanic.org
URL: http://www.pewhispanic.org/

**Refugee Council USA**
1628 16th St. NW
Washington, DC 20009
(202) 319-2102
FAX: (202) 319-2104
E-mail: info@rcusa.org
URL: http://www.rcusa.org/

**United Nations High Commissioner for
Refugees**
Case Postale 2500
CH-1211 Genève 2 Dépôt, Switzerland

(011-41) 22-739-8111
FAX: (011-41) 22-739-7377
URL: http://www.unhcr.org/cgi-bin/texis/
vtx/home

**Urban Institute**
2100 M St. NW
Washington, DC 20037
(202) 833-7200
URL: http://www.urban.org/

**U.S. Committee for Refugees and
Immigrants**
2231 Crystal Dr., Ste. 350
Arlington, VA 22202-3711
(703) 310-1130
FAX: (703) 769-4241
URL: http://www.refugees.org/

**US/Mexico Border Counties
Coalition**
310 N. Mesa, Ste. 824
El Paso, TX 79901
(915) 838-6860
FAX: (915) 838-6880
E-mail: david@acr-dc.com
URL: http://www.bordercounties.org/

# RESOURCES

The U.S. government provides most of the statistical information concerning immigration and naturalization. Much of the information comes from branches of the U.S. Department of Homeland Security (DHS). Beyond the websites of the DHS branches, a primary source of data is the annual *Yearbook of Immigration Statistics*, an online publication of the U.S. Citizenship and Immigration Services. Other DHS reports that provide valuable data include *Estimates of the Unauthorized Immigrant Population Residing in the United States: January 2011* (Michael Hoefer, Nancy Rytina, and Bryan Baker, March 2012), *Refugees and Asylees: 2011* (Daniel C. Martin and James E. Yankay, May 2012), and "U.S. Legal Permanent Residents: 2011" (Randall Monger and James Yankay, April 2012).

Another important source of government data on immigration is the U.S. Census Bureau, which collects and distributes information about the nation's population. Helpful reports and data sets include *Statistical Abstract of the United States: 2012* (2011), the frequently updated *American Community Survey, National Population Projections: Summary Tables* (December 2012), and *The Foreign-Born Population in the United States: 2010* (Elizabeth M. Grieco et al., May 2012).

Other government data sources that were central to the compilation of this volume include "Foreign-Born Workers: Labor Force Characteristics—2011" (May 2012) and "Employment Projections—2010–2020" (February 2012) by the U.S. Department of Labor's Bureau of Labor Statistics; *Attorney General's Annual Report to Congress and Assessment of U.S. Government Activities to Combat Trafficking in Persons, Fiscal Year 2011* (January 2013) by the Office of the Attorney General; *Trafficking in Persons Report* (June 2012) by the U.S. Department of State; *Annual Report: October 1, 2010–September 30, 2011* (November 2012) by the Labor Department's Office of Foreign Labor Certification; and *The Condition of Education 2012* (Susan Aud et al., May 2012) by the U.S. Department of Education's National Center for Education Statistics.

Independent nonprofit organizations that study immigration were also instrumental in the production of this book. The Pew Hispanic Center, a project of the Pew Research Center whose goal is to promote understanding of the U.S. Hispanic population, regularly issues reports and data on immigration. Among those used in this book were *Net Migration from Mexico Falls to Zero—and Perhaps Less* (Jeffrey Passel, D'Vera Cohn, and Ana Gonzalez-Barrera, April 2012), "Unauthorized Immigrants: 11.1 Million in 2011" (Jeffrey Passel and D'Vera Cohn, December 2012), *Unauthorized Immigrants: Length of Residency, Patterns of Parenthood* (Paul Taylor et al., December 2011), *Statistical Portrait of Hispanics in the United States, 2011* (Seth Motel and Eileen Patten, February 2013), and *Up to 1.7 Million Unauthorized Immigrant Youth May Benefit from New Deportation Rules* (Jeffrey S. Passel and Mark Hugo Lopez, August 2012).

The Center for American Progress was also the source for important data on numerous aspects of the immigration issue, including information appearing in "Immigrants Are Makers, Not Takers" (Marshall Fitz, Philip E. Wolgin, and Patrick Oakford, February 2013), *Raising the Floor for American Workers: The Economic Benefits of Comprehensive Immigration Reform* (Raúl Hinojosa-Ojeda, September 2012), "The Facts on Immigration Today" (July 2012), and *The Economic Effects of Granting Legal Status and Citizenship to Undocumented Immigrants* (Robert Lynch and Patrick Oakford, March 2013). The Migration Policy Institute's *Immigration Enforcement in the United States: The Rise of a Formidable Machinery* (Doris Meissner et al., January 2013) provides an in-depth look at the federal government's border-security and other immigration enforcement efforts.

The Center for Immigration Studies' *Immigrants in the United States, 2010: A Profile of America's Foreign-Born Population* (Steven A. Camarota, August 2012) and the Heritage Foundation's *The Fiscal Cost of Low-Skill Immigrants to the U.S. Taxpayer* (Robert Rector and Christine Kim, May 2007) both offer important views on the controversial issue of the costs of immigration to the native-born population and to government coffers. The Brookings Institute's *Immigrant Workers in the U.S. Labor Force* (Audrey Singer, March 2012) provides detail about the role of immigrant workers in the economy at large and in specific industries, the Kauffman Foundation's *Then and Now: America's New Immigrant Entrepreneurs, Part VII* (Vivek Wadhwa, AnnaLee Saxenian, and F. Daniel Siciliano, October 2012) examines the role of immigrant entrepreneurs in the United States, and the Institute of International Education's *Open Doors Report on International Educational Exchange* (2012) offers recent and historical data on international student populations.

Important information about the challenges facing border counties in the U.S. Southwest came from the US/Mexico Border Counties Coalition report *At the Cross Roads: US/Mexico Border Counties in Transition* (Dennis L. Soden et al., March 2006), and important information about the repopulation of rural areas by Hispanic immigrants came from Patrick J. Carr, Daniel T. Lichter, and Maria J. Kefalas, in "Can Immigration Save Small-Town America? Hispanic Boomtowns and the Uneasy Path to Renewal" (*The ANNALS of the American Academy of Political and Social Science*, May 2012).

# INDEX

of refugees in U.S., 75

visa application backlog, employment-based, 80(*t*5.1)

*See also* Labor force

Employment Eligibility Verification, Form I-9

employer requirement for, 18, 21

sample of, 19*f*–21*f*

Employment-based visas

application backlog, 80(*t*5.1)

waiting time for, 79–80

Endangered Species Act, 90

Enforcement. *See* Law enforcement

English learners (ELs)

costs of supporting, 101

in schools, 102(*t*6.3)

students in Los Angeles schools as, 121

Enhanced Border Security and Visa Entry Reform Act

nonimmigrant visas prohibited by, 25

VWP security threats and, 90

"Enhanced DHS Oversight and Assessment of Interagency Coordination Is Needed for the Northern Border" (GAO), 91

Entrepreneurs

foreign-born, 102

immigrants' contributions to U.S. economy, 121–123

Entry

exclusion, grounds for under IMMACT, 22–23

immigrants denied entry, 10, 12

immigrants denied entry by reason for denial, 11*t*

legal entry documents, waiting time for, 79–80

refugees, material support denials, 66

*See also* Admissions

Entry-exit system, 24

Ester, Karma, 22

*Estimates of the Unauthorized Immigrant Population Residing in the United States: January 2011* (OIS), 81–82

Ethiopia, 71

Ethnic diversity, 106–107

Europe region, 67

E-Verify system

Alabama's House Bill 56 and, 29

Arizona law mandates use of, 88

cases, 24*f*

description of, use of, 23–24

Legal Arizona Workers Act and, 28

participation in, 86

Exclusion, grounds for under IMMACT, 22–23

Executive Order 120 (New York City), 119

Executive Order 9066, 13

Expedited removal

asylum claims controversy, 72

under IIRIRA, 23

**F**

"The Facts on Immigration Today" (Center for American Progress), 32–33

Families

adults who are parents of minor children, by immigration status, 84(*f*5.4)

family-based LPR status, 41–42

family-based visas, application backlog, 80(*t*5.2)

family-based visas, waiting time for, 79–80

follow-to-join asylum, 69

household size, native/foreign-born populations, 38*f*

household type, native/foreign-born populations, 37*f*

immigrant, statistics on, 33–34

income by native/foreign-born/citizenship status, 42*f*

refugee application process and, 66

reunification, seven-category preference system for, 14

Family Services Collaborative, 116

Federal Bureau of Investigation (FBI), 24

Federal government

control of immigration, total, 9

definition of immigrant, 37

federally assisted programs, anti-immigrant discrimination in, 153

illegal immigration, responses to, 85–87

role in immigration, beginning of, 8

Secure Fence Act, 89–90

spending on refugees, 75

unavailability of benefits to unauthorized immigrants, 98

Feere, Jon, 23

Fees, visa, 57

"Fees and Reciprocity Tables" (Bureau of Consular Affairs), 57

Females, 22

Fertility rates

among immigrant women, 33

in Mexico, 83

Fields of study

of foreign students, 57

of international students by place of origin, 61*t*

Filipino immigrants, 12

*Final Report* (Select Commission on Immigration and Refugee Policy), 15

*Final Report: Japanese Evacuation from the West Coast 1942* (DeWitt), 13

*The Fiscal Cost of Low-Skill Immigrants to the U.S. Taxpayer* (Rector & Kim), 93

Fiscal Policy Institute, 122–123

Fitz, Marshall, 96–97

Fix, Michael, 121

Florida

police detention of individuals for immigration violations, 25

refugee arrivals, 67

Florida, Richard, 107

Follow-to-join asylum

asylees, by country of nationality, 71(*t*4.8)

description of, 69

number of admissions, 71

Food-processing companies, 114, 116

Forbes.com, 122

Ford, Gerald R.

Domestic Council Committee on Illegal Aliens, 15

termination of Executive Order 9066, 13

Foreign nationals

denied entrance, returns/removals, 63

denied entrance to U.S., 58–60

foreign-student monitoring system, 24

returns/removals of, 60

Foreign students. *See* Students, foreign

Foreign workers, temporary

H-1 visa program, 52–54

H-2 visa program, 54–56

statistics on, 52

*The Foreign-Born Population in the United States: 2010* (Grieco et al.), 31

Foreign-born workers, 123

"Foreign-Born Workers: Labor Force Characteristics—2011" (BLS), 35

Form AR-3 card, 17

Form I-9, Employment Eligibility Verification

employer requirement for, 18, 21

sample of, 19*f*–21*f*

Form I-151, 17

Form I-551, 17

Foster care, 75

14th Amendment

on birthright citizenship, 83, 84–85

equal protection clause of, 28

France, 66

*Freeman, Chy Lung v.*, 8

*FY 2012 Summary of Major Activities* (PRM), 75

**G**

Gang of Eight, 125

GAO. *See* U.S. Government Accountability Office

Garcia, John C., 89

GDP. *See* Gross domestic product

Geary Act, 9

Gender

flow of LPRs by, 48(*t*3.12)

refugee arrivals by, 68

refugee arrivals by age, gender, marital status, 69*t*

Gentlemen's Agreement, 9, 10

Geography of immigration, 110–116

Georgia, 88

CPSIA information can be obtained
at www.ICGtesting.com
Printed in the USA
FFOW05n0716280913

9 781569 957912